What Manner of Woman

Essays on English and American Life and Literature

The publication of this work has
been aided by a grant from the
Andrew W. Mellon Foundation.

THE GOTHAM LIBRARY
OF THE NEW YORK UNIVERSITY PRESS

The Gotham Library is a series of original works and critical studies published in paperback primarily for student use. The Gotham hardcover edition is primarily for use by libraries and the general reader. Devoted to significant works and major authors and to literary topics of enduring importance, Gotham Library texts offer the best in literature and criticism.

Comparative and Foreign Language Literature:
Robert J. Clements, Editor
Comparative and English Language Literature:
James W. Tuttleton, Editor

What Manner of Woman

Essays on English and American Life and Literature

Edited by
Marlene Springer

New York · New York University Press · 1977

Copyright 1977 by New York University

Library of Congress Catalog Card Number: 76-53876

ISBN: 0-8147-7777-5 (cloth)
       0-8147-7779-1 (paperback)

Library of Congress Cataloging in Publication Data

Main entry under title.

What manner of woman.
   (The Gotham library)
   Includes bibliographical references and index.
   1. English literature—History and criticism—
Addresses, essays, lectures. 2. American litera-
ture—History and criticism—Addresses, essays, lec-
tures.   3. Women in literature—Addresses, essays,
lectures.   I. Springer, Marlene.
PR151.W6W5   820'.93'52   77-8331
ISBN 0-8147-7777-5
ISBN 0-8147-7779-1 pbk.

Manufactured in the United States of America

List of Contributors

Martha Banta, Professor of English, University of Washington

Nina Baym, Professor of English, University of Illinois at Urbana-Champaign

Catherine M. Dunn, Professor of English, California State University, Northridge

Ann S. Haskell, Associate Professor of English, State University of New York at Buffalo

Carolyn G. Heilbrun, Professor of English, Columbia University

David J. Latt, Assistant Professor of English, Rhode Island College

Gina Luria, Assistant Director of the Program on Women, Northwestern University

Charles G. Masinton, Professor of English, University of Kansas

Martha Tait Masinton, free-lance editor, Lawrence, Kansas

John J. Richetti, Professor of English, Rutgers University

Elizabeth Schultz, Associate Professor of English, University of Kansas

Marlene Springer, Associate Professor of English, University of Missouri-Kansas City

Ann Stanford, Professor of English, California State University, Northridge

Irene Tayler, Associate Professor of Humanities, Massachusetts Institute of Technology

James W. Tuttleton, Professor of English, New York University

Contents

Introduction

Marlene Springer

Ruskin once posited that literature is the expression and even the yardstick of society. This symposium explores the accuracy of this yardstick, especially as it measures one-half of society— women—in Britain and America. The resurgence of feminism has forced critics and students alike into a new awareness of the way women are treated in literature, and the way scholars have handled this treatment. There was a time when such a distinguished critic of the novel as Ian Watt could observe that "the marriage of the protagonist usually leads to a rise in the social and economic status of the bride, not the bridegroom," and conclusively attribute this pattern to the preponderance of women in the novel-reading public, thus completely ignoring the more pertinent legal explanation that a woman's money in the eighteenth and nineteenth centuries was almost totally controlled by the men in the family—were a heiress to marry a butler, she could find herself reduced to working as a chambermaid; Mr. B. faced no such consequences. Today's new consciousness requires, however, that such extenuating legal circumstances, for example, be recognized. And students' interest requires that professors have ready and accurate answers to questions concerning the portrayal of women in literature in fields historically and culturally removed from their own specialties. Because such answers are not now readily available, this collection of original essays is designed to provide in one volume a chronological examination of these portraits in specific historical-cultural frames by outlining, albeit briefly, the sociological, political, philosophical, and occasionally the legal climate informing the aesthetic view of women. Frankly, the purpose of this book is not to offer still another startling new specialized perspective on the literature—though some of these essays are indeed exploratory and excitingly controversial. Rather, the volume proposes to provide students and professors alike with a convenient compendium and overview, thereby serving as a useful critical tool as well as provoking new ways to look at familiar works by writers historically and currently recognized as major figures in our literary history. Because of this deliberate focus on "recognized" figures, the essays will often, by necessity, deal with the masculine image of women; all too often the historical period presents few examples of women now regarded as major authors. The volume cannot attempt to reverse history, or even redress the fact that traditionally our definitions of women have come from men. Hopefully, however, it can serve as a major first step in correcting the current and former masculine bias in histories of literature by bringing women, both as characters and as authors, out of the footnotes and into the text.

This emphasis on culture as well as literature has prescribed a variety of specialized authors, which in turn leads to a valuable eclecticism in approach: some essays are developed thematically, others chronologically; some are omnibus essays, dealing with large groups of authors, others are deliberately restrictive, singling out four or five major writers and then providing the reader with ways to apply the approach toward these outstanding figures to the works and times of lesser authors; some develop a specific, original thesis, or suggest new ways of responding to familiar literature, while others attempt to consolidate masses of scholarship into usable form. With such a diversity of approaches, there is always the danger of disunity. The collection avoids this thematically by its uniform attempt to relate literature to culture, and structurally by its chronological coverage; every major literary period in British and American literature is treated, with more freedom deliberately allowed in developing the modern period, in which the literary explosion has not yet had time to settle out. Nonetheless, there must be, in any symposium of such scope, some sacrifices made to the demands of space, theme, and critical preference. Pre-Raphaelite and modern poetry, for example, are regrettably but unavoidably neglected here, as are probably some readers' favorite novelists. On the other hand, cultural trends, the realities of university curricula, and the uniqueness of the literature itself have justified one extremely valuable nonchronological addition: the essay on the treatment of black women. Given the wealth and cultural importance of black literature, no collection attempting to give a representation of American writing would be complete without it.

Recognizing the deliberately broad scope of the symposium—literature and history, British and American, medieval to modern—one could scarcely hope for one definitive pattern to recur in all the essays. Yet, perhaps not unexpectedly, out of the planned multiformity some definite workable theses about the portrayal of women do emerge. Primarily, when reading these essays chronologically and thus digesting centuries of major works, one is forcefully struck by the discrepancy between reality and aesthetics where women are concerned. The extent of this disparity is not paralleled in the case of men, and cannot be accounted for by weakness of imagination or the inevitable distinctness of literature and life. There are variations in degree, of course, and periodic exceptions. Ann Haskell, in her treatment of medieval women, assures us that our popular beliefs about medieval life are reliable, but they are also fractional. For example, while women have a secondary position in the ideal society of the romances, the memorial brasses depict figures of equal stature; yet, redressing the balance, the Wife of Bath with her multiple marriages and strong personality is more anomalous in the literature than the life. And Catherine Dunn, in her essay on the Renaissance, argues against any real disparity: by and large the literature late in the period does reflect real women and their changing position in society. Dunn notes, however, that the pattern is irregular, and that there are curious omissions: writers portray very few women rulers positively, though there was a paragon on the throne; and learned women rarely appear, even though their number was increasing, and the quality of their minds was recognized. When one moves forward to another British queen, Victoria, the variation between the actual and literary also narrows, but for quite the opposite reason: rather than art imitating life, life begins to imitate art. As I observe in my essay on the Victorian period, this alliance, rare in its totality, blurred the distinction between the ideal and the real. For lack of any viable alternative, the Victorian middle-class woman, enshrined by the cult of chastity, looked to as a moral guardian, feared for the power worship confers, and often sacrificed to propriety, became the Victorian heroine. The stereotypes of literature became inter-changeable with the realities of the household.

But while the literary and the literal occasionally converge, the essays illustrate that for the most part the idealization inherent in the romances, or the misogyny exemplified by James I and the Restoration wits, for example, always remain powerful, distorting forces upon the characterization of women. As a result, one is tempted to generalize, women in literature often are symbols rather than people. This is especially true, as John Richetti demonstrates, in the Restoration, with its strong preference for generality. It also holds, as Irene Tayler and Gina Luria note, in English Romantic poetry, where women, in addition to being sources of inspiration, traditional muses in effect, frequently appear as sister images or mirror images of the poet; rather than being merely inspirational, they are projections, imaginative extensions of the poet himself. Nor is the phenomenon limited to the British. Martha Banta observes how frequently women are depicted as symbols of American civilization. Just as the image of American society in the years after the Civil War tended to be warped past recognition, so were American women given literary representations that were controlled by the erroneous notions of the men in charge. Simultaneously, both the true worth of women and that of society were victims of an imagined ideal wide of the mark (which, in turn, often concealed impulses the male imagina-tion chose to ignore). Consequently, the writings from the Gilded Age reveal, often inadvertently, abundant accounts of frustrated energies striving to be used, and used well. Several of the best novelists consciously recognized what was happening. In the novels of James and Howells, for example, are often found (aptly enough, at dead center) "women *waiting* to be used and to make the best of their own value"—but women who are forced to admit the futility of their wait since they, together with the quality of American life they represent, are victims of "faulty economics, misdefined value, wasted force." Still, even in the freewheeling 1920s with its revolutionary change in manners, the best American writers of the period, James Tuttleton contends, seem most sympathetic to the stereotypical "womanly woman," the woman as life-sustaining nurse to her family. And the Masintons find a ramification of this pattern in modern American fiction: "The male hero is shown as experiencing his time in whatever manner the novelist defines that time, while the female characters whom he encounters are exempted from the burden of contemporaneity and allowed refuge either in myth or in stereotypical female roles."

This process of symbolization, of course, is not without a countercurrent, as Richetti's essay proposes. He argues that "woman as moral topic becomes woman as metaphor; from woman as the center of a moral-rhetorical occasion the literary tradition moves to examining female experience as a revealingly intense version of human experience in general." Essays chronologically following indicate that women novelists, especially, carry this current into the early nineteenth century, and it continues to reappear as feminist writers gain force later in the period both in England and America. Yet even modern feminist writers, the Masintons remind us, face the major technical problem of how to make interesting a character whose life has been socially controlled and is thus without free choice; and the predominant trend in English and American literature has been to view women more as archetypical than typical.

Even while remaining on the whole a vehicle of metaphor rather than a subject, the female character in literature is, certainly, still endowed with many of the complex guises and motivations that normal living requires. Feminine sexuality, for example, has been a troublesome question ever since Teiresias ruled in favor of the female pleasure principle. The Canterbury pilgrims consider it in various forms; Catherine Dunn quotes Drayton's early complaint against the double standard; Richetti defines the "democracy of desire" in Restoration comedy, and discusses Gulliver's outrage because "the redeeming virgin aspect of the female stereotype is a fraud." But by the Victorian period, Grundyism and the union of passion with guilt saturated society. The conspiracy of silence about female sexuality which continued to dominate literature well into the twentieth century was institutionalized during the lengthy reign of a queen who was "not amused" by any references to carnality. (Victoria's distaste for discussion of human sexual response aside, Nina Baym's essay provides an interesting sidelight on my discussion of nineteenth-century morality. She contends that a woman's aversion to sex was probably more pragmatic than prudish, given the dangers of childbirth and problems of contraception.)

Considering these explorations of female sexuality, as well as the related, recurring insistence on woman as womb, it would seem logical that marriage also be a serious literary concern; yet here too the essays now corroborate what most of us long suspected: sexual campaigns are deemed artistically interesting; the term in office is not. David Latt finds that there are few poems on married love in the seventeenth century, with *Paradise Lost* a notable exception. In Restoration comedy, marriage is funny, superficial, and a trap. And while the women's novels of the 1790s did venture a critical examination of the institution of marriage, they did not set a strong pattern for the future. Similarly, though Ann Stanford, in her essay on seventeenth- and eighteenth-century America, can pertinently cite the matrimonial and maternal poems of Anne Bradstreet, the topic is not later pursued by the best literature. Baym reminds us that in the major works of the American Renaissance, there is a dearth of women; moreover, the omission was of little concern. When women do appear, they are often merely dehumanized intellectual or sexual symbols. Hawthorne and Dickinson are exceptions, but the point remains intriguingly valid and raises important questions about the validity of the "American" vision. By the end of the century, Banta argues in her discussion of James, "the American male has wed his business. . . . The American businessman's true home is Downtown on Wall Street, while, almost surreptitiously, he maintains a second establishment Uptown on Fifth Avenue where his mistress is kept, busying herself with matters of culture and society during the long periods of his absence from her side." By the beginning of the twentieth century, the uptown mistress has hardened into Hemingway's American bitch. Tuttleton, in his comments on Fitzgerald, says that Fitzgerald was deeply troubled by the rich girl who did not subscribe to the conventional role of wife and mother, and that he and other postwar writers began to depict an intense hostility between men and women that had always been absent in the American novel.

Carolyn Heilbrun's essay, deliberately narrowed to focus on this important question of marriage in major modern literature, explores the results of this hostility, and the fact that it has been studiously ignored when it disrupts what is supposed to be domestic harmony. It is her controversial, provocative contention that in the premodern period, marriage was allowed to enter into literature only as an acknowledged condition which remained either unobserved or only superficially examined. Post-Victorian literature, in contrast, refuses to take marriage for granted, and demands that its defects be exposed. Modern writers have "established that the unexamined marriage, like the unexamined life, is not worth living, and that Eros alone will not sustain an institution which has lost, or totally transmuted, its social and economic justification." The Wife of Bath laughed, and married again; the ache of modernism, as Hardy called it, proscribes both her resiliency and her sense of humor.

The possibility that marriage will become a social and economic anachronism is frequently adumbrated in literary and cultural history—especially when examining the evolving legal, educational, and economic status of women. As Latt, Tayler and Luria, and several others note, women's legal status is sometimes difficult to determine, or is, for all practical purposes, nonexistent. That women were classed with idiots and children for several centuries by British jurisprudence is a familiar fact; the ramifications of that belittling process are not such common knowledge, and are examined by Richetti, Tayler and Luria, and me in the course of discussing literary works where knowledge of the legal system gives added perspective—a perspective unfortunately absent from much contemporary criticism.

The economic position of women is clearly influenced by their legal position, and obviously tied inextricably to their marital status. Once again, the essays illustrate that the facts frequently refute the literature to an abnormal degree. Ann Haskell discovers that while the romance literature of the medieval period often represents the women as simply "existing," the Paston letters and other historical papers prove that they were not only often solely responsible for rearing families, but also were overseers of large estates, with all the economic, agricultural, labor, martial, and legal problems that entailed. All of this while their husbands lived protectedly at their universities and later worked at their professions or businesses in the cities. And contrary to common assumption, as a corollary to this independence a change of marriage partners was common in medieval England. Such freedom and economic power are surprising, and are far removed from the condition of the nineteenth-century woman, British and American. Nina Baym observes that in spite of romantic trappings, the chief reason for marriage in nineteenth-century America was economic; the concentrated effort to make a "suitable" match, and the discouraging alternatives portrayed in the governess novels on one economic level and the working-class fiction on another, indicate that the same was largely true in England. Moreover, statistics cited by the essayists indicate that economically the women were often much worse off than the fiction or they themselves realized. But as the financial possibilities for women improved, economic justifications for marriage declined, and we are conveniently back at Heilbrun's essay.

The historical development of the education of women, and the concomitant portrayal of the intellectual heroine, cannot offer such neat symmetry, but the essays do expose some interesting, helpful patterns. Medieval women-gentry were literate, and their libraries contained courtly literature, most of which depicted their fictional counterparts as leisurely, nonintellectual women who were content to go a-Maying or minister to the sick. The late Renaissance narrows somewhat the distance between the literary and the actual, since both Shakespeare and Spenser, at least, create heroines in the new mold—positive, strong, often well educated. But Latt discusses the rise of misogynist literature and the corresponding decline in the standard of women's education, social status, political participation, and economic position in the seventeenth century, a decline that continues through the Romantic period, with (as Tayler and Luria intriguingly argue) crucial effects on the literary productivity of women and the development of the novel. Now systematically excluded from training in the classics, women could not readily gain access to the main body of learning, as well as the creative lore and technique, which were needed by those who aspired to become poets. But the novel, as a new genre, offered more freedom with fewer requirements; and lack of classical training was not such a hindrance. The result was that the novel rather than poetry became the main vehicle for their introspection and their representations of themselves as women. Moreover, these women writers, excluded as they were by personal and social circumstances from developing the high art of poetry, turned the novel toward a new purpose. They created, perhaps unknowingly, a new emphasis in art, based on the developing interest in individual experience (inner and outer), yet focused on the forces of a social milieu.

The Victorian period saw the proliferation of women's books by women, but with their authors now sheltered from wide experience as well as education, too many of them were silly novels by silly novelists, to paraphrase George Eliot. But in addition to the voluminous output of Charlotte Yonge and colleagues, the period produced some of history's best writing by, for, and about women, all done in spite of the formidable antibluestocking atmosphere. Charlotte Brontë's books, for example, protest against men who fancy women's minds something like those of children, and *Middlemarch* is Eliot's testimony to the difficulties both of writing about and of being an intellectual woman in an era when reputable doctors and educators were warning that anything as strenuous as a classical education "would be physically dangerous, taxing both the reproductive organs and the smaller brain of the female beyond their strength." Even worse, such an education would seriously damage a woman's chances in the marriage market, which, given the complexity of customs, was a serious threat. Unmarried and insolvent, her alternative as a "redundant woman" (i.e., single) was to be a governess, and wretched, as any reader of Charlotte Brontë knows.

The situation in America was parallel. Ann Stanford notes that though women were taught to read, learning was low on the list of priorities, far behind housewifery, and, of course, a dowry. Anne Bradstreet was born early and wealthy enough to share the residual ideal of the learned lady that Catherine Dunn has outlined in her discussion of Elizabeth's England, and she was singled out for her learning. Immediately following her time, however, few women were able to obtain any sort of higher education. Though Mt. Holyoke in 1837 pioneered in offering to women a curriculum comparable to men's, such schools were as rare as the portraits of learned women in literature. Martha Banta, in discussing late nineteenth-century America, contends that the forms taken by anti-intellectualism in the fiction are legion and sometimes quite subtle with only infrequent praise granted to handsome minds: "What stands out is that the good head (where it *is* admired) has usually been severed from the physically enticing body."

Even in a decapitated condition, however, women in both history and literature have rebelled. Although Catherine Dunn points out that during the sixteenth century women took their "first tottering steps toward modern feminism," and Latt argues that dissenting religious groups in the seventeenth century nurtured their independence, they in effect remained preschoolers until the nineteenth century. The essays here make no attempt to record fully the rich political history of the struggle for women's rights, but the very nature of the book brings that crucial struggle into relevant focus from time to time. The evidence of social and medical history indicates that feminism erupted in the last decade of the eighteenth century because improved living conditions permitted women at last to turn from the problems of survival for themselves and their children to a consideration of their lot as human beings. Tayler and Luria study the effects of Wollstone-craft's "dazzling" *Vindication of the Rights of Women,* the most provocative, notorious, and influential feminist outcry up to that time. This renewed consideration of woman's place touched upon in the eighteenth-century essay, the dismal revelations concerning it, and the attempts to find a private niche of one's own somewhere in the social structure are topics explored further as I discuss the turbulent times of Victoria, a woman ardently against the "wicked folly of 'Woman's Rights.'" Many joined Victoria's crinolined ranks, but a vocal minority refused to serve, and women moved, kicking and screaming both for and against, into a new consciousness.

Both the effect of this new consciousness, and the entrenched patterns and stereotypes in Anglo-American literature that these essays delineate, are strikingly mirrored almost in reverse in Elizabeth Schultz's examination of black American literature. She demonstrates that black women and black literature stand both inadvertently and deliberately opposed to the traditions surrounding them. For example, Schultz notes that the black American woman is set apart by her struggle for survival against both racism and sexism. Her slave and alien status therefore put her far from the nineteenth-century white woman of leisure. As a consequence, while white women submitted to the cultural stereotype of passivity and femininity, the black women became burdened with the stereotype of masculine aggressiveness. While white women in Victorian America and after were revered for their inestimable chastity, the black woman became a victim of opposite sexual myths. Or, white women are often plastically beautiful in traditional fiction, and, in early black American fiction, Schultz has discovered that the black woman was too; usually portrayed as the Tragic Mulatto, she fulfilled the criteria for the conventional nineteenth-century fair lady. But in contemporary black literature the dichotomy is reestablished, for the black woman is constantly contending with an image of ugliness—an image which, though built by white society, has also affected the black community's judgment of her worth. And the contrasts continue at almost every level, forming a fitting correlative for the reductive thinking necessary for nourishing stereotypes.

Women in books versus women in life; their functions as symbols rather than persons in literature and often in society; their sexuality both actual and assumed; their legal, economic, and intellectual status, as it was and as it was ignored, are primary topics then, in the essays collected here. Looking backward, one thing becomes abundantly clear: art has yet to capture the feminine mystique in a way comparable to its taming of the hero. Even given the accepted, and still debated, discrepancy between art and life, as a yardstick for the woman's lot in society literature has too often been abnormally defective—and pejorative. These essays cannot correct the rule; but by exploring the social, psychological, and literary dialectic that has produced the woman's place, they do hope to determine her measure, assess her manner, and thereby provide a compact, comprehensive survey of her world, both real and imagined.

There remains only the note of thanks. In a book such as this, contributed to so well by so many, acknowledging some would be unjust to others. I will single out only two: Irene Tayler for her immensely helpful suggestions about both people and process in the initial stages of the book, and especially Haskell Springer, who not only gave me the moral and intellectual support I anticipated, but who also was still in his suffering.

—M. S.

1.

The Portrayal of Women
by Chaucer and His Age

Ann S. Haskell

Early in its history, medieval popular literature was dominated by the aristocracy and by men. But by the late fourteenth century, English society was in a state of transition: emphasis was shifting from the upper to the middle classes, from the religious to the secular, and from life on the independent manor to the integrated life of the city. And with these changes elsewhere came the inevitable literary innovations.

It is important to recall that the prominence of the middle class was a recent phenomenon and that previously the literature had dealt with it infrequently. Important figures in literature were, for example, King Arthur and his host of associated aristocratic characters, who first appeared in English in Layamon's *Brut,* probably written in 1205, and Alexander the Great, whose best-known English representation, *King Alisaunder,* is dated about 1300. Along with experimentation in form and style, the new social climate emphasized a class of people for whom literary traditions had not yet been established. Therefore it was possible to write about not only the lives of ordinary people in general, but about women too. Nevertheless, the chivalric traditions remained alive and coexisted for some time with the new. Chaucer, for example,

1

used the older, established traditions, such as the romance, side by side with those he was creating. Consideration of women in the late fourteenth-century literature, then, must include those in romances.

The term "romance" has always suggested knights and high adventure. In the popular imagination the chivalric scene is peopled with armored men who are eminently brave; their opponents, human and superhuman, who are impressive in both dimension and ferocity; and their ladies, who are fragile, virtuous, and completely predictable in behavior. The idealized society-that-never-was, displayed prominently in the romances, is a showcase for the hero—highborn, titled, and property owning. All other roles are supportive: opponents, the more formidable the better, attest to his bravery; subordinates buttress his position of power; and ladies are passive receivers of and foils for his activities as lover and rescuer. The knight in armor is the essence of chivalric medievalism and woman is a single part of his supporting structure.

The pattern for the knight as representative of medieval English chivalry is depicted in the romantic fiction, romantic art, and even the romantic history of the era. A particularly striking contrast between the real and ideal in late English medieval society may be seen by comparing the memorial brasses and illustrations for the romances during the period. A good example of the brasses is that for Sir Symon Felbrygge and his wife Margaret, dating from 1416 and located in Felbrigg, Norfolk. Symon and Margaret are represented within two areas of identical size, and both are depicted in full figure, of the same height, and canopied with identical arches and heraldic crests in matching size and placement. The secondary position of women in the ideal society is well illustrated by a fifteenth-century miniature in Froissart's Fourth Book of Chronicles, covering Richard II's latter years on the throne, "Knights and Ladies Riding to the Tournament in London" (Harley Ms. 4379, fol. 99), for instance. The women in the scene are placed on the far side of the knights whom they accompany, making one of the ladies visible only from the waist up and the other three from the shoulders upward. All are dressed alike, and their plastic, expressionless faces, turned toward the knights, are identical. By contrast, the knights are depicted in the foreground of the scene, each wearing a highly individualized suit of armor, carrying a shield painted with his own coat of arms, and mounted on a horse covered with a cloth of ornate, distinctive pattern.[1]

Why a specific ideal is requisite for a certain society at a particular time in its history is enigmatic; the reason late medieval England still needed a chivalric ideal is not likely ever to be known exactly. Nevertheless, it was a stimulating, transitional—and therefore perhaps uneasy—milieu, needing the security of a former golden age. The discrepancy that existed between the ideal in art and the real in life is significant and the difference is even discernible within the art itself late in the period, when the romance becomes a subject of satire in, for example, Chaucer's Canterbury tale of Sir Thopas [2] or the *Tournament of Tottenham*.[3]

The popular concept of medieval life is only a small part of the whole picture. In addition to brief intervals of high adventure, there was the endless struggle simply to survive. There were not only the knighted, wellborn and wealthy, but the nameless, baseborn and poverty-racked. And besides the ladies of the upper classes, there was a host of other women: weaving gildswomen, serving girls, wives of the newly affluent middle class, women agricultural workers, and femme sole traders who operated small businesses.[4]

Even before the Age of Chaucer, which challenged the supremacy of the romance, there had always been other secular literary genres. (An example is the fabliau, a brilliant, short literary form of French origin, the best English examples of which are Chaucerian.[5]) Nevertheless, the romance was most pervasive, and even today the literature of the Middle Ages is popularly synonymous with knightly adventure and that slippery modern invention, courtly love.[6] According to the latter tradition, there was a religion of love, which was coupled with humility, courtesy, and adultery, and which, in treating woman as a nearly unattainable love object, effectively dehumanized her. This lifeless puppet figure, who offers no competition to the hero-knight's center stage, continues to be equated with medieval woman.

The vast majority of medieval women, poor and illiterate, left no record of themselves, except obliquely through inventories, rolls, and other official papers. There is, however, a body of letters written by medieval women of the gentry, a class whose men were knighted, who lived in castles, and who were the real-life counter-parts of romance heroines. The correspondence of the Pastons, dating principally from the fifteenth century, gives us details of a family who lived near Norwich, and whose wealth included the estate of Sir John Fastolf and Caister Castle. The Paston Letters reflect the violence, uncertainty, and lawlessness of the times: illegal seizure of property by any group whose strength was sufficient to wrest it from its owners, slow and inefficient legal redress, pirate raids from the nearby North Sea, rape, and outbreaks of the plague. These letters, augmented by the Stonor, Cely, and Plumpton correspondence, clearly illustrate the dicho-tomy that exists between late medieval literary portrayal of women in romances and living women in the corresponding social stratum. (I have discussed this body of letters more fully elsewhere.[7])

The life-styles of women such as the Pastons offer the reason for their independence: the husbands lived first at their universities and later in cities, where they pursued their businesses or professions, while the wives lived on and managed the family estates in the country. The women were responsible for raising families, which were sometimes large, as well as overseeing the operations of landholdings, which were frequently several and far apart. These women were emotionally and physically sturdy, capable of fending off armed attacks, running agricultural opera-tions, selling crops and buying provisions for large numbers of people, arbitrating labor disputes and collecting rents, coping with violence, and knowledgeably handling legal matters.

The heavy responsibilities of estate and family management for women of the gentry were undertaken in the face of several handicaps. First, these women were not formally educated for their jobs, as were their husbands, though the control of such extensive landholdings as those of the Pastons was formidable. The men in such families typically studied law, degrees in which the Pastons took at Cambridge University. Second, they had the frequent inconvenience of pregnancy, though childbearing was an obvious sign of femininity and could have prevented accusations that their behavior was masculine or, in some instances, possibly even hysterical, a condition thought to result from a wandering, unused uterus *(hystera)* pressing on the brain.[8] Fear of such charges is seen in these women's frequent resort to action through a male "screen," another impediment in the midst of heavy and time-consuming duties. Religious and social responsibilities added to the list of obligations for ladies of the landed gentry. Furthermore, such women were literate and their libraries contained courtly literature; clearly, they had encountered their fictional opposite numbers, whom they little resembled.[9]

The literary view of medieval women is inconsistent, both because of the writers' varied, individual ideal views of women, and because of the influence of clerical antifeminists. The Prologue of the Wife of Bath's Tale is concerned with the clerical sexist tradition and is a good point of access to the subject.[10] The melange of nonclerical writers consists of perspectives as diverse as those of the Knight of La Tour Landry, offering practical didacticism; the subjective religious visions of Margery Kempe and Julian (or Juliana) of Norwich; the prescriptive views of the Goodman of Paris; the advice for living a strait, religious existence, according to the philosophy of the *Ancrene Riwle*'s author; the lofty yearnings of Charles d'Orléans; and the nostalgic view of women vis-à-vis men drawn by Sir Thomas Malory. Additional views of women are found in saints' legends, such as the story of St. Cecilia in Chaucer's Second Nun's Tale, and feminine allegorical personifications, such as Lady Meed in *Piers Plowman.*

Though paradoxically the period produced, among other romances, the brilliant *Sir Gawain and the Green Knight* (c. 1375-1400), by the late English Middle Ages there are indications that the romance (if not obsolete) is definitely obsolescent.[11] Chaucer could already satirize the genre as passé, and within the century Malory was to write the *Morte Darthur* (c. 1469), the stunning finish to both a form and the ideal it celebrated, with conscious, bittersweet nostalgia. The representation of women also changed. They were portrayed as individuals, rather than as types, and their characters explored in depth; they could finally occupy the literary prominence once reserved for men only.

In general, later medieval literature includes more information about people of both sexes than the earlier literature. But beginning noticeably with Chaucer, the lives of women especially are accessible through literature. Typically, the nonallegorical, secular literature of the English Middle Ages had portrayed its women first, in hierarchical social order, i.e., in a framework of classes from queen to peasant; second, in moral stratification, i.e., in a range from saint to sinner; third, in a literary spectrum, i.e., from the two-dimensional, plastic type-character to the fully drawn, unique individual. While it is true that these characteristics are appropriate in a way to all literary characters, there are differences for their application to medieval women. Most importantly, the three features are clearly interdependent. The lady portrayed as a virtuous, inaccessible ideal seems to have been more stereotypical than the lower-class woman, but on close examination it becomes apparent that women such as the miller's wife in the Reeve's Tale are locked into roles as much as, say, the emperor's daughter in *William of Palerne*. It is, then, a matter of formality, a dimension of distance, rather than type, that makes the woman in the romance seem less accessible to the reader than the woman in the fabliau. The formidable quantity of romance, dealing with identifiable, important people, conveys a feeling of greater weight. The fabliau, an economical genre, (English examples of which are Chaucer's Miller's, Summoner's and Friar's tales), deals with distinctly common people. Because its plot is paramount, the fabliau contains character portrayals that are lean. Further, the quantity of fabliau text is not great. The comparison of fabliaux and romances presents a situation in which the social hierarchy obscures the literary hierarchy.

For women characters in late English medieval literature, moral stratification was usually a condition of sexual behavior. While male characters might be judged in relation to the entire gamut of morality, a woman's physical virtue superseded all other moral considerations. Indeed, physical virtue was so important that it could apparently cancel out other varieties of error.[12]

While the change in portrayal of women from early to later medieval literature is great, it is not a complete transformation. The lower-class woman is still remarkably absent as an active literary character. The covert manifestations of her presence are everywhere—the lavendered sheets, the meals, the needlework. In *Sir Gawain and the Green Knight*, for example, the hero's clothes were embroidered "As many burde ther aboute had ben seven wynter in toune" (614). Here a queen's clothes were laid out for her, there a hero's horse fed, and wine brought to a king—all by unknown, nameless people, by unseen hands. An entire group of people were nonexistent as leading characters for the authors of their time, and the romances, products of earlier conventions, retain the unseen serving women of early Middle English.

Since the correlation of virtue and social standing had been a foregone conclusion, it is the extremes of the society that have offered the least possibility for variation: if a woman were poor she was expected to be more vulnerable to temptation than a woman of higher birth; if she were a queen she was expected to be a shadowy sketch of the Virgin. It is not so much the actual matching of social rank, moral classification, and literary fullness— we can think of many exceptions—as the expectation of these correlations. When they are broken we need explanations. Sometimes the explanations worked to reinforce degrees of depravity or virtue, to strengthen serf as saint or queen as que*a*n. For example, purity bestowed on a peasant woman, such as the incorruptible old woman in the Friar's Tale, or Griselda in the Clerk's Tale, made the quality all the more remarkable. Or the nobility of an aristocratic woman, such as the queen in *Sir Launfal,* might intensify her sinfulness.

It is when the literature moves away from the extremes or moral expectation and the boundaries of society, with their rigid typecasting, into the middle class that the variation in literature, resulting from the exploration of good and bad, can take place. The middle class in general and its women especially were an untapped literary resource.

Beyond the various moral and social stratifications, what do we know of the specific work and activities of medieval women from Chaucer and his contemporaries? We learn, for one thing, almost nothing of their mothering. Children appear briefly where they are required to fill slots, but they are nameless and usually without dialogue. The infant lying in his cradle in the darkened bedroom in the Reeve's Tale is the marker by which the bed swapping is accomplished, and the occasion of the child's death prior to the time of the story is one means by which the deceptive nature of the friar in the Summoner's Tale is exposed. But we find nothing concerning the relationship between a fourteenth-century mother and her children.

The lady's role was simply to exist. Emily, in the Knight's Tale, for example, does nothing; she engages in pastimes, literally to "pass the time." She goes for walks, picks flowers, inspires love but does not give it. Likewise, we learn how other unoccupied ladies—Dorigen in the Franklin's Tale, Criseyde in the *Troilus,* Euridyce in *Sir Orpheus,* the host's wife in *Gawain*—amuse themselves. Dorigen plays games, Criseyde's household maidens tell stories and sing songs, the Wife of Bath's queen and her court ponder what women want most, while Malory's Guinevere goes a-Maying. Pertelote, portrayed as a romance lady, is learned in plant lore, one of the few meaningful occupations for ladies, part of the noblesse oblige of ministering to the sick.

In the houses of the bourgeoisie there is closer contact between women and their servants, with the actual overseeing of households by their mistresses. The merchant's wife in the Shipman's Tale calls her husband to dinner when the servants announce that it is ready; the Summoner's friar gives his order for capon directly to the goodwife; the wives of the gildsmen are sufficiently well off to bring along a cook while traveling. And wives of the conspicuously prosperous in Chaucer's canon normally advertise their husbands' wealth. They wear their affluence like billboards, demanding public recognition for their status by preceding the rest of the congregation in church at making offerings, as shown by the Wife of Bath, the gildsmen's wives, and the Reeve's Tale's miller's wife, who was "as digne as water in a dich."

The poverty of lower-class women can be judged by their scale of material values. The marginal wealth of the poor woman in the Friar's Tale is seen in her valuing a just reward for the summoner even above the price of her pan. And the frugal existence of the widow in the frame of the Nun's Priest's Tale is earned by her services as a dairywoman and her spartan living conditions. Three lines in the Pardoner's Tale enumerate other occupations for lower-class medieval women—"tombesteres/ . . . frutesteres,/ Syngeres with harpes, baudes, wafereres"—without elaboration. Even Chaucer, who makes the characters of women vastly more accessible to us than did his predecessors, leaves many areas of their day-to-day activities out of his tales; it is our copious body of appended historical criticism that makes us think otherwise.[13]

Of the actual social states of women, we have miscellaneous data revealed through the literature. The widow, for example, we know little about from the literary context. The mother of the Prioress's boy martyr, the old woman of the Friar's Tale, and Criseyde, for example, are all widows, yet we have scant information about the practical affairs of their lives. As literary characters they have little in common except the status of widow, and, hence, vulnerability. The source of their incomes is not revealed, though the Wife of Bath illustrates that one route to comfortable widowhood is financially advantageous marriages in youth. Except for the Wife of Bath's self-imposed urgency, pressure to remarry seems to be altogether absent in the lives of Chaucerian and other fictive widows late in the period, in contrast to the speed of remarriage for real women in the late English Middle Ages.

Some aspects of courting are revealed. Alisoun in the Miller's Tale, though only sufficiently far up the social ladder to warrant the rank of mistress with a lord, is highly desirable for marriage to a carpenter, lower down the scale. In fact, she seems to be following the path of her senior counterpart, Alice, Wife of Bath, in preparing for later financial security. From the Reeve's Tale we learn that a wife's dowry and lineage (even from a priest) are much more important than her legitimacy, though paradoxically the spoiling of her daughter's virginity, a literally salable item, is of real moment. A maidenhead is more precious than married parents. In the Miller's Tale we learn that the open wooing of Alisoun by Absolom is only a nuisance and is, incidentally, renewed proof for her husband of her continuing worth. On the other hand, the physical liaison with Nicholas must be covert because of the husband's jealousy.

From the literature we see that extramarital relationships were common, though the range of reactions to them varied from resignation (Miller's Prologue) to jealousy (Merchant's Tale) to death (Manciple's Tale). In the Shipman's Tale an affair merely gives the wife a temporary handicap, rather than putting her permanently out of action.

Of greater significance than the extramarital affairs themselves is the fact that in this literature the woman is invariably the strayer. "Who hath no wif, he is no cokewold," the Miller says in the Prologue to his Canterbury tale (A 3152). While many men in Chaucer's canon are portrayed as lusty, no lecher is a married man. The consistent pattern is that of wife deceiving her husband. Though men might be generally represented as lecherous, they are not depicted in specific affairs or revealed as adulterers, in direct contrast to the literary treatment of women characters. This fact, considered with the previously discussed concept of the supremacy of bodily virtue for women, may be attributable to the lack of contraceptives in the Middle Ages; the resulting pregnancies for women were obvious revelations of their behavior. Men had no such indisputable betraying device and could, in fact, even be known as "chaste maidens" in the language of the Middle English romances and religious treatises.

Chaucer's literature frequently reveals keen interest in the strength of women, rather than their weakness. He stresses this fact through such characters as Griselda, Constance, Prudence, Virginia, and May. Though he has frequently constructed his tales on the bases of old stories, he has almost always strengthened his versions of the original female characters. The sparkling Wife, his most positive creation of a strong woman, is also noteworthy because Chaucer has used her to express some of his own important social beliefs, including forceful ideas about women. Because he was a member of the middle class himself, his consideration of such subjects as gentilesse must have been of personal as well as of general societal importance to him. Using a woman who was also a member of the middle class to present his ideas is one of his distinct innovations. The mouthpiece is truly the message.

That a woman's active sexuality was equal in importance to chastity is an idea that Chaucer enunciates through Alice. In her Prologue she says:

> "Wher can ye seye in any man
> That hye God defended mariage
> By expres word? I pray yow, telleth me.
> Or where comanded he virginitee?"
> (D 59-62)

Furthermore, she is a statement on the subject in her own right, for there is no other Chaucerian character more fully drawn or more attractive, there is no other secular woman among the Canterbury pilgrims, nor is there a woman like Alice elsewhere in Middle English literature.

The concept of virtue's being inherent rather than inherited, a property of the truly gentle rather than the gentleborn, is voiced most emphatically in the Wife's tale. Chaucer has reiterated the idea several times. There is the short poem we know as "Gentilesse": "ther may no man . . . / Bequethe his heir his vertuous noblesse" (16-17). And the Franklin's Tale also explores the idea (F, 1607-12, 1472 f., 1526 f.). But Chaucer's strongest statement on the subject of gentilesse concerns the rights of women. It is the pillow speech delivered by the Wife of Bath's tough old hag who turns tender young beauty, the implicit promise Alice makes to her own prospective suitors. With this vignette Chaucer connects gentilesse, masculine superiority, chivalry, and the romance. Feature for feature, all of the elements of feminine subservience in the romance are presented. Using an older, converted story, Chaucer discusses:

1. Rape—The knight's ravishing of a woman unable to escape the attack renders him similarly powerless, first at the mercy of the queen and her ladies; next before the old crone (only by means of whose answer he escapes death); and ultimately before the superiority of all women, to which he must not only admit, but surrender himself.

2. Class superiority—The hag attacks his class bigotry and addresses the question of true gentilesse, specifically singling out the paradox of Arthurian knights, ostensible protectors of all the weak, who preferred the highborn, the beautiful, and the young.

3. Physical beauty—She tests the importance of physical beauty by literally opposing it to virtue, which she presents in the form of a lifetime choice.

4. Masculine superiority—She blasts the concept of male intellectual supremacy by hanging his very life on the string of woman's wit.

5. Constriction of choice—Finally, by winning the knight as a gift from the queen (in the same way women were often handed over as prizes in the chivalric tradition), the old woman opens the whole odious question of arranged marriages, undoubtedly one of the bitterest experiences for a medieval woman. (The Paston Letters vividly reveal the harsh consequences of a woman's refusal of an arranged marriage and of a woman's marrying the man of her choice against her family's will.[14] Young Elizabeth Paston,

who rebelled against her family's choice of an old, disfigured widower to be her husband, was locked in and physically abused, while Margery, who betrothed herself to the Pastons' bailiff, was locked out of the house and thereafter excluded from the family as if actually dead.) The forced marriage implies payment in kind for the knight's imposition of physical sexuality during the rape. He pleads: "Taak al my good, and lat my body go" (D 1061), complaining specifically of the hag's looks, age, and social status. He says, "Thou art so loothly and so oold also,/ And therto comen of so lough a kynde" (D 1100-1101).

The discomfort of the knight, turning on the skewer of his own bigotry—"He walweth and he turneth to and fro" (D 1085)—before yielding totally to the superiority of a woman and of women, is the epitome of romance reversal. Chaucer's treatment of the central character of the romance, the knight, is a statement of the demise of the genre. And his attack on the dying literary form strikes at its weakest point, its portrayal of women. A comparison of the tale with its analogues reveals an especially important change made by Chaucer: the rape is unique to the Wife of Bath's Tale. The knights in other versions magnify their courtesy by marrying the woman, whereas Chaucer's knight, a rapist, has no courtesy to redeem and his crime has determined his life, including marriage.

At a distance of hundreds of years, we have difficulty in judging how well medieval woman was represented in the literature of her time. But we do know that one of the most misunderstood areas of her life is embodied in the phrase "happily ever after," concerning the quality and length of marriage in the Middle Ages—for while we cannot determine the emotional climate of these marriages, we do have information regarding their longevity.

Since divorce is our society's method for terminating marriage prior to death, it is popularly assumed that in the absence of divorce as we know it in the Middle Ages, marriages always lasted until death. While lifetime marriage existed for a large percentage of medieval people, it should be recalled that average lifespans were much shorter than today's, owing to frequent deaths in childbirth, wars, and epidemics. It was not at all uncommon for a given couple to have several marriages each during their lifetimes, accounting for a shifting marriage group of people, maybe half a dozen adults and many more children, loosely related through the marriage at one time of one couple in the group. Furthermore, while rules for marriage were particularly convoluted, it was these very complications that could provide legitimate bases for dissolution of marriages, should one partner so desire. For example, consanguinity (the degree of blood relationship of a couple) or even variation of words spoken in wedding vows could be used as evidence of the marriage's illegitimacy.[15] Change of marriage partners was common and a recognized fact in medieval England. Hence, the Wife of Bath's several marriages would have been of far less interest to her society than to ours.

The coexistence of two very different major types of popular literature, which represent women so differently, is difficult to reconcile after so many centuries. Yet the contrast itself is valuable. In the work we refer to as the *Morte Darthur*, Malory reveals a sentimental yearning for a world in which the hero, an armored knight, was the center. It is the kind of longing indulged in by people in every age when surveying social changes of which they are not a part. Though we can discern only the general nature of those changes, it is unquestionable that Malory was reacting to a real shift in the balance between the sexes. He nostalgically presented an old form and defended old sentiments in an era in which they were outmoded. In contrast, Chaucer was at once creating new forms and enunciating contemporary ideas, and challenging the old sentiments by reinterpreting the genres that gave them literary expression.

Notes

1 For the Felbrygge brass, see Muriel Clayton, *Catalogue of Rubbings of Brasses and Incised Slabs* (London, Victoria and Albert Museum, 1968), plate 17; the miniature is printed in G. G. Coulton's *The Chronicler of European Chivalry* (London, 1930), p. 28.

2 Chaucer references are to F. N. Robinson's *The Works of Geoffrey Chaucer*, 2d. ed. (Boston, 1957), unless otherwise noted.

3 This and several other romances may be found in *Middle English Verse Romances*, ed. Donald B. Sands (New York, 1966). For a convenient survey of literature of the period, consult Albert C. Baugh's comments in Volume I of *A Literary History of England*, 2d ed., printed separately as *The Middle Ages* (New York, 1967).

4 Sylvia Thrupp, *The Merchant Class of Medieval London (1300-1500)* (Chicago, 1948), pp. 170-73; A. Abram, *Social Life in England in the Fifteenth Century* (London, 1909), p. 131 f.; and Eileen Power, "The Position of Women," in *The Legacy of the Middle Ages,* ed. C. G. Crump and E. F. Jacob (Oxford, 1926), pp. 401-33. On romance women see M. A. Gist, *Love and War in the Middle English Romances* (Philadelphia, 1947), p. 11 f.; and A. E. Harris, *The Heroine of the Middle English Romances, Western Reserve University Bulletin,* n.s., 21 (1928), p. 5 f. Consult also such studies as Kathleen Casey's "The Cheshire Cat: Reconstructing the Experience of Medieval Woman" in *Liberating Women's History,* ed. Berenice A. Carroll (Urbana, 1976), pp. 224-49.

5 See such collections as R. Hellman and R. O'Gorman's *Fabliaux* (New York, 1965).

6 See E. T. Donaldson's "The Myth of Courtly Love," in his *Speaking of Chaucer* (New York, 1970), pp. 154-63.

7 "The Paston Women on Marriage in Fifteenth-century England," *Viator* 4 (1973), 459-71. The subject is dealt with fully in my forthcoming book, *Medieval Women and Marriage.*

8 Vern Bullough, "Medieval Medical and Scientific Views of Women," *Viator* 4 (1973), 498.

9 H. S. Bennett, *The Pastons and Their England,* 2d ed. (Cambridge, 1932), pp. 261-62, iii, 112-13; G. G. Coulton, *Medieval Panorama* (Cambridge, 1938; repr. New York, 1955), p. 627; A. B. Ferguson, *The Indian Summer of English Chivalry* (Durham, 1960), p. 182 f.

10 See Robert A. Pratt's notes to the Wife of Bath's Prologue in *The Tales of Canterbury* (Boston, 1974), p. 268.

11 Compare Chaucer's sophisticated versions of the fabliaux, which appeared long past their heyday.

12 Power, "The Position of Women," p. 404, discusses the body-is-all theory.

13 I do not wish to imply authorial responsibility here, but simply to point out a misimpression. See, for example, the voluminous scholarship directed toward each detail of the Prioress's existence. A. C. Baugh lists some of these articles in his bibliography of Chaucer (New York, 1968).

14 See Haskell, "The Paston Women," pp. 466-68.

15 F. R. H. Du Boulay, *An Age of Ambition: English Society in the Late Middle Ages* (New York, 1970).

2.

The Changing Image of Woman in Renaissance Society and Literature

Catherine M. Dunn

In sixteenth-century England men and women of all classes engaged in a lively controversy about women—their moral character, their capabilities, and especially their place in the scheme of society.[1] The traditional social theory had viewed women, regardless of rank, solely as wives and mothers. The law, too, had dictated that a woman's first commandment was submission and obedience to her husband.[2] Furthermore, women were considered inferior not only in power and position, but in nature as well. Some writers denied them a "private will,"[3] and a few even questioned the possibility of a woman's having a soul.[4] Morally they were evil, since they were descendants of Eve, though for the propagation of the race they were a necessary evil. Some writers did grant women a limited goodness, while only a very few thought them morally equal or even superior to men.[5] Intellectually they were also seen as limited; most Englishmen, including women themselves, thought that a woman was by nature incapable of higher learning, being framed by God only for domestic duties.

Though these negative attitudes continued to dominate throughout much of the period, doubts gradually stirred in the minds of Renaissance men and women about the injustices of this accepted way of life, with the result that by mid-century a change is evident, the product in part of humanism, that leavening which brought so many other changes to the Renaissance. The first effects appear in the upper levels of society; for when the education of the gentleman was no longer merely a matter of skill at arms and courtly manners but of solid knowledge based on the classics, the gentlewoman, too, could and did seek to share in the new learning. Simultaneously this activity at the top produced reverberations down through the middle and lower levels of society, where social conditions, especially the rise and expansion of the mercantile class, were even more conducive to change. At first the increasing demand of women for education and greater freedom brought suspicion and antagonism, as well as a flood of satire and books of advice to wives on marriage and their duties. But with time the controversy subsided, and in general the woman's role continued to be primarily that of wife and mother.

Nevertheless, there were some significant gains, most notably in the woman's right to choose her own husband. Formerly, the parents had maintained absolute authority in the choice of husbands for their daughters, the selection usually being made on the basis of social and economic considerations. But during the last decade of the century the literature began to criticize these arranged marriages for the unhappiness they often caused. A broadside ballad from 1591, excerpted below, provides a notable example. Written about an actual case that aroused much interest, it presents in very sympathetic terms the story of a young girl condemned to die for the murder of her rich old husband:

> On knees I prayde they would not me constrain;
> With teares I cryde their purpose to refrain;
> With sighes and sobbes I did them often moue,
> I might not wed whereas I could not loue.
> . . . .
> You parents fond, that greedy-minded bee,
> And seeke to graffe vpon the golden tree,
> Consider well and rightfull iudges bee,

And giue you doome twixt parents' loue and mee.
I was their childe, and bound for to obey,
Yet not to loue where I no loue could laye.
I married was to much and endlesse strife;
But faith before had made me Strangwidge wife.

. . . .

You Denshire dames, and courteous Cornwall knights,
That here are come to visit wofull wights,
Regard my griefe, and marke my wofull end,
But to your children be a better friend.[6]

Emotional appeals such as this may have been a factor; at any rate, a change occurred in the social customs surrounding marriage as women demanded a greater voice. As a consequence, it became more and more necessary for the suitor to gain the favor of the woman first, and then the consent of her parents.[7]

This development clearly marked an important advance in the social role assigned to women. In her person, however, the Renaissance woman, despite her altering position and attitudes, was still expected to conform to the historical ideal. Above all she was to be chaste in thought and action.[8] This virtue was especially important for gentlewomen, who, because of their delicate constitution and rich diet, were supposedly more susceptible to temptations against chastity than women of lower station.[9] Also much praised were those virtues attendant upon chastity: modesty, humility, constancy, and especially temperance. In addition the woman/wife was to be pious, patient, kind, and sweet. Hopefully she was beautiful as well, although beauty was chiefly mentioned in connection with the highborn lady. Her behavior was carefully prescribed. She was to tend to her household duties industriously, so as not to waste her husband's goods; she must be silent much of the time and not speak out or argue, so as not to be considered a shrew; and she must never be witty or clever lest she become a shameless temptress of men.

These moral and intellectual qualities belonged as much to the ideal woman of an earlier age as they did to the woman of the sixteenth century. What sets the Renaissance woman, primarily the gentlewoman, apart from her predecessors was, appropriately enough, her learning. Indeed, the education of women was a matter of increasing concern by mid-century. A pioneer in advocating such education was Richard Mulcaster, master of the Merchant Taylors School of London. In his important treatise on education entitled *Positions* (1561),[10] Mulcaster still reflects some of the prejudice of his time in such passing remarks as "naturally the *male* is more worthy" (p. 133) and "the bringing vp of young *maidens* in any kynd of learning, is but an accessory by the wayes" (p. 134). And the prejudice lingers too in his justification of the training of women on the basis of man's duty to them:

> Are they not the seminary of our succession? the naturall frye, from whence we are to chuse our naturall, next, and most necessarie freindes? The very selfe same creatures, which were made for our comfort, the onely good to garnish our aloneness, the nearest companions in our weale and wo? the peculiar and priuiest partakers in all our fortunes? borne for vs to life, bound to vs till death? (p. 168)

Still, he admits that young maidens often have "aptnesse" and achieve "excellent effects" when taught (p. 167), and so he would educate them in those subjects which will prove no "let [to] their most laudable dueties in marriage" but will rather "bewtifie them, with most singular ornamentes" (p. 169). These are chiefly *"reading* well, *writing* faire, *singing* sweete, *playing* fine," and "skill of languages" (p. 179), specified later as the learned languages, apparently Latin and Greek (p. 181). Needlework, of course, is included (p. 177), but so are drawing, philosophy (presumably logic), and rhetoric.[11]

Mulcaster will allow girls to attend the public grammar schools, though he prefers private tutors. Quite surprisingly, these tutors may occasionally be women, who are "fittest in some respectes," though men teachers generally "frame them best, and . . . will bring them vp excellently well" (p. 167). He recommends that the education normally continue until about the age of thirteen or fourteen, although the girl's aptitude and "the state and abilitie" of her parents may allow for a longer time spent in study (pp. 181-82). He is of course thinking primarily of the daughters of middle-class and wealthy families who will eventually be wives and mothers, though he does recognize that different "callings" require different kinds of education. Here he includes, quite unusually, women who must learn a trade in order to support themselves. Of major concern is the education of a girl born to be a ruler, or the wife of one, for she needs great gifts and special training so as to be able to care for the country and to bring honor to herself (p. 180).

Even earlier than Mulcaster in advocating more education for women was the great Spanish humanist, Juan Luis Vives, brought to England by Queen Catherine as tutor to the Princess Mary. He set forth his theories in a treatise commissioned by Catherine entitled *de Institutione Feminae Christianae* (1523).[12] Though he grants that a woman is "a frayle thinge, and of weake discretion" (sig. 9ᵛ), Vives nevertheless asserts that differences in intellectual power are individual, not sexual. And so, while a young lady should learn to spin, weave, sew, paint, and cook (sigs. 4ᵛ-5ᵛ), she should also study, to the full extent of her ability, grammar and rhetoric, scripture, the Church Fathers, and classical writers such as Plato, Plutarch, Livy, Cicero, and Seneca (sig. 11ʳ).

As a result of the efforts of Mulcaster, Vives, and other writers on education, it was at last conceded that women had minds equal to those of men. As Ruth Kelso points out:

> . . . however restricted and orthodox a view was presented of certain commonly praised virtues in women, these men of the renaissance were ready to derive woman's true greatness and equality with men from her intellectual gifts, her capacity to profit by the study of books, to engage in speculation on high matters, and to invent, the greatest gift of all. (p. 30)

To be sure, not everyone was so enthusiastic about women's capabilities, and they were still often hampered by less favorable opportunities for education and travel,[13] by disbelief in their competence, and by social restrictions of all kinds. But the pendulum was definitely beginning to swing. Writers cited learned women of ancient times as models of what could be achieved by education,[14] and many contemporary women were emerging to join their number.

Among those who made impressive achievements in learning were several women rulers. One to be prominently singled out was Elisabetta Gonzaga, the Duchess of Urbino, celebrated by Castiglione as "so comely and grave a Majestie, . . . so great and so vertuous a Ladie" (sig. Aiiii). In the same work Duke Julian de Medicis extols the praises of several others:

> And to goe out of Italy, remember ye, in our dayes we have seene Anne French Queene, a verie great Ladie, no lesse in vertue than in state: and if in justice and mildnesse, liberalitie and holinesse of life, ye lust to compare her to the kinges Charles and Lewis (which had been wife to both of them) you shall not find her a jotte inferior to them.
>
> Behold the Ladie Margaret, daughter to the Emperor Maximilian, which with great wisdom and justice hetherto hath ruled, and still doth her state.
>
> But omitting all other, tell me . . . what king or what prince hath there beene in our daies, or yet many yeares before in Christendom, that deserveth to be compared to Queene Isabel of Spaine. . . . [There] hath not beene in our time in the worlde a more cleare example of true goodnesse, stoutnesse of courage, wisdom, religion, honestie, courtesie, liberalitie: to be briefe, of al vertue, than Queen Isabel.[15]

Isabella's youngest daughter Catalina, destined to become Queen Catherine of England, the first wife of Henry VIII, was also a woman of considerable accomplishment.[16] Besides the usual feminine skills she also learned heraldry, genealogy, history, horsemanship, and falconry; she was carefully instructed in the classics, in Roman history, in civil and canon law, in the Christian Latin poets, and in the Church Fathers. To humanists like Vives and his master Erasmus, Catherine appeared "a miracle of feminine learning." [17]

Exemplary though Catherine may have been, however, to sixteenth-century Englishmen there was only one true paragon: Elizabeth. She was extravagantly celebrated in poetry and prose, in drama, in art, and in music, not only as an excellent and virtuous sovereign but especially as a woman of unique mind and learning.[18] These gifts were evident even when she was a young girl, as her tutor Roger Ascham testifies. Setting forth her dedication to learning and her mastery of classical and modern languages as a model, he concludes that, most praiseworthy of all, she has such "excellency of learning" as "scarce one or two rare wits in both the universities have in many years reached unto." If only others would imitate her example, England could become "for learning and wisdom in nobility, a spectacle to all the world." [19]

Countless Renaissance ladies of lesser rank also earned reputations for their learning. Early in the century the most noteworthy examples were Margaret, Elizabeth, and Cecily, the daughters of Sir Thomas More. Margaret became an especially brilliant scholar, but all More's daughters learned Latin, Greek, logic, philosophy, theology, mathematics, and astronomy.[20] Later in the period appeared such learned women as Lady Jane Grey, who was commended by Ascham in *The Scholemaster* for her ability in Greek (fol. 11[v]); and the daughters of Sir Anthony Cooke, especially Anne, who became the mother of Sir Francis Bacon, and is said to have been associated with her father in teaching the young king, Edward VI.[21] Other extraordinary women patronized literature: Mary Sidney, the Countess of Pembroke, an author and the center of a literary coterie; Lady Elizabeth Carey, a kinswoman and patroness of Spenser; her daughter Elizabeth, author and patroness of Thomas Nashe—the list could be extended with the names of ladies from many of the great houses all over England. But it was to be expected that such women would emerge during the reign of a queen as learned and as favorable to literature as Elizabeth, for in her court an uneducated woman would have been decidedly out of place.

While this degree of learning was not found among the mercantile and craftsman classes, these women too found their roles in English society changing as the century progressed. Louis B. Wright points out that women in the Middle Ages had borne their share of responsibility; yet the commercial expansion in the early Renaissance, which led to more widely distributed wealth and a rapid multiplication of the middle class, augmented the responsibilities and obligations of women (pp. 202-3). At the same time, the break with earlier medieval conventions and with the Church of Rome brought about increased liberties for women as well as new attitudes regarding marriage and the home. That they had, by the end of the century, considerable independence is clearly evidenced by contemporary records. For example, the records of the Stationers Company reveal successful women printers and booksellers, most of whom had inherited their husbands' trades.[22] Women were admitted to some guilds on an equal footing with men; they served as shop managers and assistants, or aided their husbands in the conduct of small businesses; and after the deaths of their husbands they frequently continued to run the shop or business alone.[23]

The middle-class woman's life at home changed as well. The reformed church, with a less conservative attitude toward all relations between the sexes, tended to give greater dignity to women. Married chastity, not virginity, was glorified, and there was a growing insistence upon the necessity for both husband and wife to maintain the virtue and integrity of the home. The wife was not to be treated as her husband's chattel, and she should share his confidence and trust. Drawing on manuals of domestic guidance for his evidence, Wright comments on this gradual improvement in the position of middle-class women: "Though the husband remained the commander, with powers of discipline if necessary, the increased emphasis upon women's spiritual and material rights paved the way that led toward theoretical equality—a position which a few writers in the early seventeenth century were already beginning to maintain" (p. 227).

This struggle of all women to rise above the subordinate role in which the traditional social mores had placed them is clearly mirrored in the literature, beginning quite early in the sixteenth century. As one would expect, the great humanist writers were in advance of their time in granting concessions to women, especially in the area of education. Sir Thomas More, for example, provides for the education of every citizen in the Utopian commonwealth. Even the least apt receive the rudiments and are introduced to good literature;[24] those more gifted, both men and women, are encouraged to continue formal education indefinitely in the hours before daybreak when they are free from manual labor (p. 129). The Utopians study such subjects as music, dialectic, arithmetic, geometry, astrology, ethics, philosophy, and religion (p. 159). Hythloday instructs them in the Greek language and literature, introducing them to writers as varied as Aristotle, Plato, Homer, Euripides, Herodotus, and Galen (p. 183). Both sexes learn agriculture and some kind of craft, the women being assigned the easier ones such as wool-working or linen-making (p. 123). The women have no role in the government of Utopia; they are of course destined to become wives and mothers, and the duty to cook and prepare the food is still theirs. But otherwise they have some semblance of equality and they are free to devote their nonworking time to intellectual pursuits.

Castiglione's *Il Cortegiano* (1528) proposes a somewhat more limited education for women in letters, arts, and virtues. However, he is one of the first, in the person of Lord Julian, to accept women rulers (sig. Ccii), citing Plato as his exemplar. Another speaker in the dialogue, Lord Gaspar, still clings to the older antifeminist position that women are "unperfect creatures" by whom the "world hath no profit . . . but for getting of children" (sig. Ggi). His view is rejected by the other men in the company, a clear sign of the changing attitude toward women. Lord Julian's response summarizes the feminine situation quite clearly: "[women] wish not to bee a man to make them more perfect, but to have libertie, and to be rid of the rule that men have of their owne authoritie chalenged over them" (Cciiii^v-Ddi).

There was very little imaginative literature published during the middle decades of the sixteenth century;[25] the few works that did appear show less concern with woman generally, let alone with her changing place in society or her education. For example, Sir Thomas Elyot in his *Boke named the Governour* (1553) discusses only the ideal prince and his courtiers, and the 1559 edition of the *Mirrour for Magistrates* also omits women entirely.

There are a few exceptions to this neglect of woman, most notably "Shores Wife," written by Thomas Churchyard and included in the 1563 edition of the *Mirrour*.[26] Jane Shore, the mistress of Edward IV, recounts her own story, admitting that her "peacocks pryde" in her own beauty was partly responsible for her tragic fate:

> There is no cloke, can serve to hyde my fault,
> For I agreed the fort he should assaulte.
>   (83-84)

Yet she does put some blame on the king, and in effect rejects a prevalent opinion that the woman, naturally evil anyway, is always at fault. Rather, Jane maintains that she is a wronged woman; instead of condemnation she deserves some sympathy, for:

> The maiestie that kynges to people beare,
> The stately porte, the awful chere they showe,
> Doth make the meane to shrynke and couche for feare,
> Like as the hound, that doth his maister knowe:
>   (78-81)

And later:

> Who can withstand a puissant kynges desyre?
>   (89)

But even more significant than this rationalizing is her anticipation of the later concern over forced marriages. Jane Shore uses her unhappy marriage as part of her defense:

> But cleare from blame my frendes can not be found,
> Before my time my youth they did abuse:
> In maryage, a prentyse was I bound,
> When that meere love I knew not howe to vse.
> . . . .
> Note wel what stryfe this forced maryage makes,
> What lothed lyves do come where love doth lacke,
> What scratting bryers do growe vpon such brakes,
> What common weales by it are brought to wracke,
> What heavy loade is put on pacientes backe,
> What straunge delyghtes this braunch of vice doth brede
> And marke what graine sprynges out of such a seede.
>   (106-9, 120-26)

In the other works of the 1560s and 1570s which present women it is much more typical to show them as wanton, fickle, or even evil. George Ferrers's account of Eleanor Cobham in the 1571 edition of the *Mirrour* is an example.[27] Not only does the Duchess confess her overweening pride, but she admits turning to magic to determine her husband's chances to succeed the king. She claims she had no intention of harming the king and that she was the

victim of Cardinal Beaufort's hatred; but the result of her action
was her exile and the Duke's death. The moral is pointedly stated,
and Eleanor thus joins the long list of "Eve" figures who are
responsible for the downfall of their husbands.[28]

While there was some discussion in *Il Cortegiano* of the disparity
in the roles of women and men, and therefore in the standards set
for them, the subject was not generally raised during these middle
years. Near the end of the century, however, in *Englands Heroical
Epistles* by Michael Drayton, there appears one of the first clearly
articulated complaints against the double standard. It occurs in
the epistle "Alice Countesse of *Salisburie* to the *Blacke Prince*" (1598).
Alice rejects the Prince's wooing in these chiding verses:

> "To Men is graunted priviledge to tempt,
> "But in that Charter, Women be exempt:
> "Men win us not, except we give consent,
> "Against our selves unlesse that we be bent.
> "Who doth impute it as a Fault to you?
> "You prove not false, except we be untrue;
> "It is your Vertue, being Men, to trie,
> "And it is ours, by Vertue to denie.
> "Your Fault it selfe serves for the Faults excuse,
> "And makes it ours, though yours be the abuse".
>
> (33-42)

The following year Samuel Daniel published a rather pedestrian
poem entitled "A Letter from Octauia to Marcus Antonius"
(1599), in which he presents Octavia reproaching her husband for
his shameful relationship with Cleopatra. Like Alice, Octavia
denounces the double standard of conduct for men and women,
elaborating at some length on this injustice and the pain and
anguish it has caused her. The most pointed passage begins with
stanza 15, as she ponders her situation in particular and the plight
of women in general in terms that are almost modern:

> I know not how, but wrongfully I know
> Hath vndiscerning custome plac'd our kind
> Vnder desert, and set vs farre below
> The reputation to our sexe assign'd:

> Charging our wrong reputed weaknesse, how
> We are vnconstant, fickle, false, vnkinde:
> And though our life with thousand proofes shewes no,
> Yet since strength saies it, weaknesse must be so.

Of the succeeding stanzas, 17 is especially scornful:

> Thrice happy you, in whom it is no fault,
> To know, to speake, to doe, and to be wise:
> Whose words have credit, and whose deedes, though naught,
> Must yet be made to seeme farre otherwise:
> You can be only heard, whilst we are taught
> To hold our peace, and not to exercise
> The powers of our best parts, because your parts
> Haue with our freedome robb'd vs of our harts.

These two poems were evidently popular,[29] which may indicate the growing concern of women with their relationship to their husbands and their place in society.

Curiously enough, during this same decade when women were articulating their newfound awareness, men were developing one of the most artificial of all literary conventions, the sonnet. The sonnet mistress was not really a part of the emerging new ideal, nor did she fit the older stereotype of the submissive paragon. True, she was praised hyperbolically for her beauty and her virtue; but she was excessively proud, even cruel, and she rejected both men and marriage for the game of wooing.

While the courtly sonneteers of the 1590s glorified their mistresses in Platonic and Petrarchan conceits, writers such as Shakespeare and Spenser were creating heroines cast in the new mold—positive, strong, often well educated, and with a significantly different attitude toward themselves and their place in society. Beatrice in Shakespeare's *Much Ado About Nothing* (1598/99) is a case in point. Ready of wit and sharp of tongue, she is a lively example of a woman breaking away from the older stereotype while confronting a society dominated by male values. For instance, Leonato rebukes her in typical masculine fashion with this warning: "By my troth, niece, thou wilt never get thee a husband, if thou be so shrewd of thy tongue" (II.i.19-21). Benedick characterizes her as "Lady Disdain" (I.i.119), "the infernal Ate in good apparel" (II.i.263), who "speaks poniards, and every word stabs" (II.i.254-55). Don Pedro, however, enjoys her merry wit, finding her "a pleasant-spirited lady" (II.ii.366). And even Benedick himself is forced to admit that she is fair, virtuous, and wise (II.iii.239-41).

It is in the matter of marriage that Beatrice especially shows her emancipated outlook.[30] Despite all her bawdy and sarcastic banter, Beatrice is not really opposed to marriage. She criticizes men, not matrimony; and, like many real women of the time, she demands the right to choose her own husband. Her critical appraisal is clearly seen in II.i. Leonato remarks: "Well, niece, I hope to see you one day fitted with a husband." To which Beatrice responds: "Not till God make men of some other metal than earth. Would it not grieve a woman to be overmaster'd with a piece of valiant dust? make an account of her life to a clod of wayward marl? No, uncle, I'll none" (59-66). This and similar criticism show she has developed a habit of analyzing all men, though this was apparently not always her practice. That she once had a romantic interest in Benedick she reveals to Don Pedro in her account of his faithlessness:

D.P. Come, lady, come; you have lost the heart of Signior Benedick.

BEAT. Indeed, my lord, he lent it me awhile; and I gave him use for it, a double heart for his single one. Marry, once before he won it of me with false dice, therefore your Grace may well say I have lost it. (285-91)

Because of this former insincerity Beatrice questions Benedick's avowal of love (IV.i.296); when he is reluctant to prove it by killing Claudio, she becomes bitterly cynical. Claudio has slandered and dishonored her kinswoman, yet the man who has just sworn he loves her will not revenge the wrong. In a state of high emotion she concludes:

But manhood is melted into courtesies, valour into compliment, and men are only turned into tongue, and trim ones too. He is now as valiant as Hercules that only tells a lie and swears it. (IV.i.321-25)

No one can dictate a marriage for Beatrice; Benedick takes up her challenge but it is not until the Hero-Claudio problem is solved that she accepts him.

Beatrice's independence of mind stands out even more vividly when contrasted with the conventional character of her cousin. Hero is the gentle, modest, romantic heroine; she is quiet, almost nonverbal at some crucial moments, and she is completely obedient to the will of her father.[31] She will no doubt be equally submissive to her husband. Beatrice herself points up this difference between them during a discussion about choosing a husband. When Antonio remarks to Hero: "Well, niece, I trust you will be rul'd by your father," Beatrice interrupts him: "Yes, faith; it is my cousin's duty to make curtsey and say, 'Father, as it pleases you.' But yet for all that cousin, let him be a handsome fellow, or else make another curtsey and say, 'Father, as it pleases me' " (II.i.53-59). But Hero can never do this. Patient and submissive, she exemplifies the virtuous woman of the older tradition.

While Beatrice is independent, she is not particularly aggressive in her relationship with Benedick. However, some of Shakespeare's heroines are romantically aggressive, a trait which obviously sets them apart as more emancipated women.[32] Helena in *All's Well That Ends Well* (c. 1602-3) is an obvious example. She is repeatedly praised as fair, virtuous, and wise. The Countess of Rousillon loves her as a daughter; the French King regards her as a "jewel" (V.iii.1); Lafeu extolls her as "dear perfection" (V.iii.18). And yet Bertram scorns her because she is not nobly born. In the words of the King:

> . . . mad in folly, [he] lack'd the sense to know
> Her estimation home.
>
> (V.iii.3-4)

For some reason Helena loves Bertram anyway, and she follows him first to Paris and then to Florence. As the complicated plot unfolds, she is shown using her virtue and her wits to win him as her husband. Like Hero, she triumphs at the end, though unlike Hero it is largely her own doing.

Olivia in *Twelfth Night* is also an aggressive heroine. Beautiful, virtuous, and wealthy, she has for nearly a year been indulging in excessive mourning for her dead brother. She has abjured the sight and company of men, rejecting repeatedly the marriage proposal of Duke Orsino. However, her romantic nature leads her to fall passionately in love with Cesario, the disguised Viola; and, abandoning her grief, she eagerly pursues "him." When Sebastian, Viola's twin brother, appears, Olivia mistakes him for her beloved and hurries him off to a marriage ceremony. Sebastian is bewildered but compliant. The confusion of identities is eventually straightened out, and Olivia finds her new husband "most wonderful."

Olivia also represents still a third facet of the new image of woman, for she is wealthy enough to manage her own household and to be economically independent. She even supports her uncle Sir Toby Belch. On a much simpler scale is the independence of Rosalind in *As You Like It* or Viola in *Twelfth Night.* These women go out into the world dressed as men and meet the challenges of life with wit and ingenuity, earning their own way and accomplishing in fact a kind of financial independence. The high-spirited Rosalind, disguised as the youth Ganymede, leaves the court under a sentence of banishment with Celia as "his" sister Aliena. In the Forest of Arden she buys a cottage, pasture, and some sheep (II.iv.91-93). Though this purchase does not really enter into the subsequent plot, it adds a new dimension to her characterization, for she manages her own household and is self-sufficient. Viola also takes refuge in male attire, in her case after being shipwrecked on the Illyrian coast and separated from her brother. She provides herself with financial protection by obtaining employment from Duke Orsino, a situation which is essential to the plot. Of course the proper goal for women is still love and marriage, and like Olivia, both Viola and Rosalind marry at the end of the plays. But through their independent positions both have the unique opportunity to learn more about the men they love without revealing themselves. When they do discard their disguises and marry, it is because they so choose.

There is yet one other group of women who are not particularly learned, but who vary in some way from the older stereotype: the warriors and the Amazons. Especially noteworthy among these is Britomart, the "lady knight" of Books III, IV, and V of Spenser's *Faerie Queene*.[33] Britomart is drawn with such nobleness of character that she stands out as Spenser's example of perfect womanhood. She is "That peerelesse paterne of Dame Natures pride,/And heavenly image of perfection" (IV.vi.24).

Foremost among her qualities is, of course, chastity, the subject of Book III, and the virtue most praised by Renaissance writers. She is described as "pure from blame of sinfull blot" (ii.23) and "the flowre of chastity" (x.6). Through this inviolable virtue Britomart overcomes all who oppose her; it serves her like the armor she wears, to protect her from the forces of lust or perverted love. Yet Spenser does not define chastity only as virginity. That is one aspect of the virtue, to be sure. But Britomart is searching for Artegall, the knight shown her in a vision as her destined husband.[34] Therefore chastity can also be a state of mind in regard to love that is pure, holy, and controlled. Ardor is not denied her; indeed when Britomart at last finds herself in Artegall's presence,

> Her hart did leape, and all her hart-strings tremble,
> For sudden joy, and secret feare withall.
>
> (vi.29)

Another striking quality of Britomart is her beauty, a beauty so overpowering that those who see her face worship her as a divinity. Thus when she removes her armor at the castle of Malbecco, the onlookers

>   smitten were
> With great amazement of so wondrous sight
> And each on other, and they all on her
> Stood gazing, as if suddein great affright
> Had them surprised.

They continue to stare,

> And euer firmely fixed did abide
> In contemplation of diuinitie.
>
> (ix.23-24)

Likewise, when Artegall split Britomart's helmet, exposing "so diuine a beauties excellence," he humbly fell down,

> And of his wonder made religion
> Weening some heauenly goddesse he did see.
> (vi.21-22)

Such was the beauty of chastity to the Renaissance mind.

Britomart has most of the other qualities so praised by the writers of the sixteenth century. She is modest, humble, constant, prudent, and temperate. She pities Scudamore whom she finds lying on the ground in silent grief over Amoret (ix.7-20). Amid the perils of the House of Cupid, she behaves with courage. She is a warrior but she is nonetheless a woman who combines bravery and strength with tenderness and warmth. Yielding none of her womanhood, she yet makes herself felt as a noble power in the larger world.

These four groups of women character types—those who want to choose their own husbands, the romantically aggressive, the economically independent, and the warriors—are not specifically portrayed as learned. Curiously, there are relatively few learned women in the literature, even though the number of educated women was increasing considerably during the last decades of the century. Shakespeare again provides the chief example, Portia in *The Merchant of Venice*. Portia is an heiress whose material resources are matched by her beauty, virtue, and intellectual capacity. The latter quality becomes crucial in the court scene (IV.i), since Portia, disguised as "a young doctor of Rome" (153), confounds Shylock and saves Antonio's life.

Before Portia appears on stage in this scene a letter from her kinsman Doctor Bellario commends her to the Duke as "a young and learned doctor" (145). It gives "his" name as Balthazar, and continues:

> "We turned o'er many books together. He is furnished with my opinion; which, bett'red with his own learning, the greatness whereof I cannot enough commend, comes with him, at my importunity, to fill up your Grace's request in my stead. I beseech you, let his lack of years be no impediment to let him lack a reverend estimation; for I never knew so young

a body with so old a head. I leave him to your gracious acceptance, whose trial shall better publish his commendation." (156-66)

Portia acquits herself well as she questions the various persons involved in the case. Even the unsuspecting Shylock exclaims the praises of the "most reverend doctor":

A Daniel come to judgement! yea, a Daniel!
O wise young judge, how I do honour thee! (223-24)

Gratiano mockingly paraphrases these words when Portia begins to prosecute Shylock instead of Antonio:

O upright judge! Mark, Jew: O learned judge!

and later:

A second Daniel! A Daniel, Jew! (317, 333)

While this scene provides the most specific evidence of her knowledge, her skill, and her agile mind, other parts of the play supplement this interpretation of Portia. From first to last she is marked by perception and wisdom; she manages everything well, from her large estate to Antonio's defense. While she may not be "the woman of woman," as one admirer described her,[35] most critics are nonetheless agreed that she combines feminine virtue with a remarkable intellectual strength.

As in the case of learned women, there are relatively few women rulers portrayed positively in major roles in the literature,[36] despite the presence of a wise and virtuous woman on the throne of England. Elizabeth appears in allegorical guise as Cynthia, or Diana, or someone similar, but rarely as a ruler. Even her identification with the Faerie Queene in Spenser's epic provides no real example, since she never appears significantly as a ruler. However, in Book V Spenser does present a series of episodes of Justice in operation which are thinly disguised allegories of events in Elizabeth's reign. The Queen herself is represented in the character of Mercilla, described in canto ix as a "gratious Queene," sitting, with Temperance and Reverence on either side, "in royal rich estate,/ Admyr'd of many, honoured of all" (stanzas 27, 32, 33).

When Artegall and Arthur arrive at court she is "about affaires of common wele,/ Dealing of Iustice with indifferent grace." Specifically, in her principal scenes she is conducting the trial of Duessa, who tried to usurp her crown. Various personified abstractions present evidence, until the time comes for Mercilla to make her judgment. True to her name, "the Briton Prince was sore empassionate" (stanza 46). Though the evidence confirms that Duessa is guilty, yet Mercilla

> would not let iust vengeance on her light,
> But rather let in stead thereof to fall
> Few perling drops from her faire lamps of light.
> (stanza 50)

At last Mercilla gives her "tempred" ruling, leading the poet into an extended praise of her compassionate justice. In words clearly intended for the real queen behind the character, he asks:

> Who then can thee, *Mercilla,* throughly prayse,
> That herein doest all earthly Princes pas?
> What heauenly Muse shall thy great honour rayse
> Vp to the skies, whence first deriu'd it was,
> And now on earth it selfe enlarged has,
> From th'vtmost brinke of the *Armericke* shore,
> Vnto the margent of the Molucas?
> Those Nations farre thy iustice doe adore:
> But thine owne people do thy mercy prayse much more.
> (x.3)

It is particularly fitting that Spenser presents his only extended illustration of a ruler in the book dealing with justice, for this is the virtue most essential to a prince, whether man or woman. Even more praiseworthy is the ruler who tempers strict justice with gentle mercy, as his depiction of Mercilla-Elizabeth affirms.

This portrayal of a woman ruler, then, joins the gallery of other women in various roles who grace the literature of the sixteenth century. They become all the more vital when one realizes that they reflect actual women and the changing position that they were beginning to have in Renaissance society. Irregular though this development was, it is nonetheless clearly discernible. Even in the early decades a kind of first phase is apparent, as some women were given the opportunity of having a superior education. Perhaps encouraged by these women and their undeniable intellectual accomplishments, other women began to articulate similar desires. Thus a second phase occurred, that of growing awareness of discrimination and even exploitation, with a concomitant expression of the need for a change. Women not only wanted an education, they wanted greater power and freedom, especially in matters of such vital concern as the choice of a husband. More and more they ventured out into the world; they often sought and gained economic independence; and in a chosen few instances they became rulers of the realm. These are not inconsequential developments. Indeed, it is by no means an exaggeration to say that during the sixteenth century, women took the first tottering steps toward modern feminism.

Notes

1 Two important works on this subject are Ruth Kelso's *Doctrine for the Lady of the Renaissance* (Urbana: University of Illinois Press, 1956) and Louis B. Wright's *Middle-Class Culture in Elizabethan England* (San Marino, Calif.: Huntington Library, 1935), especially chaps. 7 and 13.

2 Before marriage a woman was legally under the control of her father, who had complete jurisdiction over her person and her property. Upon her marriage everything passed automatically to her husband, according to laws that were still essentially feudal. See Doris Mary Stenton, *The English Woman in History* (New York: Macmillan, 1959), especially pp. 57-66.

3 See, e.g., Edmunde Tilney, *A brief and pleasant discourse of duties in mariage, called the Flower of Friendshippe* (1568), sig. Bvi[r].

4 Chilton Latham Powell, *English Domestic Relations 1487-1653* (New York: Columbia University Press, 1917), p. 150.

5 For a contemporary discussion of women as a necessary evil, see Stefano Guazzo, *La ciuil conversatione* (1574), translated by George Pettie as *The Civile Conuersation of M. Steeuen Guazzo* (1581), sigs. 64[v]-65[v]. Castiglione, in *Il Cortegiano* (1528), presents an urbane summary of this position in the words of Lord Gaspar. See Sir Thomas Hoby's

translation, *The Covrtyer of Covnt Baldessar Castilio* (1561), especially sigs. Cciiv-Cciii. However, Castiglione also has several of his characters support the more positive view of women, especially Lord Julian on sigs. Cciii-Cciiiiv. A work which considers women good in a limited way is Juan Luis Vives, *De officis mariti*, translated by Thomas Paynell as *The Office and duetie of an husband* (1553?), especially sigs. U2, Q8. Henry Cornelius Agrippa presents the argument for women's superiority in *De nobilitate & praecellentia foemine sexus* (1529), translated by David Clapam as *A Treatise of the Nobilitie and excellencye of woman kynde* (1542).

6 Thomas Deloney, "The Lamentation of Mr. Pages Wife of Plimouth, who, being forc'd to wed him, consented to his Murder, for the love of G. Strangwidge: for which they suffered at Barnstable in Deuonshire," in *The Works of Thomas Deloney*, ed. F. O. Mann (Oxford: Clarendon Press, 1912), pp. 482-85, lines 17-20, 57-64, 69-72.

7 See, for example, the wooing of both Hero and Beatrice in Shakespeare's *Much Ado about Nothing*.

8 For an informative discussion of the double standard regarding chastity from early to modern times see Keith Thomas, "The Double Standard," *Journal of the History of Ideas* 20 (April 1959), 195-216. See also Kelso, *Lady of the Renaissance*, p. 25.

9 Kelso, *Lady of the Renaissance*, p. 24; Castiglione, *Il Cortegiano*, sig. Ggi.

10 The full title is: POSITIONS WHEREIN THOSE PRIMITIVE CIRCVMSTANCES BE EXAMINED, WHICH ARE NECESSARIE FOR THE TRAINING vp of children, either for skill in their books, or health in their bodie.

11 Cf. Castiglione, *Il Cortegiano*, sig. Ccii, where Lord Julian recommends the more traditional subjects: "sight in letters, in musicke, in drawing, or painting, and skillfull in dauncing, and in devising sports and pastimes...."

12 An English translation by Richard Hyrde appeared in 1541, with the title: *A Very Frvteful and pleasant boke callyd the Instrvction of a Christen woman*. The references are to this edition.

13 Cf. Mulcaster, *Positions*, p. 212.

14 Mulcaster's list is typical, including Sappho, Portia, Cornelia, and many lesser-known women. See pp. 173, 180-81.

15 Sigs. Ffii-Ffiiv. "The Ladie Margaret" was Margaret of Burgundy, to whom Agrippa dedicated his treatise on the superiority of women.

16 Cf. Garrett Mattingly, *Catherine of Aragon* (Boston: Little, Brown, 1941), pp. 8-9.

17 Ibid., p. 9.

18 See E. C. Wilkins, *England's Eliza* (Cambridge, Mass.: Harvard University Press, 1939).

19 *The Scholemaster*, fol. 21r-v.

20 R. W. Chambers, *Thomas More* (New York: Harcourt, Brace, 1935), p. 181.

21 Stenton, *English Woman in History*, p. 131.

22 One example is Mistress Toye, whose name appears over a period of at least three years. An entry for February 11, 1556, mentions the burial of her husband Robert. On October 13, 1556, she presents George Besshoppe as an apprentice; on June 24, 1559, she presents Thomas Robynson as her apprentice for nine years. (Edward Arber, *A Transcript of the Registers of the Company of Stationers of London 1554-1640 A. D.* [London, 1875]. I:35, 39, 118.) Her name also appears with some frequency on the various lists of members as an active participant in Company affairs (e.g., Arber, I:46, 49, 61, 86, 130).

In the first volume alone of Arber there are two other examples mentioned: Grace Cater, a "Wedowe Cytizen and stacioner of London," took John Spynser as an apprentice on September 29, 1564; and Joan Sutton, the widow of Edward Sutton and also a "Cetizen and stacioner of London," took William Kinge as her apprentice on August 24, 1569 (Arber, I: 254, 397).

23 Wright, *Middle-Class Culture,* p. 204.

24 *Utopia,* ed. Edward Surtz, s.j., and J. H. Hexter, *The Complete Works of St. Thomas More* (New Haven: Yale University Press, 1965), 4: 159. All references in the text are to this edition.

25 This fact probably reflects the unsettled religious and political questions since chronicles and religious tracts abound. Queen Mary Tudor had no particular impact as a woman, and though she was a pupil of Vives and a learned woman, she earned her place in history more for her attempts to return England to Roman Catholicism than for her scholarship.

26 In *Churchyards Challenge* (1593) he says that he wrote the tragedy "in King Edwardes daies," i.e., 1547-53 (sig. *ᵛ).

27 The full title is: "How Dame Elianor Cobham Duchesse of Glocester for practising of witchcraft and sorcery, suffred open penance and after was banished the realme into the Yle of Man." Bibliographical evidence suggests that this work may have been written before 1559.

28 Another example, though a less sinister one, is Lucilla in John Lyly's *Euphues* (1579), who is fickle and wanton, and comes to an appropriately sad end.

29 Daniel's poem was reprinted five times in twelve years, while Drayton's was reprinted thirteen times before the poet's death in 1631.

30 Cf. Juliet, who also wants to marry the man she loves. She is, however, a much less vigorous example than Beatrice; and because of this as well as the circumstances of her life, which demand a Hero-like obedience, her exercise of choice leads to her death. In a much lighter vein, Hermia in *Midsummer Night's Dream* also risks death to marry the man she loves. She actively pursues Lysander through the merry mixups of the play, and with the aid of a love potion and Duke Theseus she finally wins him. Hermia, too, is a much less vigorous and independent character than Beatrice, though she is somewhat more romantically aggressive.

31 Like Hero in some ways is Ophelia in *Hamlet*. She, too, does exactly as her father wishes, even telling a lie to protect him (III.i.133). This complete dominance by her father prevents her from developing the independence and strength she needs to survive in the corruption of the Danish court. Without it she is too vulnerable to any adversity; she can only go mad, and die. Perhaps not too incongruous in this group is a persecuted heroine like Hermione in *The Winter's Tale*, who suffers because of the unfounded jealousy of her husband, Leontes. Shakespeare allows her, like Hero, to defend herself briefly before she, too, "dies" of grief. But he does not use her as a spokeswoman for feminist ideas. Instead he has her pretend to be dead for sixteen years, patiently waiting for Leontes to repent. A seemingly unlikely candidate for this group is Katharina, the fiery-tempered heroine of *The Taming of the Shrew*. And yet at the end of the play she is deemed the most submissive of the three brides, and actually lectures the others most soundly on their conjugal duties.

32 While the aggressive heroine in one sense marks a more advanced phase in the emergence of the new concept of woman, it was not in fact a later chronological development. About 1590, when women first began in earnest to demand the right to choose their own husbands, the aggressive heroine had also appeared. Thomas Lodge's *Scillaes Metamorphosis,* appearing in 1589, was the first to feature the feminine wooer and may have suggested the idea to Shakespeare, whose *Venus and Adonis,* probably written during the winter of 1592-93, was the most notable example of this type of heroine. Shakespeare derives much of his material from Ovid's *Metamorphoses,* but the essential feature of the reluctant Adonis was apparently his own contribution, as none of the classical or Renaissance versions of the myth has this situation. Adonis is ordinarily portrayed as the willing lover of Venus, though the earlier poems do put the emphasis on her love for him. In Shakespeare's poem the focus is on Venus throughout, on her emotions, her unsuccessful entreaties, her frustrated attempts to seduce him, and her grief when he is slain.

33 Another example is Hippolyta in *Midsummer Night's Dream.* Her marriage to Theseus provides the frame for the main plot, but her position as Queen of the Amazons is not a particularly significant factor.

34 In one sense, Britomart is an "aggressive heroine" because she seeks for Artegall; yet she does not go to the extremes of behavior that Venus, Olivia, or Helena do.

35 This is the attitude of many nineteenth-century women admirers of Portia, who praise her extravagantly. See, e.g., Mrs. F. A. Kemble, *Atlantic Monthly,* June 1876. Portia is not, however, completely free from more traditional traits; for, despite her independent nature, she is determined to stand by the command in her father's will to marry the man choosing the proper casket.

36 There are some queens, for example, in the various history plays of Shakespeare, and Titania, the Queen of the Fairies, and Hippolyta, the Queen of the Amazons, in *Midsummer Night's Dream.* But these women are not generally shown as rulers and their roles are often comparatively insignificant. Lady Macbeth is a negative portrayal, for she has a definite impact on her husband's actions before he becomes king, yet she has very little afterward. Goneril and Regan both exercise considerable power as rulers in *King Lear,* but again they totally negate the values as both women and rulers that the Renaissance upheld. Cleopatra, on the other hand, is not so easily categorized. In the first half of the play Shakespeare stresses the woman more than anything else. Cleopatra assumes some leadership in the scenes relating to the Battle of Actium, but her impact is mostly negative, especially when she turns her "fearful sails" and flees (III.xi.55). However, she does at least think like a queen in her negotiations with Caesar, pressing whatever claims she can to protect Egypt. And in outwitting Caesar of his expected triumph in the final scene, she dies like a queen.

3.

Praising Virtuous Ladies:
The Literary Image and
Historical Reality
of Women in
Seventeenth-century England

David J. Latt

"England is a paradise for women, and hell for horses" was a commonplace often uttered by travelers from the Continent after they had visited the English court. Compared with their sisters in France, Germany, Spain, and Italy, aristocratic English women during the reigns of Henry VII (1485-1509) and Henry VIII (1509-47) appeared especially outspoken, learned, and influential. In point of fact, they did not always have the freedoms they seemed to possess, but in England some of the advantages of the Renaissance were enjoyed by a few women.[1] Margaret Beaufort, Countess of Richmond and Derby (Henry VIII's mother), Lady Elizabeth Russell, Lady Ann Bacon, Mildred Cecil, Katharine Killegrew, Margaret Rowlett (the daughters of Sir Anthony Cooke), and Margaret Roper (Sir Thomas More's daughter) were all exemplary models of Renaissance learning. During the reign of Elizabeth I

(1558-1603), the status of women in English society was heightened by Elizabeth's achievements and by her encouragement of other women. Few English monarchs ruled through so many turbulent and triumphant years. Her diplomacy turned England into a major European power; her support of mercantile interests greatly expanded English trade; and her defeat of the Spanish Armada in 1588 (albeit with the aid of the weather) gave England a sense of territorial security it had not enjoyed for some time.

Such advancements notwithstanding, the accession of James I in 1603 changed matters radically. Raised in conservative Scotland, James Stuart disliked the increased respect and responsibility English women had begun to enjoy. A well-known anecdote about James indicates the extent of his antagonism toward the "learned lady." When a young woman was about to be presented to James, his counselors praised her, saying that she was accomplished in Latin, Greek, and Hebrew. James's response was only to ask, "But can she spin?" [2]

The court of Charles I (1625-49), on the other hand, did not condone misogyny. Henrietta Maria enhanced the status of women by demanding that her courtiers adopt the platonizing attitudes popular at the time in France. The Queen wanted women to be seen in heightened terms and in an idealized environment. The masques and pastorals of the period testify to her influence, for in both genres women are elaborately praised for their ability to refine the grosser sensibilities of men. Henrietta Maria made fashionable the idea of the affective power of feminine virtue.

I

In the literature of the early seventeenth century, especially in the work of the major poets, John Donne, Ben Jonson, Thomas Carew, John Suckling, John Milton, and Andrew Marvell, women most often appear either as models of generalized virtue or as examples of the feminine roles of daughter, wife, and mother. When women are not shown in a domestic context, they are presented as models for men as well as for women.[3] In Donne's verse epistle beginning "Faire, great, and good," the Countess of

Salisbury is praised as a model for mankind of the potential God has placed in all individuals.[4] By allowing men and women "to study" her, she provides them with the means of becoming "great," whereby they may take the first step toward pleasing God himself.[5] Such a relationship between exemplary women and mankind is implicit in all of Donne's verse epistles to the Countesses of Bedford and Salisbury, in Jonson's poems to the Countess of Rutland and Lady Aubigny, and in Milton's *Arcades*. If mankind chooses to improve itself it need only follow the pattern of virtuous behavior practiced by the women praised by the poets.

Women were said to have the ability to influence the character not only of mankind but also of Nature itself. In Andrew Marvell's *Upon Appleton House,* an elaborate encomium of the retired parliamentarian-army hero Thomas Fairfax, his daughter Mary Fairfax is said to reform Nature itself. Like Eve before the Fall, Mary actually tends the garden; and as in Eden, because she helps it become more beautiful, Nature gratefully responds by offering her the pleasures of its flowers, brooks, and meadows:

> Therefore what first *She* on them spent,
> They gratefully again present.
> The meadow Carpets where to tread;
> The Garden Flow'rs to Crown *Her* Head;
> And for a Glass the limpid Brook,
> Where *She* may all *her* Beautyes look.
> (697-702)

Her superlative character and her ability to affect her environment are means to the end of fashioning her into the model bride. As her mother, Lady Anne Vere, was won by Thomas Fairfax and as her ancestor Isabel Thwates was rescued from the nunnery by William Fairfax, so Mary will soon find her proper place as a wife.

While the virtues Oliver Cromwell had developed in retirement could be turned to public use when they were needed—Marvell so argues in *The Horatian Ode*—Mary Fairfax's will not be. From reading *Upon Appleton House,* as from reading Donne's and Jonson's verse epistles to women and the elegiac praises of great women by Carew, Lovelace, and Milton, one would expect that women would be urged to work actively for the public good. Since Mary

Fairfax improved the garden around Appleton House, it would be logical to expect that she might be encouraged to use her considerable gifts to ensure the public weal. However, it is quite clear from the conclusion of *Upon Appleton House,* as from Donne's "Epistle to the Countess of Huntington" (1610), Jonson's "Eupheme," Milton's *Comus,* and many prose tracts that women were, in fact, forcefully urged *against* such participation. Even Daniel Tuvil, for example, who in his strong defense of women, *Asylum Veneris* (London, 1616), agrees with the Roman law that both women and men should be "publikely praised" (p. 137) in funeral orations, does not advocate the public service of women. Like John Swan in *Speculum Mundi* (London, 1635), Tuvil maintains that a woman's only proper sphere of activity is in her household.

The exclusion of women from the world of public affairs was so complete that I. L., the author of a compendious survey of English civil law, *The Lawes Resolution of Womans Rights* (London, 1632), notes that women not only have nothing to do with making laws, they more often than not have no knowledge of them: "they have nothing to do in constituting Lawes, of consenting to them, in interpreting of Lawes, or in hearing them interpretated at lectures, leets or charges, and yet they stand strictly tyed to mens establishments, little or nothing excused by ignorance" (p. 2).

In *Christian Oeconomie* (London, 1609), written by M. W. Perkins and translated by Thomas Pickering, as in many of the marriage manuals of the period, there is an emphatic declaration that women should remain at home, leaving business and travel to their husbands. Since their responsibilities are purely domestic, Perkins insists, there is no need for women to venture out into the town, except as it is necessary to supply the needs of the household. Even in works by men that praised women, such as *The Excellencie of Good Women* (London, 1613) by Barnaby Rich, women were praised solely for their domestic skills. Under no circumstances would Barnaby Rich encourage a woman to participate in public affairs. The only women who would be found "abroad," he says, are harlots (see p. 24). So strong was the admonition that women refrain from exercising public power that Thomas Carter in his *Christian Common Wealth: Or, Domesticall Dutyes* (London, 1627) urged wealthy men not to give their daughters inheritances, as that would undermine their husbands' authority over them (see p. 155).

Women, Carter and others argued, should have no authority except that given them by their husbands or fathers.

In the early part of the seventeenth century, then, women were praised for being upholders of what may be called the virtues of restraint. Rather than actively working in the political or theological worlds, women were expected to correct the world's immorality by being static *exempla*. Richard Crashaw eulogizes Mary Magdalen and Saint Teresa for such a reason. In Donne's verse epistles, the women he addresses are praised for their withdrawal from public life.[6] The Countess of Bedford preserves her virtue by retiring to the country. Her value to the society increased as she moved farther away from the affairs of public life. Removed from the world, Donne says, the Countess can function as a moral guide for all mankind.

It can be argued that discouraging women from actively pursuing public lives for themselves was a way of insuring their subordination, a means of dictating their passivity and thus their assured domination by men. In larger terms, such subordination may be a reflection of a male fear of the power of women. A passage from Joseph Swetnam's *The Araignment of Lewde, Idle, Froward, and vnconstant women* (London, 1617),[7] an extremely popular attack on women, voices some of these fears in his unqualified warning to beware of women: "Eagles eate not men till they are dead but women deuour them aliue, for a woman will pick thy pocket & empty thy purse, laugh in thy face and cutt thy throat, they are vngratefull, periured, full of fraud, flouting and decit, vnconstant, waspish, toyish, light, sullen, proude, discurteous, and cruell."[8] The warnings articulated by Swetnam and others gave great energy to the prohibitions against women's participation in public affairs. Orthodox religious thought maintained that women were intellectually inferior to men and had a greater carnal susceptibility. If women left their homes and demanded a voice in public policy, many writers concluded that God's Plan would be violated; the result could only be the destruction of order, reason, and justice.[9]

With the insistence on feminine passivity and the prevalent attitude that women should remain "indoors," individual women were effectively isolated from one another, thereby enforcing their dependence on their husbands, who in turn were then able to limit their social contacts, making themselves the focus of their wives' intellectual and emotional lives. Moreover, the gradual exclusion of women from mercantile or crafts' trade further increased the domestication of women and their dependence on men.[10] The terms of praise developed in the poetry of the time clearly supported and glorified that dependency.

II

If women had little effective power in the contemporary world, their effect on men in romantic relationships was substantial. *Or,* so the secular love verse of the period would suggest. In poetry, as in life, women have been accorded their greatest significance when they are lovers. The Renaissance, Petrarchan tradition had emphasized women's spiritual attractions. In the lyrics of Sir Thomas Wyatt and Henry Howard, Earl of Surrey, a male poet-lover acknowledges the way in which his lover has refined his sensibilities by turning him to a higher, neoplatonic love. In the seventeenth century numerous poems follow the Petrarchan mode and eulogize women for their spiritualizing influence.[11] In general, however, seventeenth-century English love poets rejected the idealizing posturing of the Petrarchans and turned instead to an analysis of psychology and sexual desire.[12] Often cynical, the lyric poetry of the Jacobean-Caroline period sought to solve the problem of what Robert Burton called "love melancholy" or what James Ferrand termed "Erotomania." [13] Whereas the Petrarchan lover seemed to be gratified by channeling the energy of his passion into poetry, the poets of the seventeenth century were rarely content to displace their sexuality in such a manner.

In Donne's *Songs and Sonnets* the acknowledgment that a woman can gratify a man's sexual needs invariably leads to greater intimacy with her and to her increased valuation.[14] In terms that echo the marriage manuals of the day, Donne argues that a woman is most valued when she has joined in an intellectual, emotional, and sexual union with a man. Curiously, however, Donne's lovers in "The Canonization," "The Good-morrow," "The Sunne Rising," and "Song: 'Sweetest love,' " like the lovers in the poems of the other secular lyricists, are not married. In seventeenth-century love poetry the emphasis is on the convivial pleasures of a relationship and not on its procreative possibilities.

In many of Donne's poems, male lovers praise their mistresses because the women's beauty, virtue, and sensuality allow the men to create a private world separable from and more perfect than the public world beyond the walls of their bedchambers. Whereas Marvell in "The Garden" argues that romantic love and women must be repudiated if a higher state of spiritual contemplation is to be achieved, Donne's speaker in "The Extasie," for example, argues the converse: without a woman, without sexual consummation, without intimacy, no higher state of experience can ever be achieved. Moreover, while in Donne's verse epistles women may be exemplars for mankind, in "The Canonization," "The Good-morrow," and "The Sunne Rising" the lovers, a man and a woman, joined together perform that function. In Donne's love poetry, for the most part, women are not loved as unobtainable, inaccessible figures of pious virtue, as they are in poems of the Petrarchan tradition such as Lovelace's "Female Glory." Among all the major secular love poets of the period, only Donne successfully integrated spiritual with sexual love. At the same time he created dynamic, positive portraits of women whose sexuality led not to the destruction but to the betterment of their male lovers.

In the work of other love poets, however, the increased emphasis on sexuality did not lead to an increased valuation of women. Anticipating developments which culminated in the libertine, Restoration misogynist verse of the Earl of Rochester, Thomas Carew and Sir John Suckling argued that while women are undeniably capable of gratifying male sexual desires, they are not always to be praised for doing so. In Carew's two poems of "Good counsell to a young Maid" and in Suckling's "Upon A. M.: 'Yield not, my Love,' " they actually warn women to beware of the protestations of male lovers. Rarely in their poetry is sexuality seen as a means of achieving greater intimacy with a woman. In their advisories to young women, they caution that men only pursue women to manipulate and use them; the love professed by eager suitors is a deceitful sham. Unlike Donne, Carew and Suckling were not able to integrate sexual needs with emotional intimacy. The one is considered by them quite apart from the other. As a result, particularly in Suckling's pessimistic "Sonnet II: 'Of thee (kind boy) I ask no red and white,' " women are reduced to the level of mere objects, capable of gratifying male sexual needs. But if women are not praiseworthy in such a situation, except that they gratuitously possess the means of masculine gratification, then neither is love itself.

As experienced by most men, Suckling insisted, the love of a woman only led to an embroilment in the pains and discomforts of passion. Moreover, while Donne praises his mistress in "Elegie XIX: Going to Bed" as being a "new-found-land," an unexplored territory of great worth, and Robert Herrick stands fixated before Julia's succulent presence, Suckling reduces feminine virtue and beauty to "meat":

> 'Tis not the meat, but 'tis the appetite
>   makes eating a delight,
>   and if I like one dish
> More then another, that a Pheasant is;
> What in our watches, that in us is found,
> So to the height and nick
>   We up be wound,
> No matter by what hand or trick.
>   ("Sonnet II," 17-24)

This is a far cry from the idealized pictures of women given in the sonnets of Sir Thomas Wyatt, Henry Howard, Earl of Surrey, and Edmund Spenser. The poem, in its emphasis on carnality, denigrates not only women, but men as well. The speaker in the sonnet finds himself unhappily manipulated by irrational forces that keep him enslaved, even though he recognizes them and can analyze them for the "kind boy."

There is nothing particularly admirable about Suckling's view of women in the poem, but equally so there is nothing admirable in the world he describes. His speakers are, more often than not, trapped by passion, even to the extent of being reduced to mere machines, with mechanical reactions ("We up be wound,/No matter by what hand or trick"). In Suckling's world the ability of human beings to react against the dictates of an irresistible force such as passion is, at best, limited. Out of that pessimism grows a callousness toward women, for they are the immediate sources of male discomfort.

Of course, doubts about mankind's potential do not have to lead to antifeminism. If time or passion impinges upon human achievement, there are other possible responses. In Marvell's "To his Coy Mistress," as in Carew's "A Rapture" and Herrick's "Corinna's going a Maying" and "To the Virgins," a speaker tries to convince a woman that a partnership of intense eroticism will counter, although not defeat, the effects of time and death. *Together*, Marvell's speaker urges, the lovers can work to overcome time. Rather than allow time to deplete all their own great gifts of beauty, youth, and energy, the lovers will consume themselves in pleasure, albeit a violent pleasure (see the concluding verse paragraph: "devour," "tear," and "rough strife").

In Suckling's poetry, however, women are not their lovers' partners, nor are they equal to men intellectually, emotionally, or sexually. They are merely necessary elements in a fixed and continuing equation. They possess the solution to what appears to be an axiomatic need. Accordingly, when Suckling addresses women in his monologues, there is no attempt to imply their personalities as do Herrick and Donne. Suckling's women merely exist, nameless and generic. They are not particular women; they could be *any* women.

In Suckling's "Upon my Lady Carliles walking in Hampton-Court garden: Dialogue," the woman, notably, is named, but she is not identified to be praised. Anonymity in this case would have been preferable. She is not addressed directly but is the subject of a dialogue between two male friends, T. C. (Thom) and J. S., who have traditionally been identified as Thomas Carew and Suckling himself. The poem is a confrontation of two very different ideas about women. On the one hand, Thom describes and praises Lady Carlisle from a platonic point of view: she is the source of many rare pleasures; music and perfume are exhaled by her as she passes by; she is a "Deity"; and her beauty is so great that men easily become her slaves. J. S.'s view of her is quite different. He hears no music and senses no perfume when she walks by. Moreover, unlike his friend Thom, he feels no transformation within himself because of her presence:

Thom.
Dull and insensible, could'st see
A thing so near a Deity
Move up and down, and feel no change?
   J. S.
None, and so great, were alike strange.
                              (18-21)

Rather, J. S. had hoped for a change *in her,* not in himself. He would have her be naked; and since she was not, he undressed her in his mind ("I was undoing all she wore"). Whereas Thom hopes for a view of a higher reality by her presence, J. S. looked lower, seeking "the parts" which please "flesh and blood." Sounding like Sir Philip Sidney's Astrophel in sonnet 71 ("But ah, Desire still cries: 'Give me some food!' "), J. S. admits to sexual desires, but whereas Astrophel struggles with the conflicting needs of spirit and flesh, Suckling's J. S. has completely resolved the conflict. Lady Carlisle can *only* be the object of his sexual desires. He will not drink the spiritually elevating influence of her beauty from her face or eyes, as did many a Petrarchan lover or as did Jonson in "Drinke to me, onely, with thine eyes"; instead he focuses his attention on "the parts deni'd unto the eyes." Altering the platonic metaphor of the woman as a "fountain," from which a man might drink virtue, Suckling uses it as a vaginal euphemism:

'Troth in her face I could descry
No danger, no divinity.
But since the pillars were so good
On which the lovely fountain stood,
Being once come so near, I think
I should have ventur'd hard to drink.
                              (40-45)

In the course of the dialogue, Suckling indirectly notes the influence writers have had in creating our perceptions of women; and he remarks how very different that literary image may be from their "reality." Responding to Thom's comment that he sensed perfumes and music emanating from Carlisle, J. S. says,

I must confesse those perfumes *(Thom)*
I did not smell; nor found that from
Her passing by, ought sprung up new:
The flow'rs had all their birth from you.
(10-13)

J. S.'s view of Lady Carlisle is not so much a matter of "realism" as
it is of a reductive materialism. In Thom's eyes she is etherealized;
her very presence, like that of Mary Fairfax in the garden around
Appleton House, has a paradisiacal effect on the environment. In
J. S.'s eyes, however, she is mere matter; her value lies in the sexual
pleasure she can bring a man. Moreover, where Thom gives her an
importance in his world (flowers turn toward her as though she
were the sun), J. S. argues that if a man does more than
momentarily adore her he is a fool. The difference between the two
men's views is indicative of a conflict in attitude toward women
that was developing during the 1630s.

Responding to such pessimism and licentiousness, Henrietta
Maria attempted to reinstill a more positive attitude toward love
and women by promoting the platonic cult of the *précieuse*. Carew's
poems "To the Queene" and "Loves Force" testify to her influence.
Addressing her, Carew says that she has defeated "wilde lust" and
the ignominious notion that *"What ever pleaseth lawfull is,"* precisely
the conclusion of his own erotic seduction poem "A Rapture."
Instead, she has shown the nation a different path

Of Modestie, and constant faith,
Which makes the rude Male satisfied
With one faire Female by his side;
Doth either sex to each unite,
And forme loves pure Hermophradite.
("To the Queene," 14-18)

"Loves pure Hermophradite" is only a more exotic figure for
Donne's true lovers united into one "abler soule." Yet Henrietta
Maria did not solve the problem of how sexual and spiritual love
could be combined. It remained for John Milton in *Paradise Lost* to
accomplish that integration. He alone of all the major poets of the
period describes romantic, sexual love within a connubial context,

thereby allowing for the integration of the need for sexual gratification, the pleasures of an intimate intellectual and emotional relationship, and the desires for procreation.

III

Given that marriage was economically, socially, and theologically important in the period and that the early seventeenth century was an era of great love poetry, it would be reasonable to expect the appearance of poems which explore the nature of the matrimonial relation. However, while there is a popular tradition of hymeneal verse, wherein a poet addresses a couple about to be wed, as well as numerous examples of poems addressed to other men's wives—Donne's and Jonson's poems to Lucy, Countess of Bedford, for example—there are few poems by husbands addressed to their wives, and none addressed by women to their husbands. Donne's *Valediction* poems may be notable exceptions, but if he is addressing his wife, why is she not named? Henry King's moving "An Exequy" is explicitly addressed to his wife; yet she is dead. Perhaps because many marriages were arranged so that aristocratic marriages were less a matter of passion than of policy, there is, then, a tradition in the period of not addressing one's conjugal mate in poetry.

The only poem devoted to investigating and eulogizing connubial love is *Paradise Lost*. Throughout the poem, Adam and Eve express their love for one another. In such instances the narrator blends his approval of connubial love with their own exclamations of contentment:

> Thou following cri'd'st aloud, Return fair *Eve*,
> Whom fli'st thou? whom thou fli'st, of him thou art,
> His flesh, his bone; to give thee being I lent
> Out of my side, nearest my heart
> Substantial Life, to have thee by my side
> Henceforth an individual solace dear;
> Part of my Soul I seek thee, and thee claim
> My other half: with that thy gentle hand
> Seiz'd mine, I yielded, and from that time see

How beauty is excell'd by manly grace
And wisdom, which alone is truly fair.
    So spake our general Mother, and with eyes
Of conjugal attraction unreprov'd,
And meek surrender, half imbracing lean'd
On our first Father, half her swelling Breast
Naked met his under the flowing Gold
Of her loose tresses hid.

(IV.481-97)

Whether or not we accept the idea that Puritan thought gave special emphasis to conjugal pleasures,[15] the fact remains that in the Divorce Tracts and *Paradise Lost* marriage is discussed in terms of the personal gratification it affords both men and women.[16] The eroticism of the above passage is similar in some ways to passages in the poetry of Carew and Herrick; the difference is in Milton's attributing sexual desire to a woman. Herrick's "A Country life: To his Brother, M. Thomas Herrick" voices a similar attitude about sexuality, but only from a male point of view. Until the Fall, Eve is not guilty of lasciviousness; rather, her sexual desires complement the affection she feels for her husband. In Milton's portrait of Paradise, man and woman equally enjoy the pleasures and intimacy of sexuality. Moreover, their affection for one another, the gratification they mutually receive, is the direct result of their fealty to God.

    It is not by chance that Milton's pean to connubial love ("Hail wedded Love") comes just after Adam and Eve's quiet prayer to God ("Thou also mad'st the Night,/Maker Omnipotent, and thou the Day," [IV.724-25]) in which they acknowledge that sexual fruition is "the Crown of all our bliss." God has provided them with the bounty of the Garden and with the unparalleled pleasures of sexuality. Moreover, in their prayer and the descriptions of their lovemaking, there is an emphasis on reciprocity. They are "mutual" helpmates in their labor in the Garden; they have "mutual" affection; and from the "mutual" pleasures of sexuality will result the bountiful populating of the earth. The satisfactions of sexuality are the fruit of God's benevolence. They are the "Perpetual Fountain of Domestic sweets," when kept pure; and they are for both man and woman to enjoy.

The delights of wedded love, however, are not merely gratuitous; they are contingent upon Adam and Eve's maintaining their proper relation to each other. Their partnership in the Garden and their sexual intimacy are based upon complementary and hierarchical abilities. Adam is superior in matters of reason, Eve in matters of affection and aesthetic sensitivity. Their genders are not equal, Milton notes (see IV.295-311). Adam's contemplative faculty is hierarchically higher than is Eve's "sweet attractive Grace," but both are necessary for the well-being of the Garden. The fact that Eve needs Adam's aid does not in any way denigrate her stature, nor is Adam degraded for needing Eve (see VIII.437-51). In Paradise each creature has abilities appropriate to its place on the scale of being. To say that Eve is "inferior" is to accept the satanic perspective, which sees the divinely ordered hierarchy as exploitive and an obstracle to the fulfillment of self. On the contrary, Eve's abilities best allow her to gratify herself and to fulfill the role assigned her by God. Thus, instead of preventing her self-fulfillment, the hierarchy facilitates it.

The relationship between Adam and Eve is not, as Satan argues, that of master and slave. Adam's guidance of Eve should be neither dictatorial nor self-serving. Only after the Fall must Eve submit to her husband's "rule." Milton's attitude toward their *post*lapsarian relationship agrees with that of the marriage manuals, which argued that because women were weaker, men had to direct their actions and thoughts. During the seventeenth century, a woman was under the supervision of her father until she married. Her mother might actually give her moral and domestic instruction, but she did so only as much as her husband had delegated his authority to her. Once married, the responsibility for her instruction passed to her husband. Moreover, while they disagreed on other matters, writers on marriage unanimously insisted on a wife's acceptance of her husband's authority.[17] However, a woman's willingness to accept that authority should grow out of her love for her husband and a concomitant recognition of the worth of his judgment. In this, Milton's view agrees with most of the liberal writers on marriage. In the postlapsarian world Eve *must* submit to the rule of her husband—that is part of her punishment for having sinned (see X.193-96)—but Milton does not expect her or any woman to unquestioningly yield to the dictates of her husband. To do so would be to deny to women what God had guaranteed to all mankind: the opportunity to give sincere "allegiance, constant Faith . . . [and] Love." Yet the final image of the poem ("They hand in hand with wand'ring steps and slow,/Through *Eden* took thir solitary way.") does not emphasize Eve's need to suffer the domination of her husband; rather, it further demonstrates Milton's forceful insistence on reciprocity and mutuality in conjugal relations, even after the Fall.

The wrangling that marks the conclusion of Book IX and most of Book X dramatizes how the pleasures of their love could degenerate.[18] Adam's accusations of Eve, his denouncements of her as the cause of his fall, are frequently noted as prime examples of misogynist sentiment. They are that, indeed, but to quote them out of the context of the poem is to potentially distort a reader's perception of Milton's attitude toward women, for the poem makes abundantly clear that Adam's accusation is misplaced. As the Son pointedly remarks in response to Adam's blaming of Eve ("Shee gave me of the Tree, and I did eat"),

> Was shee thy God, that her thou didst obey
> Before his voice, or was shee made thy guide,
> Superior, or but equal, that to her
> Thou didst resign thy Manhood, and the Place
> Wherein God set thee above her made of thee,
> And for thee, whose perfection far excell'd
> Hers in all real dignity: Adorn'd
> She was indeed, and lovely to attract
> Thy Love, not thy Subjection.
>
> (X.145-53)

Adam has only himself to blame for his fall. Yet Milton is not content simply to assign culpability. His defense of Eve and of women in general is made stronger by having her dramatically implore Adam to cease raging against her, a plea that follows the most vituperative misogynist statement in the poem:

> O why did God,
> Creator wise, that peopl'd highest Heav'n
> With Spirits Masculine, create at last

> This novelty on Earth, this fair defect
> Of Nature, and not fill the World at once
> With Men as Angles without Feminine,
> Or find some other way to generate
> Mankind? this mischief had not then befall'n.
> (X.888-95)

Against such malice, Eve is sympathetically portrayed as contritely returning only affection:

> Forsake me not thus, *Adam,* witness Heav'n
> What love sincere, and reverence in my heart
> I bear thee, and unweeting have offended,
> Unhappily deceiv'd.
> (X.914-17)

And, thinking that God's punishment of death will be exacted against them shortly, she asks Adam to again become her partner, not now in happiness but in woe:

> While yet we live, scarce one short hour perhaps,
> Between us two let there be peace, both joining,
> As join'd in injuries, one enmity
> Against a Foe by doom express assign'd us,
> That cruel Serpent.
> (X.923-27)

Adam relents, responding to the affection in her plea. He can no longer be angry with her, once she has admitted her own culpability and asked for his aid. She is once again "submissive" and willing to accept his guidance. Eve, like Adam, must reaffirm her place in the cosmic hierarchy before she can become regenerate. Eve must acknowledge that Adam is her guide, just as he must acknowledge that God is his.

Culpability for the Fall is a complex matter, beyond the scope of this essay, but the point must be made that Milton treats Eve sympathetically. Unlike conservative theologians, Milton rejects the notion that woman was the cause of all of man's woes. This point is reemphasized later in the poem when Adam remarks to

Michael, after seeing the seduction of the Sons of Seth by the Daughters of Cain, that "still I see the tenor of Man's woe/Holds on the same, from Women to begin." Michael quickly corrects him, arguing that, again, the fault is in men who would become undisciplined, giving in to carnal excesses: "From Man's effeminate slackness it begins,/ . . . who should better hold his place/By Wisdom, and superior gifts receiv'd" (XI.632-36).[19]

In moving from the prelapsarian pleasures of the Garden to the harsh toil of a postlapsarian world, Milton's portrayal of women correspondingly shifts. In Paradise, Eve is Adam's "helpmate," working with him among the plants, preparing their meals, and welcoming guests. She is a perfect fellow worker, but more importantly, given Adam's complaint to God that he is lonely (see VIII.357-66, 379-97), she is his perfect companion, for out of the intimacy of their relationship they enjoy emotional, sexual, and intellectual gratifications. Milton's emphasis changes, however, when the poem moves to a consideration of their relationship after the Fall. Her importance then is no longer as a *wife*, but as a *mother*.

In Michael's history of mankind women are the biological, passive agents of God's Plan. Eve is a crucially important element of that Plan, for, as the Son announces the prophecy of retribution against Satan, women will bring about the Serpent's punishment: "Between Thee and the Woman I will put/Enmity, and between thine and her Seed." In Books XI and XII the history of that seed is traced by Michael, first in the vision and then in a narration when Adam's sight fails. But there are few women in that history. With the exception of the daughters of Cain and Mary, there are no women named directly; only the sons of women are discussed at length: Cain, Abel, Noah, Nimrod, Abraham, Moses, Joshua, David, Solomon, Christ, the Disciples. There is no mention of Sarah, Rebecca, Susanna, Rachel, Esther. The Seed that we watch germinate is a male one.

Milton's focus on male action in that history coincides with the more conservative tradition which ignored feminine achievement and thereby implicitly argued against the active participation of women in public affairs. By not mentioning the women prophets and rulers of the Bible, Milton ignored the precedents for feminine public action. Although the implication of the Divorce Tracts is that women are entitled to the same pursuit of pleasure as men, their equity with men has severe limits and does not extend beyond a domestic context.[20] We have already noted a similar attitude in the verse epistles of Donne and Jonson. By the time of Milton's composition of *Paradise Lost* and *Paradise Regained,* however, the subject had become the source of a considerable controversy. Among nonconforming sects, particularly the Quakers, and some radical political groups,[21] there was a growing sense of the legitimacy of female participation in political and ecclesiastical matters. Margaret Fell Fox, the cofounder of the Quakers, and others argued that women could speak of God's Word as effectively as could men and that there was substantial biblical justification for female ministers. The issue still has currency today as the controversy over the ordination of women demonstrates.

While Milton's *Paradise Lost* went a long way toward establishing marriage as a fit subject for poetry, his focus on Adam and Eve's prelapsarian relationship raises serious questions about the ability of postlapsarian men and women to achieve the heights of connubial gratification enjoyed by "our first Parents." Michael's history of mankind, which is intended to inform Adam of God's Plan and therefore focuses only on those relationships pertaining immediately to that Plan, chronicles no successful, intimate relationships. Moreover, notwithstanding the emphasis on the mutual companionship of men and women in marriage in the argument of the Divorce Tracts, the conclusion of *Paradise Lost* and the figure of Mary in *Paradise Regained* clearly indicate that to Milton the feminine role of mother has a greater importance in the history of mankind than does the role of wife. Fortitude, piety, and the procreative ability of women are thereby given prominence over sexuality and companionship in marriage.

IV

In the seventeenth century, then, women were praised chiefly for their domestic capabilities and for their ability to function as static, passive exemplars of virtue. Because of historical developments, shifting economic structures, and the prescriptions of marriage manuals and courtesy books, seventeenth-century English women, though encouraged to work for the moral betterment of society, were consistently discouraged from becoming actively, directly involved in matters of public importance. The common assumption that women were by nature licentious, intellectually limited, malicious, and loquacious prevented their being urged to participate in society in any but the most limited of ways. When confined in their kitchens and nurseries or elevated to a straitening spirituality, women were praised in poems and essays. In the works of poets such as John Donne, Robert Herrick, and John Milton, the seventeenth century's "modern" awareness of sexuality led to an increased valuation of women, but for the most part the new acknowledgement of human sexual needs only added to the fear and antagonism male writers felt toward women.

Only among the members of the fringe groups of English society were women allowed to take on larger political and religious responsibilities. Basic to early Quakerism was the belief that "all are one in Christ." There is no difference in the spirit, said Margaret Fell and George Fox, between men and women.[22] Fifth Monarchists, Ranters, Independents, and Baptists agreed. The suppression of these groups was partly due to their advocacy of the equality or near-equality of women. Among the Quakers and Independents, women were often ranked as important members of the practicing clergy. No major poet praised the exploits of women warriors, politicians, or religious leaders. Some essayists—Thomas Heywood, for instance—did praise such women. But in his *A Curtaine Lecture* (London, 1637), *The Exemplary Lives and Memorable Acts of Nine the most Worthy Women of the World* (London, 1640), and the very lengthy compendium *Gunaikeion: or, Nine Bookes of Various History. Concerninge Women Inscribed by the Names of the Nine Muses* (London, 1624), Heywood does not argue that women should be called upon in his own day to aid England in its troubles.

The seventeenth century, a great era of turmoil and revolution, must be seen as formulating two important views of women; and these views, though contrary, have prevailed to our own time. On the one hand, the seventeenth century continued what may be called the frivolization of women. Although Henrietta Maria's advocacy of *préciosité* revitalized aspects of the Petrarchan tradition and momentarily heightened the status of women, the view that women had the power to be a spiritualizing influence easily degenerated. The neoplatonic context given to women quickly became diffused, so that women were said to possess only a trivial and emotionally charged religiosity. Misogynist satirists gleefully degraded women's spiritual power and sincerity by suggesting that their faith was of a lower order, inferior to the faith of men. On the other hand, the advocacy by Quakers and others of women's right to promote God's Word and to work actively in the world laid the foundation for the later development of the women's rights movements.

Notes

All quotations from the major writers of the period were taken from the following standard texts; all references to line numbers and page numbers have been placed in the body of the text: Thomas Carew, *The Poems with His Masque "Coelum Britannicum,"* ed. Rhodes Dunlap (Oxford: Oxford University Press, 1957); John Donne, *The Elegies and the Songs and Sonnets,* ed. Helen Gardner (Oxford: Oxford University Press, 1965) and *The Satires, Epigrams and Verse Letters,* ed. W. Milgate (Oxford: Oxford University Press, 1967); Robert Herrick, *The Poetical Works,* ed. L. C. Martin (Oxford: Oxford University Press, 1963); Ben Jonson, *The Complete Poetry,* ed. William B. Hunter, Jr. (New York: W. W. Norton, 1963); Henry King, *The Poems,* ed. Margaret Crum (Oxford: Oxford University Press, 1965); Richard Lovelace, *The Poems,* ed. C. H. Wilkinson (Oxford: Oxford University Press, 1953); Andrew Marvell, *The Poems and Letters,* 2 vols., ed. H. M. Margoliouth (Oxford: Oxford University Press, 1967); John Milton, *Complete Poems and Major Prose,* ed. Merritt Y. Hughes (New York: The Odyssey Press, 1957) and *Complete Prose Works,* volume 2 (New Haven: Yale University Press and London: Oxford University Press, 1959); Sir John Suckling, *The Works (Non-Dramatic),* ed. Thomas Clayton (Oxford: Oxford University Press, 1971); Henry Vaughan, *The Complete Poetry,* ed. French Fogle (New York: W. W. Norton, 1964).

1 For a discussion of the status of English women during the sixteenth and seventeenth centuries see Rev. James Anderson, *Memorable Women of the Puritan Times,* 2 vols. (London: Blackie and Son, 1862); George Ballard, *Memoirs of Several Ladies* (London, 1752); Ben Barker-Benfield, "Anne Hutchinson and the Puritan Attitude Toward Women," *Feminist Studies* I (1972), 65-96; Carroll Camden, *The Elizabethan Woman: A Panorama of English Womanhood, 1540 to 1640* (London: Cleaver-Hume Press, and New York: Elsevier, 1952); Jean Elizabeth Gagen, *The New Woman: Her Emergence in English Drama, 1600-1730* (New York: Twayne Publishers, 1954); Alice Clark, *Working Life of Women in the Seventeenth Century* (London: Routledge, and New York:

Dutton, 1919); Jessie Bedford [Elizabeth Godfrey], *Home Life Under the Stuarts: 1603-1649* (New York: Dutton, and London: Grant Richards, 1903); Christina Hole, *The English Housewife in the Seventeenth Century* (London: Chatto & Windus, 1953); Charlotte Kohler, "The Elizabethan Woman of Letters" (Ph.d. dissertation, University of Virginia, 1936); Ella Caroline Lapham, "The Industrial Status of Women in Elizabethan England," *The Journal of Political Economy* 9 (Dec. 1900-Sept. 1901), 562-99; Margaret Phillips and W. S. Tomkinson, *English Women in Life and Letters* (rpt., New York: B. Blom, 1971); Chilton Latham Powell, *English Domestic Relations 1487-1653* (New York: Columbia University Press, 1917); Myra Reynolds, *The Learned Lady in England: 1650-1760* (Gloucester, Mass.: Peter Smith, 1964); William Brenchley Rye, *England as Seen by Foreigners in the Days of Elizabeth and James the First* (London: J. R. Smith, 1865); Levin L. Schucking, *The Puritan Family: A Social Study from the Literary Sources,* trans. Brian Battershaw (New York: Schocken Books, 1969; 1st German ed., 1929); Doris Mary Stenton, *The English Woman in History* (London: Allen & Unwin, and New York: Macmillan, 1957); Roger Thompson, *Women in Stuart England and America: A Comparative Study* (London: Routledge & Kegan Paul, 1974); Francis Lee Utley, *The Crooked Rib* (Columbus: Ohio State University Press, 1944); Ian Watt, *The Rise of the Novel* (Berkeley and Los Angeles: University of California Press, 1962); Violet A. Wilson, *Society Women of Shakespeare's Time* (London: John Lane, 1925); Louis B. Wright, *Middle-Class Culture in Elizabethan England* (Ithaca, N.Y.: Cornell University Press, 1963).

2 Quoted by Camden, *The Elizabethan Woman,* p. 43. James I's misogyny is evident in his "A Satire Against Woemen" which concludes with the following stanzas:

> Even so all wemen are of nature vaine
> And can not keepe no secrett unrevealed
> And where as once they doe concaive disdaine
> They are unable to be reconcealed
> Fullfild with talke and clatters but respect
> And often tymes of small or none effect.
>   Ambitious all without regarde or shame
> Butt anie measure given to greede of geare
> Desyring ever for to winne a name
> With flattering all that will them not forbeare
> Sume craft they have, yett foolish are indeede
> With lying whiles esteeming best to speede.

The text is from the edition by Allan F. Westcott, *New Poems: From a Hitherto Unpublished Ms (Add. 24195) in the British Museum* (New York, 1911). H. M. Richmond in his important book on Stuart love poetry,

The School of Love (Princeton, N.J.: Princeton University Press, 1964), comments on Henrietta Maria's influence on Charles I's court in her advocacy of platonic love (p. 261).

3 In "An Elegie, On the Death of Mrs. Cassandra Cotton, only Sister to Mr. C. Cotton," Richard Lovelace pointedly describes Cassandra Cotton in narrower terms. She is a model *only* for women, as the application at the end of the elegy makes clear:

> Virgins, if thus you dare but Courage take
> To follow her in Life, else through this Lake
> Of Nature wade, and breake her earthly bars,
> Y' are fixt with her upon a Throne of stars
> Arched with a pure Heav'n Chrystaline,
> Where round you Love and Joy for ever shine.
> (47-52)

4 In many of the funeral sermons of the period, a procedure similar to John Donne's is used. John Ley, the Vicar of Chester, for instance, uses Jane Ratcliffe as a "patterne of Pietie" in his sermon delivered on the occasion of her burial in 1640. Similarly, John Clarke in his *Holy incense for the sensers of the saints* (London, 1634) uses Anne Ayscovgh as an example for all mankind. She was a Protestant martyr during the reign of Queen Mary, and Clarke takes her admonition to "Pray, Pray, Pray" as a lesson for all; see also Hannibal Ganon's sermon on Lady Frances Roberts, *The Praise of a Godly Woman* (London, 1627).

5 Barbara K. Lewalski's *Donne's "Anniversaries" and the Poetry of Praise: The Creation of a Symbolic Mode* (Princeton: Princeton University Press, 1973) should be consulted for a thorough and brilliant analysis of Donne's development of women, particularly of Elizabeth Drury, as symbolic figures.

6 In his epistles to male friends, Donne's concerns are quite different. When he addresses men he jokes about current news, refers to travels abroad or to business trips, and talks about intimacies of his own life. E. G., S. B., I. L., and he are all men of the world. On the other hand, the countesses addressed by Donne are isolated by their virtue. The exemplary qualities Donne sees in his male friends make them good companions; in the women those qualities set them apart from other human beings.

7 Stenton, *English Woman in History,* p. 141 and Gagen, *The New Woman,* pp. 9-10 suggest that Swetnam's attacks on women in the early part of the century and the emphasis on feminine passivity were in response to the advances women had made during Elizabeth I's reign. In the course of the century, literally dozens of misogynist works were published in England; in fact, works on women, defending and attacking them, became a minor genre in the period.

8 p. 16. The two major misogynist works in the seventeenth century,

Swetnam's, and Francis Osborne's *Advice to a Son,* went through many editions. From 1615 to 1660 Swetnam's *Araignment* was published twelve times; in 1656 alone there were five editions of Osborne's *Advice.* None of the defenses of women enjoyed the popularity of these works. Importantly, however, women began to defend themselves in the seventeenth century. Following the lead of Jane Anger, Rachel Speght, *A Movzell for Melastomvs* (London, 1617), Constantia Munda [pseud.], *The Worning of a Mad Dogge, or a soppe for Cerberus* (London, 1617), Ester Sowernam [pseud.], *Ester hath hang'd Haman* (London, 1617), and the anonymous playwrights of *Swetnam the woman-hater arraigned by women* (London, 1620) responded to Swetnam's *Araignment,* denouncing him for his malicious slander. Later in the period, the pseudonymous Mary Tattlewell and Ioanne Hit-him-home attacked another misogynist, John Taylor, in their lengthy and articulate *The Womens Sharpe Revenge* (London, 1640).

9 During the 1640s the prohibitions against feminine participation in public affairs had a greater urgency, especially in the area of public preaching. In Daniel Rogers's *Matrimonial Honour* (London, 1642), the anonymous *The Parliament of Women* (London, 1640), *A Discoverie of Six women preachers* (London, 1641), and *The Diseases of the Times* (London, 1640?) women actively seeking to reform the church and state are vehemently denounced. There is also evidence to suggest that women, more so than ever before in English history, assumed a more active role in the processes of social revolution. Ellen A. McArthur, "Women Petitioners and the Long Parliament," *English Historical Review* 24 (1909), 698-709, and Keith Thomas, "Women and the Civil War Sects," *Past and Present* 13 (1958), 42-62, have demonstrated the importance of women in radical sects during this period. Yet much earlier, in Gervase Markham's popular *Country Contentments, or the English Huswife,* first published in 1615, a woman is praised as she may be "an example, an incitment and spurre vnto all her family." That example should be private, however, for Markham goes on to add: "I do not meane that herein she shoud vtter forth that violence of spirit which many of our (vainely accounted pure) women do, drawing a contempt vpon the ordinary Ministery, and thinking nothing lawful but the fantazies of their own inuentions, vsurping to themselues a power of preaching and interpreting the holy word, to which only they ought to be but hearers and beleeuers, or at the most but modest perswaders, this is not the office either of good Hous-wife or good woman. But let our english Hus-wife be a godly, constant, and religious woman, learning from the worthy preacher & her husband" (p. 2). The opposition to women's public activity, then, had a long history in English thought. The events of the civil wars only increased the stridency of that opposition.

10 In an important study early in the twentieth century, Alice Clark surveyed the economic developments which affected the status of

women and she concluded that there was a noticeable "decline in the standard of women's education and in their social and economic position" (p. 303) in the seventeenth century. Even in those areas, such as brewing and midwifery, in which women had worked for centuries, when they became controlled by professions or were put under the governance of guilds, women invariably were excluded.

11 Among the many examples of poems in the Petrarchan mode, Henry Vaughan's "Les Amours," "To Amoret," "To his Friend. Being in Love," the poems of Henry King, and Milton's Italian sonnets II, III, and V offer a good sense of the way in which women were praised for their spiritualizing influence.

12 Earl Miner's *The Cavalier Mode* (Princeton: Princeton University Press, 1971) and Richmond's *The School of Love* examine that increased concern and consider its implications.

13 Ferrand's *Erotomania, or A Treatise Discoursing of the Essence, Causes, Symptoms, Prognostics, and Cure of Love, or Erotique Melancholy* (Oxford, 1640) sees love in terms similar to Robert Burton's *Anatomy of Melancholy* (Oxford, 1621); in both works, love is a physical and mental disease, to be cured by abstinence or purgatives. In Ferrand's words, "Love is little better than meere madnesse" (p. 230).

14 The largest part of Donne's love poetry advocates the integration of spiritual and sexual love; accordingly, women are praised by the speakers of the *Elegies* and the *Songs and Sonnets*. However, in some of the poems in the *Songs and Sonnets,* Donne presents speakers who have failed in that integration; see "Song: 'Goe, and catche a falling starre,' " "The Curse," and "Loves Alchymie."

15 In two seminal articles, "The Puritan Art of Love," *Huntington Library Quarterly* 5 (1942): 235-72 and "Hail Wedded Love," *Journal of English Literary History* 13 (1946): 79-97, William and Malleville Haller established the view that Puritan theologians placed special stress on the role of a woman as a wife and that stress brought about the heightened status of women. In his important book, *Milton and the Idea of Matrimony: A Study of the Divorce Tracts and "Paradise Lost"* (New Haven: Yale University Press, 1970), John Halkett argues that the Puritan attitude was not noticeably different from that found in the works of Anglican divines. It is clear, whichever view one takes, that Protestantism in general saw marriage as being at least equally important for its convivial delights as for its procreative function.

16 The subtitle to *The Doctrine and Discipline of Divorce* (London, 1643) emphasizes Milton's concern with the happiness of both men and women in marriage: "RESTORED TO THE GOOD OF BOTH SEXES, From the bondage of Canon Law, and other mistakes, to Christian freedom, guided by the Rule of Charity."

17 That authority was frequently compared to Christ's over the church or to the state's over the individual. Until the nineteenth century, in fact, it was still considered a *treasonable* offense in English law to kill

one's husband. See Halkett's *Milton and the Idea of Matrimony* for a thorough discussion of these matters.

18 The confrontation of Samson and Dalila in *Samson Agonistes* also demonstrates how the pleasures of connubial love could be turned to contentious hatred when hierarchical relationships and fealty to God are not maintained.

19 Importantly, while Samson in *Samson Agonistes* and Adam in *Paradise Lost* are susceptible to concupiscence, in *Paradise Regained* Satan angrily rejects the suggestion that such a temptation be used on Jesus. "Set women in his eye and in his walk," says Belial (II.153); to which Satan quickly answers:

> because of old
> Thou thyself dot'st on womankind, admiring
> Thir shape, thir color, and attractive grace,
> None are, thou think'st, but taken with such toys.
>
> . . . .
>
> Beauty stands
> In th'admiration only of weak minds
> Led captive; cease to admire, and all her Plumes
> Fall flat and shrink into a trivial toy,
> At every sudden slighting quite abasht:
> Therefore with manlier objects we must try
> His constancy.
>
> (II.174-77; 220-26)

20 Even in a domestic situation, Milton believed that men should have authority over women; see *Doctrine and Discipline of Divorce* II: xv.

21 See Keith Thomas, "Women and the Civil War Sects." Margaret Fell Fox in *Womens Speaking Justified by the Scriptures* (London, 1666) has one of the most concisely presented arguments in support of female preaching; see my facsimile reproduction of *Womens Speaking* published by the Augustan Reprint Society (Los Angeles, Berkeley: University of California Press, 1977). For examples of women writing in support of nonconforming sects, see Judith Eedes's *A Warning to all the Inhabitants of the Earth* (London, 1659) and Katherine Chidley's *The Justification of the Independent Churches of Christ* (London, 1641).

22 The following works should be consulted for fuller discussions of the Quaker position on women preaching: William C. Braithwait, *The Beginnings of Quakerism*, 2d ed., rev. by Henry J. Cadbury (Cambridge: At the University Press, 1955) and *The Second Period of Quakerism*, 2d ed., rev. by Henry J. Cadbury (Cambridge: At the University Press, 1961); Isabel Ross, *Margaret Fell: Mother of Quakerism* (London: Longmans, Green, 1949); Arnold Lloyd, *Quaker Social History: 1669-1738* (London: Longmans, Green, 1950). In addition, some Quaker works themselves are very much worth consulting: George Fox, *The*

Woman Learning in Silence (London, 1656) and *This is an Encouragement To All the Womens-Meetings* (London, 1676); Richard Farnworth, *A Woman forbidden to speak in the Church* (London, 1654); George Keith, "Post-script" to *The Woman-Preacher of Samaria* (London, 1674); Patrick Livingston, "Some Queries to them that deny Womens speaking in the Church" in *Truth Owned and Deceit Denyed* (London, 1667). The advocacy of women's independence in matters of religion promised not only disruptions in the church but in the home as well. Following George Fox, in *The Woman-Preacher of Samaria* George Keith argues that if a woman disagrees with her husband's religious principles, then she should leave him, "for *she ought rather to obey God than Man. And in Christ Jesus there is neither Male nor Femal but all are one in him,* as the Apostle said" (p. 24).

4.

The Portrayal of Women in Restoration and Eighteenth-century English Literature

John J. Richetti

Charles II landed at Dover on May 25, 1660, and on August 21 he issued patents to Thomas Killigrew and William Davenant to form acting companies and build two playhouses. Both of these companies made theatrical history by including a number of actresses to play women's roles for the first time ever on the English public stage. One would like to be able to say that the presence of real women on the stage marked a correspondingly new attitude toward the portrayal of that sex. But such seems not to have been the case. The substitution of women for the beardless youths of the Elizabethan stage was a social rather than a literary or psychological event. The new and looser moral standards of the Restoration court which reopened the theaters permitted actresses, but mainly to enliven presentations of very old aesthetic and dramatic norms that reflected a quite traditional view of women. Indeed, the Restoration stage was itself only partly a novelty, for it included

65

numerous revivals of Elizabethan and Jacobean plays and translations and adaptations from the French neoclassic theater. New
plays shared with revivals and translations various attitudes
toward the representation of characters of both sexes; these
attitudes must be considered before one can understand the
presentation of women in both dramatic and nondramatic literature.

Traditionally and necessarily, all drama tends to generalize and
typify the people it presents. Because of limited time and space, the
unique complexity accorded to individuals has to be foreshortened
and simplified. Those tendencies of drama were accepted and
indeed reaffirmed by the theory which governed the literature of
the seventeenth and eighteenth centuries. Moreover, the theory of
literature which stretched back to Aristotle considered the general
more important and meaningful than the particular and favored
the universal over the merely specific and historical. As Aristotle
said in the *Poetics,* "Poetry is something more philosophic and of
graver import than history, since its statements are of the nature of
universals, whereas those of history are singular." [1] The continuing
force of that dictum is reflected in the literary tradition of
neoclassicism, which came to govern Restoration literature.

Because of that preference for generality, the female personalities one meets in Restoration literature suffered, in a way,
more transmutation than the various males. Much more than man,
woman was an established type, a clearly defined character in the
recurring human situation as understood by western culture. In art
as in life, women were male appendages, restrictively identified as
daughters, wives, mothers, or mistresses. More generally, in playing
those social roles, any female character participated to some extent
in a cultural stereotype which ran continuously through the most
familiar documents of European civilization. In the Scriptures, the
Church Fathers, the medieval philosophers, and the literary
tradition stretching from the Greeks, woman was portrayed with
some consistency as a necessary evil. For patriarchal Greeks as for
medieval schoolmen, women were unfortunately the only means
available to perpetuate the race. Except for that function, they
were dangerous creatures, embodiments of the irrational and the
uncontrollable, summaries of human weakness and corruption
whose failings were described in a long tradition of misogynistic

literature. Christianity added sexual disgust to the patriarchal condescension and homoerotic preferences of antiquity, and St. Augustine's famous despairing comment, *"inter feces et urinam nascimur,"* turns woman into a more than symbolic reminder of human imperfection. That disparagement seems to have been modified somewhat in the Middle Ages by the cult which developed around the Virgin Mary and by the love poetry written in the twelfth century by the Provençal poets. But even the extravagant amatory and pious conventions thus established depended upon the traditional view of woman. The Virgin, the distant and unattainable beloved of the Troubadours, and the spiritualized female inspiration of Dante and Petrarch were the corrective antitheses of those corrupt embodiments of human weakness, Eve and Pandora. The Virgin Mary and her sisters merely served by their rare purity to emphasize the grossness of the type, of women in general; they were the pure exceptions who proved the filthy rule.

One can find numerous examples of that cultural stereotype in the English literature of the seventeenth and eighteenth centuries. It could hardly have been otherwise. But as the period progresses, as the eighteenth century ripens along with the middle-class civilization of England, the promise implicit in the presence of actresses rather than squeaking lads begins to be fulfilled. Within the neoclassic aesthetics that demanded generality and the cultural tradition that defined the female truth in satirical and moral terms, one can observe an emerging counter-mythology of women which leads eventually by the middle of the eighteenth century to the creation of a distinctively modern kind of heroine and the expression of a new female consciousness, or at least to a new awareness of the value of female experience on the part of a male-dominated culture. The transition is perhaps best described this way: woman as moral topic becomes woman as metaphor; from woman as the center of a moral-rhetorical occasion, the literary tradition moves to examining female experience as a revealingly intense version of human experience in general.

The reasons for that transformation are complex and probably beyond definitive formulation. Perhaps what it is customary to call English empiricism is important in breaking down old cultural stereotypes; perhaps the combined force of English Protestantism and English political theory with their heightened sense of the value of the individual is also crucial. Perhaps the development of a substantial middle class in England, which in turn created a female leisure class that read books and for whom books were deliberately written, is the most important factor. Social historians have yet to settle the question, but the literature of the period does provide a set of documents which marks with some clarity a revision of the traditional view of women. Of special interest are the ways in which the stereotypes are modified and perhaps transformed by the modifications and transformations of the literary types which articulate them. The history of the changing attitudes toward women in English literature from the Restoration into the eighteenth century is a matter, in large part, of the change from an aesthetic preference for generality of representation to an increasing interest in the particularized facts of social experience.

Let us turn to stereotypes first and to an extreme, nearly absurd kind of artistic generality. The last place one might expect to find convincing representations of women (or of human beings as normally understood) is Restoration heroic tragedy. Like Hollywood spectaculars, these plays proposed to overwhelm their audiences by splendid rhetoric and pageantry. Character in that sort of enterprise becomes another means of arousing the audience; it is as broadly conceived as the spectacle and matches the rest of the play in scale. Thus, in Dryden's massive ten-act epic, *The Conquest of Granada* (1669-70), women play a crucial role, and the love they excite in the men is of appropriately grandiose inspirational dimensions. Indeed, love and war are exactly parallel activities, and the noble Moors eventually lose their city to the Spaniards because they fail at love.

In the course of a plot far too complicated to summarize, numerous lovers pass and repass as the battle for the city swings along. Two women are central in the play and represent the two halves of the cultural stereotype. The infinitely cunning Lyndaraxa promises love to various enamored Moors. She exploits them to gain power and wealth for herself, and she articulates a cynical self-consciousness about that noblest of passions. Long-suffering Almahide, on the other hand, loves the outrageously noble Almanzor and strikes any number of pathetic attitudes in the course of events, refusing to deny her love for him or to violate her duty as the wife of Boabdelin, King of Granada. Lyndaraxa has no passions except avarice and ambition; Almahide reconciles passion and domestic duty. Love, selfish and selfless, spins the absurd complications which comprise the play. Love provokes the heroes, undoes the villains and weaklings, and drives the star of it all, Almanzor, to his greatest heights of rhetoric and valor. It seems fair to say that the audience who endured such spectacle responded to the power of love and the broadly conceived women who embody and promote it because such emotional and moral simplicities were a thrillingly exaggerated revision of reality. The diarist John Evelyn's sister wrote that she found the play "so full of ideas that the most refined romance I ever read is not to compare with it: love is made so pure, and valour so nice, that one would imagine it designed for an Utopia rather than our stage." [2]

As different as they are, however, Almahide and Lyndaraxa both illustrate the compulsive center of female personality that the stereotype always enforces. Lyndaraxa pretends to be spontaneous, but she exploits female variability for her own designs. She tells one of her anxious lovers who asks for assurance that she will love him even if he loses an impending battle:

> I know not what my future thoughts will be:
> Poor women's thoughts are all *extempore.*
> Wise men, indeed,
> Beforehand a long chain of thought produce;
> But ours are only for our present use.

(Part I.IV.ii)

Lyndaraxa's villainy lies precisely in her denial of that outline of female behavior, and her variations are controlled and focused on a clearly conceived and utterly selfish goal. Almahide is a heroine because of the purity of her compulsions and the resolute stillness of her solution to the dilemma posed by the conflict of duty and passion. Almanzor and the other male stars of heroic tragedy are such by means of violent external action, or at least by virtue of their unabashedly public rhetoric. Almahide, as she explains in this soliloquy, is heroic by means of an internalized action, nothing less than heroic self-denial and repression:

But Heaven, which made me great, has chose for me,
I must the oblation for my people be.
I'll cherish honour, then, and life despise;
What is not pure, is not for sacrifice.
Yet for Almanzor I in secret mourn!
Can virtue, then, admit of his return?
Yes, for my love I will by virtue square;
My heart's not mine, but all my actions are.
I'll like Almanzor act; and dare to be
As haughty, and as wretched too, as he.
What will he think is in my message meant?
I scarcely understand my own intent:
But, silkworm-like, so long within have wrought,
That I am lost in my own web of thought.

(Part I.I.ii)

Such female introspection is frequent in these plays, but Dryden is really more interested in the effects that women have on men than in women themselves. Almahide defines herself as a secret and private version of the public male hero, Almanzor. Dryden's greatest play, *All for Love* (1667), allows women to share the public space that men occupy without neglecting the examination of those unsettling effects women cause. By their demands, Cleopatra and Octavia interrupt the heroic career of Antony, but these women are more than conventional obstacles. By current standards, they are perhaps the most satisfying women in all of Restoration tragedy.

Dryden manages to make Cleopatra and Octavia moving and dignified figures by providing them with wonderfully restrained and controlled language; the rant of heroic tragedy is exchanged for a consistently powerful understatement. When Antony sorrowfully discards her, Cleopatra simply refers us to a passion too large for words:

Then must we part? Farewell, my cruel lord!
The appearance is against me; and I go,
Unjustified, for ever from your sight.
How I have loved, you know; how yet I love,
My only comfort is, I know myself:

I love you more, even now you are unkind,
Than when you loved me most; so well, so truly
I'll never strive against it; but die pleased,
To think you once were mine.

(IV)

The most truthful moment in the play also depends upon unspoken feelings which the lines invite us to imagine. It is an incident Dryden added to the story as he received it: the meeting between Octavia and Cleopatra after Antony has agreed to forsake Egypt, a brief but marvellous scene in which, as Dryden himself remarked in his preface, "though the one were a Roman, and the other a queen, they were both women." To return to some initial terms, the scene is the meeting of opposite ends of the cultural stereotype: the virgin-mother and the temptress. These extremes are, in effect, revised in the course of the scene by Dryden's dramatic skill. Caught in social and sexual roles, both women self-consciously exercise what power they have. Octavia, in Dryden's sly stage direction, comes up close to Cleopatra:

> I would view nearer
> That face, which has so long usurped my right,
> To find the inevitable charms, that catch
> Mankind so sure, that ruined my dear lord.
> CLEO. Oh, you do well to search; for had you known
> But half these charms, you had not lost his heart.

Octavia declares that tricks like those are the last thing a Roman matron would care to know. Cleopatra answers that she is proud of her charms because they have earned her Antony's love:

> And when I love not him, Heaven change this face
> For one like that.
> OCTAV. Thou lov'st him not so well.
> CLEO. I love him better, and deserve him more.
> OCTAV. You do not; cannot: You have been his ruin.
> Who made him cheap at Rome, but Cleopatra?
> Who made him scorned abroad, but Cleopatra?
> At Actium, who betrayed him? Cleopatra.

Who made his children orphans, and poor me
A wretched widow? only Cleopatra.
CLEO. Yet she, who loves him best, is Cleopatra.
If you have suffered, I have suffered more.
You bear the specious title of a wife,
To gild your cause, and draw the pitying world
To favour it: the world condemns poor me,
For I have lost my honour, lost my fame,
And stained the glory of my royal house,
And all to bear the branded name of mistress.
There wants but life, and that too I would lose
For him I love.
OCTAV. Be't so, then; take thy wish. (EXIT)

(III)

The pathos is shared equally, for these characters confront one another as women rather than as embodiments of good and evil. Wife and mistress possess passion without being totally possessed by it; the cultural antithesis that wife and mistress represent is merely part of the characters' histrionic equipment, and they both work within the antithesis, playing with the emotional force each receives from it. These women talk about themselves; Antony is merely the excuse and occasion for *their* self-display.

On the surface, Restoration comedy is a much more promising field in which to observe the erosion of the female cultural stereotypes. As comedies, the plays are permitted a domestic and social realism denied by the operatic conventions of heroic tragedy. In the comedies of Congreve, Vanbrugh, and Dryden, for example, women are more than generalized figures who express or inspire titanic emotions. They exist in society and control money and the social power it commands. They are out for marriage, but marriage in these plays is a social convenience whose interference with natural urges is the main source of fun for the audience. The women in these relentlessly "honest" plays are as comically uneasy within that institution as the men; there is in effect a democracy of desire at work. And even desire itself is as comic as marriage. The cynical calculations of a Lyndaraxa to manipulate sexuality for political power become for Dryden's Doralice in *Marriage à la Mode* (1673) a faux-naive examination of the inevitable cycle of desire and disgust. When Palamon, her would-be lover, wishes they had enjoyed each other at least once, she replies:

> For aught I know, 'tis better that we have not; we might upon trial have liked each other less, as many a man and woman, that have loved as desperately as we, and yet, when they came to possession, have sighed and cried to themselves, Is this all? PALA. That is only, if the servant were not found a man of this world; but if, upon trial, we had not liked each other, we had certainly left loving; and faith, that's the greater unhappiness of the two. (V.i)

The witty point is that desire is as great a trap as marriage, and the recurrent joke of Restoration comedy is on those men and women who are unable to see that urbane truth. In fact, these comedies are anti-satirical and their dominant characters are beyond such moral and emotional simplicities as the traditional representation of women enforces. Thus a character like Vanbrugh's Heartfree in *The Provok'd Wife* (1697) who indulges himself in traditional satiric attacks like the following is necessarily slated for ironic conversion to love and domesticity:

> I always consider a Woman, not as the Taylor, the Shoomaker, the Tire-woman, the Sempstress (and which is more than all that), the Poet makes her; but I consider her as pure Nature has contriv'd her, and that more strictly than I should have done our old Grandmother Eve, had I seen her naked in the Garden; for I consider her turn'd inside out. Her Heart well examin'd, I find there Pride, Vanity, Covetousness, Indiscretion, but above all things, Malice; Plots eternally aforging, to destroy one-anothers Reputations, and as honestly to charge the Levity of Mens Tongues with the Scandal; hourly Debates, how to make poor Gentlemen in love with 'em, with no other intent, but to use 'em like Dogs when they have done; a constant Desire of doing more mischief, and an everlasting War, wag'd against Truth and Good-nature. (II)

By the fourth act, Heartfree can declare to his Belinda that she has "made a Convert" of him and that he's "grown a Fool: I cou'd be fond of a Woman." Belinda thanks him, "in the Name of the whole Sex" and warns him that a month of possession may bring him to polite indifference: "Well, you Men are unaccountable things, mad till you have your Mistresses; and then stark mad till you are rid of 'em again." Belinda accepts Heartfree, but only after proving her superior urbanity, her sharper ironic distance from sexuality. There is no sexual repression in sight in Restoration comedy, but the freedom such license makes possible for its characters, male and female, is an urbane contempt for human instability rather than anything that might be called sexual liberation.

It is hardly surprising that women in Restoration comedy tend to have a certain strength the men tend to lack. Comedy in general often presents women as the calm possessors of sexuality, residing in it and at home with its demands, exercising the social power it can give them if they manage it wisely. Congreve's two heroines, Angelica and Millamant, in *Love for Love* (1695) and *The Way of the World* (1700) respectively, are as urbane and witty about social and sexual matters as anyone in Restoration comedy, and yet they may be said to preserve themselves from the moral contagion of the age and the implicit moral superiority of its playwrights. Congreve is the most delicate wit in that rough crew of dramatists, and his two most memorable women are interesting because the delicacy of their self-consciousness sets them apart from their dramatic worlds. Angelica resides quite comfortably in the background of her play, watching with bemused tolerance the various silly intrigues and marital-financial schemes which constitute its plot. Quite unlike most other heroines of the genre and the age, she is the strongest and most capable character in the play, testing her weak if likable lover, Valentine, and rewarding him in the end for his constancy by means of her cunningly arranged power. She pretends to favor Valentine's father, Sir Sampson Legend, and manages to tear up the bond by which that disapproving parent hoped to disinherit his son. Angelica's modesty as she solves the hero's problem and delivers herself is quite transparent: "Had I the world to give you, it could not make me worthy of so generous and faithful a passion; here's my hand, my heart was always yours, and struggled very hard to make the utmost trial of your virtue" (V).

Angelica seems untouched by the sexuality destructively ram-

pant in Restoration comedy; her sights are on her own standards of
constancy rather than on that impatient, mechanical, and thereby
demeaning passion which the others in the play care about. In *The
Way of the World,* Millamant is the same sort of self-contained and
implicitly mysterious personage—a person in fact, surrounded by
mere "characters." She and her worthy suitor, Mirabell, recognize
each other as self-conscious equals. Their marriage is a dramatically foregone conclusion from the moment in the fourth act when
Mirabell continues the quotation from Suckling with which
Millamant has bewildered her awkward country suitor, Sir Wilful
Witwoud:

> "Like Phoebus sung the no less amorous boy."
> Enter MIRABELL.
> MIR. "Like Daphne she, as lovely and as coy."
> Do you lock yourself up from me, to make my search more
> curious? or is this pretty artifice contrived to signify that here
> the chase must end, and my pursuits be crowned? For you can
> fly no further.

Millamant protests that she will "fly, and be followed to the last
moment." She expects to "be solicited to the very last, nay, and
afterwards." In fact, she will "never marry unless I am first made
sure of my will and pleasure."

These lovers give each other pleasure by means of wit and self-
conscious irony. There is absolute equality between them; both are
aware of the dynamics of desire and power which obtain in male-
female relations, and each recognizes the rights of the other. That
recognition neutralizes the destructive effects of the sexual dynamic, for the urbane perspective thus achieved is a way of
acknowledging power without the vulgar need to exercise it. In the
customary world of Restoration comedy, full of solipsistic fops,
sexually deluded dowagers, and raving libertines, Millamant and
Mirabell share a self-conscious urbanity which frees them even
from their own potentially comic humanity.

That urbanity is, perhaps, rather cold and repellent, and such
self-possession is only possible in the smugly self-contained world of

Restoration comedy. Exceptional women like Millamant and Angelica are promoted, in a sense, and allowed to enter the charmed circle of male urbanity, to share the Horatian bemusement that is a male prerogative. The ordinary females in Restoration comedy inhabit the old stereotypes, but they pose no threat to that male world. Misogynistic satire, like Heartfree's in *The Provok'd Wife,* is in bad taste, a set of banalities that the urbane ideal renders unnecessary. The writers of these comedies seem to serve and to reflect a serene order, a leisure-class, urban, male-dominated society where exceptional heroines such as Congreve's may easily be allowed to share power.

But there is a good deal of satirical disparagement of women in Restoration poetry, and profane wits like Rochester and Dorset condemn the sex as a matter of course and cultural habit. The minor lyrics of the time are full of innumerable Phyllises, Daphnes, Dorindas, and the like, mistresses praised and reviled according to whim. There is a distinctive ferocity about some of these love complaints, although even the most brutal of them have that ample cultural precedent mentioned before. One of the standard and classical turns of these libertine lyrics is a protest against the falsification of women by amatory pastoralism, a protest directed at men who are foolish enough to believe in the fictions of love. Thus, Rochester turns away from love and the confining biological realities that it supports:

> Let the Porter, and the Groom,
>   Things design'd for dirty Slaves;
> Drudge in fair Aurelia's womb,
>   To get Supplies for Age and Graves.
>   ("A Song," 1691)

The sexual disgust in that stanza has both cultural and moral force behind it. In their most interesting moments, libertine lyrics combine the gay triviality of their form with a fierce satiric revulsion worthy of Juvenal or St. Jerome. Such poets seem as disgusted with their own lack of moral purpose as with the distressing realities of sexuality and procreation. In these poems, the combination of the format and the moral content dramatizes the desperate instability of the latter. A poem by Charles Sackville, Earl of Dorset, is notable for that ironic disparity:

> Tell me, Dorinda, why so gay,
> Why such embroid'ry, fringe, and lace?
> Can any dresses find a way,
> To stop th' approaches of decay,
> And mend a ruin'd face?
>
> Wilt thou still sparkle in the box,
> Still ogle in the ring?
> Canst thou forget thy age and pox?
> Can all that shines in shells and rocks
> Make thee a fine young thing?
>
> So have I seen in larder dark,
> Of veal a lucid loin;
> Replete with many a brilliant spark,
> As wise philosophers remark,
> At once both stink and shine.
>   (c.1680)

Whatever urbanity the poem begins with is traded for the brilliant vulgarity of that last stanza, an image of the desperate decadence one feels in reading these lyrics. Libertine wits like Rochester and Dorset tell us more about the inadequacy of their own promiscuity and dissipation than about their female targets. The fear of women and the self-hatred implicit in all misogynism are obtrusive in these lyrics.

One looks in vain in Dryden's poetry for something approaching that misogynistic force. Although he translated part of Juvenal's satires, Dryden never himself wrote a satire on women. Rather, the females to be found in his verse are most prominent in poems of praise, where they make their appearance as domesticated versions of the virgin whose purity redeems mankind. Such is the wonderfully extravagant center of "To the Pious Memory of the Accomplish'd Young Lady, Mrs. Anne Killigrew" (1686), a lady whose talents as a poet and painter combine in Dryden's elegant hyperbole to reproach the present immoral time:

What can we say t'excuse our *Second* Fall?
Let this thy *Vestal,* Heav'n, attone for all!
Her *Arethusian* Stream remains unsoil'd,
Unmixt with Foreign Filth and undefil'd,
Her Wit was more than Man, her Innocence a Child!

As that curious last line makes clear, Dryden's heroine is as remarkable a hybrid of active strength and passive receptivity as she is a slightly blasphemous combination of the Virgin Mary and classical poetess-vestal. Anne Killigrew's fancied achievements are exactly parallel to the ambitions of Dryden's poetry. The small truth with which Dryden began (Anne Killigrew wrote poems, painted pictures, and died young) is a convenient occasion for celebrating the power of the arts (and Dryden's poem) to reimagine the world, to present it in stately and totally splendid fashion. Anne Killigrew is the positive half of the female stereotype, but wittily appropriated and transformed by the baroque energies of Dryden's imagination. What the poem celebrates is Dryden's power and daring in constructing and elaborating the fiction which makes Anne Killigrew an artistic prodigy who wrote and painted by divine instinct; her sex is presented as part of the wonder of it all. In a sense, her virtue and her art coexist so perfectly only so Dryden can be witty about that desirable paradox in a series of graceful classical and biblical tableaux. There is an inevitable condescension in all this hyperbole. Anne Killigrew was hardly the divinity the poem elaborates, and the disparity implicit in Dryden's unrestrained use of her little career works to make his wit all the more obtrusive.

Restoration poetry reveals any number of attitudes toward women, from grim misogyny to fulsome praise. But the condescension of Dryden's spacious ode is always in the air. In a famous critical aside, Dryden chided Donne for affecting "the metaphysics, not only in his satires, but in his amorous verses, where nature only should reign; and [he] perplexes the minds of the fair sex with nice speculations of philosophy, when he should engage their hearts and entertain them with the softness of love." [3] Implicit in Dryden's casual joke is a confidence about the nature of women, a serious trust in their existence as a moral and emotional type. Even the most violent libertine denunciations share that confidence. No matter how angelic or revolting, women are always available for male purposes; they can be counted upon to enact certain roles.

In the early eighteenth century, a somewhat less confident view of women and another use of the moral-rhetorical opportunity they provide appears in the works of Pope and Swift, notably the latter. A disgust with human bodies and their functions is a recurrent and notorious theme in Swift's works, but a quite traditional one if we remember the Christian emphasis on such matters that was his cultural inheritance. Especially memorable and relevant to our purposes is Gulliver's horrified close-up view of the enormous bodies of the Brobdingnagian court ladies in the second book of *Gulliver's Travels* (1726):

> ... they would strip themselves to the skin, and put on their smocks in my presence, while I was placed on their toilet directly before their naked bodies, which, I am sure, to me was very far from being a tempting sight, or from giving me any other emotions than those of horror and disgust. Their skins appeared so coarse and uneven, so variously coloured, when I saw them near, with a mole here and there as broad as a trencher, and hairs hanging from it thicker than pack-threads; to say nothing further concerning the rest of their persons. Neither did they at all scruple while I was by to discharge what they had drunk, to the quantity of at least two hogsheads, in a vessel that held above three tuns. The handsomest among these maids of honour, a pleasant frolicsome girl of sixteen, would sometimes set me astride upon one of her nipples, with many other tricks, wherein the reader will excuse me for not being over particular.

Gulliver also remarks that "a very offensive smell came from their skins," but quickly qualifies that by reminding us of his acute sensitivity when faced with fifty feet of perfumed woman. He notes further that he found their "natural smell" much more bearable and compliments the Queen and his little nurse, Glumdalclitch, "whose persons were as sweet as those of any lady in England." Gulliver's disgust has sexual undertones and seems to be composed partly of his own guilty repressions in the face of those fascinating and yet necessarily repulsive bodies. By the time *Gulliver's Travels* is

over, Gulliver has nearly suffocated in the embraces of a female
Yahoo and fainted with disgust in the arms of his wife when she
greets him upon his final return to England. Gulliver is unbalanced
by his experience of human extremes. He loses his belief in the
civilized and relative cleanliness of the Queen of Brobdingnag,
Glumdalclitch, and the unperfumed maids of honor, and he sees
women only in terms of the degraded and unmediated natural
state of the Yahoos, especially their sexual and excremental
aspects.

Gulliver's violent disgust resembles Strephon's in Swift's poem,
"The Lady's Dressing Room" (1730). Strephon violates the female
mysteries of Celia's chamber and finds the ultimate and degrading
secret emanating from her close-stool. He is punished "for his
Peeping," and becomes blind "to all the charms of Female Kind."
Not so the narrator, in the poem's closing lines:

> Should I the Queen of Love refuse,
> Because she rose from stinking Ooze?
> To him that looks behind the Scene,
> *Satira's* but some pocky Queen.
> When *Celia* in her Glory shows,
> If Strephon would but stop his Nose;
>
> . . . .
>
> He soon would learn to think like me,
> And bless his ravisht Sight to see
> Such Order from Confusion sprung,
> Such gaudy Tulips rais'd from Dung.

The satiric point in this poem and in *Gulliver's Travels* is complex.
The poem's narrator invites ironic examination of his cheerful
conclusion by phrases like "stinking Ooze" and "gaudy Tulips." It
cannot simply be said that Gulliver's and Strephon's disgusted
discoveries are balanced and essentially negated by a tolerant
civility which accommodates itself to human process. In Swift's
works, women are more than a golden opportunity for the
discriminating satiric intelligence, even though they illustrate the
problems of human nature with special clarity. Gulliver and
Strephon somehow expect a great deal of women and are all the
more outraged by the disparity between expectations and reality.

Swift arranges matters so that the reality they encounter is the necessary opposite of their extreme expectations. Celia emerges from her dressing room like a "Goddess ... array'd in Lace, Brocades and Tissues," and Gulliver's cratered giantesses have been preceded in the book by the flawless skins of the delicate Lilliputian ladies and indeed by those of "our English ladies, who appear so beautiful to us, only because they are of our own size, and their defects not to be seen but through a magnifying glass, where we find by experiment that the smoothest and whitest skins look rough and coarse, and ill coloured." As Gulliver himself points out in that rational moment, the lesson is that all these matters are relative. But that relativity does not survive the horror of the child-man Gulliver, thrown back into a nightmare world of gigantic maternal shapes and disturbing odors.

The quality of the disgust that the female body especially excites in Swift's works returns us to some initial terms and permits us to say that Gulliver and Strephon are outraged because they discover that the redeeming virgin aspect of the female stereotype is a fraud. It is that violent contrast between cultural expectation and natural reality which is responsible for the brutal disgust in Swift's works. The rational relativism of Gulliver and the narrator of "The Lady's Dressing Room" breaks down in the face of the shocking disparities Swift's art arranges for them, and the lesson of Swift's satires seems to be that whoever forgets those disparities is a fool. His satires are, in fact, obsessively concerned not so much with female instability or loathsomeness as with fraud. Christian moralist that he was, Swift was moved to rage by the pretension and pride of what his King of Brobdingnag calls "the most pernicious race of little odious vermin that nature ever suffered to crawl upon the surface of the earth."

Women are the perfect target from such a moral perspective because they exemplify pretense. Society values women as beautiful objects, encourages them to adorn themselves, uses them as models of perfection and intimations of divinity, and yet the Christian tradition identifies women as the embodiments of human corruption. "Last week I saw a woman flayed," says the narrator of Swift's *A Tale of a Tub* (1704), "and you will hardly believe how much it altered her person for the worse." Swift's mad author in that work speaks of the disparity between fair surface and horrible interior as if it were a newly discovered scientific curiosity and goes on to assert that whoever can "find out an art to sodder and patch up the flaws and imperfections of nature, will deserve much better of mankind, and teach us a more useful science, than that so much in present esteem, of widening and exposing them." Swift's satires are arranged to record his moral shock over such deliberate ignorance and colossal inconsistency. The overvaluation of women that Swift exposes is a sign of a profound kind of moral blindness, a social and cultural symptom of moral stupidity.

Pope has a lighter touch, and there is at first glance none of this extreme disgust with women in his works. Swift's hugely moral contempt seems exchanged for amusement. When Belinda in "The Rape of the Lock" (1714) concludes her toilette, she issues forth, a goddess like Swift's Celia but delicately qualified in that divinity by Pope's art of implication:

> Not with more Glories, in th' Etherial Plain,
> The Sun first rises o'er the purpled Main,
> Than issuing forth, the Rival of his Beams
> Launch'd on the Bosom of the Silver *Thames*.
> Fair Nymphs, and well-drest Youths around her shone,
> But ev'ry Eye was fix'd on her alone.
> On her white Breast a sparkling *Cross* she wore,
> Which *Jews* might kiss, and Infidels adore.
> Her lively Looks a sprightly Mind disclose,
> Quick as her Eyes, and as unfix'd as those:
> Favours to none, to all she Smiles extends,
> Oft she rejects, but never once offends.
> Bright as the Sun, her Eyes the Gazers strike,
> And, like the Sun, they shine on all alike.
> Yet graceful Ease, and Sweetness void of Pride,
> Might hide her Faults, if *Belles* had Faults to hide:
> If to her share some Female Errors fall,
> Look on her Face, and you'll forget 'em all.
>
> (Canto II.1-19)

Belinda is a creature of ironic magic, created by the transforming cosmetic mysteries which end canto I and precede her progress up the Thames to the seat of political power at Hampton Court.

Pope's lines see to it that the reader marvels over her resemblance to the real, the serious, and the substantial, but also that he never forgets her trivial, self-serving, and ultimately synthetic nature as manufactured goddess of beauty. Instead of dismantling or flaying Belinda and reducing her to natural and revolting facts, as Swift would have done, Pope examines the subtle flaws in her personality. She floats to Hampton Court, to gossip, tea, and flirtation in the same language used to describe the progress of epic heroes on the way to destiny. She rivals the sun in her glory, the cross on her breast reduces religious differences to a cult of ecumenical sexuality, and her face cancels any ethical discriminations we might otherwise be able to make about her. As this passage makes clear, Belinda's self-absorption makes the mock-heroic tone possible. As Pope presents her, Belinda is crucially unaware of her triviality, and the temporary loss of discrimination Pope says she induces is a reflection of her inability to be anything except the synthetic goddess. The satiric point here is that women, as represented by Belinda, have no identity except a social-sexual one. Absorbed completely in being what society tells them nature intended them to be, women lack a personal self, a particular reality.

> Nothing so true as what you once let fall,
> 'Most Women have no Characters at all.'
> Matter too soft a lasting mark to bear,
> And best distinguish'd by black, brown, or fair.

So begins "Epistle II, To a Lady" (1735), Pope's examination in verse "of the characters of women," which goes on to dramatize the comically invariable discovery of the merely social-sexual underneath the superficial variety of female personalities. Men, the poem explains, have various "Ruling Passions," women only two: the "Love of Pleasure, and the Love of Sway." In the poem's terms, women are taught by "Nature" (we would say, I suppose, "culture") that they exist to please, to give "pleasure." It follows that they must elevate pleasure (sexuality, for the most part, is what Pope's word suggests) to an ethical imperative. But women are further instructed by "Experience" that men seek to deny them the pleasure they themselves are designed to provide; hence marriage and other confining male institutions. And, therefore, women are impelled to seek power so that they may ensure their own pleasure. Such analysis is reminiscent of the sexual politics of Restoration comedy.

But the overall satiric ambition and effect of Pope's poems is to present women as embodiments of disorder, unable to distinguish between their own desires for pleasure and power and ethical categories, not so much evil as naively self-absorbed. Self-absorption which blinds one to ethical disorder is potentially, of course, a very serious matter, and is the recurrent theme of eighteenth-century satire at its most profound. It is appropriate, therefore, that Dullness in *The Dunciad* (1728, 1743) should be a goddess; for the subject of that poem is, in the end, the social and moral triumph of self-absorbed disorder. The progress easily seen in Pope's work leads naturally from the engaging silliness of Belinda to the vision of Dullness in the revised *Dunciad* of 1743 as the primordial, anarchic human substance whose reestablishment leads to "Universal Darkness."

From her throne, Dullness beholds with pleasure "the Chaos dark and deep" over which she presides, and she sees it with the kind of vain and self-deluded satisfaction one expects from a mad dowager in Restoration comedy:

> All these, and more, the cloud-compelling Queen
> Beholds thro' fogs, that magnify the scene.
> She, tinsel'd o'er in robes of varying hues,
> With self-applause her wild creation views;
> Sees momentary monsters rise and fall,
> And with her own fools-colours gilds them all.
>
> (I.79-84)

The paradox in these lines returns to Swiftian and indeed classic satiric themes. Woman embodies nature in all of its unorganized and disorderly plenitude; she is the opposite of moral form and civilized order and stands for an absurd kind of self-created disorder. It is no matter that Belinda seems to be the sun goddess, the center of a glittering civilization. To have her way, she and her friends in "The Rape of the Lock" are ready to reduce it all to a chaos Dullness would love:

Sooner let Earth, Air, Sea, to Chaos fall,
Men, Monkies, Lap-dogs, Parrots perish all!
                    (Canto IV.119-20)

But Pope and Swift are in this regard, and in others, islands of
resistance to the drift of their times. The lesser literary monuments
of the first half of the eighteenth century mark the definite
beginning of distinctly tolerant and even respectful attitudes
toward women. The literary decline of the court and its libertine
ethos and the virtual disappearance of the cynical sexual realism of
Restoration comedy are related facts. As power, economic and
cultural, shifts toward the commercial classes and bourgeois ideals
replace aristocratic myths, literary developments such as sentimental drama and domesticated romance occur in which women are
opportunities not for moral revelation but for the rich pathos
implicit in their exploitation and almost inevitably wretched fates.
Quite often, the romance and drama of the early eighteenth
century linger over the plight of women in a male world, tricked
and then abandoned for following their natural tendencies for
passion and fidelity. Here, to take a famous example, is Nicholas
Rowe's Jane Shore in the tragedy that bears her name (1714):

Mark by what partial justice we are judged:
Such is the fate unhappy women find,
And such the curse entailed upon our kind,
That man, the lawless libertine, may rove
Free and unquestioned through the wilds of love;
While woman, sense and nature's easy fool,
If poor weak woman swerve from virtue's rule,
If, strongly charmed, she leave the thorny way,
And in the softer paths of pleasure stray;
Ruin ensues, reproach and endless shame,
And one false step entirely damns her fame.
In vain with tears the loss she may deplore,
In vain look back to what she was before,
She sets, like stars that fall, to rise no more.
                                        (I.ii)

The very qualities that make woman the perfect satiric target—
"sense and nature's easy fool"—now establish her as the perfect

literary tool for exciting pathos and creating rich emotional moments. There is, moreover, an implicit political element in Jane Shore's pathos; she is a lower-class woman exploited by upper-class males, the cast-off mistress of Edward IV. Similar arrangements and purposes are the staple of much of the amatory fiction of the early part of the century, a tradition which may be said to come to a spectacular head in Richardson's *Pamela* (1740).

The publication of *Pamela* marks the beginning of what is now called the novel, and the emergence of that genre is the single most important event in the century for the representation of women in literature. In theoretical terms, the novel is a preference for the literal and the actual over the generalized representations that neoclassical literary theory enforced. In certain eighteenth-century English novels, it is fair to say that women are depicted in their socio-historical particularity, no longer merely or largely opportunities for male moral-rhetorical display, or even primarily tools for creating emotions in a special literary context. Lacking real social power, deprived of public responsibilities, and largely confined to domestic and personal experiences, women thereby possess the kind of particularized consciousness the novel, as a literary genre, tends to value. From the newly established novelistic perspective, the chaotic self-absorption the satiric tradition identified as the root of female unworthiness becomes the sign of an authentic personality.

This is not to say that a book like *Pamela* gives up the pathetic opportunities or abandons the stereotype of the virgin redeemer. The strategy of the book and of the genre is often to use the particularity of experience to promote the old stereotype in new and more convincing fashion, from inside as it were, from the point of view of the woman. The plot of *Pamela* is itself evidence of that; the heroine moves from being a pathetic outsider, threatened by a world of male violence and sexuality, to the role of reforming and inspiring spouse. As the newly married Mr. B. exclaims:

> You cannot, my dear life, be so happy in me, as I am in you. O how heartily I despise all my former pursuits and head-strong appetites! What joys, what true joys, flow from virtuous love! joys which the narrow soul of the libertine cannot take in, nor his thoughts conceive! And which I myself, whilst a libertine, had not the least notion of! [4]

That is dreadful stuff in itself, but if one thinks about the trick Pamela has managed, such passages are exhilarating. The greatness of *Pamela* lies in its rendering of Pamela's helplessness and enclosure; she is surprised not just by the eager Mr. B. but by her own quite obtrusive sexuality. Surrounded not simply by the externals of her impossible social and legal situation, Pamela makes her way around her own internal sexual bewilderment by suppressing it and diverting into dominance those unruly instincts that the satiric tradition identifies as the nature of the feminine condition. Pamela delays gratification and represses desire in an heroic fashion; she manages in her book to make herself into the redeeming virgin. What is new and striking is that instinctive self-management, that self-control for social power and position.

Obviously, Pamela is a heroine for both sexes. She is the middle-class, Protestant self which defines itself by a series of tactical refusals and delays, which examines inner and outer circumstances and waits for the profitable moment to invest its energies, which represses instinct to promote social position. She is a respectable version of Defoe's two heroines, Moll Flanders and Roxana, whose overt criminality and explicit subversion of the masculine world make them more attractive but far less plausible figures.[5] In truth, Richardson's significance as a portrayer of female experience can be measured by looking at some other heroines fashioned by male novelists of the time.

Defoe's two indomitable women claim to be surrounded by desperate circumstances and do indeed endure specifically female trials. They are seduced, forced into crime and a sort of defensive prostitution and mercenary marriage; they have children, marry, and speak at length of the woe that is in marriage. Roxana, for example, develops a clearly articulated ideology of freedom which outlines with subversive vigor her desire to "be a *Man-Woman;* for as I was born free, I wou'd die so." [6] One of her lovers proposes marriage and its attendant submission, arguing "that a sincere Affection between a Man and his Wife, answer'd all the Objections that I had made about the being a Slave, a Servant, *and the like;* and where there was a mutual Love, there cou'd be no Bondage; but that there was but one Interest; one Aim; one Design; and all conspir'd to make both very happy." [7] Roxana's answer to that conventional wisdom is contemptuous of the male dominance and female risk such arrangements involve:

Ay, said I, *that is the Thing I complain of;* the Pretence of Affection, takes from a Woman every thing that can be call'd *herself;* she is to have no Interest; no Aim; no View; but all is the Interest, Aim, and View, of the Husband; she is to lead a Life of perfect Indolence, and living by Faith (not in God, but) in her Husband, she sinks or swims, as he is either Fool or wise Man; unhappy or prosperous; and in the middle of what she thinks is her Happiness and Prosperity, she is ingulph'd in Misery and Beggary, which she had not the least Notice, Knowledge, or Suspicion of.[8]

But Roxana and Moll are female impersonators, not simply strong and self-reliant but unperturbed by the implications of female experience. For them, sexuality is simply an available and efficient means for self-advancement and survival. As their tendency toward multiple identity in their stories indicates, they are playing at being women. They are essentially male creations, characters who use their dreadful female problems as opportunities for demonstrating their skill and cunning in survival. They remain to all intents and purposes untouched by the special quality of female experience.

One can find other examples of male appropriation of female experience, but the most striking in this regard is John Cleland's notorious Fanny Hill, who narrates her own *Memoirs of a Woman of Pleasure* (1749). Her description of sexual adventures is a relief for anyone who has tried to read the demi-pornography of minor female novelists like Aphra Behn and Eliza Haywood.[9] Instead of the joyless and inevitably destructive turbulence of sex which their novels feature, Fanny gives us charmingly varied accounts of elegant copulations, erotic dances in which males and females are equal recipients of pleasure. But Mrs. Behn's and Mrs. Haywood's tiresome accounts of sexual disaster seem to be an artless recognition of the realities of sex for eighteenth-century women, or at least of its emotional resonances. In some way, these popular writers tell a truth about sex: their novels dramatize it as a self-destructive female urge that involves submission to dominant and treacherous males; sex leads to brutal punishment for violation of male property rights and often results in disease and death. Fanny Hill advances the opposing male myth which reverses the moral commonplaces surrounding sex, making it a therapeutic exercise that actually retards disease and death by transforming sexual organs into a utopian landscape where bliss is eternally renewed. Here is one quite explicit example:

> Then she lay exposed, or, to speak more properly, displayed the greatest parade in nature of female charms. The whole company, who, except myself, had often seen them, seemed as much dazzled, surprised, and delighted, as anyone could be who had now beheld them for the first time. Beauties so excessive could not but enjoy the privileges of eternal novelty. Her thighs were so exquisitely fashioned, that either more in, or more out of flesh than they were, they would have declined from that point of perfection they presented. But what infinitely enriched and adorned them was the sweet intersection formed, where they met, at the bottom of the smoothest, roundest, whitest belly, by that central furrow which nature had sunk there, between the soft relievo of two pouting ridges, and which in this girl was in perfect symmetry of delicacy and miniature with the rest of her frame. No! nothing in nature could be of a beautifuller cut; then, the dark umbrage of the downy sprigmoss that over-arched it bestowed, on the luxury of the landscape, a touching warmth, a tender finishing beyond the expression of words, or even the paint of thought.[10]

A great novelist like Fielding is less crude and less obviously "male" in his approach to women than a pornographer like Cleland. But at first glance, the women in *Joseph Andrews* (1742) and *Tom Jones* (1749) seem as artificial and functional as Cleland's complaisant mannequins. They serve the needs of Fielding's comic plots and fall into deliberately symmetrical and traditional oppositions. Either hypocritical and lustful like Lady Booby, Bridget Allworthy, and Lady Bellaston, or angelically virtuous like Joseph's Fanny and Tom's Sophia, they bring us back to cultural stereotypes. Fielding, however, manages a social and moral realism that extracts complexity even from those stereotypes and satiric commonplaces. Sophia is the most revealing of his characters in this regard.

Fielding's presentation of Sophia and the situation surrounding her in the novel is of a piece with the complexities of *Tom Jones* itself. The book is, on the one hand, a self-declared "history," a novel in the full sense of the term which treats matters such as morals, manners, and social class in an informed and comprehensive way. On the other hand, the narrator is consistently ironic about the specifics of his story, always concerned to maintain a controlling distance from events and characters and to move them away from the social actualities his narrative uncovers and toward moral generality and the larger unity of his comic plot. Thus, Sophia is the daughter of a West Country squire, "a middle-sized woman; but rather inclining to tall." But her face and figure are described by the narrator in several pages of arch hyperbole: "for, lo! adorned with all the charms in which nature can array her; bedecked with beauty, youth, sprightliness, innocency, modesty, and tenderness, breathing sweetness from her rosy lips, and darting brightness from her sparkling eyes, the lovely Sophia comes!" [11] Such beauty has its effect, and Tom Jones falls in love with Sophia; but social and financial realities intervene. Blifil, the odious heir to Mr. Allworthy's estate, is preferred by Sophia's father to the penniless and illegitimate Tom. Sophia is an ironically idealized woman caught in the harshly rendered facts of property marriage and social ambition in the eighteenth century. Squire Western aspires to found a dynasty and create a lordly estate by combining his property with Allworthy's. Sophia is a means to that end, unable to marry without her father's consent and liable to disinheritance if she refuses. She is rescued from disaster only by the benificence of the narrator, who arranges matters so that Tom's legal status as Allworthy's true heir is revealed. Sophia marries for love at last; she gets away with expressing rebellion against male authority and exercising sexual preference. But she does that only after the comic plot intervenes to reverse a real social dilemma and to neutralize the subversive implications of Sophia's independent gestures. *Tom Jones* deals with female problems but solves them ironically by means of a traditional and "comic" celebration of love and marriage.

Such a summary is, perhaps, a bit unfair to Fielding. *Tom Jones* is a notably frank work in its treatment of female sexuality. It features a number of women who assert themselves sexually for their own pleasure and power, and without suffering melodramatic reprisals. The narrator, to be sure, invites our laughter and moral scorn for some of them, like Di Western, the grotesque lady politician; Brigid Allworthy, the secretly lustful old maid; and Lady Bellaston, the eager purchaser of Tom's favors. But there is one chapter of startling domestic realism in *Tom Jones* that deserves our attention, since it marks very clearly those grim aspects of female existence in the eighteenth century which should qualify our laughter and moral scorn even for Fielding's female grotesques and identify their behavior as reasonable defenses against male power. Chapter 4 of Book 7 is "a picture of a country gentlewoman taken from the life," a brief account of Sophia's mother, the late Mrs. Western. The narrator explains that she "had been a faithful upper-servant all the time of their marriage" and that Squire Western "had returned that behaviour by making what the world calls a good husband." That consists of swearing at her occasionally, never beating her, and seeing her only at meal times:

These, however, were the only seasons when Mr. Western saw his wife; for when he repaired to her bed, he was generally so drunk that he could not see; and in the sporting season he always rose from her before it was light. Thus was she perfect mistress of her time, and had besides a coach and four usually at her command; though, unhappily, indeed, the badness of the neighbourhood and of the roads made this of little use; for none who had set much value on their necks would have passed through the one, or who had set much value on their hours, would have visited the other. Now, to deal honestly with the reader, she did not make all the return expected to so much indulgence; for she had been married against her will by a fond father, the match having been rather advantageous on her side; for the squire's estate was upward of £3000 a year, and her fortune no more than a bare £8000. Hence, perhaps, she had contracted a little gloominess of temper, for she was rather a good servant than a good wife; nor had she always the gratitude to return the extraordinary degree of roaring mirth, with which the squire received her, even with a good-humoured smile. She would, moreover, sometimes interfere with matters, which did not concern her, as the violent

drinking of her husband, which in the gentlest terms she
would take some of the few opportunities he gave her of
remonstrating against. And once in her life she very earnestly
entreated him to carry her for two months to London, which
he peremptorily denied; nay, was angry with his wife for the
request ever after, being well assured that all the husbands in
London are cuckolds.

For this last, and many other good reasons, Western at
length heartily hated his wife. . . .[12]

That picture of married life among the rural leisure class can
stand as the dreadful alternative to the comic solution that
Fielding's book arranges. And Fielding's awareness of domestic
issues led him to write in *Amelia* (1751) a story of sustained
domestic realism and to portray women who do not fit the comic
categories he used in the earlier novels. A quite revolutionary
example in that book is one Mrs. Matthews, who seduces the
heroine's husband and actually remains a sympathetic character.
But even in *Amelia,* Fielding is still committed to traditional
generality and concerned to shape his materials toward a controlled and coherent moral purpose. To a large extent, Fielding's
moral psychology is interested in the comically predictable aspects
of behavior, and his novels tend to exclude the kind of extended
portrayal of women which seeks to understand their special
mysteries and unique problems.

It is, in fact, very difficult to find a fair rendering of those
problems in the eighteenth-century novel, even in the work of
female novelists. In *Evelina* (1778), for example, Fanny Burney
confronts her heroine with the problem advertised on the title
page, how to gain "entrance into the world." Evelina has been
excluded by male forces, her father, Sir John Belmont, refusing to
acknowledge his secret marriage to her mother. That unfortunate
lady has died at Evelina's birth, and she has been raised by a pious
clergyman in the country. Evelina is thereby without stable social
identity, and the book is her tour of various comically rendered
social milieux, from the lower-middle class aspiring vulgarity of the
Branghtons and Mr. Smith to the brutal diversions and sexual
advances of aristocrats like Sir Clement Willoughby. She is
eventually delivered from social uncertainty by coincidence and by

the force of her own moral instincts. She saves a young man from suicide, befriending him in spite of the dangerous misinterpretation such friendship subjects her to, and that young man turns out to be her brother. The sight of the kneeling Evelina melts her obdurate father, and she is restored to her rightful place as heiress, able now to marry her graciously constant aristocratic lover, Lord Orville. Evelina, in short, suffers patiently and inspires male deliverance; her instinctive moral qualities restore her social rights. She is untainted by her adventures along the way, quite unchanged from the poor innocent she was at her beginning. Beneath the often quite brutal social satire of *Evelina*, there is a totally conventional sentimental plot in which female virtue is rewarded for maintaining its moral attitudes in the face of turbulent social experience. Evelina strikes those lovely and ineffectual poses the male world admires; she is therefore admitted to all its privileges.

I think only Richardson's *Clarissa* (1747-48) among the great novels of the century offers a character who defines a specifically female kind of behavior and refuses the male resolutions that save or damn other women in fiction. *Clarissa* is quite simply the most profound rendering of a woman that eighteenth-century literature has to offer, or at least the most successful dramatization by a male writer of the notion that female experience is a special and meaningful category. And to some extent, Richardson was aware of that special mission of his book and his heroine, although hardly in modern terms. He declared in a postscript that his "great end" was to promote Clarissa as a Christian heroine in an age of growing skepticism and immorality. To speak precisely, her Christian heroism is a matter of resisting the contradictory demands of property marriage and sexual freedom, destructive alternatives which constitute the outer limits of female behavior in the upper-middle-class world of the novel.

The implications surrounding sexual freedom and property marriage are a recurrent topic in eighteenth-century literature. They are expressed with memorable clarity in Boswell's *Life of Johnson* (1791). Johnson puts the traditional case against female sexual freedom with candor: women, he says more than once to Boswell, are the basis of property; marriage ensures the order of society and the peaceful and legal transmission of property. Adultery throws all that in doubt. "Confusion of progeny constitutes the essence of the crime; and therefore a woman who breaks her marriage vows is much more criminal than a man who does it. . . . I asked him if it was not hard that one deviation from chastity should so absolutely ruin a young woman. JOHNSON. 'Why, no, Sir; it is the great principle which she is taught. When she has given up that principle, she has given up every notion of female honour and virtue, which are all included in chastity.' " [13]

Clarissa exemplifies the heroism Johnson would have admired in a woman, and indeed he was one of the great champions of Richardson's book. But there is a sense in which Clarissa's personality is also a matter of very precise resistance to male demands. In refusing both marriage and cohabitation, Clarissa identifies them as eighteenth-century male provinces. In heroically denying what modern readers might consider her own deepest sexual inclinations and spurning the domestic compromise others suggest, she redefines the chastity Johnson thought essential into something distinctly her own. She reclaims chastity and makes it into a definitively female trait, a sign of self-possession and apartness rather than a guarantee of male dominance.

Clarissa is above all a shrewdly intelligent character whose moral heroism is grounded in an exact understanding of the social and personal consequences of action. Pressed by her family to marry the rich and odious Solmes, she tells her mother that such compulsion violates her upbringing: ". . . for although I am to be treated by my brother, and through his instigation, by my father, as a slave in this point, and not as a daughter, yet my mind is not that of a slave. You have not brought me up to be mean." [14] Mrs. Harlowe's answer and Clarissa's reply tell us that the daughter understands the moral surrender marriage itself involves for women:

So, Clary! you are already at defiance with your father! I have had too much cause before to *apprehend* as much. What will this come to? *I,* and then my dear mamma sighed—*I,* am forced to put up with many humours— . . .

I am extremely affected on my mother's account—more, I must needs say, than on my own. And indeed, all things considered; and especially, that the measure she is engaged in, is (as I dare say it is) against her own judgment, she *deserves* more compassion than myself. Excellent woman! What pity, that meekness and condescension should not be attended with the due rewards of those charming graces! Yet had she not let violent spirits (as I have elsewhere observed with no small regret) find their power over hers, it could not have been thus.[15]

The most violent spirit Clarissa has to deal with is Lovelace, a character whose rampant sexuality is grounded in the traditional satirical and libertine distrust of women. What he seeks is to extract from Clarissa the unstable and compulsive core of the female personality that the cultural tradition posits. Lovelace sees her in symbolic terms, as a woman whose improbable virtue threatens the traditional male definition of female personality. Just before Lovelace finally rapes Clarissa, he writes to his friend, Belford: "Is not *this* the hour of her trial—and in *her,* of the trial of the virtue of her whole sex, so long premeditated, so long threatened? Whether her frost be frost indeed? Whether her virtue be principle? Whether, if once subdued, she not be always subdued?" [16] As Anna Howe, her friend, perceives and as Clarissa herself reveals indirectly, she is indeed drawn to Lovelace, and the most compelling part of the book for modern readers is the struggle that takes place as she resists and he pursues.

In spite of her inner urges, Clarissa resists successfully. Lovelace has to resort to drugs and to rape, and the scene in which she confronts him afterward is the beginning of her triumph. As Lovelace himself reports it to Belford, she declares herself untouched and quite beyond his notions of female psychology:

> As I told thee, I had prepared myself for high passions, raving, flying, tearing, execration. . . . But such a majestic composure—seeking me—whom yet, it is plain, by her attempt to get away, she would have avoided seeing—no Lucretia-like vengeance upon herself in her thoughts—yet swallowed up, her whole mind swallowed up, as I may say, by a grief so heavy, as, in her own words, to be beyond the power of speech to express—and to be able, discomposed as she was to the very morning, to put such a home question to me, as if she had penetrated my future view—how could I avoid looking like a

fool, and answering, as before, in broken sentences, and confusion? . . .

O Belford! Belford! whose the triumph now! HERS, or MINE? [17]

In the volume and a half that follows, Clarissa triumphs as no other heroine of the age quite manages to do. In effect, she perfects a new way of writing which implies a new way of being. In literary terms, she drops her analytic novelistic style and the perspective it commands. She may be said to refuse to continue as a character in the stories the male world has tried to write for her. Neither a martyr to parental authority and the pawn of economic necessity in the Harlowes' scenario, nor a half-willing sacrifice to her own desires in Lovelace's combination of satire and romantic comedy, Clarissa chooses to be the star of her own distinctively female book, which might well be called the legend of St. Clarissa. For Clarissa elects to die, flying in the face of common sense (and of biological reality, one might add). She arranges an extended pious tableau, herself at the center, surrounded by worshippers and former enemies begging for forgiveness. She writes ten "posthumous" letters to be distributed after her death, and these form the scripture that completes the work of general redemption her death serves. Part of the letter she writes to Lovelace can stand as a conclusion and a reminder that even in the spiritual melodrama over which she presides there is still a strong trace of the triumph of the female will that she represents:

> So, sir, though no thanks to your *intention,* you have done me real *service;* and in return I wish you happy. But such has been your life hitherto, that you can have no time to lose in setting about your repentance. Repentance to such as have lived only carelessly, and in the omission of their regular duties, and who never aimed to draw any poor creatures into evil, is not so easy a task, nor so much in our power, as some imagine. How difficult a grace then to be obtained, where the guilt is premeditated, wilful, and complicated!
>
> To say I once respected you with a preference, is what I ought to blush to own, since, at the very time, I was far from thinking you even a moral man; though I little thought that

you, or indeed that any man breathing, could be—what you have proved yourself to be. But indeed, sir, I have long been greatly above you: for from my heart I have despised you, and all your ways, ever since I saw what manner of man you were.[18]

In the context of this essay, Clarissa is the ultimate woman in eighteenth-century English literature because she seizes the male initiative, transforming her sexual and social degradation into an occasion for her own moral-rhetorical display and replacing the female stereotype with a profoundly independent and transcendent humanity far beyond mere sexual identity.

Notes

1 *The Basic Works of Aristotle,* ed. Richard McKeon (New York, 1941), p. 1464.

2 Cited by James R. Sutherland, *English Literature of the Late Seventeenth Century* (Oxford, 1969), p. 61.

3 *Of Dramatic Poesy and Other Critical Essays,* ed. George Watson (Everyman edition, 1962), "A Discourse Concerning Satire," II, 76.

4 *Pamela,* ed. William M. Sale (New York, 1958), p. 379.

5 *The Fortunes and Misfortunes of the Famous Moll Flanders* was first published in 1722, and *Roxana, The Fortunate Mistress* in 1724.

6 *Roxana,* ed. Jane Jack (Oxford English Novels, 1964), p. 171.

7 Ibid., p. 149.

8 Ibid.

9 For a discussion of that tradition, see my *Popular Fiction Before Richardson: Narrative Patterns 1700-1739* (Oxford, 1969), chaps. 3 and 4.

10 *Memoirs of a Woman of Pleasure,* introduction by Peter Quenell (New York, 1963), pp. 194-95.

11 *Tom Jones* (Modern Library edition, 1950), p. 109.

12 Ibid., p. 277.

13 *Boswell's Life of Johnson* (Oxford Standard Authors edition), pp. 393-94.

14 *Clarissa, or, The History of A Young Lady* (Everyman edition, 1962), I: 102.

15 Ibid., pp. 102-3.

16 Ibid., III: 190.

17 Ibid., pp. 220-21.

18 Ibid., IV: 436-37.

5.

Gender and Genre: Women in British Romantic Literature

Irene Tayler and Gina Luria

Sir William Blackstone's description of the legal status of the married woman in his *Commentaries of the Laws of England* would seem to reflect the attitude toward women generally in Britain throughout the Romantic period: "The husband and wife are one person in law; that is, the very being or legal existence of the woman is suspended during the marriage, or at least is incorporated and consolidated into that of the husband: under whose wing, protection and *cover,* she performs everything." [1]

This is a description of what the Common Law called "coverture," the suspended or "covered" status of women during marriage: as Ray Strachey wittily put it, "my wife and I are one, and I am he." [2] In fact, through the function of equity, the law did provide married women with somewhat greater protection or independence than Blackstone's position would seem to allow—though not much. Women could, for example, receive the protection of premarital contracts, or trusts, which were, however, likely to be negotiated on their behalf by their families.[3] But even then their legal status was subsumed to that of their husbands, though their property might be protected.

Although an injured husband could obtain divorce under certain circumstances, until 1857 a wife could not. As a married woman she could neither sue nor be sued; even the money a female writer earned belonged to her husband; and the children, too, until they reached majority, belonged to their father who could, if he chose, refuse their mother the right to see them. Such was the experience of Caroline Norton, née Sheridan, a granddaughter of the great playwright; and it was partly her consequent pamphlets and public struggle to change the law that led to the bill that passed in 1857 reforming the marriage and divorce laws of England.[4] The traditional view that a woman was "incomplete" or "unrespectable" if she did not marry reflected in part the fact that the family was itself a microcosmic government, with correspondingly political assumptions about authority and obligation. Marriage reform was accordingly a corollary of the wider parliamentary reforms of the mid-nineteenth century.

The situation had been no better on the Continent; indeed recent history had provided celebrated precedent for some of Norton's behavior to Caroline, for when George I ascended the throne in 1714, he came from Hanover without a wife. Here is J. H. Plumb's brief account:

> There was no Queen: she had been divorced. Bored by her husband and irked by his infidelities, Sophia Dorothy of Celle had listened too eagerly to the supplications of a handsome adventurer. . . . She was prepared to elope with him. . . . On 28 December 1694 Sophia Dorothy was divorced and shut up in the castle of Ahlden where she remained until her death thirty-two years later. Never again did she set eyes on her husband or children. George ignored her appeals for pardon.[5]

Queen or commoner, woman's "very being" was indeed "incorporated and consolidated" into that of her husband or father, at least in law. But the confinement is emblematic of woman's condition at that time in literature, too, though with one important difference: in literature women were authors as well as subjects, and to that extent able to modify the terms of their subjugation in art and—gradually—in life. That they were writers of limited range, however, a look at their work in different genres shows at once. The critic and poet Yvor Winters used to say in his classroom lectures that although women made on the whole poor poets, they made good novelists because "what a novel needs above all is *bulk*." It would seem that the Romantic period in English literature might provide the grounds for such a contention (though not for Winters's reasons: Scott surely depends more on bulk than Austen), for whereas the period provided such important women novelists as Austen, the Brontë sisters, and even Mrs. Radcliffe and Mary Shelley, no woman was a major poet.

Genre was, then, to some extent a function of gender, and a major cause of that situation lay in contemporary assumptions about women's education. Far more debilitating for women even than their legal status—at least from the point of view of the history of literature—was the poverty and narrowness of their education, especially their systematic exclusion from training in the classics. As Father Ong has observed in *The Barbarian Within,* "the Latin world was a man's world," and not only because of its clerical derivations: "The monopoly which Latin exercised in formal education combined with the structure of society in the West up until the past few generations to give the language its strangest characteristic. It was a sexually specialized language used almost exclusively for communication between male and male." Girls went to school with boys only while they learned English grammar. They were dropped as soon as the boys moved on to Latin. Ong notes: "This pattern is closely connected with the position of women in society and with the fact that until recently the learned professions, where Latin was used, were closed to them."[6]

As Ong remarks elsewhere, until well into the nineteenth century "learning Latin took on the characteristics of puberty rite, a *rite de passage* or initiation rite: it involved isolation from the family, the achievement of an identity in a totally male group (the social), the learning of a body of relatively abstract tribal lore inaccessible to those outside the group."[7] Those outside the group were the lower classes, servants, and women. Thus the main body of learning, content as well was technique, was transmitted in a language and literature not available to women.

Such learning was essential to those who wished to become serious writers, especially of poetry. Vivid evidence is provided by Coleridge: at the outset of his *Biographia Literaria,* where he is sifting through his own poetic beginnings, he congratulates himself on his good fortune in having had a Latin master at once sensible and severe. The classical grounding was thorough:

> He early moulded my taste to the preference of Demosthenes to Cicero, of Homer and Theocritus to Virgil, and again of Virgil to Ovid. He habituated me to compare Lucretius, . . . Terence, and above all the chaster poems of Catullus, not only with the Roman poets of the, so called, silver and brazen ages; but with even those of the Augustan era: and on grounds of plain sense and universal logic to see and assert the superiority of the former in the truth and nativeness, both of their thoughts and diction.[8]

And although we can glimpse threads of romantic dogma in the fabric—the unquestioned value of "nativeness," for example—the effect of the whole was to prepare the reader of poetry, and certainly the writer of it, to know what he was about in classical terms. Composition, even in an opium dream, was pretty sure to be *composition:*

> I learnt from him, that Poetry, even that of the loftiest and, seemingly, that of the wildest odes, had a logic of its own, as severe as that of science; and more difficult, because more subtle, more complex, and dependent on more, and more fugitive causes. In the truly great poets, he would say, there is a reason assignable, not only for every word, but for the position of every word; . . . In our own English compositions, (at least for the last three years of our school education,) he showed no mercy to phrase, metaphor, or image, unsupported by a sound sense, or where the same sense might have been conveyed with equal force and dignity in plainer words.[9]

Clearly the plain dignity so achieved was born from no simple stirring of the heart, and this was of course one of the grounds on which Coleridge took exception to Wordsworth's claim that he had found for poetry "a more permanent, and far more philosophical language" in the example of that used by men in "humble and rustic life." Coleridge frames his own position by paraphrasing Sir Joshua Reynolds' "Good taste must be *acquired,* and like all other good things, is the result of thought, and the submissive study of the best models." [10]

Of course Wordsworth's own position is far less simple than he sometimes allowed it to appear, for even in the 1800 Preface, although "all good poetry is the spontaneous overflow of powerful feelings," still "Poems to which any value can be attached were never produced on any variety of subjects but by a man who, being possessed of more than usual organic sensibility, had also thought long and deeply." [11] And even more telling, in a way, is his concept of the "Silent Poet," one who despite powerful feelings, sensibility, and thought, lacks the "accomplishment" of verse:

> Oh! many are the Poets that are sown
> By Nature; men endowed with highest gifts,
> The vision and the faculty divine;
> Yet wanting the accomplishment of verse,
> (Which, in the docile season of their youth,
> It was denied to them to acquire, through lack
> Of culture and the inspiring aid of books,
> Or haply by a temper too severe,
> Or a nice backwardness afraid of shame)

—such men "live out their time" and "go to the grave, unthought of." [12]

In fact, Wordsworth in these lines is unwittingly describing the denied "accomplishment," if not necessarily the "gifts," of those of his female contemporaries who aspired to be writers; they were to remain, at best, Silent Poets. There were, of course, a few more fortunate individual women: Fanny Burney might have learned Latin from Dr. Johnson. But at the age of twenty-two, when Johnson proposed the enterprise to her, Burney was already sufficiently aware of the hostility her knowledge of Latin might be expected to arouse in others. Accordingly she refused the offer, remarking that it would be foolish "to devote so much time to acquire something I shall always dread to have known." [13]

Anna Laetitia Barbauld, whose father was a dissenting minister and headmaster of an exemplary boys' school, finally persuaded him "despite his ordinary prejudices against learned women," to help her learn Latin and Greek, and to allow her the use of his library. But the result for Anna was intellectual isolation, for her brother was educated away from home and she was herself kept carefully apart from the schoolboys.

Maria Edgeworth's education was broad, but distinctly unliterary: she was early and thoroughly immersed by her father in political economy, constitutional law, and European history; but the effect was to bend her interest toward nonfiction to the extent that she was "unaware at the time of truly contemporary English poetry." [14] And despite her tremendous significance in the development of the nineteenth-century novel, she disparaged the genre, explaining in her "Advertisement" to *Belinda:* "The following work is offered to the public as a Moral Tale—the author not wishing to acknowledge a Novel.... So much folly, errour and vice are disseminated in books classed under this denomination." [15]

Edgeworth's contemporary, Jane Austen, was moved by this statement to a pointed reply. In Chapter 5 of *Northanger Abbey* she vows: "I will not adopt that ungenerous and impolitic custom so common with novel writers, of degrading by their contemptuous censure the very performances, to the number of which they are themselves adding." [16]

Yet Austen herself was caught in the ambivalence she protested. Despite a paucity of biographical information about her, we do know that her awareness of her own limitations as an artist touched on this very question of her lack of a classical education. In her letter of December 11, 1815, to James Stanier Clarke, replying to his suggestion that she might create the character of a clergyman along the lines of Beattie's Minstrel, "Fond of, & entirely engaged in Literature—no man's enemy but his own," Austen writes:

I am quite honoured by your thinking me capable of drawing such a clergyman as you have the sketch of in your note of Nov. 16th. But I assure you I am *not*. The comic part of the character I might be equal to, but not the good, the enthusiastic, the literary. Such a man's conversation must at times be on subjects of science and philosophy, of which I know nothing; or at least be occasionally abundant in quotations and allusions which a woman, who, like me, knows only her own mother tongue, and has read little in that, would be totally without the power of giving. A classical education, or at any rate a very extensive acquaintance with English literature, ancient and modern, appears to me quite indispensible for the person who would do justice to your clergyman; and I think I may boast myself to be, with all possible vanity, the most unlearned and uninformed female who ever dared to be an authoress.[17]

Intentional irony aside, such an apology from one of the most intelligent writers of the period points clearly to the profound gulf which still separated men and women as to both aspiration and achievement. Despite her great natural gifts, Austen found herself limited by her lack of either the factual-scientific education of a Maria Edgeworth or the classical and literary training of any English public school boy.

Although not formally educated beyond the requisite "letters and numbers," Austen and her female contemporaries certainly read in English, encouraging the enormous proliferation of circulating libraries and women's magazines after mid-century.[18] As Austen's heroines demonstrate, poetry, especially the "modern" poetry of Thomson, Young, Gray, Cowper, and Crabbe, was an important element in a young woman's life. Women's letters of the period, to say nothing of their novels and what poems they did write, are full of allusions, paraphrases, "lifts" from Shakespeare, Milton, "The Vanity of Human Wishes," and the works of Pope. Women were reading poetry, but deprived of that *sine qua non* for high literary enterprise, the classical education, not many were writing poems.

It would seem that the rising interest in the concept of "natural genius" ought to have encouraged women to channel their talents into poetic form. Consider, for example, what Charlotte Brontë has to say by way of explaining the nature of her two sisters' genius, especially Emily's:

In externals [Emily and Anne] were two unobtrusive women; a perfectly secluded life gave them retiring manners and habits. In Emily's nature the extremes of vigour and simplicity seemed to meet. Under an unsophisticated culture, inartificial tastes, and an unpretending outside, lay a secret power and fire that might have informed the brain and kindled the veins of a hero; but she had no worldly wisdom. . . . Neither Emily nor Anne was learned; they had no thought of filling their pitchers at the well-spring of other minds; they always wrote from the impulse of nature, the dictates of intuition, and from such stores of observation as their limited experience had enabled them to amass.[19]

Charlotte's analysis reverberates with the "givens" of romantic theory as summarized in William Duff's *Essay on Original Genius* (1767). "Genius naturally shoots forth in the simplicity and tranquillity of uncultivated life," he maintains:

The truth is, a Poet of original Genius has very little occasion for the weak aid of Literature: he is self-taught. He comes into the world as it were completely accomplished. Nature supplies the materials of his compositions; his senses are the under-workmen, while Imagination, like a masterly Architect, super-intends and directs the whole. . . . It may be easily conceived therefore, that an original Poetic Genius, possessing such innate treasure . . . has no use for that which is derived from books, since he may be encumbered, but cannot be enriched by it.[20]

But although such romantic theory greatly influenced women as novelists, it had little practical effect on their poetry.

There were, to be sure, a few women poets. Some wrote, anonymously, poems to be used as fillers for magazines and newspapers: Mary "Perdita" Robinson is an example. Occasionally a woman like Charlotte Smith or Felicia Hemans emerged to win the praise of her contemporaries: on Christmas Eve 1802 Wordsworth, reading sonnets, chose a telling list of authors—Milton, himself, and Charlotte Smith. And in 1835 he saw fit to group Felicia Hemans with Scott, Coleridge, Lamb, and Crabbe as recently dead authors to be mourned, writing:

Mourn rather for that holy Spirit,
Sweet as the spring, as ocean deep;
For Her who, ere her summer faded,
Has sunk into a breathless sleep.[21]

Even the "rustic genius" Ann Yearsley found an audience of more than a thousand subscribers to her first volume of poetry and was compared to Robert Burns, though only after Hannah More had provided her with a dictionary, a spelling book, a grammar, and editorial assistance.

The historical fact is that woman's importance in Romantic poetry was not as writer, but rather as muse for the male poet. We shall consider the implications of this fact later, but one of its causes, at least, should be clear by now: the women who wrote poetry did so (as John Stuart Mill later put it) as "self-educated men." One crippling effect of that self-education showed in their frequent unanimated reliance on the conventional postures of classical tradition, a function of their awareness of debility. They lacked, in Wordsworth's phrase, "the accomplishment of verse."

But fiction, growing up in a time of the emerging woman, included women in its earliest development (Aphra Behn, Mrs. De la Rivière Manley, Defoe's *Moll Flanders,* Richardson's *Clarissa,* and Fielding's *Amelia),* offering a place for women both as writers and subjects in a way not true of poetry. Moreover, when women as a group turned to novel writing, they could leave their sense of debility behind; the novel, still in process of creating its conventions, offered more nearly equal opportunity to learned and unlearned. So increasingly women acted on this new advantage; accordingly, it was in their novels rather than in their poetry that their introspection and consequently their representations of themselves as women reached full development—a development that may be said to have turned the direction of the novel toward a new purpose, that of modifying (as suggested earlier) the terms of woman's "incorporated" condition.

Historians of the novel have long observed that between Sterne and Scott the majority of English novelists were women, although Scott's immediate contemporary, Jane Austen, is the only one much read today. Yet she seems oddly out of place among the male greats: F. R. Leavis, quick to assert that she is indeed "one of the truly great writers, and herself a major fact in the background of other great writers," cannot quite locate her antecedents. He postulates Richardson and Fanny Burney, but seems to sense a fuller context that he does not actually define: Burney, he admits, is not "the only other novelist who counts in her formation":

> she read all there was to read, and took all that was useful to her. . . . If the influence bearing on her hadn't comprised something fairly to be called tradition she couldn't have found herself and her true direction; but her relation to tradition is a creative one. . . . Her work, like the work of all great creative writers, gives a meaning to the past.[22]

What, then, *was* Austen's "tradition"? It was Sir Walter Scott himself whose shrewd assessment of his own times brought him closest to defining it for us. His analysis of current changes in the novel appeared in the *Quarterly Review* in a discussion of Austen's recently published novel, *Emma* (1815):

> A style of the novel has arisen within the last fifteen or twenty years, differing from the former in the points upon which the interest hinges; neither alarming our credulity nor amusing our imagination by wild variety of incident, or by those pictures of romantic affection and sensibility, which were formerly as certain attributes of fictitious characters as they are of rare occurrence among those who actually live and die. The substitute for these excitements . . . was the art of copying from nature as she really exists in common walks of life, and presenting to the reader, instead of the splendid scenes of an imaginary world, a correct and striking representation of that which is daily taking place around him.[23]

Scott is in fact pointing to a shift that had occurred in the relationship between the writers of the new novel (mainly women) [24] and their readers (many of them women): "He who paints a scene of common occurrence, places his composition within that extensive range of criticism which general experience offers to every reader." In this context the lack of a public-school education hinders the audience as little as it had the author. And it is from the point of view of this newly enfranchised readership that Scott assesses Austen's latest work: "The author's knowledge of the world, and the peculiar tact with which she presents characters that the reader cannot fail to recognize reminds us something of the merits of the Flemish school of painting." [25] This aesthetic—the appeal to what "the reader cannot fail to recognize"—has of course a considerable history: Scott has virtually paraphrased Dr. Johnson's praise of Shakespeare as the poet of nature faithfully mirroring manners and life, with the significant difference that Scott has reversed Johnson's emphasis on the general and placed it, in keeping with his time, on the individual detail.

Like the Flemish painters, Austen depicts quotidian reality consciously shaped to reveal the richness of individual life. Her peculiar genius, as Leavis partially suggests, was to make art of the "new" women's novel, and in doing so she may be seen to have laid the groundwork for the Victorian novel. Walter Allen judges Austen's subject matter to be "in a sense trivial—stated very superficially, it is always a young woman's finding a husband," yet vows that she is "with Dr. Johnson, the most forthright moralist in English." [26] Moralist with a trivial subject? The discrepancy exists in Allen's eye, but not in the eyes of Austen's contemporaries: the moral and legal issues surrounding marriage were in her time under increasingly serious review,[27] and the novel provided a public forum for airing women's positions on the subject.

Scott's date for the new "style" of novel—it had arisen "within the last fifteen or twenty years"—connects Austen with the turbulent decade of the 1790s, during which not the least significant occurrence was the emergence of a new feminism. Englishwomen's anger at their exclusion from learning and power extends back in time at least to Catherine of Aragon. Yet Mary Wollstonecraft's dazzling *Vindication of the Rights of Woman* (1792) was more provocative, notorious, and influential than any previous feminist outcry. In her lesser-known works of fiction, as much as in her polemic, Wollstonecraft sought to describe, define, ameliorate within the limits of the possible the lives of her female contemporaries. Thus perhaps even more significant for the history of the woman's novel than Wollstonecraft's feminist dogma is the example of her early novel, *Mary, A Fiction* (1788), in which Wollstonecraft, then still "unencumbered" by much book learning, presented a young Englishwoman's response to her condition, and in doing so provided a prophetic vision of the emerging genre.

Like many of her female contemporaries, Wollstonecraft was ignorant of the techniques needed to fill her pitcher at the wellspring of other minds; that came, in a rush, later. Rather, when moved by the "secret power and fire" within her, she sat down to write a novel, but a novel with a difference. In her "Advertisement" to *Mary* she explained her intentions:

> In delineating the Heroine of this Fiction, the Author attempts to develop a character different from those generally portrayed. This woman is neither a Clarissa, a Lady G-, nor a Sophie. In an artless tale, without episodes, the mind of a woman, who has thinking powers is displayed. The female organs have been thought too weak for this arduous employment; and experience seems to justify the assertion. Without arguing physically about possibilities—in a fiction, such a being may be allowed to exist; whose grandeur is derived from the operations of its own faculties, not subjugated to opinion but drawn by the individual from the original source.[28]

There are several radical implications here. First, the statement of self-consciousness, the intended emphasis on perception rather than (as in the sentimental novel) reaction. Second, the almost offhand, matter-of-fact statement about the "weakness" of women as they are viewed—and as they generally are. Third, the insistence, which is borne out in the tale, on the primacy, the potential "grandeur," of a young woman's "thinking powers," directed toward an understanding of her own existence. One thinks of Austen's Emma Woodhouse, Fanny Price, Anne Elliot—and eventually of Eliot's Dorothea Brooke and Henry James's Isabel Archer.

Even Wollstonecraft, however, was slow to recognize the revolutionary potential of the mutating genre: in the *Rights of Woman* she publicly cavilled against the practice of women, particularly young women, reading novels. But coincidental with this almost mandatory warning against the slop pails of sentimentality were evidences of her own increasing interest in fiction as a feminist forum. Besides *Mary* there is Wollstonecraft's intense self-analysis in the letters to

Imlay; her significant work as an editor of Johnson's *Analytical Review*, which took contemporary fiction seriously and in which Wollstonecraft commissioned other novelists, like Mary Hays, to review the new novels; there is as well her tutelage of Hays and her support of other experimental women writers such as Eliza Fenwick and Mary "Perdita" Robinson. Finally, there is the evidence of the sheer weight in numbers of novels by women published throughout the 1790s—novels which, whatever the writers' political affiliations, addressed themselves to the central question that Wollstonecraft had early proposed: what are the rights of woman?

The first right, it appears, was the freedom to consider the institution of marriage critically, and indeed from a woman's point of view. Thus there emerges a flock of novels surveying the social landscape with an intense concern for daily activity and social reality. "I have sent you the Gossip's Story to review," writes Wollstonecraft to Hays; "The great merit of this work is, in my opinion, the display of the small causes which destroy matrimonial felicity and peace." [29] Novels abound with illegitimate births, consenting seductions, filial rebellions, economic worries, even expressions of feelings as mundane as boredom. Set against this welter of the actual is the suggestion of a new ideal: a strong young woman who can define the values that determine her fate and can make them stick. An example would be the heroine of Hays's controversial novel *Memoirs of Emma Courtney* (1796). Fighting against a loveless marriage, seeking economic and intellectual independence *and* the sexual love of the man she chooses, Hays's Emma achieves none of these. But through her, Hays herself (learning perhaps in part from the *Caleb Williams* of her other mentor, William Godwin) manages to make heard the crying need for reform in women's education, sexual rights, and freedom of mind. Accordingly a later Emma, the heroine of Austen's novel, can defend with assurance the life of a well-endowed old maid: "I am not only not going to be married at present, but have very little intention of ever marrying at all," she says; having already fortune, employment, and consequence, "I have none of the usual inducements of women to marry." [30] She chooses otherwise in the end, of course, but Austen's point about the importance of financial independence to the autonomy of women has been quietly made.

A second and corollary right was the freedom to examine with some critical openness the quality of a woman's life after marriage. In novel after novel we are shown examples of the married state that challenge the romantic clichés and provide vivid evidence of the importance of mature and intelligent choice. Thus Susan Ferrier's *Marriage* (1818) is stocked with a variety of male-female relationships in which the bad relationships turn the women into automatons or witches, whereas the good relationships allow them to flourish as people—further evidence of how little was a young woman's finding a husband seen as a morally trivial subject. The whole moral structure of her life was governed by the conditions of marriage.

Another right newly achieved by women was the right to appeal, just as the rising middle class as a whole was appealing, to nature as norm at a time when "the law of nature" was in process of being redefined along lines that were less hierarchical, increasingly egalitarian. Man's true nobility in the new view depended not on his birth, but on his virtues—an important index to which lay in his capacity to feel elevated when in the presence of nature. If the man of sensibility was the true aristocrat, why was not the woman of sensibility his equal? This appeal had the immediate value of providing women with the dignity and self-esteem to challenge the injustices of their present condition—a fact seized on and illustrated by women novelists—while at the same time implicitly undercutting the rationalizations of male dominance as they are embodied in "the law of nations," and hence in the laws—both written and assumed—of family relations. The heroine of Helen Maria Williams's *Julia* (1790) is prepared by her "virtue," her sense of her own "native dignity" achieved in the presence of Nature, to suffer whatever she must in her pursuit of a proper marriage:

> ... the beams suddenly spread their light over the whole lake, except where long deep lines of shadow were thrown from the rocks on its surface. Julia gazed upon the objects which surrounded her with a transport of mind which she had never felt before.... It is in such moments as these that the soul becomes conscious of her native dignity.... In the country, the mind borrows virtue from the scene.[31]

Laura Montreville, heroine of Mary Brunton's novel *Self-Control* (1810), is similarly enabled, by her "elevation" in response to the natural environment, to wrestle with the experience of her lover's dishonorable attempts to seduce her:

> ... in a solitary village, remote from her equals in age and rank, Laura necessarily lived much alone, and in solitude she acquired a grave and contemplative turn of mind. . . . conversant with the grand and sublime in nature, her sentiments assumed a corresponding elevation.[32]

In choosing her own life she cuts across the public assumptions about authority and obligation to achieve at least in part self-governance. The cost in personal anguish is necessarily high, for her choice reveals the discrepancy between the laws of nature and of nations.

The epitome of the young woman in touch with true moral values and able to enforce them, to reintegrate the disorder about her, is Austen's Fanny Price, the heroine of *Mansfield Park*. Long considered Austen's emblem of her recantation of the "spirited woman"—Elizabeth Bennet and Marianne Dashwood, for example—Fanny is in fact the most radical and rebellious of all the Austen women. Like many of her fictional contemporaries, she is isolated from the world she lives in by her lesser birth, formal education, and breeding. (At the beginning Mrs. Norris and Sir Thomas even worry about the possibility of her contaminating the four Bertram children.) Self-educated, with only the intermittent support and encouragement of Edmund, Fanny is led from a love of books to love of nature—a love which Austen makes clear is both a source of her inner strength and a further evidence of it:

> all that was solemn and soothing, and lovely, appeared in the brilliancy of an unclouded night, and the contrast of the deep shade of the woods. Fanny spoke her feelings. "Here's harmony!" said she, "Here's repose! ... When I look out on such a night as this, I feel as if there could be neither wickedness nor sorrow in the world; and there certainly would be less of both if the sublimity of Nature were more attended to, and people were carried more out of themselves by contemplating such a scene." [33]

When Fanny refuses to marry for social advantage, despite enormous moral and psychological pressure (the most painful being Sir Thomas's accusation of filial ingratitude), that inner strength is in effect allowing her to challenge an entire social structure and expose the flimsiness of its values. Indeed it is Fanny even more than Edmund who represents the qualities by which the elect achieve "ordination." Thus she, a lone woman, emerges as the "privileged guardian" [34] of Mansfield Park, the moral teacher of all those around her, including Sir Thomas who long before had questioned the value to his family of taking her in.

Finally, there was the right to open political dissent, as in Hays's *Emma Courney,* Amelia Opie's *Adeline Mowbray* (1810), Charlotte Smith's *Desmond* (1792) and *The Young Philosopher* (1798); and perhaps most clearly in Wollstonecraft's own last and unfinished novel, *The Wrongs of Woman; or Maria.* The realities of life, and especially of a woman's life, are shown by Wollstonecraft to be sordid and harsh: the heroine tells her tale from the confines of the madhouse in which her husband has lawfully imprisoned her. In this world of social outcasts, a microcosm of the great world, the prison maid, Jemima, is a kind of Everywoman whose history implicates the entire society that produced her; she and Maria, despite their difference of social class, are equally vulnerable.

Sociological evidence for the accuracy of Wollstonecraft's critical perception may be found in Mary Ann Radcliffe's *The Female Advocate, or an attempt to recover the rights of women from male usurpation* (1799) and Pricilla Wakefield's *Reflections on the present condition of the female sex; with suggestions for its improvement* (1798). But Austen, too, expresses the issues for us. At the end of *Mansfield Park,* summarizing the events that follow from Henry Crawford's running off with Mrs. Rushworth, Austen draws a pointed conclusion:

That punishment, the public punishment of disgrace, should in a just measure attend *his* share of the offence, is, we know, not one of the barriers, which society gives to virtue. In this world, the penalty is less equal than could be wished.[35]

Such inequality is clearly a political matter, and is reiterated throughout Austen's canon in the fates of such figures as Lydia Bennet Wickham or Colonel Brandon's "niece" Eliza.

Few female novelists of the period made the connection between anger and action as did Wollstonecraft, Hays, and Charlotte Smith. Yet the aesthetic seriousness of even those women who opposed Wollstonecraft (like Jane West, Elizabeth Hamilton, Hannah More) reveals the changing mode of female fiction. Women writers theorized publicly about the genre: Mary Hays in the pages of the *Monthly Magazine* took Dr. Johnson to task for his assertion in *The Rambler* that the novel should remain general and universal; she criticized Richardson for the unrealistic "airy fantasy" of his *Clarissa.*

Wollstonecraft's contribution had been, then, to redirect the energies of the novel, to use the medium to exploit the force of her perceptions. And from *Mary* on, these perceptions turned more strongly into convictions bolstered by voluminous reading and a wide acquaintance with thinkers like William Godwin and Thomas Holcroft. Thus Wollstonecraft and her female contemporaries became convinced that given a world in which women were denied equal status, education was the key to significant change. But until the gates of the universities and libraries swung open to women on equal terms with men, what better way to educate women, to help them transform themselves and live with greater perceptiveness and self-awareness, than through the novel which was everywhere being devoured—to quote Hannah More—like a "complicated drug"?

Here, then, was the rationale for a novel about woman's experience: it would teach, ennoble, and enrich her. Even those novelists who, like shy Mary Brunton, publicly denigrated their own success as novelists—

> I would rather, as you know, glide through the world unknown, than have ... fame, however brilliant. To be pointed at—to be suspected of literary airs—to be shunned, as literary women are, by the more pretending of their own sex, and abhorred, as literary women are, by the more pretending of the other!—my dear, I would sooner exhibit as a rope-dancer [36]

—vigorously attacked any denigration of the status of the novel itself. No longer should this (acknowledgedly) women's literature take aesthetic second place:

> Why should an epic or a tragedy be supposed to hold such an exalted place in composition, while a novel is almost a nickname for a book? . . . I think a fiction containing a just representation of human beings and of their actions—a connected, interesting, and probable story, conducting to a useful and impressive moral lesson—might be one of the greatest efforts of human genius. Let the admirable construction of fable in Tom Jones be employed to unfold characters like Miss Edgeworth's—let it lead to a moral like Richardson's—let it be told with the elegance of Rousseau, and with the simplicity of Goldsmith—let it be all this, and Milton need not have been ashamed of the work.[37]

Rather, it was necessary to rehabilitate the genre to allow it the dignity accorded the traditional forms. But the mode of such amelioration would be Romantic rather than Augustan; it would focus on a direct and intuitive perception of the ordinary, encouraging introspection rather than offering prescription. Thus, as the novel evolved through the decade from Wollstonecraft to Austen, what emerged was woman's version of the shift from mirror to lamp, her analogue to the poetry of the male Romantic poets, insofar as both are defined by their intense concern for self-exploration and self-determination.

This heightened self-awareness in the women novelists was one response to their legal position, to their suspended existence under law; but the political situation had a further striking effect on the literary one. When we turn to the works of male poets, we find woman there, too, "incorporated and consolidated," but this time through an extension of her traditional role as the poet's muse. He for Poetry only, she for the Poetry in him was ever the case. Now the muses of Romantic poetry have a further trait that significantly extends the implications of the tradition, namely, their repeated appearance as sister image or mirror image of the poet. Often they are not even so much his inspiration as they are his projection, the imaginative extension of himself. In Blake woman is the prophet's emanation.[38] For Wordsworth it is Dorothy, his sister, who "maintained for me a saving intercourse/ With my true self" and "preserved me still/ A poet," to quote his own grateful account in *The Prelude*.[39] We might find a kind of parallel, also, in Coleridge's Eolian harp that is at once "some coy maid half yielding to her lover" and a figure for the poet himself played on by "flitting phantasies"; and again in "Kubla Khan" the "damsel with a dulcimer" is in one sense a projection of the poet, a muselike power that "In a vision once I saw," whose song the poet must revive in himself if he is to "build that dome in air."

Byron, of course, is widely assumed actually to have had an affair with his half-sister Augusta, but he also idealizes the self-sister relationship in his poetry, chiefly in the figures of Astarte in *Manfred* and Adah in *Cain* (he named his only legitimate child Augusta Ada). And Shelley offers a subtle and provocative variation on the Narcissus myth in his "Alastor," a poem in which the autobiographical elements are manifest. The young poet, wandering "obedient to high thoughts" and in search of "strange truths," had a vision in his sleep, "a dream of hopes that never yet/ Had flushed his cheek." What he sees—and falls in love with, and searches for relentlessly until his death—is a feminized image of himself.

> He dreamed a veiled maid
> Sate near him, talking in low solemn tones.
> Her voice was like the voice of his own soul
> Heard in the calm of thought; its music long,
> Like woven sounds of streams and breezes, held
> His inmost sense suspended in its web
> Of many-coloured woof and shifting hues.
> Knowledge and truth and virtue were her theme,
> And lofty hopes of divine liberty,
> Thoughts the most dear to him, and poesy,
> Herself a poet.[40]

The case parallels that of Byron's Astarte, whom Manfred describes this way:

> She was like me in lineaments—her eyes—
> Her hair—her features—all, to the very tone
> Even of her voice, they said were like to mine;
> But softened all, and tempered into beauty:
> She had the same lone thoughts and wanderings,
> The quest of hidden knowledge, and a mind

To comprehend the Universe: nor these
Alone, but with them gentler powers than mine,
Pity, and smiles, and tears—which I had not;
And tenderness—but that I had for her;
Humility—and that I never had.
Her faults were mine—her virtues were her own—
I loved her, and destroyed her! [41]

Manfred destroyed Astarte, presumably, by the fact of his illicit love—"Thou lovedst me/ Too much, as I loved thee," he tells her spirit, "though it were/ The deadliest sin to love as we have loved." Shelley's poem, however, goes beyond the social question of incest to the deeper psychological issue and develops the implications of sister-love—it is a form of self-love or narcissistic isolation. What emerges finally is an admonition to heed the implications of the Narcissus myth, to recognize how dangerous, how destructive is that spirit of solitude.

The danger was real for Shelley. Biographical evidence shows that he felt himself to be a disciple of Mary Wollstonecraft. Indeed, his first wife, Harriet, considered that a good part of Mary Godwin's appeal for Shelley lay in the fact that she was Wollstonecraft's daughter: "She heated his imagination by talking of her mother, and going to her grave with him every day." In any event, having read most of Wollstonecraft's works before or during the first year after his elopement with her daughter, Shelley embodied and celebrated Wollstonecraft in the striking figure of Cythna, the heroine of his outspokenly feminist epic *The Revolt of Islam*. Yet—and here we see the extent of Shelley's "danger"—even Cythna is represented as the hero's, Laon's, "own shadow, a second self. . . ." Indeed, before pressure from his publisher forced Shelley to rework their relationship, he had cast Cythna as Laon's sister, and the drama reverberates with this organizing principle. Accordingly—and despite his avowed intentions—Shelley subverts the communal implications of Wollstonecraft's ethic and her plea for woman's autonomy. To understand that is to understand a great deal both about Shelley and about the assumptions that shaped much of major Romantic poetry.

In his carefully developed article "Incest as Romantic Symbol," Peter Thorslev, Jr., concludes:

there is a very real sense in which the only love possible for the Romantic hero—for Chateaubriand's René, for the Byronic hero as epitomized in Manfred, for Shelley's poet-hero in *Alastor, Laon and Cythna* or *Epipsychidion*—is an incestuous love. First, it symbolizes perfectly this hero's complete alienation from the society around him; and second, it symbolizes also what psychologically speaking we can call his narcissistic sensibility, or, more philosophically speaking, his predilection for solipsism.[42]

Even Keats can provide some support for such a view, for example in *Endymion*, where although Peona is not the object of Endymion's romantic love, she does function as a kind of normative or balancing extension of himself, as well as supportive confidante:

> Who whispers him so pantingly and close?
> Peona, his sweet sister: of all those,
> His friends, the dearest.[43]

It is in her bower that he first finds "slumbrous rest":

> But, ere it crept upon him, he had prest
> Peona's busy hand against his lips,
> And still, a sleeping, held her finger-tips
> In tender pressure.[44]

"Thus, in the bower,/ Endymion was calmed to life again." In this view, too, it seems appropriate that the lovestruck Endymion, struggling for a way to understand his passion for the Moon, should say "Thous seem'dst my sister," [45] adding, a few lines later, "Thou wast the charm of women, lovely Moon!" [46]

Jerome McGann, in a comment on Byron's literary treatment of women, really defines the case for all the major Romantic poets: "The female counterparts of Byron's heroes . . . correspond exactly to the state of the hero's soul which they inhabit. They objectify the passionate impulses in the man whose imagination made them what they are. This is as much to say that none of them are truly 'persons.' " [47] The point is that in a period whose aesthetic sanctified the uniquely individual experience, and in a genre commanded almost exclusively by male writers, the "female" became little more than metaphoric extension—"female counterpart," objectified impulse.

This self-seclusion was not only sexual or intellectual, but social: consider how little is romantic poetry a poetry of community, as compared with Augustan or Victorian poetry, for example. The issue is a central one in Wordsworth, that most sublimely egotistical of Romantic poets; he seems to have understood the implications of his egotism and fought to overcome it. "My difficulty," he says, came "from a sense of the indomitableness of the spirit within me. . . . I was often unable to think of external things as having external existence. . . . Many times while going to school have I grasped at a wall or tree to recall myself from this abyss of idealism to the reality." Yet he felt equally the obverse difficulty—that of finding too little reality in one's own spirit: "In later periods of life I have deplored, as we all have reason to do, a subjugation of an opposite character. . . ." [48] The problem is to balance a sense of inner with a sense of outer, and to find a relationship between them. In the 1802 Preface Wordsworth had undertaken in several added paragraphs to define the work of the poet somewhat more fully than his 1800 Preface had done. He used the occasion to emphasize the issue of community: "The Poet binds together by passion and knowledge the vast empire of human society," "carrying everywhere with him relationship and love." [49] Yet after his brother's death in 1805, Wordsworth condemned his own continued "distance from the Kind," associating it by implication with the immature "Poet's dream," a "fond illusion" of the as yet un- "humanized" soul. [50]

This is not the place to reopen discussion of the perplexing question of Wordsworth's relationship to Dorothy; [51] but to ask whether it was overtly incestuous or merely disturbingly close is already to suggest that from the point of view of the present essay it hardly matters. What does matter is that in the same years during which Wordsworth was struggling to achieve for himself a better balanced sense of the relation between self and other, that is, to achieve a more responsive and responsible sense of community, he was modifying the kind of relationship he had with his sister— first by expanding his "family" at Grasmere to include Coleridge and the Hutchinson sisters and his own brother John, then by marrying Mary Hutchinson in 1802 and fathering children. After John's death he threw himself even more vigorously into the proprieties, at least, of family and community life. That his poetry suffered as his egotism was wrestled down (it *was* wrestled down at least in this one expression of it, his disturbing closeness to Dorothy) may suggest how very deep was the connection in Wordsworth between his best poetry and what Thorslev has called "narcissistic sensibility" or "solipsism." What Thorslev claimed as the only love possible for the Romantic hero—an incestuous love of his sister—appears to have been precisely the love that was necessary to Wordsworth's poetic success: it was the egotistical sublime as expressed in the poet's inner life, the source of his art.

The point is that when the poets of the Romantic period conceived of the female, especially (as was rare) the female *poet*, it was mainly as extension of a male counterpart: her place in the high rank of poetry was secured by the fact that she was a kind of feminized alter-ego of the male poet. The novel, of course, had none of those high-flown claims as genre that would make it inaccessible to female writers; indeed women had always been stigmatized as novel readers; what more logical than that they should in turn provide this feminized food for their own audience? The surprise is that they managed to develop through the genre a new dignity both for it and for themselves. Blackstone's interpretation of the law—that the "very being" of a woman is "incorporated and consolidated" into that of her husband—finds its artistic expression, however ironically, in the romantic poet's view of his own relationship to his muse. But it finds no such expression in the romantic novel as written by women.

Thus it was that women in the Romantic period not only provided powerful imagery for one of the most prominent features of the period as a whole—its creative egocentricity—but were themselves initiators of a new direction in art, of what was to become a major mode, the Victorian novel. (Even Mrs. Radcliffe reveals in her famous "explained" conclusions a concern for the life we actually live, as opposed to the appearance seized on by heightened sensibility.) In this way we may see how the women of the Romantic period—closed off by personal and social circumstances from the high art of poetic genius—created a countermovement that drew on the growing concern for individual experience (inner and outer), yet focused it on the facts of shared daily life, insisted on the forces of social context. In this way too we may see how Jane Austen is emphatically "of her time" and not, as so often assumed, aloofly behind it. And Mary Shelley's *Frankenstein* may be read as Romantic Woman's ultimate judgment on the alienated artist of male romanticism:[52] however altruistic his motives, in isolation he creates monsters—the very embodiment of his alienation—that destroy his home and everything he loves. Put another way, the novel suggests that to realize oneself as "one person in law" is to find oneself morally and emotionally alone, at incalculable loss to self and other, to civilization and human growth. This was the lesson that women in British Romantic literature had both to learn and to teach.

Notes

1 Book the First (Oxford, 1765), p. 442.
2 Ray [Rachel] Strachey, *The Cause* (London, 1928), p. 15.
3 See Mary R. Beard, *Woman As Force in History* (New York, 1947), especially chap. 4; and Leo Kanowitz, *Woman and the Law: The Unfinished Revolution* (Albuquerque, 1969), especially chap. 3, "Law and the Married Woman."
4 This is matter for the Victorian chapter of the present book; but interested readers may find the Nortons' story briefly summarized in Josephine Kamm's *Rapiers and Battleaxes* (London, 1966), pp. 23-28.
5 *The First Four Georges* (London, 1956), p. 41.
6 Walter Ong, *The Barbarian Within* (New York, 1962), p. 211.
7 Ong, *The Presence of the Word* (New Haven, 1967), p. 251.
8 *Biographia Literaria*, ed. J. Shawcross (Oxford, 1967), I: chap. 1, p. 4.
9 Ibid., pp. 4-5.
10 Ibid., II: chap. 16, p. 26n.
11 "Preface" to the *Lyrical Ballads*, II: 387-88. All citations of Wordsworth, except those to *The Prelude*, are from Ernest de Selincourt and Helen Darbishire, eds. *The Poetical Works of William Wordsworth*, 5 vols. (Oxford, 1940-49 [Vols. I-III, 2d. ed., Helen Darbishire, 1952-54]), and are cited by work, volume and page.
12 "The Excursion," I, 77-91; de Selincourt V: 10-11.
13 As quoted in Josephine Kamm, *Hope Deferred: Girls' Education in English History* (London, 1965), p. 104.
14 Marilyn Butler, *Maria Edgeworth: A Literary Biography* (Oxford, 1972), p. 153.
15 Maria Edgeworth, *Belinda*, 3d ed. (London, 1811), I: 5-6.

16 *Northanger Abbey,* ed. R. W. Chapman (Oxford, 1926), I: 37.

17 *Jane Austen's Letters to Her Sister Cassandra and Others,* ed. R. W. Chapman (Oxford, 1932), II: 443. That women's exclusion from the privileges of male education affected their capacities as visual artists, too, is made clear in Ann Sutherland Harris and Linda Nochlin's excellent *Women Artists: 1550-1950* (New York, 1976).

18 These women's magazines not only differed in content and emphasis from men's magazines, but also translated any Latin quotations used in reviews of new books.

19 "Biographical Notice of Ellis and Acton Bell, by Currer Bell" [i.e., Emily and Anne by Charlotte Brontë] in Charlotte Brontë, *Life and Works of Charlotte Brontë and her Sisters* (London, 1873), V: xv-xvi.

20 William Duff, *An Essay on Original Genius,* 1767 ed. in facsimile reproduction, ed. John L. Mahoney (Gainesville, Fla., 1964), pp. 271, 281-82.

21 "Extempore Effusion upon the Death of James Hogg," IV: 277-8.

22 F. R. Leavis, *The Great Tradition* (Garden City, N.Y., 1954), pp. 13-14.

23 Sir Walter Scott, "Review," *Quarterly Review* 14 (1815), 192-93.

24 See Winifred Husband's "The Lesser Novel in England," (M.A. thesis, University of London, 1922), for a nearly complete listing by title, author, and year of novels written in England during the last half of the eighteenth century. There were, of course, important male novelists in the period, of whom several—Godwin, Holcroft, Lewis, Bage—evinced in their political radicalism at least an implicit feminism that was eagerly seized on and developed by the women novelists as they set about writing their new mode of "women's fiction." (Holcroft's *Anna St. Ives* [1792], for example, is a political study of a young woman's options, and was widely read and manifestly influential.) Later in the period as august a figure as Scott responded to the very shift defined in his review of *Emma,* for in female characters such as Jeanie Deans he portrayed women actively participating in the significant trivia of the "common walks of life." For a more detailed discussion of the development of the "partisan novel" at the end of the century see Marilyn Butler's excellent *Jane Austen and the War of Ideas* (Clarendon, 1975), and Gary Kelly's exemplary *The English Jacobin Novel 1780-1805* (Clarendon, 1976).

25 Scott, "Review," p. 197.

26 *The English Novel* (New York, 1958), p. 115.

27 See Ian Watt, *The Rise of the Novel* (Berkeley, 1959), chap. 5.

28 *Mary, A Fiction* (London, 1788), pp. 1, 3-4.

29 Reprinted in *The Love Letters of Mary Hays,* ed. A. F. Wedd (London, 1925), p. 240.

30 *Emma,* ed. R. W. Chapman (Oxford, 1926), p. 84.

31 (London, 1790), I: 80-81.

32 (London, 1810), I: 11.

33 *Mansfield Park,* ed. R. W. Chapman (Oxford, 1926), I: 113.

34 Ibid., III: 355.
35 Ibid., p. 468.
36 Quoted in Anne Katharine Elwood, *Memoirs of the Literary Ladies of England* (London, 1843), II: 216.
37 Ibid., pp. 220-21.
38 For an extended discussion of the rather special case of Blake's view of women, see Irene Tayler's "The Woman Scaly," *Bulletin of the Midwest MLA* 6 (Spring 1973), 74-87.
39 *The Prelude*, XI, 341-42, 346-47; 2d ed., ed. Ernest de Selincourt, rev. Helen Darbishire (Oxford, 1959), pp. 419-421.
40 "Alastor," 11. 151-61; *The Complete Works of Percy Bysshe Shelley*, ed. Neville Rogers (Oxford, 1975), II: 48.
41 *Manfred*, II, ii, 106-18; *The Works of Lord Byron*, ed. E. H. Coleridge (New York, 1966), *Poetry*, IV: 106.
42 *Comparative Literature Studies* 2 (1965), 41-58. The passage quoted here occurs on p. 50.
43 *Endymion*, I, 407-9; *The Poetical Works of John Keats*, ed. H. W. Garrod, 2d. ed. (Oxford, 1958), pp. 76-77.
44 Ibid., II, 443-46; Garrod, p. 78.
45 Ibid., III, 145; Garrod, p. 132.
46 Ibid., 1. 169; Garrod, p. 132.
47 *Fiery Dust: Byron's Poetic Development* (Chicago, 1968), p. 189.
48 Notes to "Ode: Intimations of Immorality," IV: 463.
49 "Preface" to the *Lyrical Ballads*, II: 396.
50 "Elegiac Stanzas," IV: 258-60.
51 Recent letters in *TLS*, responding to Donald H. Reiman's reading of "'Tis said that some have died for love" *(TLS*, September 13, 1974, 979-80), show how lively the issue remains.
52 It is worth noting that Victor Frankenstein's fiancée Elizabeth is called his "more than sister," and further that the entire story, the framing device, is delivered by Walton in letters to his own sister, who had also been as a mother to him in his youth.

6.

Angels and Other Women
in Victorian Literature

Marlene Springer

The Victorian Temper, The Victorian Frame of Mind, Victorian Prelude, Victorian People and Their Ideas, are all titles that reflect an essential fact about the period in English history from about 1837 to the turn of the century: it was the age of a woman. Slowly it became an age of *the* woman. In the sixty-four years of Victoria's reign, her presence and effect on British life, for better and for worse, was ubiquitous. She was a crucial force in a period, and a nation, in a state of unprecedented change: machines were instigating a revolution, destroying the previous century's relatively slow pace and secure faith in the status quo, and creating for the Victorians a new era, a new society. Darwin in science, Strauss and others in theology, forced the English to reconsider their place not only in the nation, but in a gigantically expanded universe and earthly chronology as well. Victoria and her subjects tried, with admirable success, to "greet the unseen with a cheer"—confident in their own ability to extend the progressiveness, glitter, and technical sophistication of the Crystal Palace to all levels of life, and to all those lands—one-tenth of the globe—which enjoyed the benevolent protection of an empire basking in a golden glow.

But confidence, assurance that progress was an important product, ability to accept industrial and religious change were not acquired easily or gratuitously; some sacrifice was inevitable—and the present pejorative implications of the word "Victorian" are the residue of those sacrifices. Progress and industrial revolution were also expensive, and the working class paid the price. Disraeli spoke of "Two Nations," the rich and the poor, and the former went to excessive lengths to make sure that it rarely encountered the latter.[1] Theological questioning and confrontation with an indifferent, perhaps even vindictive evolutionary process underscored a need for stability at some more immediate level; thus the home became the new temple. Enshrined in this temple by the cult of chastity, looked to as a moral guardian, feared for the power that worship confers, and often sacrificed to propriety, was the Victorian Woman. An alliance—rare in its totality—of art and life produced a creature in whom the distinctions between fiction and fact were blurred; the stereotypes of literature became interchangeable with the realities of the household. Lacking any viable alternatives, the Victorian woman became, by necessity, and sometimes by choice, a Victorian heroine; and the age of the woman, with all of its ironies, was at hand.

Victoria said that her success as a queen depended in large part on the morality of her court and the harmony of her domestic life; and she severely resisted what she saw as threats to virtue and the home. Speaking with the royal and androgynous pronoun, she said, "We are anxious to enlist everyone who can speak or write to join in checking this mad, wicked folly of 'Women's Rights' with all its attendant horrors, on which the poor feeble sex is bent, forgetting every sense of womanly feeling and propriety." In a rare example of unity, the larger intellectual community agreed with the Queen's position on both the dangers of reform and the nature of the sex. In the face of such unanimity, the Victorian woman came to believe—almost. For the mere fact that Victoria needed to remind and admonish reveals that the stereotype lived and breathed, but often consumptively. The feminist "Shrieking Sisterhood" could not be ignored, and the derogatory label ironically became an apt metaphor, on both the private and public levels. Privately, the shrieks were born of the muted and barely understood psychological disturbances inevitable in a system where repression, particularly sexual, was the norm. Publicly, the shrieks came from men and women who protested that one could only be eligible for goddess status after having been declared legally dead and sexually spiritualized.

The loyal opposition, however, though vocal, and right, was attempting to storm a formidable historic citadel and lacked the support of most of the captives within. Even the leading feminine intellects of the day—George Eliot and Harriet Martineau, to name two—refused to support the drive for suffrage, some even preferring to believe what science, literature, and tradition told them: women were "lesser men," "blinder motions bounded in a shallower brain," as Tennyson says in "Locksley Hall." Lacking education, denied experience, the sheltered woman came to fear an alternative freedom, and kept the circular effects of repression in motion. When any author or politician dared to tamper with the locks on her own cell, she often responded with a protective fit of morality, giving us further proof that the women themselves were true believers, effectively helping to keep the myth and the reality closely aligned.

The energies directed toward maintaining the tradition of the "subordinate sex," and even reconstructing and reenforcing it as it came under increasingly strenuous attack, were legion. They took every important generic form in literature—discursive prose, poetry, fiction—and came from the various branches of learning—philosophy, theology, science, psychology, medicine, jurisprudence. In philosophy, Auguste Comte, whose Positivist theories were influentially circulated in the 1830s and long continued in vogue, ordained woman as the Moral Providence in his new order, with the Intellectual Providence assigned to the male Priesthood. Contending that with women "the consecration of the rational and imaginative faculties to the service of feeling has always existed spontaneously," Comte argued that women have unconsciously preserved medieval traditions and saved moral culture. Now that the heart is recognized as reigning over the intellect, women will assume their rightful position as objects of veneration. The flag of Positivism will depict a young mother, carrying her infant *son*. Woman is to be the moral guide, who rears the children, renounces all property, and has no work away from the home.[2]

Nor did the tradition of male superiority, ingrained in social institutions and supported by public opinion, lack important defenders as the century progressed. Herbert Spencer, for example, in his *The Study of Sociology* (1873) argued that sex differences could best be explained by assuming "somewhat earlier arrest of individual evolution in women than men; necessitated by the reservation of vital power to meet the cost of reproduction." Female energy spent in reproduction was not available for intellectual development.[3] By the end of the century, when Havelock Ellis began to plan his major work, *Studies in the Psychology of Sex,* the question of what actually constitutes a "woman" had become so complex that he had to do a preliminary study, *Man and Woman* (1894). His conclusions are predictably nebulous, but he does join Spencer and his party with such claims as "women dislike the essentially intellectual process of analysis; they have the instinctive feeling that analysis may possibly destroy the emotional complex by which they are largely moved and which appeals to them"; or, "girls are aided by a better memory and a variety of emotional and moral qualities which involve a greater docility. Boys, however, possess other qualities which contain the promise of ultimately greater intellectual development." [4]

Thus the superstitions and taboos of the past gained philosophical and scientific respectability. The medical world strengthened the image. William Acton, in his popular work *The Functions and Disorders of the Reproductive Organs* (1857), outlined the predominant ideology when he assured his readers that women are by nature modest and sexually passive. "Love of home, children, and domestic duties are the only passions they feel. . . . She submits to her husband, but only to please him; and but for the desire of maternity, would far rather be relieved from his attentions." Legally, too, the Victorian woman was regarded as a frail vessel in need of what came to be debilitating protection. The Matrimonial Clauses Act, vehemently opposed as a threat to the sanctity of the home, was not passed until 1857. Prior to its passage, divorce was possible in England only by going through ecclesiastical courts, civil courts, and the House of Lords. With the "Divorce Bill," men could get a divorce for proven adultery; women had to prove adultery plus some additional grievance such as cruelty, desertion, sodomy, bestiality, or rape. (Not until the Matrimonial Causes Act of 1923 was the double standard removed.) Without a divorce, a wife was legally bound to even the cruelest of men; until 1884 she could be imprisoned for refusing conjugal rights, and not until 1891 did the courts decide that a husband had no right to detain his wife forcibly in order to obtain restitution of those rights. Thus, once married, women became legal slaves—until the Married Women's Property Act of 1882, they could not even hold property. Being legally a minor did have its advantages, though: a husband and wife could not be convicted of conspiracy, because they were one person. And since it was a legal presumption that a wife acts under the command, actual or implied, of her husband, she was excused from punishment for certain offenses committed in her husband's presence—for example, theft, burglary, and housebreaking; but a wife could be punished for treason, murder, and violent theft, for these are prohibited by the laws of nature.[5] But the laws that ostensibly protected, obviously suppressed. Suffrage, though tied to property laws for men, was denied even the property-holding woman until 1918; the only important office a woman could hold was the Crown; the legal and medical professions were by and large closed, though by the mid-1870s the few women doctors were at least accepted. For much of the century, however, the married woman's property, liberty, earnings, children, even her conscience belonged to her husband.[6] Yet to remain single made one an "odd woman," and marriage was unquestionably considered the greater good.

While being scientifically and legally defined, the role of the Victorian woman was also being created, and disseminated to the mass audience, by the sentimental and chivalric school. Books of "advice to young ladies," all aimed at the middle class, abounded; Dr. John Gregory's *A Father's Legacy to His Daughters* (1774), popular for over one hundred years, postulated that a woman's life was one of suffering and that her personal virtues were humility, chastity, delicacy, and beauty. Mrs. Sarah Ellis's "Women of England" (1839) went into sixteen editions in its first two years. It and her subsequent tracts, "Daughters of . . .," "Wives of . . .," "Mothers of . . .," all advised women to take the only natural role, subservience. She warned the daughters of England: "The first thing of importance is to be content to be inferior to men—inferior in mental power, in the same proportion that you are inferior in bodily strength." To the wives she says: "At home it is but fitting that the master of the house should be considered as entitled to the choice of every personal indulgence, unless indisposition or suffering on the part of the wife render such indulgences more properly her due; but even then they ought to be received as a favor, rather than claimed as a right." [7] (Any flagrant deviation from this norm risked being met with almost hysterical opposition such as in Mrs. Lynn Linton's "The Girl of the Period" [*Saturday Review*, March 14, 1868]. It was a vehement attack against the militant women of the period—and Mrs. Linton made a career of praising demure females over "strong minded women"—"drawing-room blights.") John Ruskin, in his "Of Queens' Gardens" (1865), and even more specifically in *Fors Clavigera*, gave perhaps the most complete summary of the classic Victorian polemic, asserting in *Fors* that a woman's work is to please people, to feed them daintily, to clothe them, to keep them orderly, and to teach them. "The right life for all woman-kind," says Ruskin, "is that of the Swiss paysanne"; but given the dominant idea that a woman's leisure is a definitive indication of status, Ruskin sees that the energies previously spent in milking must now be spent in "sweet ordering, arrangement, and decision" so that the house will be a place of peace, "the shelter, not only from all injury, but from all terror, doubt, and division" ("Queens' Gardens"). And it is from Ruskin that woman received her most eloquent coronation:

> And whether consciously or not, you must be, in many a heart enthroned: there is no putting by that crown; queens you must always be; queens to your lovers; queens to your husbands and your sons; queens of higher mystery to the world beyond, which bows itself, and will forever bow, before the myrtle crown, and the stainless scepter, of womanhood.[8]

Carlyle, in a letter of February 9, 1871 demonstrates his complete agreement with Ruskin:

> I have never doubted the true and noble function of a woman in this world was, is, and forever will be, that of being Wife and Helpmate to a worthy man; and discharging well the duties that devolve on her in consequence, as mother of children and mistress of a Household, duties high, noble,

silently important as any that can fall to a human creature; duties which, if well discharged, constitute woman, in a soft, beautiful, and almost sacred way, the Queen of the World, and, by her natural faculties, graces, strengths, and weaknesses, are every way indicated as specifically hers. The true destiny of a Woman, therefore, is to wed a man she can love and esteem; and to lead noiselessly, under his protection, with all the wisdom, grace, and heroism that is in her, the life prescribed in consequence.

In spite of the strength and moral certainty of the Establishment, however, rebellion was not entirely stifled. Among the prose essayists, John Stuart Mill, in his *On the Subjection of Women* (1869), argued conclusively for an end to the legal and social repression. Addressing many of his arguments to the issues of enfranchisement and property rights, Mill contended that women are not queens but rather the last legal slaves; and he used his formidable intellect and Benthamite logic to prove the cultural insanity of classing women with idiots and children. On this topic he was heard, caricatured, and conveniently relegated to the back bench—ironically to become the voice of prophecy—while his more conventional opponents, Ruskin and Carlyle, were left in control of the field.

While Mrs. Ellis, Ruskin, and Carlyle delineated the Victorian woman in prose, Coventry Patmore's *The Angel in the House* (1854-56) was the great poetic celebration of womanhood and domestic bliss.[9] Daring to contest the conventional belief that bourgeois marriage was inherently unpoetic material, he drew confidence from Wordsworth's rustics and turned the ostensibly mundane subject into an apotheosis of married love. Occasionally banal, always sentimental, the prologue and twelve cantos of the first volume, "The Betrothal," and the equally long second volume entitled "The Espousals," celebrate a married harmony fostered primarily by the saintly, submissive woman. Inspired by Patmore's first wife, whom he regarded as so much a saint that he always kept the anniversary of her death as a day of seclusion and prayer, the heroine (Honoria) is the man's "most effectual means of grace,/ and casket of . . . worldly bliss." "Her disposition is devout,/ Her countenance angelical," modesty is her chief grace, and "in mind and manners how discreet!" *(A in H,* I,58-59). The poem illustrates Patmore's belief (subscribed to in the abstract by most Victorians) that married love was an indispensable civilizing power, and that a true husband and a true wife can realize a fullness of love in each other that is analogous to God's love for man. Women are to be not only a glory to man—in "The Weaker Vessel" *(Religio Poetae,* 1887), Patmore was later to write that woman only loves and desires to become what her husband loves and desires her to be—but also a constant reminder of the divine in him; the honor instinctively accorded her is man's unconscious recognition of her place in the divine plan. Obviously, Patmore's celebration of the connubial sacrament is overdrawn, but his Honoria was taken to be on the whole a realistic possibility. Many Victorians tried to be, or to have, Honoria; the book sold a quarter of a million copies before Patmore's death in 1896.

Victorian womanhood as portrayed by Patmore gained wide acceptance—but there were also poetic explorations of the shadow side of the pedestal.[10] Tennyson's *The Princess* (1847) and Elizabeth Barret Browning's *Aurora Leigh* (1857) close ranks with Mill, and address the implications of domestic consignment. The middle-class housewife's day as revealed in Mrs. Beeton's *Book of Household Management* (1863) was just as boring then as now; directing the usual three to seven servants and handling other domestic duties could probably be finished in two hours. The potential of the remaining hours of leisure was virtually negated by the propriety which demanded that a woman be accompanied whenever she left her house. In such circumstances, women's education and social freedom became increasingly topical. In *The Princess* Tennyson addresses the question of women's education, but with a mixture of classic liberalism and expedient conservatism.

Tennyson's personal and artistic treatment of women is both complex and extensive. Jane Carlyle once noted the diffidence of Tennyson's response to women, saying: "Alfred is dreadfully embarrassed with women alone—for he entertains at one and the same moment a feeling of almost adoration for them and an ineffable contempt! adoration I suppose for what they might be—contempt for what they are!" And W. D. Paden, in *Tennyson in Egypt,* has noted that in his adolescent verse there is only one woman who is both attractive and attainable. His early women are weary, isolated, mysterious, neurotic; and his contempt for them is more evident than his admiration.

With *The Princess,* however, Tennyson at least tried to come to terms with one pressing contemporary problem facing women: their lack of formal education, and the consequent destiny of the intelligent woman in a society which admired silence more than sagacity in its women. The poem itself is a disturbing mixture of frivolity, seriousness, philosophical contradiction, and, in the early sections, mockery of the feminist position. The hero—a medieval prince—is making the traditional quest, this time in search of a living grail, Ida, a woman betrothed to him at birth. (Tennyson himself was ambivalent about arranged marriages; he scorned commercial unions, but here he supports the idea of marriage settled at birth, apparently believing that true love could flower in the asexual innocence of childhood.[11]) Ida has become the virgin-superior of a remote women's university, and the Prince's life is threatened when he deceptively enters the fortress. The machinations of the plot include a jealous lesbian relationship, a battle between the hero and Ida's brother, an abandoned infant, and a series of "weird seizures" by the Prince (added by Tennyson in his fourth edition in 1851) which enable him conveniently to escape any unpleasant reality—especially those realities involving sexual politics. The Prince loses the battle only to win the prize, an Ida whose gush of love for someone else's child has released her true femininity. Women, the Prince assures Ida, are not men's inferiors, but complementary opposites: "For woman is not undevelopt man,/ But diverse." The sexes must never reverse roles, but rather learn from each other, he gaining "in sweetness and in moral height," she receiving "mental breadth" without losing "the childlike in the larger mind." But the poem is not entirely the capitulation it appears. The extreme view of the Prince's father ("Man is the hunter; woman is his game./ The sleek and shining creatures of the chase,/ We hunt them for the beauty of their skins;/ They love us for it, and we ride them down") is flatly rejected. And before Ida enthusiastically embraces her "natural" role as wife, mother, and moral guide, she does voice decidedly liberal, and eloquent, arguments for equality, calling for "everywhere/ Two heads in council, two beside the hearth,/ Two in the tangled business of the world,/ Two in the liberal offices of life,/

Two plummets dropt for one to sound the abyss/ Of science and the secrets of the mind." The poem ends, however, with a plea for patience in bringing about reforms, and it is this tone that is to dominate Tennyson's later poetry. As his responsibilities as sage increased, and perhaps as he became better acquainted with the Queen, his hope for an educated woman as a "diverse" equal gradually receded in favor of a woman who is much the lesser man: a modest, obedient, patient Enid, a prelapsarian Elaine, a Guinevere groveling at the feet of an Arthur who comes to lecture, and forgive "as Eternal Gods/ forgive." The fatal, neurotic woman of the earlier period is replaced, the proud, self-sufficient Ida marries, and by the time of *Idylls of the King* his answer to the "woman question" clearly defines him as a "worthy laureate of his beloved queen." His earlier mysterious maidens have become, as Lionel Stevenson notes *(PMLA* 63: 243), matter-of-fact literary stock characters; the distance between what women are and what they can be has narrowed, and they become most important for the spiritual and social direction they provide.[12] Hallam Tennyson quotes him on his unreserved conviction of woman's redemptive destiny:

> She must train herself to do the large work that lies before her, even though she may not be destined to be wife or mother, cultivating her understanding not her memory only, her imagination in its highest phases, her inborn spirituality and her sympathy with all that is pure, noble and beautiful rather than mere social accomplishments; then and then only will men continue to hold her in reverence.[13]

It should be said, however, that Tennyson cannot be too much faulted for his conservative position, taken even in one of his most liberal poems, for his feminine counterpart, Elizabeth Barrett Browning, chooses the same resolution for her feminist poem *Aurora Leigh* (1857) as Tennyson did for *The Princess.* Unlike Tennyson, and despite her disapproval of much of the propaganda for the cause, Mrs. Browning was a fighter for women's rights. In "Casa Guidi Windows" she notes that the Crystal Palace offered "No help for women sobbing out of sight/ Because men make the laws"; and *Aurora Leigh,* with its 11,000 lines of blank verse, was her clarion call against the oppression of women—especially those who wanted careers. Even more than *The Princess* the poem is weighted with melodrama: the orphaned heroine temporarily refuses her destined husband in favor of a career as an artist; the blindly idealistic hero attempts to put his social theories into practice by marrying a waif (Marian) who has been on the dole ever since she ran away from an alcoholic mother who tried to sell her to a lecherous gentleman; a scheming lady disrupts the Two-Nation marriage and sends Marian off to Australia with the lady's maid; Marian falls into white slavery after she has been tricked off the boat, and is abandoned in Paris; the hero is tragically blinded (Browning was heavily influenced by *Jane Eyre*); Aurora is inevitably transformed into a willing wife after her feminine instincts have been revitalized by Marian's illegitimate child and Romney's blind helplessness. But unlike the Princess, Browning's heroine does not give up her career—she has both career and husband. Nor does Marian, the counterpart to Tennyson's Psyche, marry and ensure a family for her child. The narrator supports her decision to refuse a convenient marriage and yet keep her child, an aspect of the poem that Coventry Patmore condemned. Moreover, Elizabeth Browning is daring enough to discuss forthrightly the ills which befall a woman who is not fortunate enough to be educated or have a protective prince. Marian does not take to the streets, but her friends do.

Browning was severely criticized for mentioning prostitution; the *Dublin University Magazine* deemed it a "closed volume for her own sex," and other reviewers called the language of the poem too coarse for a respectable woman to read. But Elizabeth replied, "If a woman ignores these wrongs, then may women as a sex continue to suffer them; there is no help for any of us—let us be dumb and die." And she was amused rather than angered when told about a woman of sixty who complained that her morals had been injured by reading *Aurora Leigh*, and that her character would be in danger if others discovered she had looked at the book.[14] But for all its moral purpose and daring, the poem has many flaws: it is grotesquely long, outdistancing *Paradise Lost*; the characters are unreal (Marian speaks in the idiolect of a middle-class damsel); the plot strained even Victorian belief; and most important, the polemic is contradictory. She proposed to write a political poem—

and did so—inveighing against conventional habits of thought throughout. Yet, like Tennyson, she felt compelled to end with a promise of happy marriage and material wealth. The fact that she did so is startling evidence of the pervasiveness of the Victorian belief in the supreme importance of married love. Ruskin himself called it the greatest poem in the language, unsurpassed by anything except Shakespeare.

The doctors, lawyers, philosophers, essayists, and poets, then, all helped produce the Victorian woman. Carefully taught to suffer and be still, flattered into believing that along with one Queen there should be a multitude of queens, kept complaisant through ignorance, the average Victorian became the stereotype she was trained to admire—and jealously protected her position. But while poetry and prose were literalizing the ideal, it was in fiction, with its generic allowances for wide-ranging study of personality, that the values of the middle class found their fullest expression.

The advent of a massive leisure class greatly enlarged the reading public, and had a profound effect on the nature of fiction. "Silly women's novels," to use George Eliot's phrase, proliferated, and the aura of ideal womanhood was protected by sheer bulk. The heroine in these novels, and even more so in the "railway" fiction of the mid-century, followed a fairly rigid formula. She was young, beautiful, and usually tall; she had to be unathletic, sometimes even physically frail so that she could faint with realistic regularity; she had to speak standard English, and belong to the middle class; she was always assumed to be inferior to men, and her primary obligation was submissiveness to authority. Governed by emotion, not reason, the heroine most often also had an extreme sensibility, but rarely was she allowed to show anger. She was intrepid when faced with moral dangers, having her intuitive morality to rely upon, but, because of her frailty, tended to physical cowardice. Finally, and above all, she had to be pure—chastity was not *a* virtue, but was virtue itself, and to lose one's virginity prematurely was the worst possible disaster.[15]

There are, of course, exceptions to this sort of heroine in the 40,000 novels the Victorians are estimated to have produced. But they are aberrations that confirm the rule. Elizabeth Sewell, Mrs. Henry Wood, Rhoda Broughton, Eliza Linton, G. W. M. Reynolds (who wrote and sold more than Dickens), Jane Brookfield—the list is interminable, as are the novels—cranked out these books, nearly all of which contained only slight variations of the popular formula. Charlotte Yonge was perhaps one of the best known of this ilk and her output was, unfortunately, only slightly atypical; she wrote more than 200 novels, even while abstaining from fiction during Lent. Though often compared to Jane Austen, her talent was very slight. She gained immense popularity because she so clearly and favorably depicted the middle class, because she could spin an interesting (though poorly constructed) story, and because she appealed to the moral impulses of the Victorians. Unlike the pure romance novels, the reading of which, doctors warned, could cause a rush of blood to the uterus and consequent intrauterine diseases, Charlotte Yonge's tractarian stories could be read not only with safety, but with righteousness. The Religious Tract Society laid down in 1863 the essential rules for healthful fiction: the stories should be moral; true to both nature and fact, free from exaggerations of character; and unexciting, leaving the spirit calm and the passions relatively unmoved. Charlotte Yonge's novels eminently qualify. And, as in the other domestic fiction, her depiction of women is fairly standard. She had an unshakable belief that men's minds were superior to women's, and women who dispensed with male protection were not favorably treated—as in, for example, her *Hopes and Fears* (1860).[16] In *The Clever Woman of the Family* (1865) she studies two bright women, one a feminist of sorts, one an invalid intellectual. The feminist, Rachel, is allowed to marry at the end, but only after she and her schemes have been brought to ridicule; Ermine is Mrs. Yonge's ideal as she lies on her ever-present couch and pens essays on education.[17]

The Charlotte Yonges of the period, then, fell into step with the Ruskins and the Carlyles, offering a fairly consistent view of woman and domesticity. Almost nine-tenths of the stories approvingly ended in marriage. Marital boredom and ensuing feminine discontent were largely ignored.[18] The major authors of the era, recognizing the "Victorian woman" as defined by the culture and its conservative spokesmen, contributed their talents to fostering the sentimental-heroine, queen-of-the-house view; but they also explored with disturbing intensity the darker side of forcing women into preconceived psychological and social roles. The ramifications of and deviations from the cultural ideal are major concerns of Dickens, George Eliot, Thackeray, Meredith, and Hardy, for example. Using the same ideal as a touchstone, Charlotte Brontë and Mrs. Gaskell, as well as Dickens and Hardy, also made bold moves outside the class structure to study wider variations: the Victorian as governess, the sentimental heroine as working girl, the sacred vessel smashed by circumstance—the fallen woman.

The best panorama of the Victorian scene, the Victorian temper, and even Victorian womanhood is of course offered by Charles Dickens. With his hundreds of characters he seems to defy categorization. His heroines, however (as opposed to his minor characters), can be classed by some representative generalities. Dickens's own attitudes toward women in general, and the Victorian ideal in particular, were complex, and as several critics have shown, dynamic. In the early novels, which reached an artistic peak in *Dombey and Son* (1846-48), he seems to concentrate on the woman Ruskin is later to define—romantic, vulnerable, childlike. It is in *David Copperfield* (1849), however, that he really begins to explore what he had begun to recognize as a contradiction in his, and his society's, attitude. On the one hand he admires the delightfully incompetent Dora. She is the young David's perfect dream, as well as the model for the Dickens child-wife: she has curls (a trait she shares with Pet Meagles, Annie Strong, and Cora Copperfield, to name a few); she has dimples (as do Pet, Bella Wilfer, *ad infinitum*); a small, delicate figure (Bella, Mrs. Copperfield); impractical accomplishments (she sings and paints); she is spoiled; she is unhappy with the practicalities of marriage; and finally, like his other child-wives, she has a surprising understanding of her own deficiencies.[19] She is a "favorite child of nature," David is told, and "her childish way was the most delicious way in the world" to him. But she is also for ornament, not for use. "Dora is only to be looked at, and on no account to be touched," David is prophetically warned as Dora tries on her wedding dress. In a rare look beyond the marriage ceremony into the frustrations of life with the Victorian heroine, Dickens shows us David facing a life of boredom, a life of marital emptiness, and admits that while eminently desirable in theory, the child-wife is impossible to live with in fact. But Dickens's answer to David's problem, after Dora's timely death, is the equally uninviting, equally sexless, long-suffering Agnes, in whom David finds "the source of every worthy aspiration I had ever had, the centre of myself, the circle of my life, my own, my wife, my love of whom was founded on a rock." Coventry Patmore could not have said it better.

Dickens, then, handles the problems inherent in his early complex attitude toward women by splitting—the toy, Dora; the saint, Agnes. The dichotomy is a metaphor for the identical paradox in the real thing: the Victorian princess—innocent, coy, beautiful, must be miraculously transformed into Ruskin's queen—moral guide, stellar example of saintly patience and godlike intuition. Nor was Dickens alone in his longing for this ideal with its correspondent pressure on the actual woman to meet it. Such heroines abound in the best of fiction—Amelia in *Vanity Fair,* Dinah in *Adam Bede,* Laetitia in *The Egoist,* innumerable Eleanor Bolds in Trollope, Caroline in *Shirley* (interestingly enough, Charlotte Brontë shares Dickens's mixture of affection for and annoyance at the child-woman). And just as Dickens's concept is the mid-Victorian ideal, so also can his progress be seen as a portent of some of the deeper exploration of the feminine psyche that is to come in George Eliot, Meredith, Hardy, or even later, in D. H. Lawrence, Doris Lessing, and Margaret Drabble. As Dickens wrote on, his view of women gained depth. This is not to say, of course, that he was initially unaware of the problem woman—one has only to look at Flora Finching, who is Dora grown old, Miss Havisham (Dora rejected), Mrs. Clennam (Dora embittered), or Miss Wade, who is not Dora at all. But the heroines of the novels in which these women appear are all allowed to avoid such permanent, severe neuroses, and begin to diverge from the stereotype toward individuality.

A hint of change occurs in *Bleak House;* the splitting still exists, with Dora changed to Ada, Agnes to Esther, but no longer are they given equal billing. Esther is still often treated as a child, but she has a free hand with adult responsibilities. And her title, "Little Woman," is indicative of her transitional position in Dickens's evolution. Little Dorrit is also a child, but as "Little Mother," she is beyond Esther. With Little Dorrit, Dickens let his ambiguous longing for the child-woman have free, purgative reign, for she brings with her all the purity and innocence of childhood, yet she is not a child, and laments being treated as one. The prostitute, with her knowledge of sexuality, recognizes Little Dorrit as the woman she is: "You are kind and innocent; but you can't look at me out of a child's eyes." Ultimately Arthur Clennam comes to the same realization: he accepts her proposal of marriage, and even is able to call her "Amy." But Little Dorrit must always retain most of her innocence—she rejects her real name—and she settles into the usual "modest life of usefulness and happiness." She becomes a mother to her sister's children and her own (though, significantly, we never are allowed to see Little Dorrit as an actual mother), a nurse to her brother, and a combination of both to Arthur.

After the cathartic experience with *Little Dorrit,* and partly, his biographers say, because of what he learned during his affair with Ellen Ternan, in *Great Expectations* (1860) Dickens was able to draw a complex woman, realistic in modern behavioral terms. Estella is Little Dorrit perverted—the Victorian ideal warped by revenge and hatred for men—an ominous exaggeration of the Sue Brideheads to come. Reared in a spiritual rather than a physical prison, she is a woman carefully taught not to love. And just as Dora's and Little Dorrit's asexuality has its appeal to David and Arthur, so, in this darker novel, does Estella's studied frigidity attract Pip. As with the earlier heroines, Estella is aware of her limitations; but here the limitations reach new sexual depths, and the awareness is correspondingly more profound. Estella is cured through suffering—that favorite Victorian concept—and almost as if to underscore the dual nature of her wound, the suffering is physical as well as emotional. The novel ends with a choice. Presented with the two endings Dickens was forced to write, we can have Estella forever estranged from Pip by a marriage to a Shropshire doctor whose claim to her stems from his protecting her from a beating (Drummle's horse was not so fortunate); or we can have Estella and Pip together. But the Victorian happy ending is compromised here by a subtle, almost prophetic hint of a marred domestic bliss that Hardy is to explore so profoundly, for Dickens describes their future in tones suggestive of the final lines of *Paradise Lost:* "I took her hand in mine, and we went out of the ruined place; and as the morning mists had risen long ago when I first left the forge, so the evening mists were rising now. . . ."

With Little Dorrit, the totally angelic wives of Dickens disappear; with Estella he makes a major foray into the darker side of human relations where great emotional expectations are shattered and love is made a vehicle for hate. He returns to the child-wife in *Our Mutual Friend,* but she is allowed to grow up to become the modern suburban housewife. Bella Wilfer starts as a "Dora," but becomes someone who wants "to be something so much worthier than the doll in the doll's house." She reads *The Complete British Family Housewife* with the assiduity of a Casaubon taking notes, and spends much time mastering the newspaper so that "she might be close up with John on general topics when John came home." Ibsen picks up the story from here.

"Men, I believe, fancy women's minds something like those of children. Now, that's a mistake," says Charlotte Brontë's heroine, Shirley—and George Eliot agrees. While Dickens was writing to the general Victorian audience, Eliot was taking the same stereotypes and forcing *her* readers to go deeper into the complexities of being Victorian and female. Rosamond, in *Middlemarch,* is the child-wife who learns to use her childishness with devastating skill, ultimately controlling her husband-parent in much the same way modern children do: she simply refuses to understand, and he resignedly gives up trying to explain further. But as brilliant as this portrait is, George Eliot's novel is even more important for the study it affords of the antithetical woman—the Victorian who found herself desperately wanting to be more than a mere social fixture in the outside world. A few exceptional women made it; George Eliot herself, Harriet Martineau, Helen Fawcett are representative. But Eliot's interest is in the multitudes of unexceptional women who have intellectual curiosity and who want to be more than Bella Wilfer, but who lack the tremendous strength of will required for rebellion against a system which denied women any education worthy of the name.

At the elementary level, girls were given the same education as boys. The duration of this training of course depended on class; the poor were barely educated no matter what the sex, yet even there schooling for girls stopped earlier. The education of the monied was always private, and for girls was in the hands of parents, or governesses, or fashionable schools. Whatever the source, the standard curriculum was music, dancing, art, German, Italian, French, English, morals, and religion. The schools varied greatly: some were quite good given their limited aims, others were very harsh (two of Charlotte Brontë's sisters died as the result of privations suffered in one of them). Nearly all provided little more than a superficial catechistic education; one of the standard texts was *Mangnall's Questions,* which posed such important queries as "What is a whalebone?" Anything more strenuous, it was argued by reputable doctors and educators, would be physically dangerous, taxing both the reproductive organs and the smaller brain of the female beyond their strength. Moreover, a classical education would seriously damage a woman's chances in the marriage market. Women were constantly urged "never to engage in masculine pursuits or to do anything to jeopardize the dignity of their rank or the delicacy of their sex." [20] The vacuous females that this system produced were evident in every drawing room, and eventually even the conservatives called for reforms, with some positive results. In 1852 Queen's College was incorporated (permission for the name, which tacitly sanctioned its endeavors, was given by Victoria), and the next year Bedford College was founded. Progress was slow, however; the Schools Inquiry Commission of 1864-68 reported that English girls' boarding-school education was still at best fragmentary, and though Oxford finally established the first of its five women's colleges—Lady Margaret Hall—in 1878, not until 1960 were the women's colleges granted the same status as the men's.

As the need for changes became more apparent, especially in the 1860s, the novels about educated, emancipated women proliferated. Florence Wilford's *A Maiden of our Own Day* (1862), Rhoda Broughton's *Not Wisely but Too Well* (1867), Charlotte Yonge's *A Clever Woman* . . . all have heroines who rebel against forced leisure. It was into this atmosphere that George Eliot thrust Dorothea Brooke—but without the oversimplification of the less-talented writers, for Eliot did not see the question merely in terms of a villainous system and suffering women, though she did agree in part with this simple dichotomy; Dorothea does suffer, and society, says Eliot, is guilty. In the first edition of *Middlemarch* she writes:

> Among the many remarks passed on her mistakes, it was never said in the neighbourhood of Middlemarch that such mistakes could not have happened if the society into which she was born had not smiled on propositions of marriage from a sickly

man to a girl less than half his own age—on modes of education which make a woman's knowledge another name for motley ignorance—on rules of conduct which are in flat contradiction with its own loudly-asserted beliefs.

But the fact that the phrase concerning women's education is not in the manuscript, and that she also expunged it from the second and subsequent editions, illustrates a complex ambivalence toward the contemporary lot of women. Influenced by her reading of Comte and F. D. Maurice, and undoubtedly scarred by the attacks on her because of her union with Lewes, she held a view of woman which was both somber and in some respects realistically condescending. She argues that women have almost no control over their own fates—and in Eliot's world few fates are happy. For a woman to try to shape her own life is to court disaster: she is hampered by both the emotional and physical disadvantages of her womanhood, by inadequate education, and, most likely, by lack of experience. The best course is a passive, loving one; the happiest woman the quiet, gentle one who finds her joys close to home.[21]

But while the passive women may be the happiest, and the Rosamonds the most powerful, there are those who reject both modes, who refuse to accept the finality of their poor educations, and who pursue androgynous horizons. Critical reaction to Dorothea Brooke has been as mixed as George Eliot's. Her creator treats her with both gentle ridicule and deep sympathy. The *Daily News* rebuked Eliot for being too sarcastic with Dorothea, and Robert Colby has since argued that Eliot sees Dorothea's saintliness as morbid and streaked with spiritual pride. *The Academy,* on the other hand, saw "her devotion and purity of intention as altogether beautiful," but the beauty "must always rest on a basis of illusion because there is no right place for their bestowal." [22] *The Academy's* attitude seems to approach Eliot's own. Modern critics continue to take widely varying stands on Dorothea, but whatever one's view, it must be agreed that in her Eliot has one of the finest explorations of the dilemmas facing the Victorian heroine who has the desire and the intelligence to be more than a good conversationalist, yet who, like most humans, lacks the will or talent necessary for true greatness. Dorothea is not a Florence Nightingale—in fact the *Edinburgh Review* called her "commonplace"—

but she has, in Arnold's sense, curiosity. Moreover, she has "a certain spiritual grandeur ill-matched with the meanness of opportunity"; and the mismatch, strengthened by the social limitations imposed by sex, is the root of her tragedy. Hampered by "that toy-box history of the world adapted to young ladies which had made the chief part of her education," entangled in the conspiracy of silence about sex which forces her to retain "very childlike ideas about marriage," she marries Casaubon with visions of an ivory tower replacing the doll's house—and the results are well known.

George Eliot's vision in *Middlemarch* for women is dark; and it continues to be so. After *Adam Bede* all the novels, except *Silas Marner,* are primarily concerned with a tragic heroine rather than hero, and all show the disability of being a woman—a handicap which does not necessarily make for tragedy, but plays a large part in defining the quality of tragic suffering.[23] At the end of *Middlemarch,* Dorothea accepts a marriage and a role which are unworthy of her, but with resigned bitterness the narrator observes that "no one stated exactly what else that was in her power she ought rather to have done." Powerless, lacking a will to greatness, uneducated yet curious, intuitive, intelligent—Dorothea stands for the many Victorian women who looked, often futilely, for a way out. The energy of this sort of personality, the buried life that Eliot hints of, sometimes surfaced in a drive for reform: most often it remained encased in lives of quiet desperation.

Dorothea Brooke, trying to alter her lot, ends in marriage and a life of indirection. Had she been equally intelligent, yet less financially secure, her prospects would have been even bleaker. She could have become a governess. The Victorian woman as governess is one more broad area treated in the fiction, and one more instance of the middle-class stereotype providing the touchstone for her portrayal. As any reader of Charlotte Brontë knows, the lot of a governess was likely to be wretched. Almost exclusively from the middle class but suddenly forced to work (the bank failures of the 1830s were especially effective in putting many well-bred women into the governess ranks), she became a creature in limbo somewhere between the Two Nations, and was always denied the privacy of either. Unmarried, and thus one of the half-million so-called "redundant women," she joined an estimated 24,700 in the profession. Her average yearly salary was thirty-five pounds, though some were paid nothing at all and had nothing to fall back on when they were dismissed. In 1849 Charlotte Brontë's Mrs. Pryor *(Shirley)* gives a description of their lot which remained valid for some time:

> I have been a governess myself a great part of my life.... when I was young, before I married, my trials were severe, poignant. I was early given to understand, that "as I was not [my employers'] equal," so I could not expect "to have their sympathy." It was in no sort concealed from me that I was held a "burden and a restraint in society." The gentlemen, I found, regarded me as a "tabooed woman," to whom "they were interdicted from granting the usual privileges of the sex," and yet who "annoyed them by frequently crossing their path." The ladies too made it plain that they thought me "a bore." The servants, it was signified, "detested me:" *why,* I could never clearly comprehend. My pupils, I was told, "however much they might love me, and how deep soever the interest I might take in them, could not be my friends." It was intimated, that I must "live alone, and never transgress the invisible but rigid line which established the difference between me and my employers." My life in this house was sedentary, solitary, constrained, joyless, toilsome. The dreadful crushing of the animal spirits, the ever prevailing sense of friendlessness and homelessness consequent on this state of things, began erelong to produce mortal effects on my constitution—I sickened. (chap. 21)

The governess was of course one of the most conspicious English wage-earning women, and because of her class she was also a familiar anomaly to the British reading public. The governess heroine as a fictional type emerged in the late 1830s and 1840s; Lady Blessington's *The Governess* (1839), a society novel turned social tract, was among the first, and others soon followed: Elizabeth Sewell's *Amy Herbert* (1844), Mrs. Sherwood's *Caroline Mordaunt* (1845), Anne Brontë's *Agnes Grey* (1847).[24] In fact, 1847 could well be termed the year of the governess, for two of fiction's most famous appeared: Becky Sharp and Jane Eyre. Both set a new fashion, for they considered themselves ladies first and dependents second; but Becky's tenure is short, and it is hard to remember that this was indeed her way into the drawing room (though through her we get a clear picture of just how inclusive a governess's position *could* be). *Jane Eyre* is left, then, as the epitome of governess novels.

To do the intricacies of Jane's character and characterization justice here is impossible; critical treatment of her is nearly as extensive as that accorded Dorothea (see for example, Q. D. Leavis's fine introduction to the Penguin edition). Briefly, then, in some ways she is still the typical heroine: Rochester insists on seeing her as "my better self—my good angel"; she escapes passion by mentally returning to her childhood and the moral reassurances of a ghostly mother who tells her to flee temptation (chap. 32); she represses her desires in favor of Arnoldian duty and pragmatic chastity (having Bertha as a frightening example of the alternative); and ultimately she receives the Victorian prizes of wealth and marriage. Nonetheless, in the novel Brontë is iconoclastic in several respects: she ignores social taboos by elevating the lowly governess to full, complex human stature, and also gives to a spinster passions questionable even in a married woman; artistically, she deliberately, as Mrs. Gaskell notes in her *Life of Charlotte Brontë*, "makes her heroine plain, small, and unattractive, in defiance of the accepted canon." Thematically, Brontë refuses to let Jane accept the child bride, father-daughter relationship Rochester initially proposes, or the unwholesome, sister-brother (though here not platonic) relationship so often found in Victorian novels that St. John offers her. And Jane's personality diverges greatly from formula. She runs rather than submit when faced with restraint. While admiring both Helen Burns and Miss Temple, she finds the spiritualized, altruistic life of the former and the well-regulated, restrained mind of the latter unobtainable and undesirable. She rejects passivity, and professes her love to Rochester first and last. She refuses secondary status of any sort, and accepts Rochester only after he is free, and (as many are quick to point out), she can offer a strong arm to replace his impotent one. And even the marriage is clearly deemed atypical: "I am my husband's life as fully as he is mine."

Brontë was to lose this optimism, this hope that men could

believe in and women accept equality; and in *Shirley* her independent heroine wins only by capitulating. "Conquered by love, bound with a vow," she lets her lover learn to rule by ceasing to govern. Nor would Jane Eyre's passion have been permissible a decade later. Kathleen Tillotson notes that by 1853 and the outcry against Mrs. Gaskell's *Ruth*, the Grundy era had arrived. *Jane Eyre* prophetically comments on both of these trends, for Brontë's conscious effort to counter the typical Victorian heroine testifies to the stereotype's entrenchment; the confused reactions Jane receives from men when she speaks to them as equals testifies still more to the gist of contemporary opinion. In this Magna Carta for governesses at least, the woman suffers, but she refuses to be still.

Jane Eyre met with wide acclaim, though some reviewers, obviously threatened by having their condescension toward working women put in such a glaring light, objected to giving a governess fine sensibilities. Mrs. Gaskell was to touch, with less talent, the same snobbish nerves, for she, though a middle-class lady herself, decided to concentrate on someone even lower than the governess, the shop girl.

Working-class fiction developed during the Victorian era into a vast genre in its own right. The plight of the working girl was repeatedly the subject of these novels, all composed in heads comfortably resting on antimacassars, and almost all informed by the Ruskinesque view of what a woman should be. The fact that Brontë in *Shirley* can ignore the working-class children going to work at dawn in the snow indicates how even the most sensitive of Victorians could literally avert their eyes; and it is easy to understand why they chose not to look. The Factory Act of 1833 prohibited the employment of children under nine except in silk mills, restricted the hours of factory children under thirteen to eight, and those of thirteen- to eighteen-year-olds to twelve. Women were given the hours the children could no longer be saddled with, and not until the Factory Bill of 1844 did women finally win a twelve-hour day.[25] The reduced hours were a mixed blessing: less work meant less pay, and in the depressed times of the forties and fifties the women themselves complained bitterly of being given more time at home to watch their children starve. Ironically enough, when the changes did begin, they were not necessarily made for humanitarian reasons, but often because their instigators, middle-class matrons, were horrified to learn that the proprieties were being violated. In 1842 the Children's Employment Commission published its first report on the barbaric conditions in the mines. An indignant public demanded change as soon as it learned that women were working around naked men (the heat of the tunnels made clothing oppressive), and that the women themselves often worked bare to the waist.[26]

Even Mrs. Gaskell, though stimulated to write her first novel by a working woman's simple question: "Have you ever seen a child clemmed to death?," was motivated by her realistic fears that the long factory hours would have disastrous effects on the woman's ability to be a wife and mother. Gaskell expanded the social range of the novel by bringing it into the factory, but her understanding of the plight of the working-class woman was painfully attained, and incomplete. Her depiction of women illustrates much about the separation of the Two Nations, and about the difficulty of imaginatively crossing over. Though none of her heroines are the simpering females of sentimental fiction (when they *do* faint, they fall hard, on paving stones, not couches), their values and speech are middle-class, and they are drawn by a middle-class pen. But while Mrs. Gaskell consistently underplayed the horrors of the environment, and with equal class blindness approved of the woman's placing all home duties first, her attitude toward the role of women in marriage, at least, gradually changed. In *Mary Barton* (1848), the women may treat their men like children, but the men are always recognized as superior; in *Lizzie Leigh* (1850) the wife is obedient in spite of her own views of right and wrong; in *Ruth* (1853), one of the earliest novels to attack the double standard, the wife is right in opposing her husband when he acts immorally; finally, in the title story of *Right at Last and Other Stories* (1860), Gaskell argues that it is the duty of the woman to take full responsibility for her actions.[27] With all her progress, however, she never approved of the "masculine" assertive woman, nor did she ever allow her own daughters to ignore the Victorian proprieties. By forcing sheltered Victorians to look briefly at the working class she did both of them a moral service, but the fact remains that even in the hands of her most talented spokesman, the fictional working woman was too obviously out of her class.

Nowhere is the circumscribed vision of the Victorian novel more evident than in its treatment of the lowest caste of Victorian femininity, the fallen woman, and the woman who turns her fall to profit, the prostitute. The distinction between a "fallen woman" and a prostitute is of course a real one, but the same sexual prudery that so protected most middle-class women from both knowledge and enjoyment also perpetrated an intense fear and indignation. In a system which made chastity *the* virtue, the woman who fell had great difficulty getting back up again, especially if she were not wealthy; and the woman who was down already had few ways to supplement a subsistence income other than "living on her beauty." Loss of chastity did not, of course, automatically mean the streets, but the distance from the bed to the pavement was not far, and it was traveled by many; there were an estimated 50,000 prostitutes in London alone. And venereal disease was rampant. In 1870 William Acton published the second edition of the best contemporary book on the subject, his *Prostitution, Considered in its Moral, Social, and Sanitary Aspects, in London and other Large Cities and Garrison Towns, with Proposals for the Control and Prevention of its Attendant Evils.* In it he estimated that one-fourth of the British military had venereal disease. Largely as the result of his earlier agitation, Parliament had passed in 1864-68 a series of Contagious Disease Acts, which required medical inspection of *women* upon police demand (previously such laws were applied only to animals). Though well-intentioned, the laws were viciously abused, and many women merely suspected of streetwalking were driven to it after the stigma of an inspection made them outcasts. Josephine Baker led the thirteen-year repeal crusade, and finally won in 1886.

On the fictional front the battle for compassion was also being vigorously prosecuted. Steven Marcus, in *The Other Victorians,* points out that the Victorian novel was a great humanizing agent, simply because it required its readers to look at the lower classes, and especially the fallen woman, as real people rather than as subhumans who, says the narrator of *My Secret Life,* do not feel the cold as much as the rest of us do. Dickens, like Mrs. Browning, realized the efficacy of exposure, and dotted his work with such women: Martha and Little Em'ly in *David Copperfield,* Nancy in *Oliver Twist,* the walk-on prostitute in *Little Dorrit,* to name a few. The purpose of almost all fictional treatments of fallen women was to turn middle-class disgust into sympathy—and the fallen are generally treated as objects of philanthropic concern. Usually the original seducer is wealthy or from the army, and the girl is duped into her first indiscretion (see, for example, Little Em'ly, Hetty Sorrel of *Adam Bede,* and Hardy's Tess and Fanny Robin). From then on the decline is steady, for she is usually pregnant, and an unemployable pariah. However, since the object is reform the portraits are almost always idealized; there are no female Bill Sikes among them, and society, as much as character, is faulted. But while the fictional fallen women often have hearts of gold, there is little poetic justice, and their fates are severe. Though Acton reports that in reality "no other class of females is so free from general [excluding venereal] disease," and that at thirty-five prostitutes are no worse off than women who toil at virtuous labor, in fiction they are almost inevitably racked with consumption, craving food or drink or both, and on the verge of suicidal despair. In fact, suicide was a commonplace fictional end, though it was not the only suitable way out of a seduced woman's difficulty: Dickens prescribes emigration and even lets Martha marry, while Eliot spares Hetty the noose in favor of transportation. Yet many must die, such as Esther in *Mary Barton.* In *Ruth* the fallen woman is even made the heroine (she has all the stereotypical features—beauty, gentleness, insipidity), but she too dies after giving her all in a typhoid epidemic.[28]

What is interesting about so many of these fictional portraits, however, is that they are so obviously still drawn as "Victorian." Seduced or willing, free or paid, they are made to judge themselves in strictly middle-class, moralistic terms. In spite of Acton's proof that many actual prostitutes were transients in the trade, their fictional counterparts see their fall as complete (note, for example, Esther's thoughts as she looks into the Barton home, "that Eden of innocence from which she was shut out," "that happy class to which she could never, never more belong"). Moreover, while they are often innocent victims, they see themselves as moral lepers who defile by their very touch: Esther screams at Mary, "you must never kiss me"; the prostitute tells Little Dorrit, "I never should have touched you"; Martha sees herself as "bad," "lost," with the river "the only thing in all the world that I am fit for, or that's fit for me." In an age controlled by Grundies of both sexes, the fictional message had to be muted: to reach the Victorian fireside, the fallen woman first had to be filled with remorse, assume her guilt; then she could be reformed, or transported—but at least she could not be ignored.

By the 1870s chastity was beginning to lose its hold on the Victorian conscience, and subconscious. In 1870 Dickens died, marking the end of an era, and *Middlemarch* was published in 1871 to signal the start of another. It is uncannily appropriate, then, that in that same year Thomas Hardy, the novelist who was to explore perhaps better than anyone in his time the implications of Victorian womanhood behind him and modern femininity before him, published his first book, *Desperate Remedies*. The novel, a melodrama, was the beginning of Hardy's search for form and character, a search that was to take him through a variety of genres and women.[29] In *Desperate Remedies* he wrote a sensation story; in *Under the Greenwood Tree* (1872) fanciful comedy; in *A Pair of Blue Eyes* (1873) romantic tragedy; in *The Hand of Ethelberta* (1876) a society novel; in *Far From the Madding Crowd* (1874) and *The Return of the Native* (1878) he found his form in rustic tragedy, and stayed with it to write his great novels. As eclectic as his canon are his heroines, for, in the course of his fifteen novels, he depicts all the general Victorian types we have been defining: the sentimental, docile heroine; the rebellious woman who refuses to stay home; the fallen woman who is no longer welcome there; the working woman who knows the viciousness of the machine; the neurotic woman who is the victim of being forced into an unnatural role. Even more impressive, however, is that Hardy was competent, and confident, enough in almost every case to take one representative, aggregate figure and move beyond the conventions he so familiarly dealt with into complexities that are only now being thoroughly analyzed. A close, concluding look at Hardy, then is particularly appropriate.

The "woman question" fascinated him throughout his life. He read widely in Comte, as well as Mill, though in a letter to Florence Henniker in 1895 he remarked that he was just getting to *The Subjection of Women*, "which I do not ever remember reading." He mentions *The Princess* in *The Mayor of Casterbridge*, and he obviously knew Ruskin. His unpublished notebooks also indicate that he possibly derived some of his insights into Jude's relationship with Sue (in *Jude the Obscure*, 1895) from reading George

Egerton's *Keynotes,* and that he was fascinated with Schopenhauer's uncomplimentary view of the sex, since he copied out long passages of the philosopher's *Studies in Pessimism.* (Hardy copied, for example, "It is only the man whose intellect is clouded by his sexual impulses that could give the name *the fair sex* to that undersized, narrow-shouldered, broad-hipped and short-legged race. . . . It is in woman's nature to look upon everything only as a means for conquering men. . . .") The man who created Tess obviously did not share this view, but his reading of both the Positivists and the pessimists certainly awakened him to both the saintly and the Kalian possibilities in women, engendering in him a stimulating ambivalence that forced him into an increasing awareness of the feminine psyche.[30]

Hardy was well aware that the prevailing feminine ideal was Patmore's submissive angel. Yet a quick survey of Hardy's characters proves him to be unimpressed with this idea of perfection; and his docile, subservient women, his versions of Amelia Sedley and Caroline Helstone, are the least sympathetic of his characters. Hardy does bow to the sentimental convention enough to let Thomasin Yeobright *(The Return of the Native)* survive in a story drenched in tragedy. But she also is made to reveal what is wrong with all such women when she sighs, "I wish all good women were as good as I"—a statement so indicative of popular taste that *Belgravia* used it as a caption. However, while he chose to treat rather cursorily the popular docile heroine, recognizing her for the bored and boring human being she was forced to be, he did not discard the tradition, but built on it, concentrating a great deal of his novelistic energy on a tangential type, the young girl who, stimulated by her reading, dreams or intrigues herself out of the mainstream of mundane propriety and into the world of the Romantic. Fancy Day *(Under the Greenwood Tree)* in comedy, and Eustacia Vye *(The Return of the Native)* in tragedy are the two Hardy women who define the range of his treatment of this type of "Romantic aspirant." Fancy's dreaming only frustrates, rather than harms her, and, to the satisfaction of many of her readers, she obtains her Dick Dewey and lives ever after.

It is with Eustacia, however, that Hardy risks a full-scale study of the dangers inherent in sentimentalizing and romantic ambition. Eustacia is a woman defined by the convention, but is artistically elevated far above it. She reminds one of Bourbon roses and marches from *Athalie,* but her heroes are Saul and Napoleon. She dreams, and turns her dreams into cosmic rebellion. Rather than be a docile wife, she refuses to be content with furze cutting, bridles at her husband's asexuality, curses the universe in a set speech from high tragedy, and goes off to the death dictated by Victorian poetic justice and Hardy's despairing view of existence. Yet the very fact that she remains an object of sympathy despite the selfishness of her dreams for a better life, that the novel supports a woman who was not "pure" when she married (Hardy conservatively vacillated on this point, wavering from revision to revision on her physical status), that we are led to hope that she actually makes her adulterous appointment with Wildeve, and that our final view of her is as a corpse whose "finely carved mouth was pleasant, as if a sense of dignity had just compelled her to leave off speaking," are indicative of Hardy's sense of the feminine predicament.

He gives unusual support to his women, then, no matter their faults; he is even more partisan when dealing with the fallen woman. He goes beyond the humane assertions of previous novelists that sexual victimization of the lower-class woman was an intolerable violation of human nature, to insist, in the tradition of *Ruth,* that a woman seduced, no matter what her social rank, can be pure, and is indeed capable of great heroism. It was a position most Victorians were unwilling to accept; the furor which followed the publication of *Tess of the d'Urbervilles: A Pure Woman* (1891) was even greater than that Mrs. Gaskell aroused.

Irving Howe, in *Thomas Hardy,* says Tess "is one of the great examples we have in English literature of how a writer can take hold of a cultural stereotype and, through the sheer intensity of his affection, pare and purify it into something that is morally ennobling." Tess, a woman Hardy unabashedly depicts as the ideal of luxuriant, irresistible sensuality, loses her virginity in a seduction-rape by Alex d'Urberville. But whether she is raped or merely seduced, Tess's fall and subsequent tragedy are unequivocal, and Hardy is equally clear in his casting of blame for Tess's position. Her fall is made possible by her helplessness and ignorance of passion; and her initial sorrow over the birth of her illegitimate child is caused not by her "innate sensations" but by her "conventional aspect." Tess had been educated out of the free, natural Jacobean morality of her mother and into the guilt of her contemporaries. But Tess ultimately comes to terms with her guilt, realizes that the source of her morality lies in the natural world, starts a new life, and meets Angel Clare.

Through Angel Clare Hardy makes his most devastating attack on the inhumanity of Victorian conventions for women. Clare demands of Tess absolute virtue. When he finds her flawed he rejects her, even though he has just confessed a worse transgression than hers, has admitted that Tess was victimized, has himself left the very church and society that dictate his harsh judgments. Tess's own newfound independence cannot withstand Angel's class-conscious righteousness. She reassumes her guilt, acquiesces to Clare's punishment for her, yet cannot stifle her inner sense that things are out of kilter. Angel comes to his humanity, but too late; custom and the President of the Immortals have their way with Tess. But Hardy has also had his way with the cruelties of the double standard, which he saw to be worsened by meanness and hysteria. Tess is by far his, and the period's, strongest study of female sexuality, and in creating her he adroitly captured in fiction the woman who is naturally sensuous, who first learns to be afraid of and then accepts her sensuality, but is not mentally or emotionally trained to manage it and is therefore destroyed. Some were glad to see her hang, but the way was opened for a more humane approach. In this novel at least, purity had at last triumphed over chastity.

Before turning to Sue Bridehead, Hardy's most complete study of the implications of the social and psychological structure which was Victorian womanhood, it is well to pause long enough to give him credit for depicting one type of woman that too often remained well hidden in the shadows of Victorian literature: the unabashed physical female who clearly understands sex for the weapon it can be—Arabella Donn (*Jude the Obscure*). With her, Hardy makes another major assault on class-oriented conventionality. The antithesis of Tess, she uses convention for her convenience. Sharing the Wife of Bath's disregard for propriety but lacking her compensatory wit, Arabella is often regarded as the villain. Though she is scarcely the heroine that D. H. Lawrence makes her, when he calls her the embodiment of his "female

principle," she does have redeeming features: she is never deliberately evil, she is more honest and straightforward with the world
than Sue, and she has insight into human character.[31] Arabella is
the easy object of nineteenth-century rejection; but she exists in a
novel which says that sex of itself has "nothing in it of the nature of
vice."

The ambiguity of her characterization is often taken as emblematic of Hardy's own perplexity over such animalistic, morally
empty sexuality. Yet in a Darwinian age when sexual selection was
an influential theory, he could not totally degrade what she
represents, and Arabella does survive his coarsening of her. She
leaves the novel as a woman whose assessment of realities gives her
a reliable, sensitive perceptiveness of Sue Bridehead's unhappiness.
It is the fleshy Arabella who speaks the book's final, tragic words of
truth.

But with Sue Bridehead, in whom much of the Victorian temper
achieves its logical result, Hardy reaches new depths. Her antecedents in Victorian tradition (Tennyson's Ida, Eliot's Dorothea) and
in Hardy are clear—as is her superiority in each case. Like
Eustacia, she romanticizes; when forced into it, she can momentarily be as docile as Thomasin; and she out-Tesses Tess in her
guilt. But Arabella she is not, and that is the kernel of her problem.

The nuances of Sue's neuroses have been amply discussed: D. H.
Lawrence loathes her as "the witch type, which has no sex";
Robert Heilman discusses her frigidity and the more universal
"threat of intellect to the life of feelings and emotions"; more
recently Michael Steig defines Sue in terms of Wilhelm Reich's
"hysterical character." [32] Sue clearly has an abnormal aversion to
sex, and, by extension, to marriage. But Hardy also explained in a
letter to a friend that "there is nothing perverted or depraved in
Sue's nature. The abnormalism consists in disproportion. . . ." It is
in illustrating this disproportion that Hardy juxtaposes the nineteenth and twentieth centuries.

Sue is most concisely explained as a woman with a twentieth-
century mind controlled by a nineteenth-century view of the self.
She is intellectually liberated, and could serve her mentor, John
Stuart Mill, as proof-positive of the legitimacy of his demands for
women's equality. But Sue has also been influenced by the Ruskins
of her age. Her intellect bridles at a social role that could promise

her no legal equality, could possibly place her among the 43 percent of Victorian women who had between five and nine children (17 percent had ten or more), and could both deny her the right to work at her level and force her to take slave wages. She develops her intellect, worships her pagan gods, lives platonically with a student, meets Jude as an equal. But she also marries Phillotson twice, is driven to confess her unmarried status to the landlady, cannot talk about sex to Little Father Time, and even beyond Victorianism, is repulsed by physical love. Ruskin reigns; Sue, in spite of her mind, remains an emotional Victorian.

The modern audience can recognize rather easily Sue's masochism, her hysteria, her fanatic frigidity, and her desire to return to her asexual childhood—a trait which so clearly ties her to those before her: Jane Eyre, Amelia Sedley, Catherine Earnshaw. (Interestingly enough, in many of these instances the symbolic "return to the womb" is not to safety; for Jane it means the terrible red room; for Catherine the oak-paneled bed where she wakes with a great grief, aware of sleeping alone for the first time; to Amelia it is a "dear little white bed" where for "many a long night she wept on its pillow"; for Sue it is a fetal position in a closet with spiders— all appropriate to an age where childhood and childbirth were deliberately painful.) We marvel at Hardy's ability to create such a character in an age ignorant of modern psychoanalysis, and to do it so skilfully that even while she tortures Jude she gains our empathy. He clearly understood the effects of decades of subjection, of hypocritical idolizing, of emotional slavery. In an age when sexlessness was an explicit ideal, Jude, "the Victorians," and even Hardy himself did not see Sue as grotesque. But Tess's black flag and Sue's sackcloth nightgown confirm Hardy's recognition of the great price paid by the second sex for the idealization and repression that were so much a part of the Victorian frame of mind.

With Sue, Hardy ushers the fictional woman out of the nineteenth century and into the next. While Victorian England was vainly trying to keep its women in idolatrous control and isolation, Hardy, by using and then transcending the age's own stereotypes, forced his public into an expanded awareness of the sex, and of sex itself. His last novel, centered on marriage, and his comment that the laws sustaining it are evidence that we "are

slaves of gross superstition" (unpublished letter to Preston Maxwell, January 6, 1912) signal the ironic end to an age which
literally revered the institution and created angels to stand guard
over it. Leslie Stephen once deemed the first commandment of
fiction to be "thou shall not shock a young lady." Hardy protested
against the charlatanry that made young ladies so fragile, and
called for candor in both fiction and life. The fictional forces of the
period were with him: George Gissing could focus a whole novel on
those "odd women" who preferred to stay single; and *Lady
Chatterley's Lover* was to answer the challenge the year Hardy
himself died. In that era of ambiguities as well as equipoise, the
stereotypes had remained the realities until the realities could
enjoy them no longer; and that past which still is too much the
present turned toward the ache of modernism.

Notes

1 So effective was the First Nation in closing out the Second that the
term "Victorian" has now come to mean almost exclusively the
middle-upper class. Almost 90 percent of the characters in traditional
Victorian fiction belong to the middle class or gentry, and the
Victorian woman, as described in this paper, is almost exclusively a
product of that class. Helpful for background material are Walter
Houghton, *The Victorian Frame of Mind* (New Haven: Yale University
Press, 1957); Jerome Buckley, *The Victorian Temper* (Cambridge, Mass.:
Harvard University Press, 1951); Maurice Quinlan, *Victorian Prelude*
(New York: Columbia University Press, 1941).

2 Basil Willey, in his *Nineteenth Century Studies* (New York: Columbia
University Press, 1949), pp. 199 ff. offers a good summary of Comte's
labyrinthine logic on this subject, and I am indebted to his study.

3 Jill Conway, "Stereotypes of Femininity in a Theory of Sexual
Evolution," *Victorian Studies* 14 (September 1970), 48. Spencer also
argued that there were acquired female characteristics, such as desire
for approval and capacity to deceive, born out of a prolonged
existence in a male-dominated society.

4 Havelock Ellis, *Man and Woman* (London: A. & C. Black, 1926), pp.
262, 261. For modern, corrective studies see, for example, Julia
Sherman, *On the Psychology of Women: A Survey of Empirical Studies*
(Springfield, Ill.: Charles C Thomas, 1971), or Janet Hyde and B. G.
Rosenberg, *Half of the Human Experience* (Lexington, Mass.: D.C.
Heath, 1976).

5 For a clear and helpful analysis of British civil law, see J. J. S.

Wharton, *An Exposition of the Laws Relating to the Women of England* (London: Longman, Brown, Green, & Longman, 1853). It is interesting to note that the rigid divorce laws did not hold true for Scotland, which had had equality in such laws for over 300 years, and where adultery and willful desertion were sufficient grounds. For additional information on the legal status of British women in the later part of the nineteenth century and on into the twentieth, see Vera Brittain, *Lady into Woman: A History of Women from Victoria to Elizabeth II* (New York: Macmillan, 1953).

6 See Duncan Crow's indispensable book, *The Victorian Woman* (London: Allen & Unwin, 1971), pp. 147 ff. Brittain's book, cited above, is also extremely valuable as it takes up the story where Crow leaves off; see, for example, pp. 95-115 for a discussion of women in the professions. For a history of the women's suffrage movement in Britain, see Midge Mackenzie's documentary entitled *Shoulder to Shoulder* (New York: Knopf, 1975).

7 Mrs. Ellis, *The Women of England* (New York: Langley, 1843), pp. 7, 32. Hannah More's *Coelebs in Search of a Wife* (1809) also long remained a model for middle-class behavior. For further information on the "ideal Englishwoman" see Alicia C. Percival's *The English Miss Today and Yesterday: Ideals Methods and Personalities in the Education and Upbringing of Girls during the Last Hundred Years* (London: Harrap, 1939).

8 For a good discussion of Ruskin's views on women, see J. A. Hobson, *John Ruskin: Social Reformer* (London: James Nisbet, 1899). Quotations from Ruskin are from his essay "Of Queens' Gardens" in *Sesame and Lilies,* and from *Fors Clavigera,* letter xlvi and letter xciv.

9 Coventry Patmore, *The Angel in the House: The Betrothed* (London: John Parker, 1854). Volume 2, subtitled "The Espousals," and published in 1856, also contains a prologue, twelve cantos, and an epilogue. For a detailed discussion of Patmore, see J. C. Reid, *The Mind and Art of Coventry Patmore* (London: Routledge & Kegan Paul, 1957). I am particularly indebted to Reid's pages 152-55.

10 Meredith's *Modern Love* offers a much more adult and disenchanted conception of the marriage relation, and, if space had permitted, a comparison of it with Patmore's poems would provide a useful contrast. The fact that Meredith's work was received with righteous indignation further indicates the wide acceptance of the Patmorian view. It should be noted, however, that poets did occasionally find they could say things in verse that were unsayable in prose. There is Robert Browning's ostensible support of adultery in "The Statue and the Bust," for example, or the suggestion of decisively sexual identity in Tennyson's "Mariana" and "Oenone," and in numerous Swinburne women.

11 Gerhard Joseph, *Tennysonian Love: The Strange Diagonal* (Minneapolis: University of Minnesota Press, 1969), pp. 108, 44-45.

12 Ward Hellstrom, *On the Poems of Tennyson* (Gainesville: University of Florida Press, 1972), p. 114.
13 Joseph, *Tennysonian Love,* p. 44.
14 Gardner Taplin, *The Life of Elizabeth Barrett Browning* (New Haven: Yale University Press, 1957), pp. 321, 312.
15 For a discussion of these points see Margaret Dalziel's invaluable study *Popular Fiction 100 Years Ago* (London: Cohen and West, 1957), chap. 9.
16 E. M. Delafield, *Ladies and Gentlemen in Victorian Fiction* (London: Hogarth, 1937), pp. 260, 275. For further study of Yonge see Vineta Colby's *Yesterday's Woman* (Princeton, N.J.: Princeton University Press, 1974), and Muriel Masefield, *Women Novelists from Fanny Burney to George Eliot* (1934; reprinted, Freeport, N. Y.: Books for Libraries Press, 1967).
17 Patricia Thomson, *The Victorian Heroine: A Changing Ideal* (London: Oxford University Press, 1956), p. 81. Thompson offers an excellent study of the effects of the feminist movement on the fictional heroine, though I disagree with her conclusion that there was no one widely shared ideal of Victorian womanhood.
18 Dalziel, *Popular Fiction,* p. 115.
19 Jane Stedman, "Child-Wives in Dickens," *Dickensian* 59 (1963), 113-14.
20 Quinlan, *Victorian Prelude,* p. 155.
21 Hazel Mews, *Frail Vessels: Women's Roles in Women's Novels from Fanny Burney to George Eliot* (London: Athlone Press, 1969), p. 197.
22 John Holmstron and Lawrence Lerner, eds., *George Eliot and Her Readers: A Selection of Contemporary Reviews* (New York: Barnes and Noble, 1966), p. 120.
23 Barbara Hardy, *The Novels of George Eliot* (New York: Oxford University Press, 1959), p. 47.
24 Robert Colby, *Fiction With a Purpose: Major and Minor Nineteenth-Century Novels* (Bloomington: Indiana University Press, 1968), p. 193.
25 For a complete discussion see Wanda Neff, *Victorian Working Women* (New York: A M S Press, 1966). Chapter 9 of Brittain, *Lady into Woman,* entitled "The Struggle For Equal Pay," gives a concise summary of the working woman's position from the late nineteenth century on, and is a fine supplement to Neff. Brittain points out, for example, that the horrible conditions for working women led to the founding in 1875 by Emma Paterson of the Women's Protective and Provident League—changed fourteen years later to the Women's Trade Union League. By 1913 there were 878,000 women trade unionists.
26 Crow, *Victorian Woman,* pp. 78-79.
27 Aina Rubenius, *The Woman Question in Mrs. Gaskell's Life and Works* (Uppsala, Sweden: A.-B. Lundequistska Bokhandeln, 1950), p. 75.

28 The reactions to *Ruth* are interesting. The Grundies were outraged; others, such as Dickens, Kingsley, and Mrs. Jamison considered it timely protest; Charlotte Brontë said that it did not go far enough, and objected to Ruth's death. See Thomson, *Victorian Heroine*, p. 134.

29 The book was inspired by an off-hand suggestion of George Meredith's. That Meredith was the man to stimulate Hardy is appropriate, for he, too, must be credited with greatly expanding the Victorian understanding of women. Space prohibits extensive treatment of his works, which are often viewed as the comic alternative to Hardy's tragedy. A few generalities can be included, however. He disdained the sentimental tradition, and early recognized the inherent falsity of forcing women into passive, domestic roles. His women are honest, direct, witty, intelligent. He asserts that chastity is a male fetish, not a natural feminine condition. But while his women are not saints, they do live the "Victorian" life, and are acutely aware of the dangers inherent in rebellion. The views on marriage expressed in the novels are essentially conservative, as he usually allows his heroines the conventional Victorian ending—but his women have the right to choose or reject marriage partners, and Meredith says that above all, women must have the strength and courage to make the choices life offers them. Timidity is their bane, a decidedly un-Victorian attitude. For further study see Alice Woods, *George Meredith as a Champion of Women and of Progressive Education* (Oxford: B. Blackwell, 1937), and Lois Fowler's *"Diana of the Crossways: A Prophecy for Feminism"* in *In Honor of Austin Wright, Carnegie Studies in English* 12 (1972).

30 In an unpublished letter to Helen Fawcett (November 30, 1906) he further reveals his mixture of conservatism and liberalism. Women should be given the vote, but not because they deserve it; he still sees them as the force for moral goodness: "I am in favour of it because I think the tendency of the woman's vote will be to break up the present pernicious conventions in respect of manners, customs, religion, illegitimacy, the stereotyped household (that it must be the limit of society), the father of a woman's child (that it is anybody's business but the woman's own except in case of disease or insanity). . . ."

31 See his interesting essay, "Study of Thomas Hardy," in *Phoenix: The Posthumous Papers of D. H. Lawrence*, ed. Edward D. McDonald (New York: Viking, 1936), pp. 398-516.

32 See Robert B. Heilman, "Hardy's Sue Bridehead," *Nineteenth-Century Fiction* 20 (March 1966), 307-23; and Michael Steig, "Sue Bridehead," *Novel* 1 (Spring 1968), 260-66.

7.

Marriage Perceived:
English Literature 1873-1941

Carolyn G. Heilbrun

"Wedding is destiny, and hanging likewise," Heywood wrote over 400 years ago. It appears that novelists, until the modern period, agreed with the proverb in all its implications: weddings, like hangings, marked the end of experience. The novelist averted his eyes from married life as from the grave: perhaps he suspected a resemblance between them. If married people reappeared in the fictional world, it was to take part in social arrangements—perhaps the weddings of their children—but not to reveal aught of marriage. No select society ever demanded stronger oaths of secrecy, or commanded silence with greater success. Odysseus and Aeneas, among others, have visited the dead and heard accounts of that state; when, in literature, we have heard an account of marriage, it has not been dissimilar. Achilles, having chosen glory and a short life, said, when dead, that to have the gift of life again he would be the lowliest peasant. "Oh, when I was single, my pockets did jingle," conveys the same emotion less elegantly. In Dante's Hell, one goes on doing what one is doing; in marriage, apparently, it is the same.

160

Courtship has been another matter. On the road to marriage, as on a voyage of discovery, the journey not the arrival matters. Whether because the earth must be peopled, which was Benedick's excuse, or because of all the economic factors that marriage alone rationalized, each journey was for a land unreported upon. Had the voyagers been eaten by savages, forced into obscene rites, or lost all memory of their homeland? Marriage, like death, seemed a bourn from which no traveler returned, not, at least, as more than a ghost of his former self.

Recently, however, we have heard from a returned voyager. He is a Victorian—what Steven Marcus, who has edited his report, calls an "other" Victorian. Here is his view of marriage, smuggled out of the uncharted land:

> I tried to like, to love her. It was impossible. Hateful in day, she was loathesome to me in bed. Long I strove to do my duty, and be faithful, yet to such a pitch did my disgust at length go, that laying by her side, I had wet dreams nightly, sooner than relive myself in her. I have frigged myself in the streets before entering my house, sooner than fuck her. I loving women . . . ready to be kind and loving to her, was driven to avoid her as I would a corpse. . . . My health began to give way; sleepless nights, weary days made me contemplate suicide.[1]

He remains married because, as he tells a friend, he would be all but a pauper without her money. His hate for his wife grows:

> Fear of the pox kept me awake some time. Then the scene I had passed through excited me so violently, that my prick stood like steel. I could not dismiss it from my mind. I was violently in rut. I thought of frigging, but an irrepressible desire for cunt, cunt, and nothing but it made me forget my fear, my dislike to my wife, our quarrel, and everything else— and jumping out of bed I went into her room.
>
> "I shan't let you,—what do you wake me for, and come to me in such a hurry after you have not been near me for a couple of months,—I shan't—you shan't,—I dare say you know where to go."

But I jumped into bed, and forcing her on to her back, drove my prick up her. It must have been stiff, and I violent, for she cried out that I hurt her. "Don't do it so hard,—what are you about!" But I felt I could murder her with my prick, and drove, and drove, and spent up her cursing. While I fucked her I hated her,—she was my spunk-emptier. "Get off, you've done it,—and your language is most revolting." Off I went into my bedroom for the night.[2]

A bit extreme, perhaps? Vulgar language, an obvious case of satyriasis, and the man is a brute. Let us, therefore, replace his obscenities with the discreet tones of Jane Austen:

Had Elizabeth's opinion been all drawn from her own family, she could not have formed a very pleasing picture of conjugal felicity or domestic comfort. Her father captivated by youth and beauty, and that appearance of good humour, which youth and beauty generally give, had married a woman whose weak understanding and illiberal mind, had very early in their marriage put an end to all real affection for her. Respect, esteem, and confidence, had vanished for ever; and all his views of domestic happiness were overthrown. But Mr. Bennet was not of a disposition to seek comfort for the disappointment which his own imprudence had brought on, in any of those pleasures which too often console the unfortunate for their folly or their vice. He was fond of the country and of books; and from these tastes had arisen his principal enjoyments. To his wife he was very little otherwise indebted, than as her ignorance and folly had contributed to his amusement. This is not the sort of happiness which a man would in general wish to own to his wife.[3]

Let us add to this paragraph the fact, carefully provided by Austen, that the Bennets have five children and were for many years in expectation of a sixth. How carefully we avert our eyes from what we like to think Austen has failed to tell us, failed, even, to observe.

Novelists, from the eighteenth century until late in the nineteenth, paid to marriage the tribute Chaucer paid to the Roman

Catholic Church: while little about it approached the ideal, no alternative was conceivable. For the novelist from the beginning, marriage, like money, class, property, and sex, with all of which it was, of course, intimately connected, was part of the landscape, part of that reality which Henry James defines for us as that we "cannot possibly *not* know." But, as James has elsewhere pointed out, "There is a traditional difference between that which people know and that which they agree to admit that they know, that which they feel to be a part of life and that which they allow to enter into literature." [4] It is my contention that marriage was not allowed to enter into literature, except as a condition universally acknowledged, but either unobserved, or glimpsed so occasionally that little was discovered beyond casual misery or boredom or both.

It is shocking at first to realize that all our tender ideas about marriage in literature are derived, not from marriage at all, but from courtship. Marriage as a subject for literature has been avoided with an assiduousness that would be astonishing if we had not always taken the presence of marriage so for granted that we have failed to notice its absence.

Why was the married state itself so little examined in premodern fiction? In the first place, marriage is quotidian. It takes an Arnold Bennett to seek to give us what he was to call a tragedy in a million acts: an ordinary life. In the second place, happy marriages, we are fond of saying, are not news. There has been, then, a sense in the novel, as in life, not that marriage might be happy, but that those within it might, with luck, survive. Shaw, as always, astonished us by announcing what we had not known we knew:

> . . . sensible people make the best of one another. Send me to the galleys and chain me to the felon whose number happens to be next before mine; and I must accept the inevitable and make the best of the companionship. Many such companionships, they tell me, are touchingly affectionate; and most are at least tolerably friendly. But that does not make a chain a desirable ornament nor the galleys an abode of bliss. Those who talk most about the blessing of marriage and the constancy of its vows are the very people who declare that if the chain were broken and the prisoners left free to choose, the whole social fabric would fly assunder. You cannot have the

argument both ways. If the prisoner is happy, why lock him in? If he is not, why pretend that he is? [5]

Before the twentieth century brought with it the cold Shavian shower of truth, we all assumed that marriage as a rewarding institution had been continually confirmed by novelists. As Forster said, speaking of the end of courtship novels, which is to say of most novels, "Any strong emotion brings with it the illusion of permanence, and the novelists have seized upon this. They usually end their books with marriage, and we do not object because we lend them our dreams." [6] The appeal of courtship over marriage as a literary subject is obvious: there is built in like the equipment in modern kitchens, suspense, danger, thwarted hopes, and a clearly understood reward—what, in earlier ages, they called the guerdon. The princess has been rescued, the dragon (money, averse parents, initial misunderstandings, competition) slain, the reward claimed. It begins "Once upon a time," and ends "they lived happily ever after." We all know this last phrase to be a fantasy, part of the fairy tale we tell only to our youngest children. Marriage, the true ending of comedy, amounts to integration into the society. As T. S. Eliot puts it:

The association of man and woman
In daunsinge, signifying matrimonie—
A dignified and commodious sacrament.[7]

That is the past. When, in the twentieth century, Eliot searched the wasteland, he found its essence to be in marriage: in "A Game of Chess," the two monologues signify matrimony as an undignified and sterile perversion.

If, surveying nineteenth-century literature, we look beyond England for a presentation of marriage as a viable relationship, Tolstoy is the first writer to come to mind, "All happy families are happy in the same way," he has told us in that famous first sentence. The way is soon made clear: Dolly struggles with the ironing board and convinces herself that her life is acceptable because it is more serene than Anna's, Kitty is moving the bedroom furniture when Levin wants to discuss his soul, Anna has been so revolted she has fled out of society altogether. A man might settle to be Levin or Oblansky—so might a woman—but what human being able to read Tolstoy's novel with intelligence would settle for being Dolly or Kitty? One would rather be Anna, and be dead, unless one yearned for life as unreservedly as did Achilles.

If, still surveying the nineteenth century, we consider life, as we did with the "other" Victorian, is there any marriage known to us we can point to as "alive"? (The difficulty even of finding an adjective with which to describe a "good" marriage is a clue to the problem: "successful" sounds like a business, or a machine; "happy," unreal, like a fairy tale, without complex human tensions; "good" connotes class achievement, as in "she made a good marriage.") The most obvious and best example has the misfortune of not being, legally, a marriage at all: nonetheless, the union of George Eliot and George Henry Lewes was, by any standard, a "good" marriage. I shall not restate here the account of how these two found each other, nor of how each did his best work while their "marriage" lasted. What is remarkable, however, is that George Eliot allows none of her heroines such a union, nor any destiny like her own. Gail Godwin has written of Eliot's heroines, "Each had intelligence, imagination, passion, and a keen desire to use her life to the fullest. Yet each fails or languishes through a mistaken sense of duty, or through death, before the book is done." [8] The question is a wide one. Graham Hough has noted that "George Eliot passed her personal life among the philosophic radicals, yet became the great novelist of the traditional sanctities of pastoral England." [9]

The traditional sanctities of pastoral England included, of course, marriage as the principal nexus of socioeconomic organization. Apart from all its connections with money and property, marriage was the only destiny possible to women who were trained for nothing else. We are all familiar with Charlotte Lucas's reply to Elizabeth when Elizabeth is horrified at her friend's decision to marry Mr. Collins. "When you have had time to think it over," Charlotte tells Elizabeth, "I hope you will be satisfied with what I have done. I am not romantic you know. I never was. I ask only a comfortable home; and considering Mr. Collins's character, connections, and situation in life, I am convinced that my chance of happiness with him is as fair, as most people can boast on entering the marriage state." [10] Who will wonder at Elizabeth's horror?

Who can dispute the clear-sightedness of Charlotte, twenty-seven, not pretty, forced to choose between nonexistence and the possibility of a place, however inadequate, in society, and with no illusions about marriage. Four decades later, a Charlotte Brontë heroine would cry out, "I have to live, perhaps, till seventy years. As far as I know, I have good health; half a century of existence may lie before me. How am I to occupy it? What am I to do to fill the interval of time which spreads between me and the grave? . . . Probably I shall be an old maid . . . I shall never marry. What was I created for, I wonder? Where is my place in the world?" [11]

So Edward Carpenter (1844-1929), one of the most perceptive and least acknowledged commentators of the period, watched the slow torture of his six sisters:

> For indeed the life, and with it the character, of the ordinary "young lady" of that period, and of the sixties generally, was tragic in its emptiness. The little household duties for women, encouraged in an earlier and simpler age, had now gone out of date, while the modern idea of work in the great world was not so much as thought of. In a place like Brighton there were hundreds, perhaps, of households, in which girls were growing up with but one idea in life, that of taking their "proper place in society." A few meagre accomplishments—plentiful balls and dinner-parties, theatres and concerts—and to loaf up and down the parade, criticizing each other, were the means to bring about this desirable result! There was absolutely nothing else to do or live for. It is curious—but it shows the state of public opinion of that time— to think that my father, who was certainly quite advanced in his ideas, never for a moment contemplated that any of his daughters should learn professional work with a view to their living—and in consequence he more than once drove himself quite ill with worry. Occasionally it happened that, after a restless night of anxiety over some failure among his investments, and of dread lest he should not be able at his death to leave the girls a competent income, he would come down to breakfast looking a picture of misery. After a time he would break out. "Ruin impended over the family," securities were falling, dividends disappearing; there was only one conclu-

sion—"the girls would have to go out as governesses." Then silence and gloom would descend on the household. It was true, that was the only resource. There was only one profession possible for a middle-class woman—to be a governess—and to adopt that was to become a *pariah*. But in a little time affairs would brighten up again. Stocks were up, the domestic panic subsided; and dinner-parties and balls were resumed as usual.

As time went by, and I gradually got to know what life really meant, and to realize the situation, it used to make me intensely miserable to return home and see what was going on there. My parents of course were fully occupied, but for the rest there were six or seven servants in the house, and my six sisters had absolutely nothing to do except dabble in paints and music as aforesaid, and wander aimlessly from room to room to see if by any chance "anything was going on." Dusting, cooking, sewing, darning—all light household duties were already forestalled; there was no private garden, and if there had been it would have been "unladylike" to do anything in it; *every* girl could not find an absorbing interest in sol-fa or watercolours; athletics were not invented; every aspiration and outlet, except in the direction of dress and dancing, was blocked; and marriage, with the growing scarcity of men, was becoming everyday less likely, or easy to compass. More than once girls of whom I least expected it told me that their lives were miserable "with nothing on earth to do." Multiply this picture by thousands and hundreds of thousands all over the country, and it is easy to see how, when the causes of the misery were understood, it led to the powerful growth of the modern "Women's Movement." [12]

In *Love's Coming of Age,* Carpenter had earlier characterized the marriages resulting from the female situation: "The man needs an outlet for his passion; the girl is looking for a 'home' and a proprietor. A glamor of illusion descends upon the two, and drives them into each other's arms." [13] By the eighteenth century, the unmarried woman had already ceased to be an economic asset [14] so that spinsters of some achievement were granted the courtesy title of "Mrs.," the mark of a woman who had achieved an adult role.[15] Spinsters were not written of, though Henry James wished that

George Eliot had left Dinah "to the enjoyment of that distinguished celibacy for which she was so well suited";[16] no one would write of them until Gissing's *The Odd Women* (1893), a novel whose title refers to the superfluity of women in an England where they could not possibly all find husbands and would not, probably, find any alternate destiny.

By the last two decades of the nineteenth century, then, the literary state of marriage was this: marriage was not really presented, but was accepted, like death, as one of the unavoidable conditions of life. Where we do see it in literature, marriage appears to be a situation like war, as Auden tells us, calling for "patience, foresight, manoeuvre." [17] Only occasionally is there a glimpse of a marriage which seems to hold the promise of life. In these marriages (there are examples in *Bleak House* and in *Persuasion,* with that uniquely happily married couple in all Austen, the Crofts), the woman is noted for being unusually competent, for sharing to a rare degree her husband's life, decisions, and adventures, and for being openly admired by him. What we notice here, of course, is that these marriages, like that of Eliot and Lewes, bear the marks of friendship. We shall return to this.

Oddly enough, the only extended view of a marriage in literature which can be said to be a union, not of equals but of comrades, is between men: Holmes and Watson. If we observe them in their adventures and their domestic life, we discover their relationship to be in accord with tradition to the extent that the husband, Holmes, is the unquestioned leader in all their doings; but at least Watson is a companion rather than an appendage or a domestic convenience. Commentators have often noted Watson's almost archetypal necessity to the detective story, but few have found his function also to be in the domestic comforts he offers Holmes—comforts, furthermore, which do not entail a large family and chintz on all the furniture. Rex Stout also identified Watson as a woman and Holmes's wife in an article designed to appear a shade more outrageous than it was.[18]

By the times Holmes came along, we were well into the so-called "modern" period. Nothing so well marks that period as its refusal to take marriage for granted or to be content only to hint at its defects. Courtship, while not abandoned, is now handled with more awareness of its ramifications. The economic and social confidence in marriage, not quite eroded, is being worn away by irony, sometimes by satire. Here is Wilde in 1895. Gwendolen, you will remember, has informed her mother that she is engaged to Mr. Worthing. Lady Bracknell's response is properly immortal: "Pardon me, you are not engaged to anyone. When you do become engaged to some one, I, or your father, should his health permit him, will inform you of the fact. An engagement should come on a young girl as a surprise, pleasant or unpleasant, as the case may be. It is hardly a matter that she could be allowed to arrange for herself." [19] The impeccable defenses of marriage have, for the most part, been breached. If not a union of equals, marriage has become at least a contract between two recognized parties acting on their own behalf. Childbirth does not necessarily result from marriage, and sexuality does not necessarily require it. For many modern novelists, indeed, it appears that marriage is necessary to the discovery of identity. Even in novels of courtship, the courtship is not a separate exercise, but the playing out of the marriage roles. There are no longer novels and plays of courtship; the subject now is marriage.

Charles Tansley sits at the dinner party, in *To the Lighthouse,* wanting someone to give him a chance to exert himself. Sitting opposite him, Lily Briscoe, the artist, understands this:

> There is a code of behaviour, she knew, whose seventh article (it may be) says that on occasions of this sort it behoves the woman, whatever her own occupation may be, to go to the help of the young man opposite so that he may expose and relieve the thigh bones, the ribs, of his vanity, of his urgent desire to assert himself; as indeed it is their duty, she reflected, in her old maidenly fairness, to help us, suppose the Tube were to burst into flames. Then, she thought, I should certainly expect Mr. Tansley to get me out. But how would it be, she thought, if neither of us did either of these things? [20]

It is this question, among others, the modern novel and the modern play begin to ask.

Writing in 1880 his second novel which, like his first, "nobody would publish," Shaw not only dubbed marriage "the irrational knot," but portrayed it for what it was: a matter of woman-purchase.[21] Susanna refuses to marry the man with whom she is living:

> "I can support myself, and may shew Bob a clean pair of heels to-morrow if I choose. . . . I confess I shouldn't like to make a regular legal bargain of going to live with a man. I don't care to make love a matter of money; it gives it a taste of the harem, or even worse. Poor Bob, meaning to be honorable, offered to buy me in the regular way at St. George's, Hanover Square, before we came to live here; but, of course, I refused, as any decent woman in my circumstances would." [22]

Shaw was ahead of his time, but not by much. In his 1908 play, *Getting Married,* the bride-to-be reads the marriage service, is shocked, and almost refuses to go through with the ceremony. In 1918, when Robert Graves married a young woman who was kept in a continuous state of anger by the attitude of the Huntingdon farmers to their wives and daughters, nature followed art: "Nancy had read the marriage service for the first time that morning, and been so disgusted that she all but refused to go through with the wedding, though I had arranged for the ceremony to be modified and reduced to the shortest possible form." [23]

Because the major critics between 1939 and 1969 have been men for whom marriage was still seen as the central fact of the social universe, the degree to which modern literature had come to question marriage in all its ramifications has for a long time gone unnoticed. Lionel Trilling, one of the most brilliant and influential of these critics, can speak for all of them when he reads *The Bostonians* as a novel written in praise of its hero and in fear of destruction of the old marital balance: James's novel, Trilling wrote, "is a story of the parental house divided against itself, of the keystone falling from the arch, of the sacred mothers refusing their commission and the sacred fathers endangered." [24] Trilling, like most of his peers, attributes to the novelists his own convictions about the immutability, the inevitability of the patriarchal structure, in whose arch marriage was certainly the keystone.

But the overwhelming fact which we must confront is that the modern novel is extravagantly marked, not only by its technical innovations and its "imagination of disaster," but also by its changed attitude toward marriage. We may still have novels like Conrad's which almost ignore marriage altogether; we may still have the occasional novel of courtship. Yet that strange double vision which accepts marriage as the proper end to a story, but cannot render marriage either real or vital or threatened as an institution, is gone. Perhaps coincidentally, marriage ceases to be an absolute economic necessity at the same time that it ceases to be taken as an inevitable stage in human development, like death. We can now see that James, in *The Bostonians,* was suggesting not only the utter misery to be expected from Verena's married life with Ransom—the end of the novel makes that quite clear, if the rest of the novel has not—but the agonizing difficulty of considering any other alternative for women. Indeed, from the beginning, James questioned marriage. The heroine of his first novel returns, in *The Princess Cassamassima,* to try to compensate for the terrible folly of her "economic" marriage to the Prince. We are left in no doubt in *The Portrait of a Lady* about Isabel's marriage, nor about her need to come to terms with the consequences of her having been married wholly for "economic" reasons. It is extraordinary that critics saw James in support of the old idea of marriage, but such is the simple fact.

If we think back upon the shocking passages from the "Other" Victorian, we are sharply reminded that the deep flaws in marriage might have been seen earlier if people had been able to be outspoken about sex and the marriage bed. There can be no question that marriage would have been a different institution had women been free to talk openly about their sexual experiences, and had their sense of their own sexuality been revealed. Yet, oddly enough, marriage began to be questioned in novels, by Hardy, James, and Meredith, for example, long before the strictures on writing about sex had been lifted. Furthermore, despite our present age's enormous emphasis upon sex, we did not begin to understand the reason for marriage's growing failure until we began to see what marriage ought to have in common with friendship, with companionship. Openness about sex was not sufficient to enlighten our views on marriage, nor was idealization of sexual relations sufficient to save it.

D. H. Lawrence, the novelist who most influenced the influential critics of our time, rejected the idea of marriage as combining passion and companionship. Friendship was rejected as the model for the Laurentian marriage. Searching always for an ideal of marriage and sexuality which might replace the shattered social institutions he observed about him, Lawrence, insisting upon the polarization of the sexes, looked more to the dark "phallic" knowledge of sex than to the gentler possibility of comradeship. This view, while giving us magnificent novels, led his followers sadly astray in their hopes for marriage. No wonder that Birkin, having achieved his sexual polarization with Ursula, returns to the idea of a love-friendship with a man. The question is one of the human need for intense relationships which may include, but which cannot be solely sustained by, sex. Martin Green, one of Lawrence's greatest admirers, has written of Lawrence's twentieth-century hypocrisy, "the erotic movement hypocrisy, of sexual heroics in a drama of fulfilment. It seems likely that in those late years when he was most publicly the prophet of sexual fulfilment, Lawrence himself was sexually passive. He got himself into the position of having to claim more sexual prowess, more masculine desire, than he had. . . ." [25]

Forster, in certain ways more revolutionary than Lawrence in ideas, though not in technique, asks of Helen in *Howards End:* "Had she ever loved in the noblest way, where man and woman, having lost themselves in sex, desire to lose sex itself in comradeship?" [26] Woman's desire for comradeship runs like a leitmotif through Forster's earlier *A Room with a View,* but in *Howards End* is seen connected to another idea. The desire for work, Margaret Schlegel says, "is a new desire. It goes with a great deal that's bad, but in itself it's good, and I hope that for women, too, 'not to work' will soon become as shocking as 'not to marry' was a hundred years ago." [27] If we put beside these comments Ansell's Byronic complaint in *The Longest Journey* that "man wants to love mankind, woman wants to love one man," [28] and the sad observance that nature wants dutiful sons, loving husbands, responsible fathers, "and if we are friends it must be in our spare time," [29] we begin to see that Forster understood that deep human need for something more than Eros, for which society provided no possibility. Men and women in Forster's novels might eschew marriage for friendship, but in so doing they placed themselves outside of the central social situation. In Lawrence's novels, as we have seen, men might look to profound sexuality for the redemption of marriage. Other modern authors, however, came to see that the lack of friendship in marriage doomed not only marriage, but women. As long as she was only Kurtz's "Intended," the woman to whom Marlow lies at the end of *Heart of Darkness* is incapable of entering the realm of adult reality. Marlow has already told his audience that women do not live in the real world. Even Conrad, then, whose fictional world almost excluded women, was aware that in promising themselves in marriage women declared themselves prepared only for lies.

C. S. Lewis, a devoted and lifelong masculinist, saw Eros and Friendship as distinct if not opposed kinds of love. Yet he conceived also of the coexistence of Eros and Friendship:

> Suppose you are fortunate enough to have "fallen in love" and married your Friend. And now suppose it possible that you were offered the choice of two futures: *"Either* you will cease to be lovers but remain forever joint seekers of the same God, the same beauty, the same truth, or *else,* losing all that, you will retain as long as you live, the raptures and ardours, all the wonder and the wild desire of Eros. Choose which you please." Which should we choose? Which choice should we not regret after we had made it? [30]

Lewis notices that in most societies friendships are between men and men, women and women, for "where men are educated and women not, where one sex works and the other is idle, or where they do totally different work, they will usually have nothing to be Friends about." [31] In marriage, as society and novelists before the modern period conceived it, husband and wife have "nothing to be friends about." Auden, who mentions marriage more than once in his essays, defined the securest foundation for a happy marriage as a "healthy mixture of physical desire and *philia,* a mutual personal liking based on common interests and values," where "the dominant feeling is of mutual respect between equals." [32] Novelists seem rarely to have had this view of the matter; nor is it frequently encountered even among essayists.

If we return to *Pride and Prejudice* with these definitions of marriage in mind, we see that the horror of Charlotte Lucas's marriage to Mr. Collins was not mainly the inevitable fumblings of their sex life, but the impossibility of their ever having between them anything resembling friendship. We anticipate that Darcy and Elizabeth will have a lovely time in bed, but we have hopes for the marriage primarily because each has chosen it (one in despite of economic and class concerns), and because we conceive the two as equal in their claims upon society and human relations. We trust there will continue to be dialogue between them. In short, they can become friends. It is barely possible that *Pride and Prejudice* has remained Austen's most popular novel, while not technically her highest achievement, not because it is "romantic," but because at its end the married pair are most nearly capable of what Auden calls "a mutual respect between equals."

A recent critic of the modern novel, looking at marriage as the old, established institution, inevitable, necessary, and unchanging as death, has distinguished between Meredith and James by observing that Meredith's young women move as inevitably toward marriage, and the ability to love, as James's heroines move away from it.[33] This distinction is less vital than at first appears. Meredith was essentially a comic, James a tragic writer: the end of comedy is integration into society, the end of tragedy is isolation. Meredith and James, however, are more alike than different in that both understand marriage to be doomed where all of. a woman's human qualities are not exercised within it. That Clara Middleton in *The Egoist* avoids marriage to Willoughby Patterne and is handed to Vernon Whitford, while Isabel Archer in *The Portrait of a Lady* perceives too late the disaster of marriage to Osmond is less important than that both women, one before the wedding and one after, learn what it is to be considered by one's husband merely an extension of his being.

The similarity of marriage and death ought to be looked at more closely. For the woman before modern times marriage is, except in rare instances, a kind of death. It is the death of her individual identity, the death of her as a person under law, her sexual sacrifice (for she enters into sexual experience ignorant, and without acknowledged desire, whatever may follow), perhaps her literal death in childbirth. In Woolf's first novel, Rachel contemplates marriage and then dies; the similarity of the two experiences is suggested. Ottoline Morrell wrote of her youth, "I didn't think of marrying then, and clung to my solitary liberty. I believe in many women there is a strong intuitive feeling of pride in their solitary life that when marriage really comes it is, to a certain extent, a humiliation." [34] Clarissa, achieving death in Richardson's novel, avoids marriage to the man who rapes her. Of the two states, death or marriage, death is preferable. Novelists before the modern period were as unwilling thoroughly to explore the one state as the other. Both states were too final.

My thesis that marriage for the modern English novelist is a failed institution in which passion is not supported by friendship is substantiated by the work of almost every major novelist writing after, say 1873, the year in which Hardy published *Far From the Madding Crowd,* and Butler began *The Way of All Flesh.* Hardy's work seems nowhere to have been appreciated for the important marriage novel that it is. James was repeiled by its "unpleasantly aggressive heroine." [35] Bathsheba passes through the possible marriage ideals. First there is the sexually exciting man whom every woman wants to spend a month with, but whom no woman should marry; she is saved from the usual marital fate by his death. Second, there is the man who wishes to make an idol of the woman he desires, bringing disaster upon himself and the woman. Gabriel Oak, the only man with whom marriage is possible, is a long time being appreciated, since he is so far from the socially accepted ideal. Readers have readily assumed Bathsheba to have compromised and Gabriel to be a fool. In fact, Hardy has emphasized the possibility of friendship and mutuality, rather than the glamour of romance. She had to learn that men who do not exploit her are not therefore less manly—most women have still to learn this. He has the wisdom to wait, since it is vitality and originality he admires.

Butler's novel has been more easily praised, since it holds up for condemnation not only marriage but the family, an institution whose glories people were earlier beginning to doubt. Butler, however, both in the marriage of Ernest's parents, and in the decision of the double hero, Ernest and Overton, not to marry, makes clear the bankruptcy of marriage as a personal institution, though it continues to serve the ends of society and business.

Escaping from marriage, Ernest, unlike his father, need not victimize his children to revenge himself upon the world for having, through marriage, victimized him.

The definition of marriage as a process of victimization is fully enunciated by the beginning of the eighties. Meredith's Clara Middleton, appearing in 1879, is explicit about what she loathes in Willoughby: his insistence upon envisioning her entirely as an extension of himself. Her father, in his turn, is prepared to trade her for a cellar of fine wine: she is the only payment he has to offer for such indulgences. We watch Clara escape the trap as eagerly as we follow the escape of any hunted creature: it is only comedy and the impossibility of thinking of an alternate career that give Clara to Vernon at the end. We know that Clara, like Willoughby's former fiancée, would marry King Kong himself to escape life at Patterne Hall. In 1881, Isabel Archer, victimized by the money that was to have freed her, is, like a Greek tragic hero, allowed to understand her destiny: women viewing marriage from the other side of the great divide are granted tragic perceptions of how fate has entangled them. By 1885, in his creation of *Diana of the Crossways,* Meredith has joined James in portraying the disasters of marriage after the fact. In 1886, James will write, in *The Bostonians,* his last courtship novel, one in which, as in Meredith's *The Egoist,* his perceptions of marital failure are cast back over the courtship.

By the nineties, the theme of marriage as the most sinister of arrangements begins to dominate the most lasting novels. In *New Grub Street* and *The Odd Women,* Gissing dramatizes the failure of marriage to serve either society or its incumbents. The hollowness of marriage is revealed in Ibsen's plays and in Shaw's rendition of their plots and themes in *The Quintessence of Ibsenism* (1891). By 1895, Wilde's *The Importance of Being Earnest* perfectly spoofs marriage *and* courtship, as we have seen, pausing on the way to notice that the polarization of sexual roles has contributed to this madness: "All women become like their mothers. That is their tragedy. No man does. That's his." [36]

Jude the Obscure, appearing the same year as *The Importance,* repeated in tragic form that play's farcical emphasis on the modern theme of the double. Sue Bridehead and Jude, fatally alike, destined for one another as only doubles can be, are so isolated and forced into their relationship that disaster, dramatized in Sue's refusal of sexual intercourse, is inevitable. Had they been free to choose one another, to choose their experience of passion, and their occupations, theirs would have been a wholly new kind of marriage. As doubles, they are drawn to one another in a situation where, given the society, the death of one, or both, is inevitable. "Marriage" is possible only to Jude and Arabella where, providing the opportunity for nothing but sexuality, it satisfies neither the man nor the woman.

The theme of the double is developed quintessentially by James in *The Wings of the Dove* (1902). James here presented, perhaps for the first time, the double as women. In doing so, he revealed that it is the disconnection between energy and power for the woman that has doomed marriage. Kate Croy has energy, health, intelligence, the discipline to do what she does not like, and an appreciation of the things of the mind. She is without power. Milly, without Kate's qualities, has power—that is, money—a longing for experience, and an appreciation of the things of the spirit. Inevitably, one must manipulate the other, using as instrument the man each loves. Milly achieves spirituality, Kate money, each at the price of marriage and love. While this great novel may be interpreted in many ways (and has been), its testimony to the cost of female powerlessness has been little noticed. The reason, no doubt, includes the inability of critics to admire energy in a woman (it is always called aggression or manipulation) since they expect and approve woman's passivity and spirituality. Milly's great and final act is not dovelike; on the contrary, it is to give power, money, the least spiritual and "feminine" of forces.

The Edwardian period, famous for its golden afternoons, also deserves fame for relentless consideration of marriage in all its disastrous aspects. The strange double standard of the premodern years has utterly dissolved: courtship no longer evolves toward a marriage shown to be despicable in the society the novel presents. Marriage, for all but Conrad, is, in the modern novel, neither ignored nor denigrated in the comic mode. The Edwardian period brought four of Forster's novels, James's major marriage novel, *The Golden Bowl*, and the works of Wells and Bennett which, whether futuristic or naturalistic, showed forth marriage's failures. In the theater, the subject of marriage is ubiquitous. Of the five plays, for example, reprinted in Gerald Weales's anthology, *Edwardian Plays,* four have marriage as their major theme, the fifth confronts it at least by implication.[37] Hypocrisy about marriage is seen as the marriage trap's chief mechanism.

The Edwardian period can be said to close with the publication of *Dubliners* (1914), *The Good Soldier* (1915), and *The Rainbow* (1915). Within *Dubliners* itself can be seen the modern period's progress toward its final realization of marriage as an analogy for death. What Joyce was to call the paralysis of Dublin life is set forth with marriage and the hope of courtship ("Evelina") and fear of entrapment ("A Painful Case") as chief marks of lifelessness. The final great story, "The Dead," displays among much else, the picture of a marriage in which the woman has never really been *seen.* A symbol to her husband, recognized at a party only by her dress, encountered only through society's protective covering (a heliotrope envelope, a glove), Greta reveals herself, and her husband's spiritual deadness, in one moment when Gabriel's desire is exposed as lust and his tenderness as condescension.

The Good Soldier, whatever is to be believed concerning the narrator's competence, is indisputably a novel about marriage's failure to serve any purpose whatever. Dowell ends by loving the mad Nancy: "I should marry Nancy if her reason were ever sufficiently restored to let her appreciate the meaning of the Anglican marriage service." [38] Perhaps the novel can be said to be critical of all upper-class life, at least in modern times. But marriage is the paradigm of that life for Ford, here and in his great tetralogy, *Parade's End.*

Lawrence's *The Rainbow* could qualify as a disquisition upon the failure of marriage. From this failure there emerges an individual, Ursula. But, once into the twenties and *Women in Love,* Lawrence can see her only as the mate for the proper man; married to him, she disappears from the novel. Lawrence tells us that the marriage succeeded, but even so he does not lie to us. He allows us to see that Ursula is an appendage, and little more. Gudrun, the artist, the woman who will not submit to marriage, has not yet been seen by critics as more than destructive.

Gudrun was prologue; with Virginia Woolf in the twenties came the first full fictional development of the woman as artist. Inevitably, she could not marry. Having presented, in *To the Lighthouse,* the cannibalism of marriage, Woolf ended her final novel, *Between the Acts,* with a marital confrontation stripped of all societal association and returned to its beginnings.

> Left alone for the first time that day, they were silent. Alone, enmity was bared; also love. Before they slept, they must fight; after they had fought, they would embrace. From that embrace another life might be born. But first they must fight, as the dog fox fights with the vixen, in the heart of darkness, in the fields of night.[39]

The figure who perceives this marital scene is La Trobe, the woman artist. Husband and wife are her creations, part of her new play, while she remains single, and, as far as is possible for human beings, autonomous.

Woolf is the only woman writer of the modern period to challenge in a profound way conventional views of marriage. Katherine Mansfield, it is true, looked at marriage and saw that it was bad, but the quality of her insights, not their innovativeness, is notable. Alone in the twenties and thirties, Woolf conceived of marriage as partaking more of friendship than of passion. Unlike George Eliot, she was able to translate into her fiction the marriage she lived. This is how Nigel Nicolson describes it:

> When two people of independent minds marry, they must be able to rely upon each other's tolerance, affection and support. Each must encourage, without jealousy, the full development of the other's gifts, each allow the other privacy, different interests, different friends. But they must share an intellectual and moral base. One of them cannot be philistine if the other is constantly breasting new ideas. They cannot disagree wildly on what is right and wrong. Above all, their love must grow as passion fades . . . particularly if they have no children.[40]

What the Woolfs experienced, and what Virginia Woolf re-created in fiction, was the need of individuality in marriage, of space: "A love affair brings human beings unnaturally together," John Bayley has written, "while marriage keeps them the right and dignified distance apart." [41] In the popular mind, and for many years among the "manly" critics, the ideal of marital passion and "togetherness" has persisted in the face of all evidence that these are the signs of a love affair, not a marriage. As views on marriage begin slowly to alter, Woolf will, I think, be seen in this regard as prescient. Mrs. Dalloway's marriage to Richard in *Mrs. Dalloway* is not ideal, in any romantic sense. Yet her decision that life with Peter Walsh would have forced them always "unnaturally together" is correct; indeed, within the novel, Clarissa can be seen to move from being Mrs. Dalloway to becoming herself, Clarissa. Surely this, rather than development toward a greater dependency, is the proper movement within a marriage. "Taking other people's reality for granted," John Bayley has also said, is "the first requirement of love." [42] But it is the requirement most breached in marriage. We know the Dalloway marriage has served both partners, for Richard brings flowers to express his love, and she herself is recognized, at the end, as triumphantly "there."

Woolf is, of course, feminist in the profoundest sense, insisting upon the autonomy of female, as well as male, persons. Rachel Vinrace, and, even more, Katherine Hilbery perfectly understand this. So, in fact, does Eleanor in *The Years,* though they all think she is sterotypically an "old maid." Whatever the problems of humanity in the twentieth century, marriage, as Austen conceived it, does not hold the solution: that much Woolf makes clear. For all her revolutionary techniques, for all her innovations in the use of time and language and reality, she is nowhere more radical than in her perception that marriage, if it is not companionship, celebrated by the breaking together of bread, is nothing. She had discovered this truth in her own marriage:

> They never experienced jealousy of another person or of a talent unshared. She deeply respected his judgement on what meant most to her, her writing; and he, lacking the flight of searing imagination and recognizing that she possessed it, shielded her, watched her fluctuating health, nurtured her genius, and with instinctive understanding left her alone in a room of her own, while he remained always available in the common room between them. [43]

Today, past the so-called modern period, Doris Lessing is the single British woman writer who questions as profoundly as did

Woolf marriage and the patriarchal society it supports. More political than Woolf in her insights, Lessing writes of the connections between marriage and the economic structure of society. It is no accident that Lessing, though she is far from a writer of comedies of manners, has called Meredith "that astonishingly underrated writer." [44] In this perception she celebrates the moment when the novel turned its back upon both patriarchy and the accepted marital conventions, and looked to the new demands women might make now upon the most unexamined of institutions. Modern writers have at last established that the unexamined marriage, like the unexamined life, is not worth living, and that Eros alone will not sustain an institution which has lost, or totally transmuted, its social and economic justification.

Notes

1 Steven Marcus, *The Other Victorians* (New York: Basic Books, 1964), pp. 91-92.
2 Ibid., pp. 93-94.
3 Jane Austen, *Pride and Prejudice* (New York: W. W. Norton, 1966), p. 162.
4 Henry James, "The Art of Fiction," in Henry James, *The Future of the Novel*, ed. Leon Edel (New York: Vintage Books, 1956), p. 25.
5 George Bernard Shaw, *Man and Superman*, act 3.
6 E. M. Forster, *Aspects of the Novel* (New York: Harcourt, Brace, 1927), pp. 86-87.
7 T. S. Eliot, "East Coker," *Four Quartets*. T. S. Eliot, *The Complete Poems and Plays* (New York: Harcourt, Brace, 1952), p. 124.
8 Gail Godwin, "Would We Have Heard of Marian Evans?" *Ms*, September 1974, p. 75. Godwin goes on to confess: "As a novelist myself—and one who has, so far, denied my heroines the crucial strengths and options I myself have needed—I am fascinated by this question of why so many of us deny our heroines what we refuse to deny ourselves."
9 Graham Hough, *The Last Romantics* (New York: University Paperbacks, 1961), p. xi.
10 Austen, *Pride and Prejudice*, p. 88.
11 Charlotte Brontë, *The Professor* (1845, 1857), chap. 10.
12 Edward Carpenter, *My Days and Dreams* (London: Allen & Unwin, 1916), pp. 30-32.
13 Edward Carpenter, *Love's Coming of Age* (New York: Modern Library, 1911), p. 80.
14 Ian Watt, *The Rise of the Novel* (Berkeley and Los Angeles: University of California Press, 1959), p. 145.

15 Hazel Mews, *Frail Vessels* (London: Athlone Press, 1969), p. 173.

16 Quoted in ibid., p. 102.

17 W. H. Auden, "Fairground," in *City Without Walls* (London: Faber and Faber, 1969).

18 Rex Stout, "Watson Was a Woman," rpt. in Howard Haycraft, *The Art of the Mystery Story* (New York: Grosset & Dunlap, 1947), pp. 311-18.

19 Oscar Wilde, *The Importance of Being Earnest,* act 1.

20 Virginia Woolf, *To the Lighthouse* (New York: Harcourt, Brace, 1927), p. 137.

21 Mona Caird, in articles in the *Westminster Review* which appeared from 1888 to 1894, found the evils of modern life to have their origin in the patriarchal custom of woman-purchase. Quoted in Amy Cruse, *After the Victorians* (London: Allen & Unwin, 1938), p. 129.

22 Bernard Shaw, *The Irrational Knot* (London: Constable, 1909), p. 220.

23 Robert Graves, *Good-bye to All That* (Garden City, N. Y.: Doubleday Anchor Books, 1957), p. 272. There is no indication that Nancy has heard of the Shaw play.

24 Lionel Trilling, *The Opposing Self* (New York: Viking Press, 1955), p. 117.

25 Martin Green, *The von Richthofen Sisters* (New York: Basic Books, 1974), p. 173. Green goes on in this passage to compare Lawrence to Max Weber, who was involved in the opposite hypocrisy.

26 E. M. Forster, *Howards End* (New York: Vintage Books, 1921), p. 311.

27 Ibid., p. 110.

28 E. M. Forster, *The Longest Journey* (New York: Vintage Books, 1962), p. 88.

29 Ibid., p. 69.

30 C. S. Lewis, *The Four Loves* (London: Fontana Books, 1960), p. 64.

31 Ibid., p. 68.

32 W. H. Auden, *Forewords & Afterwords* (New York: Vintage Books, 1974), p. 64. The same definition is repeated on p. 101.

33 Donald David Stone, *Novelists in a Changing World* (Cambridge, Mass: Harvard University Press, 1972), p. 135.

34 *Memoirs of Lady Ottoline Morrell,* ed. Robert Gathorne-Hardy (New York: Knopf, 1964), p. 72.

35 Stone, *Novelists,* p. 77.

36 Wilde, *Importance of Being Earnest,* act 1.

37 *Edwardian Plays,* ed. and with an introduction by Gerald Weales (New York: Hill and Wang, 1962). The plays are: Maugham, *Loaves and Fishes;* Hankin, *The Return of the Prodigal;* Shaw, *Getting Married;* Pinero, *Mid-Channel;* Granville-Barker, *The Madras House.*

38 Ford Madox Ford, *The Good Soldier* (New York: Vintage Books, 1951), p. 236.

39 Virginia Woolf, *Between the Acts* (New York: Harcourt, Brace, 1941), p. 219.

40 *The Letters of Virginia Woolf: Volume II: 1912-1922,* ed. Nigel Nicolson and Joanne Trautman (New York: Harcourt Brace Javanovich, 1976), p. xiii.
41 John Bayley, *The Characters of Love* (New York: Basic Books, 1960), p. 229.
42 Ibid., p. 273.
43 *Virginia Woolf Letters: Vol. II,* p. xiv.
44 Doris Lessing, *A Small Personal Voice* (New York: Knopf, 1974), p. 28.

Images of Women in
Early American Literature *

Ann Stanford

The period of our early literature covers roughly 200 years—from the arrival of the Pilgrims at Plymouth and of women in the Jamestown colony in 1620 to the early years of the republic just after 1800. The literature itself embraces almost half a continent, from the growing cities of the seaboard to the western frontier, from the clustered villages of New England to the widespread plantations of the South.

The writings of the period were mostly pragmatic in purpose— to argue, exhort, or record; the women who appear in much of what was written in both North and South are real women moving through the pages of journals and accounts of travel, sermons, and books of right conduct. Only in the early eighteenth century do fictional women begin to appear in the form of writers of letters to the newly burgeoning presses in various cities, letters written most often by men, but signed with women's names. It was for local newspapers or in pamphlets printed by local presses that American

* This essay was written in part under a grant from the National Endowment for the Humanities.

authors wrote most of their poetry and fiction up until the waning years of the eighteenth century. In those last years American writers began to turn to the novel, and adopting the English sentimental mode, they showed women most often as victims of seduction or as captives of the native American tribes.

The actual lives of women during these centuries varied. Their circumstances depended on whether they lived in the northern, middle, or southern colonies, or near the older settlements or on the frontier; whether they came from the upper, middle, or lower classes or were Indians or slaves; and whether they lived in the country or the city. A few generalizations may, however, be made.

From the first the family was an important unit in the colonies. As soon as the early New England villages began to expand, families moved out into the newly opened lands, often in closely related groups. With such dispersal, the established government and the church, even in New England, became less significant in the structuring of society than was the family.

Within the family, women held a place outlined and restricted during the seventeenth century by a literal interpretation of the Bible; they were to be proper helpmeets to their husbands. Nonetheless, they were important in the family structure. In New England, and often in other colonies, they ruled their households, second only to their husbands; they were given charge of servants and children, often even of whole farms when their spouses were away. Moreover, upon the deaths of husbands and during the minorities of their children, many women continued to supervise farms and a wide variety of businesses.

Because there was generally no system of primogeniture in America, except for a time in the South, accumulated lands were often subdivided among the sons of a family until they became too small for further division. Parents then needed to provide for their sons an education in a profession or trade or some other means of livelihood. For their daughters a suitable dowry of money or goods was arranged at marriage. Women were not educated to go into trades or professions, but in keeping with their ordained role, were trained in the skills of the household. Generally, in New England and in families who could afford education, girls were taught to read. But since reading and writing were often taught separately, many could read who had not learned to write. Higher education was closed to women, though a few women became fairly well educated through reading and with the assistance of tutors; Mercy Warren, for example, was educated along with her brother.

Overlying the economic and familial roles of women was the class system brought from England and the class and caste system developed in the South during the eighteenth century. Even where primogeniture was not practiced, or perhaps because it was not, the rank of a family as a whole was important. Even that humble band of farmers and tradespeople who formed the colony at Plymouth were conscious of such distinctions; William Bradford describes how the original plan for producing crops as a commune had to be abandoned in part because it did not allow for differences of rank and age. In John Winthrop's *Journal* gentility takes precedence over sex as a means of ranking. His pages show the greatest deference toward the Lady Arbella Johnson, the person of highest rank in the great immigration of 1630. She occupied the "great cabin" on the ship *Arbella*, which had been renamed in her honor. Until 1769 the students in classes at Harvard were seated according to rank by birth; John Adams, for example, was fourteenth in his class, and he owed even that modest place to his mother's side of the family.[1]

From the beginning, at least in the settlements most in touch with England, particularly in the cities and the areas along the Atlantic coast, the styles of England were followed in clothing and furniture, household decoration, and other arts. As early as 1647 Nathaniel Ward's *Simple Cobler of Aggawam* satirized the effort made by Puritan women to be in fashion, ridiculing their dress and their inquiries about what the Queen was wearing at court.[2] Styles in literature likewise came from abroad. It was easier to obtain books from England than from other colonies, and the depiction of manners in English books and newspapers served as models for the colonists. The provincial attempts of Americans to imitate the manners of the English upper classes became part of the satire in such late eighteenth-century pieces as Trumbull's *Progress of Dullness* and Royall Tyler's *The Contrast* just as they had in the earlier work of Ward. These and other writers of the later period, like Dr. Benjamin Rush and Charles Brockden Brown, could show that even though the biblical restrictions on the role of women had lost force, women were still restricted by manmade law and custom and were subject to the psychological and physical domination, and sometimes oppression, of men in the form of seducers, captors, or unsympathetic fathers or husbands.

Indeed, much writing in both the seventeenth and eighteenth centuries attempted to indicate the acceptable roles and attitudes of women over the 200 years of changing values. Women depicted in the early literature are forthright, earthy, and capable. Toward the end of the period, as luxuries increased and styles in literature changed, they are more often shown as lacking in education, often oppressed, given to expressions of vaporous sentiment, and dependent upon fathers, lovers, and husbands. The forms of literature also changed during the period, moving from scattered accounts of women in journals, sermons, and pamphlets, through the beginnings of native storytelling in the Indian captivity narratives and fictional letters to newspapers, and finally to the representation of women as major characters in the tales and novels of the dawning age of fiction.

Because of the reportorial nature of the writings of the seventeenth and much of the eighteenth century in America, however, the images of women in the literature are often accounts of real women, usually brief and fragmented. In relatively few pieces of writing do we find the focus on one woman over a period of time that occurs in imaginative literature. Hence, in looking for such images, especially during the seventeenth century, we may best gain an overview from the rare longer pieces that reflect the lives of individuals. The women at the center of these are Anne Hutchinson, Anne Bradstreet, Mary Rowlandson, and Sarah Kemble Knight. All were educated New Englanders representative of the upper or middle classes. All but Anne Hutchinson told their own stories.

In 1637 the Reverend John Cotton in the meetinghouse at Boston turned to his devoted parishioner, Anne Hutchinson, and reminded her of the whole sum of woman's duty. "The Lord hath indued yew with good parts and gifts fitt to instruct your Children and Servants and to be helpfull to your husband in the Government of the famely," he said. Admittedly Mistress Hutchinson had helped her sisters, he continued, turning to the women of the congregation, but "let not the good you have receved from her, make you to reaceve all for good that comes from her; for you see she is but a Woman and many unsound and dayngerous principles are held by her." [3] Thus in a dramatic moment in the Boston meetinghouse Cotton defined and circumscribed the orbit within which woman might comfortably move—the orbit of piety, house-wifery, service to neighbors, and assistance and obedience to the husband or father, who represented within the family the authority of both church and state.

The story of Anne Hutchinson and her attempt to transcend this narrow round was told in the pamphlet war that developed as an accompaniment to the outbreak of the Civil War in England. In the controversial tracts Anne Hutchinson became the first woman extensively portrayed in the literature of New England. She became an almost fictional personage, denounced as a Jezebel by the Bay colonists and depicted as victim by their antagonists, who attempted to discredit the congregationalist form of church organization developed in the Bay.

In 1644 a London publisher brought out Governor Winthrop's defense of the Bay Colony's conduct in the Hutchinson affair in a pamphlet titled *A Short Story of the Rise, reign, and ruine of the Antinomians, Familists & Libertines, that infected the Churches of New-England: ... Together with Gods strange and remarkable judgements from Heaven upon some of the chief fomenters of these Opinions; And the lamentable death of Ms. Hutchison.* The *Short Story* was a mere collection of documents pertaining to the trial and excommunica-tion of Anne Hutchinson; however, in its second edition, published later that year, Thomas Weld, the colonial agent in London, tied the whole together with a lengthy introduction, in which he spared no detail to discredit the erstwhile prophetess. Winthrop had compared her countenance during the trial to Daniel's "lions . . . let loose." Weld attacked her through womanly, satanic, and serpentine images. Her errors were "brats hung up against the Sunne" which the Antinomians "hatched and dandled." Her weekly lectures let loose venom which diffused through the veins and vitals of the people. The miscarriage which Anne Hutchinson, who had already borne at least fourteen children, underwent after the ordeal of the trial and the rigorous journey to Rhode Island, Weld viewed as a judgment of God, for she "brought forth not one . . . but . . . 30 monstrous births . . . at once." The thirty monsters were comparable to the thirty erroneous opinions added up against

Mrs. Hutchinson during her interrogation. Weld viewed her death at the hands of Indians "neare a place called . . . Hell-gate" as a proper judgment of God, asserting that the Indians in those parts had not killed other settlers. Obviously, Weld comments, "Gods hand is the more apparently seene herein," and he concludes, "Thus the Lord heard our groanes to heaven, and freed us from this great and sore affliction."

The government of the Bay Colony was hostile toward the Antinomians because the latter represented a threat to the rigid patriarchal union of ministers and magistrates who ruled the colony. Anne Hutchinson's party was strongly supported by women, many of whom she had nursed through childbirth or illness. Eventually their enthusiasm for her teaching brought about the downfall of the Antinomian movement itself, for her followers brought their husbands to her meetings. Thus she was left open to the charge of teaching men as well as women, contrary to the admonition of St. Paul. Mrs. Hutchinson violated Puritan doctrine in other ways as well. Her belief in revelation and the indwelling of the Holy Spirit threatened to set the guidance of the heart over that of duly constituted authority, the revelations of women over the intellectual arguments of the ministers.

In the accounts of her contemporaries, most of them her adversaries, Anne Hutchinson is portrayed as an imperious and argumentative woman, intelligent, serving her neighbors, but stubborn and determined to have her own way, a woman who gloried in her power and her sense of personal revelation, and who even took hope from the afflictions of excommunication and exile. She is matriarchal in the leadership of her family. Little is said of that husband who came with her to the new world, uprooting himself from the comfortable house and business in Alford. William Hutchinson is quoted once, however, in the report of the emissaries from the Boston church to the exiles in Rhode Island: "mr Hutchison tould us he was more nearly tied to his wife than to the church, he thought her to be a dear saint and servant of god" (Hall, p. 392).

Although Hutchinson's love for his wife may have bordered on the sin of caring too much for one who was a mere creature, conjugal love itself was one of the attributes required of Puritans, for the Bible commanded spouses to love one another. For this reason, young Puritans, though their parents arranged marriages for them, were not forced into those in which mutual love might not be possible. Both Anne and William Hutchinson and their younger contemporaries, Simon and Anne Bradstreet, furnish examples of devoted married love.

Anne Bradstreet represents far more than this, however. Her life and her published work illustrate the process of immersion in a new environment, at first seemingly strange and hostile, which becomes in time the landscape of home. She is also the representative, *par excellence,* of the educated, intellectually vigorous immigrant who made up the first generation of settlement in New England. Coming as they did from the Old World, these first immigrants had a broader world view than that of their immediate descendants. Moreover, Anne Bradstreet was educated by tutors in the house of the Earl of Lincoln in the generation that followed the death of Queen Elizabeth, and she had absorbed the ideas of mighty projects—both literary and worldly—that the great writers of that preceding age had propounded. Nevertheless, unlike Anne Hutchinson, Bradstreet was careful not to go outside the limits permitted women in the patriarchal society. She admitted the superiority of men, albeit sometimes ironically, and conformed in almost every outward way to the ideal reiterated in countless sermons and pamphlets of advice to married women throughout the century.

She herself set forth the ideal in an epitaph on her mother, Dorothy Dudley, who died in 1642. Dorothy Dudley, wrote her daughter, was a pious woman, an obedient wife, a loving instructor of her family, and a good neighbor; and she presided justly over a large household of children and servants, giving reward or punishment as their conduct deserved. Anne Bradstreet, too, according to John Woodbridge, the editor of her book *The Tenth Muse* (London, 1650), practiced similar virtues. He praises her pious conversation and her management of her household. Her poems were written, he adds for the benefit of a society dedicated to industry, only in moments "curtailed from her sleep and other refreshments." [4]

Although Woodbridge sets forth Mistress Bradstreet's conformity to the pattern of ideal Puritan wife, her fame as spread by *The Tenth Muse* depended upon her learning. Even so, her "learned" poems all too often were weakened by her recognition that she was writing as a woman invading territory considered "masculine." [5] In the "Prologue" she denies that she is a poet in the epic sense, or a historian, though she included much that passed as knowledge in the quaternions and she attempted the history of the world in her "Four Monarchies."

The woman she reveals in her personal poetry is more at ease. She appears to be much in love with her husband. Several of the love poems sent to Simon while he was away on public business describe him as the sun that warms his spouse the earth; the lonely wife speaks of the children who "through thy heat I bore" and begs him to return. The invitations to return are playful, good-natured, and above all sensual, taking their erotic imagery from the Song of Solomon via Francis Quarles's elaboration in *Sions Sonets,* a dialogue between the bride and the heavenly bridegroom. In bringing biblical imagery to an earthly love, Anne Bradstreet increases the impression of a passionate regard. In her appeals for him to return, she set forth a theme which must have been echoed many times by the wives of the planters in North and South, whose men were often away for long periods as statesmen, merchants, soldiers, or lawyers or ministers on circuit.

As a mother, Bradstreet at times takes a candid, earthy view of the problems of rearing children. During the first childless years of marriage she had longed for children; after her four boys and four girls were born she cared for them skillfully and lovingly, and they all lived to maturity. There is no question of her devotion to her children and grandchildren; yet she is also able to describe the desperation of a parent trying to quiet a crying child, the discomforts of the nine months of pregnancy, and the sufferings of the mother in childbirth, as well as the fear of dying at such a time. In describing such pangs and fears, the mother need feel no Freudian guilt at sometimes depicting the child as seeming to delight in tormenting her, for the child according to Calvinistic doctrine is "stained from birth with Adam's sinful fact" and hence naturally depraved. This somewhat antagonistic view of the child is adopted only in "Childhood," part of a series that recounts the good and bad of each of the four ages of man. In other writing, such as the family elegies, the prose, and certain poems of the notebooks she expresses her continuing love for her children.

"Before the Birth of one of her Children" attempts to retain the all-important love of her husband even in death. The poem is directive rather than moving; the only figure in it, her request that Simon "kiss this paper for thy love's dear sake," is an exaggeration perhaps picked up from a romance. Nevertheless, her fear that she might die in childbirth and her concern for her children in that event are intensely serious; this personal valedictory, like some of the poems in her notebooks, was meant more for utility than for art. (The risk of death must certainly have been in the minds of women facing childbirth during the early period. In a study of the population of the Plymouth Colony in the seventeenth century, John Demos estimates that slightly fewer than one in five deaths among adult women resulted from causes connected with childbirth. In other words, the mother died in an average of one in thirty births.[6])

Later, in the poem "In reference to her Children," Anne Bradstreet shows more of her usual wit as the mother both concerned for her children and proud of them. In some ways the later poem resembles "The Author to her Book" where she describes her attempts to make the book presentable just as she would wash the face of a child and dress it up before letting it out in public. In other passages, too, she responds to her children with pride or understanding. *Meditation X* seems surprisingly modern; she writes that all children differ, and "those parents are wise that can fit their nurture according to their Nature."

Bradstreet demonstrates an ability constantly to adjust to nature and her environment in other ways too, perhaps one of the traits of character needed by a woman on the frontier of civilization. Born a member of the gentry and raised in the household of the Earl of Lincoln, where her father held the high post of steward, the sight of the New World must have been even more depressing to her than to emigrants from less wealthy and cultivated backgrounds. Bradstreet admits that her "heart rose" against the New World and new manners at her first coming into the country, but "finding it was the will of God" she submitted. The flexibility which allowed her to bow to the inevitable helped her through the difficult early days of settlement, the several moves from a settled community to a new plantation, and the long absences of her husband. No doubt she was sustained in the New World also by her love of learning and of writing.

Anne Bradstreet had few feminine models to follow in her dedication to literature. There had been women who wrote during the sixteenth century among the queens and aristocrats, women like Queen Elizabeth and the Countess of Pembroke, but Anne Bradstreet was the first woman to write with professional perseverance. Her dedication was not without opposition. Her comment in the "Prologue" that she was liable to censure by "each carping tongue/Who says my hand a needle better fits" was followed by a plea to the masculine sex to "grant some small acknowledgement" of women's accomplishment. She made the plea after saying what everybody knew—"Men can do best, and women know it well." However, in her elegy on Queen Elizabeth she went farther in her feminist pose: "Let such as say our Sex is void of Reason,/ Know tis a Slander now, but once was Treason."

Despite her outbursts in the "Prologue" and the elegy on Queen Elizabeth, she avoided the fate of Anne Hopkins, the wife of the Governor of Connecticut, who lost her understanding by "giving herself wholly to reading and writing," according to the journal of Governor Winthrop. Had Mrs. Hopkins but "attended her household affairs, and such things as belong to women, and not gone out of her way and calling to meddle in such things as are proper for men, whose minds are stronger . . . she had kept her wits and might have improved them usefully and honorably in the place God had set her" (April 13, 1645).

In contrast, despite a lifelong devotion to learning, Anne Bradstreet apparently wholly embraced the position within the household to which the religious and social beliefs of her society assigned her. In size, the Bradstreet family, with its eight children, was typical, the average number of children per family in the first generation at Andover being 8.3. Recent demographic studies, particularly those of Philip J. Greven, Jr., at Andover and John Demos at Plymouth, have revealed that the early colonists in the country towns of Massachusetts were healthier and longer-lived than historians had heretofore suspected. Of every 1,000 children born in Andover between the years 1640 and 1669, from 890 to 917 survived to age 10, and 877 to 907 lived at least to age twenty.

Nearly four-fifths of the men lived to be at least fifty. The records for women were less complete, but indicate that nearly three-fourths of the women reached fifty, more than half reached sixty, and over a third reached seventy. The survival of both partners in marriage was greater than a scattered reading of journals may have led us to believe. Of the first-generation men, 67.6 percent had only one wife; in the second generation this figure increased to close to 75 percent. John Demos, finding similar figures at Plymouth, comments, "The old stereotype of the doughty settler going through a long series of spouses one after the other needs to be quietly set aside." [7]

Though the country towns during the first decades of settlement were generally healthy, the newer towns were occasionally subjected to the danger of conflict with the native Americans. Unfortunately, there are few pieces of writing from the early years that look at such clashes from a viewpoint other than that of the colonists. Accounts of troubles with native Americans occur in the literature in journals and in various histories of the Indian wars, but most vividly in the form of a new genre, the Indian captivity narrative. The first and most popular of these, after John Smith's account of his captivity in Virginia, grew out of the war waged against the settlers in western Massachusetts and the upper Connecticut Valley by King Philip, the son of Massasoit, in 1675-76.[8] Published in 1682, it was called significantly *The Soveraignty and Goodness of God, Together with the Faithfulness of His Promises Displayed; Being a Narrative of the Captivity and Restauration of Mrs. Mary Rowlandson.*

Mrs. Rowlandson was the wife of a minister in the frontier settlement of Westfield. During February 1676, while the Reverend Rowlandson was away from home, the Indians captured Mrs. Rowlandson with her wounded six-year-old child, along with her other children, Mary, age ten, and Joseph, sixteen. The wounded child died, but the others were saved, as was Mary Rowlandson herself after eleven weeks among the Indians. Upon her return to her own people Mrs. Rowlandson set down her account of her adventure "to declare the Works of the Lord, and his wonderfull Power in carrying us along, preserving us in the Wilderness, while under the Enemies hand, and returning of us in safety again." [9]

The story was immediately popular. It had everything—a pious and educational purpose, to show how through God's providences not only Mary Rowlandson, but the English settlement of western Massachusetts and the upper Connecticut had been saved; moreover, it was a good story of adventure in a day when publishers stressed sermons and pamphlets of religious controversy along with an occasional ponderous history. The experience itself—capture, adjustment, and escape or redemption—provided a good narrative sequence. To this Mrs. Rowlandson added an uncanny eye for detail, a simple and direct style with some of the cadence of biblical narrative, and a pattern of metaphor which suggested for the soul a descent into Hell, a redemption, and return.

Moreover, Rowlandson wrote as a woman who had undergone an ordeal to which women and children were especially subject, for the men who protected them were often killed rather than taken. Rowlandson in making her archetypal journey into the "vast and desolate wilderness," that "pit," thus represents the individual Christian and more particularly, the woman under duress. Her readers could see her as a woman undergoing various trials of her strength, piety, mother-love, industry, and her sense of individual worth.

Mrs. Rowlandson's experiences were typical of those in other narratives. During the first hard days of captivity she performed feats of strength and determination. She herself was wounded in the side; yet she managed to carry her wounded daughter, sometimes on foot sometimes on horseback, during the two-day trek to the Indian village. At night she sat with the child on her lap warmed only by a campfire while the snow fell around her. She stayed constantly with the child till she died several days later and was buried by the Indians. Even after the restoration of the remaining family, however, Mrs. Rowlandson grieved over the lost child and its burial far from other Christians.

The reiteration of Mrs. Rowlandson's pious reliance on God is woven continuously into her narrative. She received her Bible as the gift of an Indian after a raiding party, and she tells how she relied on the comfort of the Scriptures, following the common practice of opening the Bible at random that through Providence she might find a passage adapted to her need. Generally she received such evidence of God's interest in her individual plight. As she tells it, the whole experience was designed to test her faith. It was only by probing the very bottom of the abyss of despair that both she and New England could regain that total reliance on God that he required to bring about their redemption.

The story of this pilgrimage into the "pit" of the wilderness is enlivened by the day-to-day account of Rowlandson's stay among the Indians, such descriptions being among the lasting values of many of the captivity narratives. Rowlandson, with a remarkable memory for detail, gives especial attention in her story to the kinds of food and shelter her captors improvised during their frequent journeys. Of particular interest also are her descriptions of her mistress, the squaw chief Weetamoo, whose stormy temper plagued Rowlandson during the captivity.

Throughout her captivity, Mrs. Rowlandson displayed the expected Puritan virtue of industry and concern for her husband and children. She made shirts and caps and knitted white stockings for Indians large and small and received pay in the form of money or food. And she refused to let her husband come in person to ransom her out of fear that he might be killed or captured.

Thus in every way Mrs. Rowlandson, no less than any character of fiction, represented the virtues expected of the women of her society—the piety, the devotion to husband and children, the practice of industry—even during her pilgrimage toward a literal redemption. It is no wonder that her story was an instant popular success and that it remained so through at least thirty editions. It introduced the genre of the Indian captivity narrative which was to continue for more than 200 years while the successive waves of settlers crossed the continent and encountered over and over again the tribes of native Americans.

Like the story of Mary Rowlandson, the other early Indian and captivity narratives were designed to show the power and goodness of God in providing for the captive an experience of redemption. In 1684 Increase Mather took up the theme by telling of the captivity of Quentin Stockwell in *An Essay for the Recording of Illustrious Providences,* and his son Cotton included the tales of Hannah Dustin and Hannah Swarton in his *Humiliations Follow'd With Deliverances* (1697). Hannah Dustin ended her own captivity by following the example of the biblical Jael; during the night she and her white companions—another woman and a youth—slew the captors with their own tomahawks and brought home ten scalps to prove their exploit. Mather reprinted the narrative in *Decennium Luctuosum* (1699), including there also the story of seven-year old Sarah Gerish, preserved by Providence in her wanderings. The narrative of Elizabeth Hanson, taken captive with several of her children at Dover, New Hampshire, in 1724, came out under the title *God's Mercy Surmounting Man's Cruelty* . . . in 1728, and expresses a similar providential view.[10]

The captivity narratives, of course, reflected the concerns and the literary proclivities of the society that produced them. During the French and Indian wars the narrators, or their editors, stressed the cruelties of the tribes employed by their enemies. The colonists used the narratives in similar fashion as anti-British propaganda during the Revolution. The style, which earlier was straightforward, became more elaborate and dramatic in later narratives, as may readily be seen in the successive editions of Elizabeth Hanson's story in 1754 and 1760, and in the revised editions of the captivity of Mrs. Johnson, first published in 1796. Richard VanDerBeets has pointed out that the stylistic changes thus revealed would continue to develop until the narratives became tales emphasizing the feelings of the narrator, at length becoming entirely fictional. Such were *An Account of a Beautiful Young Lady, Who Was Taken by the Indians and Lived in the Woods Nine Years* (1787); *The Narrative of the Singular Adventures and Captivity of Mrs. Thomas Berry* (1800); and *The History of Maria Kittle In a Letter to Miss Ten Eyck* (1797) by Ann Eliza Bleecker, "an outright novel of sensibility." [11]

The narrative of Mary Rowlandson summed up the piety of the earliest settlers. It expressed their belief that God as first cause brought about all the events of this world, however trivial, speaking to his people through the revelations of the Bible and the signs to be found in everyday living if one could but read them right. But the destruction of the frontier towns and the scattering of their closely knit congregations hastened the changes already creeping over New England. With the decline of the close village community and the scattering of households over more isolated farmsteads, the family gained even more influence as the primary social group. At the same time, the family was losing power over the individual because holdings of land had been subdivided as far as possible, and the sons of a family were no longer forced to delay marriage while waiting for an inheritance in land. Economic diversification was increasing throughout the colonies, and sons in the northern and middle colonies were increasingly drawn into various trades.[12]

At the same time the intense Calvinism which had inspired the early planters of New England was breaking down. Churches gradually expanded to admit more men and women into full participation as church members. The world became increasingly viewed as subject to natural laws, and God retreated farther from the direction of the world's everyday affairs.

The change from a world in which woman's role was determined by biblical models did not result in any widespread altering of the lives of women; the laws still placed many restrictions upon them, especially with regard to control of property, and custom barred them from entering the professions. The change in attitude probably made it possible, however, for some women to move about in the world with greater ease. At any rate, in the early years of the eighteenth century we see a woman making the arduous journey from Boston to New York by horseback, not for the glory of God or under compulsion, but on business, and, we suspect, out of curiosity.

Sarah Kemble Knight was a third-generation American, daughter of a Boston merchant. Of her husband, Richard Knight, little is known, but he seems to have been away from home when Madam Knight made her journey. The records show that Madam Knight maintained a large household, consisting of her mother and daughter, an only child, together with several lodgers. The house also contained a shop, probably run by Madam Knight or her servants. The industrious woman also made a business of copying legal documents, and with the knowledge of law so gained, went on her travels in order to settle the estate of a cousin. During her five months' absence, she kept a journal of her travels and those she met along the way—women and men from all social classes— innkeepers, the extremely poor, country bumpkins, ministers, middle-class travelers, the Dutch merchants of New York, and even the governor of Connecticut. All these she describes in a lively style in which passages of wry wit alternate with detailed sketches of people, places, and customs.

A portrait of Madam Knight herself emerges from these

impressions—a solid, respectable, outspoken, upper-middle-class matron, whose unshakable sense of her own rank and self-worth does not deprive her of humor. Her view of the world is shrewd and lively; concern with religion has been reduced to comments on meetinghouses and ministers. She speaks wittily rather than intolerantly of other religions; when crossing a river in a canoe, she fears a wetting from which she will rise "at the best like a holy Sister Just come out of a Spiritual Bath in dripping Garments." [13] Sunday, on which Mary Rowlandson was so loath to serve her captors, is mentioned just once, as a reason for not describing the port at Milford.

Occasionally Madam Knight mingles with her wit an attempt at understanding and sympathy for those of other backgrounds. Her description of Bumpkin Simpers, who enters a store to buy a ribbon for his friend Joan Tawdry, is perhaps her most humorous, but she pauses after her ridicule to say that these people have as large a portion of "mother witt" as those brought up in the city, only they lack education and conversation.

Madam Knight apparently had both. The *Journal* includes fairly skillful original poetry that suggests acquaintance with Dryden and his contemporaries. Her practice of giving characters descriptive names may have come from reading the popular *Pilgrim's Progress*. She refers to the romances of *Parismus* and the *Knight of the Oracle* by the Jacobean Emmanuel Forde, both still popular as pamphlets much reduced from their original length. In addition, her satiric tone, her tolerant amusement with herself and the foibles of others, her reference to God as her "Great Benefactor," all suggest an acquaintance with the works of the dawning age of enlightenment. Probably through wide reading and her function as a copier and witness of legal documents, she was better educated than other women of her class and time. Moreover, Madam Knight was more independent and curious about books and the world than most of her sisters and certainly more active in affairs outside the household.

Nevertheless, she is conscious of her frailties as a woman, fearful of crossing rivers and timid when her guide outdistances her in the dark. In such travels through the night, Madam Knight foreshadows the romantic age to come. She describes the dark ride through the forest in a way that suggests the gothic scenes in

Irving. And while riding among the trees after the moon has risen, she dreams of the castles and cities she has read about far away in Europe. Hers is an early example of that longing for a European civilization they have never seen that imbues Americans both in and out of literature from Irving to Henry James and beyond.

The nearest to another land Madam Knight can get is New York, and she delightedly records the customs there. Her purchases, at least those she records, reflect her business rather than any so-called feminine interest in clothes; she bought one hundred reams of paper. And she returns at last to her mother and daughter who apparently with the help of servants managed the household while its mistress was away.

More typical, perhaps, of Boston society at this period are the events recorded in the diary of Samuel Sewall, over the period 1674-1729. In it we encounter almost everyone of importance in the city, though the passages most often reprinted concern his courtship of Madam Winthrop, the widow of Major-General Wait Still Winthrop. Sewall not only gives a portrait of the lady herself, but a glimpse of the way time and money were spent by the upper classes in Boston *circa* 1620. The haggling over a marriage contract was typical of what went on before marriage among people of property at that time. A widow received a life estate in a third of her husband's property; she could also receive additional money or property by will. Even though she might reserve the right to will the latter when she remarried, her new husband would have the disposal of the income from all her property so long as she lived. Widows were thus apt to bring more money to a marriage than a parent could give any one of his daughters; hence widows were popular. The high value placed on widows and on a large marriage portion may be seen in one of the jocular advertisements placed in the New England *Courant* for January 29, 1722. In it several journeymen represent themselves as looking for wives. Those who may apply are "Old Virgins" with £500, or young widows who have estates from their first husbands, or young ladies with estates in their own hands.

With the advent of such colonial newspapers as the *Courant* we come to a new period in American writing. The periodicals, with their pages to be filled at regular intervals, offered the opportunity for American writers to try their hands at short pieces of various kinds. Often these took the form of poetry or letters to the editor printed over pseudonymous signatures.

Early in 1722 the *Courant* began to publish fictitious letters concerned with particular problems of women. One letter complains of a whorehouse located across the street from a church. Others purport to be from women in despair over the cruel treatment they receive from their husbands. Abigail Afterwit complains of nonsupport; Hortensia, that her husband beats her. Betty Frugal is about to be flattered into a marriage for her money. Fanny Mournful says her father beats her since he married a new wife; Belinda complains that the young man courting her is too bashful. Dulcimira defends the fair sex against recent antifeminine comments in the newspaper.

The women who present themselves in these letters are among the earliest fictional characters in American literature, perhaps the first. Although stereotyped, they present as part of their satire real problems of women, who, because of the law, rarely possessed the means to escape the domination of a father or husband even though he be improvident or cruel. Moreover, such ministers as Cotton Mather still pressed submission upon women as a religious duty.

More fully developed as a "character" than these early women of the *Courant* is Benjamin Franklin's Silence Dogood. In creating Silence, the young Franklin seized the opportunities that lay in a series of letters from the same person. By arranging for her to be brought up and carefully tutored by a minister, he provided her with an unusually broad education for a woman, which enabled her to write and speak with assurance. By presenting her as a widow with her own income from her boardinghouse, he gave her the independence to speak as the head of a household on private and public issues; further, by starting out with her biography, witty enough to produce the praise of the editor and his circle, Franklin insured the continued welcome of Silence in the *Courant*.

Unlike the women who appeared in the journals, tracts, and narratives of the seventeenth century, this first important fictional character in American literature represents the middle or lower middle class of artisans, mechanics, and tradesmen rather than the upper class of magistrates, important ministers, and wealthy merchants. In her unsecluded role, Silence sees a wide vista of

Boston life. She comments as a spokeswoman for Franklin on the problems of society, among others those of widows left in poverty, and she proposes as a solution a mutual aid society. Like other women appearing in the *Courant,* Silence blames many of women's faults on the system of society which has a double standard of sexual morality and places the property and prosperity of women in the hands of men. Franklin was to repeat similar sentiments later in his "Speech of Polly Baker." On the other hand, Franklin in three fictional letters to his own paper the Pennsylvania *Gazette* (July-September 1732) satirized women who affect life-styles above their stations and who spend their time in dispensing gossip.

During Franklin's long life he wrote innumerable essays and letters in which comments on women or advice to women occur, ranging from the early satires to the playful letters to Madame Helvetius and Madame Brillon during his stay in France. He so constantly and skillfully adapted both style and content to circumstances and audience that a study of his attitudes toward a variety of women should provide material for a lengthy study. Ancillary to such study would be the brief portraits of women scattered through the *Diary* of Samuel Sewall and those in the writing of William Byrd II of Virginia. Throughout Byrd's diaries we catch glimpses of the lives of women on the plantations of the South, as well as the well-known view of women in the backwoods of North Carolina in *The History of the Dividing Line,* a type of portrait which continued into the twentieth century with the writing of Erskine Caldwell and William Faulkner. Evidence that the women of the South, no less than those of the North, objected to their inequality under the law may be seen in "The Lady's Complaint" published in the Virginia *Gazette,* Williamsburg, October 22, 1736. Its author asks for equal laws that "neither Sex oppress;/ More Freedom give to Womankind,/ Or give to Mankind less."

The most fully developed fictional satire after the *Dogood Papers,* however, is that in John Trumbull's *The Progress of Dullness* (1772-73). Published shortly after Trumbull's graduation from Yale, the *Progress* is a satire on the education provided for both sexes, portraying Miss Harriet Simper as a companion piece to sketches of Tom Brainless and Dick Hairbrain. Harriet is interested only in clothes, beaux, and gossip. When she reads at all, she reads novels like *Clarissa* or *Pamela*. Dreaming of romance, Harriet's fate, like that of so many fictional eighteenth-century ladies, is to find her beauty fading, and she contents herself at last with the dull parson Tom Brainless. Trumbull's satire depicts Miss Simper as a provincial version of the society women in the satires of Pope and Lady Mary Wortley Montagu and other English writers of an earlier period.

Harriet Simper's choice of the novels of Richardson as models for her conduct is repeated by heroines in other American literary works. *Pamela, Clarissa,* and the *History of Charles Grandison* were immensely popular in America, where no native novels were produced till near the end of the century. Young women were continually warned by preachers and moralists to shun the reading of novels and plays, which gave the wrong impression of the world. The world was a place of earnest endeavor; marriage was a serious business. The young Trumbull grieves that ladies' "reading is confined/ To books that poison all the mind;/ Novels and plays (where shines displayed/ A world that nature never made)." Benjamin Rush, the noted Philadelphia physician and essayist, likewise advocated education as an aid in subduing the "passion for novels." Novels, he told the students of the Young Ladies Academy in Philadelphia in 1787, "hold up *life,* it is true, but is not as yet *life* in America," the intrigues of British novels being far removed from American manners.[14] Despite such warnings, the sentimental novel, the novel of seduction, had arrived, and it was only a matter of time until American writers followed the lead of the English novelists.

The first such American novel, William Hill Brown's *The Power of Sympathy* (1789), is, like its English forerunners, an epistolary romance. Brown attempts to counter the usual American criticism of novels by stressing a moral lesson; he warns young women against seduction by showing its terrible effects on the seduced one, her family, and her true love. Seducers he confines to the most odious corner of Hell. The story is filled with betrayed maidens who die in childbirth or shortly thereafter or go mad or whose lovers commit suicide. The number of such incidents make the novel less an entertainment than a grim case history; indeed, one of its most notorious incidents was based on a recent true story of the seducing of a young woman by her sister's husband. Similar novels followed, the best known being *Charlotte, a Tale of Truth* (1791) by Susanna Rowson, and Hannah Foster's *The Coquette* (1797). Shorter tales of seduction may be found in various colonial newspapers, an example being "Caroline, or the Seduced American" in the Philadelphia *Minerva* for January 14 and January 21, 1797.

The rise of the tales of seduction in America during the eighteenth century coincided with an increase in premarital sexual intercourse. In real life, however, the resulting conceptions were usually followed by marriage, rather than by illegitimate births. A graph of premarital conceptions in Hingham, Massachusetts, from 1650 to 1850 shows a fairly smooth rising curve of early births after less than six months of marriage, reaching its peak in the 1780s, at which time 20 percent of births occurred after six months of marriage and over 30 percent in less than eight and a half months. The curve for both types of birth descends smoothly to 1850, where it is no higher than it was in the 1680s.[15] The rising curve may reflect the weakening of parental authority over marriages. This occurred when marriage no longer involved primarily a settlement of the real property of a family on young couples. The change reflected the increasing importance of other more movable forms of wealth.[16]

A more serious effort to understand and improve the conditions of women than any previous writer had attempted was made by Charles Brockden Brown at the turn of the century. Brown's first work *Alcuin* (1798), a dialogue, discusses the problems of women—their confinement in the home, their lack of control over property, their lack of the power to vote, their insufficient education. He includes arguments favoring divorce and describes a utopia of women, where the sexes mingle on an equal basis. In this society the differences in sex are confined to procreation; otherwise the sexes dress in the same way and join in all areas of work and government.

Brown attempted to express some of the ideas from *Alcuin* and those from his study of psychology in his novels. The first two, *Wieland* (1798) and *Ormond* (1799), combine the gothic and sentimental modes. The settings and atmosphere are intricate; the winding paths in the former and the narrow complex of city streets in the latter provide a dense and intrusive background, suggesting an analogy to the complexities of the mind. The mutual interest of the sexes in learning and art he demonstrates in the little group at the center of *Wieland* and in *Ormond.* In the latter Constantia Dudley has been educated in the classics, then learns French and Italian during her seclusion while the plague rages in Philadelphia. Ormond hesitates to marry, for he believes that marriage should be between intellectual equals. Constantia likewise seeks intellectual as well as physical companionship in marriage. Brown's heroines, with their "masculine" minds, are not mere sentimentalists easily overcome by fear or by the dark pre-Byronic charms of their pursuers. For Brown, background, experiences, and education are all important in the development of character, an idea he received from such English liberals as William Godwin and Mary Wollstonecraft. Hence in his careful probing into the history of his heroines, he develops women characters more complex and rich than any of his countrymen would for several decades to come.[17]

With the work of Brown we come to the end of the early period of our literature. With Brown, whose books influenced later writers in England and America from Shelley to Poe, we are launched upon the period when works of fiction will at last replace the earlier less imaginative forms of literature as mirrors of women.

Looking back, we have noted that during our first two centuries, this country produced very little bellelettristic literature. The emphasis in New England and even in the Middle Colonies, where religious emphasis was strong, was on piety and utility. Though in New England both men and women could read, learning for women was far down the list of desirable attributes after a knowledge of housewifery, sewing and knitting, simple bookkeeping, and a dowry. Yet when a woman by her own efforts in reading and writing became skilled in knowledge, she could be praised. Anne Bradstreet, who was born early and wealthy enough to share the last glow of the ideal of the learned lady that flourished in the time of Queen Elizabeth, was singled out by her contemporaries for her learning. Following her time, however, few women were able to attain so good an education, or at least few demonstrated it for the world to see. So we have observed writers from Sarah Kemble Knight to Charles Brockden Brown pleading the desirability of giving more education to women.

With the increased emphasis on education and on the primacy of reason, piety became a less important requirement for a wife.

We may contrast the qualities of a good woman as given in Cotton Mather's *Ornaments for the Daughters of Zion* (1692)—piety, skill in housewifery, love for and obedience to a husband—with the qualities of the heroines in Brown—serenity, fortitude, and learning are foremost, followed by ability in the graces of music and art. And of course, like all heroines of the novels of seduction, the ladies must be beautiful and wellborn. Though the novels are based on seduction and romantic attachment, the fruits of such encounters rarely enter the story. Devotion to family becomes devotion to parents—for example, Colonel Manly and Maria in Royall Tyler's play *The Contrast* (1787) obey and revere their parents; Constantia is devoted to her father, however burdensome he becomes, in *Ormond*. Whereas in the seventeenth century love meant love within marriage, the focus of the late eighteenth century is on courtship and its hazards. Stories end with the death of the seduced and sometimes the seducer, or marriage. Even Brown, who in *Wieland* concluded his story with the madness and death of Wieland and the destruction of his family, added a postscript in the form of a happy marriage between Clara Wieland and Pleyel.

But Brown's novels are in some ways even farther from reality than the seventeenth-century portraits of Anne Hutchinson. If we turn to the eighteenth century to see what real women were doing, we find that except for the wealthier classes their work and position were similar to what they had been earlier. Women were still bearing many children and managing large households. In the cities they helped their husbands in their businesses and often carried them on after their husbands died. Women were keeping shops and running printing businesses, shipping firms and docks, growing seeds, and keeping taverns, or working as servants or as slaves. During the Revolution women ran the farms and plantations with the help of servants who were not away at war. They boycotted English products and clothed themselves in homespun. Throughout the century women were moving westward with their husbands, settling the frontier, occasionally undergoing the kind of captivity made familiar by Mary Rowlandson and Elizabeth Hanson. For women of wealth there was more leisure, but their responsibilities were still great. Among these classes marriage was usually based on a suitable marriage contract involving gifts of money or property on both sides. Even William Hill Brown's sentimental hero, Harrington, acknowledges this when he hesitates a long time before deciding to marry a young woman without a dowry.

During the entire period letters and journals show women as they viewed themselves going about their daily affairs. The letters of Abigail Adams and of Mercy Warren furnish examples of the kind of lives women were leading just before and during the foundation of the republic. Eliza Lucas Pinckney describes in her letters her experiments with introducing new plants, particularly indigo, in an effort to break the one-crop dependency of the South. Phillis Wheatley, born in Africa and carried as a child into slavery, produces the first book written by a black in America, containing poetry that made her for a brief while a celebrity in Boston and English society.[18]

The women of the literature of the seventeenth century, when they appear at all, are large, heroic figures: Anne Bradstreet, the first genuine American poet, beside whom "others souls . . . dwelt in a lane"; Anne Hutchinson, who for a brief time was the most powerful resident of Boston, overshadowing John Winthrop and the ministers, whose exile and death made her a tragic heroine brought down by her own intense visionary outspokenness; Mary Rowlandson, the representative Puritan, the determined protagonist of an archetypal journey. Even the more comic figures, the women briefly described in Nathaniel Ward's *Simple Cobler* as "gant bar-geese, ill shapen, shotten shellfish, Egyptian hieroglyphics, or at best . . . French flirts of the pastry" overshadow in their fantastic appearance the women of fashion in the century to come.

The eighteenth century witnesses a decline in the stature of the women in popular literature. Silence Dogood, witty and independent as she is, remains a commentator. Harriet Simper is not only uneducated, but perhaps ineducable. The women of the Indian captivity narratives have lost much of the independent self-reliance of such heroines as Mary Rowlandson and have come to suffer from the emotional vapourings of the heroines of sentimental novels, while the heroines of the sentimental novels have become pretty toys to be broken by the seducers who abound. Even the best of them, the heroines in the novels of Charles Brockden

Brown, respond to circumstance rather than move as self-propelled individuals in the world, and occupy in any tale only the brief period between adolescence and marriage.

Notes

1 Janet Whitney, *Abigail Adams* (Boston, 1947), p. 7.
2 George Francis Dow, *Every Day Life in the Massachusetts Bay Colony* (Boston, 1935; reissued, New York, 1967) is a good source for information on the life-style of the period.
3 David D. Hall, *The Antinomian Controversy 1636-1638: A Documentary History* (Middletown, Conn., 1968), pp. 370-71. All quotations regarding Anne Hutchinson are from this source.
4 *The Works of Anne Bradstreet in Prose and Verse,* ed. John Harvard Ellis (Charlestown, Mass., 1867; reprinted, Gloucester, Mass., 1962), p. 84. All quotations from Anne Bradstreet are from this source.
5 Kenneth A. Requa has an excellent essay on "Anne Bradstreet's Poetic Voices" in *Early American Literature* 9 (1974), 3-18.
6 *A Little Commonwealth: Family Life in Plymouth Colony* (New York, 1970), p. 66. Philip J. Greven, Jr., in *Four Generations: Population, Land, and Family in Colonial Andover, Massachusetts* (Ithaca, N.Y., 1970), pp. 27-28, points out that while 15.9 percent of the women in the first and second generations at Andover died between the ages of twenty and thirty-nine, the years of childbearing, the mortality was greater among men between those ages, with a death rate of 18.4.
7 Greven, *Four Generations,* pp. 26-29; Demos, *A Little Commonwealth,* pp. 67, 192-95.
8 For a history of King Philip's War and its aftermath, see Douglas Edward Leach, *Flintlock and Tomahawk* (New York, 1958).
9 Charles H. Lincoln, ed., *Narratives of the Indian Wars* (New York, 1913), p. 134. The Rowlandson narrative is reprinted in Richard VanDer-Beets, *Held Captive by Indians: Selected Narratives, 1642-1836* (Knoxville, Tenn., 1973), pp. 41-90.
10 The narrative of Elizabeth Hanson as it was revised in the English edition of 1760 is reprinted by VanDerBeets, ibid. pp. 130-50. VanDerBeets in his "Introduction," pp. xi-xxxi, provides a valuable insight into the development of the Indian captivity narrative over its entire history, and I am indebted for much of the material included here to that work, as well as to his articles "The Indian Captivity Narrative as Ritual," *American Literature* 43 (1972), 548-62; "A Surfeit of Style: The Indian Captivity Narrative as Penny Dreadful," *Research Studies* 39 (1971), 297-306; and " 'A Thirst for Empire': The Indian Captivity Narrative as Propaganda," *Research Studies* 40 (1972), 207-15.

11 VanDerBeets, *Held Captive*, p. xxiii. On style in the Indian captivity narratives generally, see Roy Harvey Pearce, "The Significances of the Captivity Narrative," *American Literature* 19 (1947), 1-20.

12 James A. Henretta, *The Evolution of American Society, 1700-1815: An Interdisciplinary Analysis* (Lexington, Mass., 1973), p. 133.

13 Malcolm Freiberg, ed., *The Journal of Madam Knight* (Boston, 1972). All quotations from the *Journal* are from this edition.

14 "Thoughts upon Female Education," in *Essays, Literary, Moral and Philosophical* (1798), pp. 75-92. Rush advocated for a woman an education that included a good knowledge of English, an ability to write "in a fair and legible hand," bookkeeping, the principles of Christianity, geography, astronomy, natural philosophy, chemistry, history, travels, poetry, and moral essays.

15 Henretta, *Evolution of American Society*, pp. 132-33. The number of cases of fornication is available from court records, inasmuch as fornication was considered a crime in early New England. The birth of a child sooner than eight and a half months after marriage was considered evidence of fornication unless the midwife testified that the infant appeared premature. See Demos, *A Little Commonwealth*, pp. 152-53, 157-59. Under these circumstances fornication was a leading crime even earlier than the 1680s. See Edwin Powers, *Crime and Punishment in Early Massachusetts, 1620-1692*, (Boston: Beacon Press, 1966), pp. 52, 404-7, 409. The penalty for fornication was generally a whipping or fine.

16 Henretta, *Evolution of American Society*, p. 133. See the following note for a reference to the return to a more conservative role for women which runs parallel to the falling curve.

17 Brown's heroines represent the liberal or even radical view of the role and capabilities of women. The triumph of the conservative view, under which women were "to be submissive, domestic, pious, and thereby re-establish their delicacy, spiritual superiority, and—most important—their restraining power over men" is traced by Patricia Jewell McAlexander in "The Creation of the American Eve: The Cultural Dialogue on the Nature and Role of Women in Late Eighteenth-Century America," *Early American Literature* 9 (1975), 252-66.

18 In addition to works already cited, references for further study include the following: *On Individuals:* Elizabeth Wade White, *Anne Bradstreet: "The Tenth Muse"* (New York, 1971); Ann Stanford, *Anne Bradstreet: The Worldly Puritan. An Introduction to Her Poetry* (New York, 1975), containing a bibliography of recent scholarship; "Anne Bradstreet: An Annotated Checklist," *Bulletin of Bibliography* 27 (1970), 34-37; Winnifred King Rugg, *Unafraid: A Life of Anne Hutchinson* (Freeport, N.Y., 1930, 1970); Peter Thorpe, "Sarah Kemble Knight and the Picaresque Tradition," *College Language Association Journal* 10 (1966), 114-21; Harriot Horry Ravenel, ed., *Eliza Pinckney* (New York, 1896);

Charles Francis Adams, ed., *Letters of Mrs. Adams, The Wife of John Adams,* (Boston, 1841, rev. ed. 1848); L. H. Butterfield et al., ed. *The Book of Abigail and John: Selected Letters of the Adams Family, 1762-1784* (Cambridge, Mass., 1975); Katherine Anthony, *First Lady of the Revolution: The Life of Mercy Otis Warren* (Garden City, N.Y., 1958); Jean Fritz, *Cast for a Revolution: Some American Friends and Enemies, 1728-1814* (Boston, 1972)—about Mercy Warren and her circle; Mercy Warren, *History of the Rise, Progress and Termination of the American Revolution* (Boston, 1805); John W. Jackson, *Margaret Morris, Her Journal with Biographical Sketch and Notes* (Philadelphia, 1949); Baroness von Riedesel, *Journal and Correspondence of a Tour of Duty, 1776-1783,* trans. Marvin L. Brown, Jr. (Chapel Hill, N.C., 1965); Caroline Gilman, ed., *Letters of Eliza Wilkinson, During the Invasion and Possession of Charlestown, S.C. by the British in the Revolution* (New York, 1839); Julian D. Mason, Jr., ed., *The Poems of Phillis Wheatley* (Chapel Hill, N.C., 1966).

General works: Mary R. Beard, ed., *America Through Women's Eyes* (New York, 1933); Mary Sumner Benson, *Women in Eighteenth-Century America: A Study of Opinion and Social Usage* (New York, 1935); Elizabeth Cometti, "Women in the American Revolution," *New England Quarterly* 20 (1947), 329-46; Elisabeth Anthony Dexter, *Colonial Women of Affairs: Women in Business and the Professions in America before 1776* (Boston, 1924); Alice Morse Earle, *Colonial Dames and Good Wives* (New York, 1895, 1962); Eugenie Andruss Leonard et al., *The American Woman in Colonial and Revolutionary Times, 1565-1800* (Philadelphia, 1962); Edmund S. Morgan, *The Puritan Family* (New York, 1966).

9.

Portrayal of Women in American Literature, 1790-1870

Nina Baym

The eighty years after the close of the Revolution saw continuous changes in American life. Besides the war itself, the subtler but ultimately more influential forces of urbanization, industrialization, and immigration exerted growing pressure throughout the period. Women of 1860 lived differently from women of 1790, and women's lives at any time varied according to social class and geographical region. A poor southern rural woman, the mistress of a flourishing plantation, the wife of a homesteader, a New England schoolteacher, a woman from a prosperous New York merchant family, an Irish immigrant, a slave, or an enterprising sporting woman in Virginia City—these lives represent an enormous range of experience.

Nevertheless, the fact of sex in a highly discriminatory society ensured some common features in the lives of women all over the nation. The duties of women on farms tended to be alike regardless of region (the South excepted), and the rapidly expanding middle class increasingly imposed its expectations on ever-larger numbers of women in towns and cities. There was a simple ideology of woman during this period: she was naturally designed for the home and the private sphere; laws aiming to keep her there were for her own benefit as well as the public good; women who felt legally or culturally restrained were unnatural; women who, for whatever reason, *had* to leave the home were pitiable and of no account.[1]

Law and custom blended in this theoretically benign protectorate. Women could not vote or hold public office anywhere in the states during this period (the first woman suffrage bill was enacted in 1869 in the Wyoming Territory). Although in some states single and widowed women might hold property, married women surrendered everything they owned to their husbands, along with rights over their persons, their children, and all future earnings (New York, for example, passed its first bill permitting married women to hold property in 1849). It was almost impossible, except in some of the newer states (e.g., Indiana), for a woman to obtain a divorce, and only a little less difficult for a man. Women had virtually no physical exercise or training, and wore clothing whose weight and constriction are almost unimaginable to the contemporary mind. A winter street costume, for example, might weigh as much as forty pounds.

Educational opportunities grew for everyone in this period, but far more slowly for women than men, especially at the college level. The first college for women to offer a curriculum comparable to that of the men's schools was Mt. Holyoke, established in 1837; the first coeducational institution of higher learning, Oberlin, had been founded four years earlier in 1833. Such schools remained rarities, as did a college-educated woman, until the twentieth century. Denied a formal higher education, women generally could not enter the professions, and as a result the ideal of self-actualization through work could not exist for them to any significant degree. A sizable minority of women did in fact work for pay, but out of necessity and at wages too low to make working life attractive.

Most working women during this period were in domestic service or the mills, or did piecework in small shops and at home. The middle-class woman who needed money shunned these occupations, but found almost no other work available. If she had some property, she might run a boardinghouse. She might teach primary school, at half the salary of her male counterpart, or she might be a paid lady's companion; governessing, the great resource of the genteel poor in England, did not develop widely in the United States. Many single and widowed genteel women simply depended on the charity of more affluent kinsmen, and lived marginal lives as wards of their brothers or uncles. Many other single women in this class never left home. There seems to have been a good deal of prostitution, but this profession—except briefly in the Far West—brought neither affluence nor independence.

If, then, a woman could find a well-off, competent, and stable man, marriage was certainly her happiest circumstance, and there is little doubt that the economic was the chief motive for marriage during this period. But if her husband proved financially unsuccessful or emotionally undependable, the married woman's life might be a good deal worse than that of her single sisters. Moreover, there were dangers: childbirth was frequent and extremely hazardous. Fewer children died in this century than before, but many still did, and the bereaved mother's grief expresses itself constantly in poetry written by women at the time. Moreover, the death rate for mothers, because of the primitive and unsanitary conditions at delivery, remained very high; it does not seem to have declined significantly in this country until after World War I, when it dropped radically. Thus every pregnancy meant a serious risk of the woman's life. Invariably, the marital situation produced a great deal of anxiety, which surfaced in that feminine distaste for sex misread by later generations as Victorian prudery. The sexual reforms advocated by the earliest feminists asked for precisely the opposite of what is demanded today: they wanted freedom from sex rather than freedom to have more of it.

By the 1850s, middle-class ideology had elevated one image of woman—the home-loving woman, pleasing, conservative, and virtuous, a comfort and delight to her husband, an ideal to her children—into a national model. Women who did not fit the mold were oddly invisible, their lives little noticed in their own day and largely unrecorded for ours. Many middle-class women, no doubt, were content within the patriarchy, while others must have found it difficult to object to the superficial flattery of the ideology. Nevertheless, motivated by growing affluence and leisure, by modernization, by change, and by the ideals of democratic individualism frequently sounded in public rhetoric, middle-class women began to rebel. This was the age of all sorts of reform movements, in many of which women were significantly involved. And this was the age in which agitation for reform in woman's life began and gathered tremendous momentum. Movements in women's education, working women's laws, marriage, divorce, and property laws, as well as the feminist movement itself, which focused on woman suffrage—all these indicated a continuing dissatisfaction and turbulence among the very women who were presumably most favored by the system. Large numbers of women began to speak and write, testifying not only to themselves but to an audience of women who heard and read them. Although the "New Woman" was not recognized and labeled until after the Civil War, she had been taking shape distinctly during the decades before it.[2]

The literature from this period that we—that is, the critics and scholars—value and teach today does not reflect this social picture, because its mode is not realism: it is symbolic, romantic, ideological, philosophical, inspirational, and mythic. We preserve, of course, only a fraction of the output of the time, but literature, having its own history and concerns, was not, even at the time, a perfect social mirror. The leading critical doctrine of the period, "literary nationalism," consisted of variations on the idea that America, newest and greatest of nations, ought to produce the greatest literature ever known. Would it imitate but surpass British models? Or would it achieve something entirely new? On this issue the critics argued, but they united in affirming an exalted mission for the young writer.

More practically, the coincidence of aggregated populations, better printing and transporting facilities, and the great increase in literacy created the opportunity for an author actually to make a profession of writing; that is, to earn his living by his pen. Before 1825 only a handful of Americans had ever tried to be professional authors; after this date, spurred by British examples (against whom, unfortunately, they had to compete), quite a large number of writers made the attempt and a surprising number succeeded. Of course, success depended on large sales, large sales on popularity, and popularity on pleasing a mass audience. Many of the successful writers were women. They wrote historical or domestic novels featuring women characters and female dilemmas. Some of these authors were unmarried, others widowed or deserted; in few cases did their lives correspond to the feminine ideal of their day. But awareness of that ideal is a major pressure in their works.[3]

Most of these women have been forgotten, perhaps deservedly so. Critics quite naturally prefer writers who think of literature as a fine art to those who think of it as a means to pay bills, and it is true that a dedicated artist is probably more likely to produce good work. Nevertheless, certain kinds of bias—a preference for stories about whaling rather than housekeeping, for example—may well have operated unjustly to exclude women's books from serious critical consideration. It is useful, as we discuss the treatment of women by major authors, to remember that by the end of the decade 1845-55, during which works appeared by Emerson, Poe, Thoreau, Hawthorne, Melville, and Whitman, everyone knew that the greatest book of the age was *Uncle Tom's Cabin* by Harriet Beecher Stowe.

The earliest major author to concern himself with women was Charles Brockden Brown, who wrote a number of gothic romances at the turn of the century, and is memorialized in literary histories as the first American professional writer. Brown began his career by publishing, in 1798, two parts of a four-part feminist dialogue called *Alcuin* (the remaining sections did not appear until 1815, after his death). *Alcuin* is a fiery document obviously influenced by Wollstonecraft, Godwin, and Paine. Its crisp, inexorably logical prose makes a strong impression even today. Its basic premise is that women, like men, are rational beings. The anatomical differences between the sexes have no bearing on their relative rational capabilities. Therefore, all sexual discrimination, whether in education, upbringing, opportunity, law, or custom, is monstrous. From the viewpoint of woman's condition, Brown condemns the entire moral, political, legal, and domestic structures of American life. The work is composed as a dialogue between Alcuin, a young man who imagines his views on women to be advanced, and Mrs. Carter, who soon shows him how backward he really is. The brilliant Mrs. Carter, a widow keeping house for her brother, dramatizes the contrast between limited female circumstance (for she is "always at home" and has had "a woman's education") and the breadth of her mind. Brown's gothic romances are not feminist, but their women characters are often very intellectual and high-minded, rather unlike the frail vessels of the typical novel written at about this time.[4] His rationalist-deist approach leads him to demonstrate feminine excellence in terms more typical of the eighteenth than the nineteenth century.

The soft domestic ideal as seen in the works of Washington Irving is more representative of nineteenth-century values. Much interested in legend and folktale, and fond of quaint and archaic matter, Irving dealt with women only occasionally when the imperatives of his narrative required it. He was better at rapid visual evocation of a feminine type than at individual portraiture. Dame Van Winkle, the famous wife whose shrewish tongue drove Rip to his solitary rambles, actually never appears in the story; the plump Katrina Van Tassel, coveted by Ichabod Crane, is described in a few sentences and otherwise is completely in the background. The rare pieces which focus on women in *The Sketch Book* (1819) are unabashedly sentimental representations of stereotype. Portraying a young maiden who dies of a broken heart when deserted ("The Broken Heart"), or a young wife whose love and support cheer and inspirit the ruined husband ("The Wife"), or an old woman who cannot survive the death of her returned prodigal son ("The Widow and Her Son"), Irving is in fact conveying different facets of the one image of woman as the being who lives for love alone. His women are always at home. Irving's use of this stereotype reflects not so much his ideas of women as his lack of ideas about them. The portraits of women in his work are among innumerable copies of the great cliché of the age.

Irving's much tougher and weightier contemporary, James Fenimore Cooper, had ideas about everything. His reputation today rests on five of the forty-odd novels he wrote—the series known as the *Leather-Stocking Tales,* whose hero is among the first and greatest personifications of the American ideal of lone self-sufficiency and harmonious interaction with the American wilderness. Women are not central to these tales, but they are present and important in each. They are invariably linked to civilization and settlement; they carry with them ties to the future and the past, not because they bear children but because they link men with one another in family and civil organizations. In this function they represent a threat—not to Leatherstocking's homoerotic chastity, as fashionable criticism has it, but to the nonsocial core of the hero's life. Leatherstocking's failure to marry throughout the series expresses the reality of his unique and transient role in American history.

At the same time that the women represent civilization, as individuals they exhibit a range of behavior which the flatness of Cooper's style tends to disguise. Overall, Cooper seems to develop three main feminine types. There is a passive, weak, dependent, fragile woman who is feeble even to the point of feeblemindness, a portrayal by no means wholly flattering of a conventional ideal (Louisa in *The Pioneers,* 1823; Alice in *The Last of the Mohicans,* 1826; Hetty in *The Deerslayer,* 1841). There is a moody, lofty, intelligent, articulate, highly sexed, and individualistic woman who is simply too pronounced a personality to have a social function and who, denied Leatherstocking's option of taking to the woods, either goes bad (Judith in *The Deerslayer)* or dies (Cora in *The Last of the Mohicans).* Finally, there is a strong, cheerful, independent, forthright, high-spirited but ladylike young woman—an adumbration of the "American girl"—who is generally the heroine (Elizabeth in *The Pioneers;* Ellen in *The Prairie,* 1827; Mabel in *The Pathfinder,* 1840; Hist in *The Deerslayer).* These women often stand out from the conventional society in which they function because of their independence, bravery, and clearheadedness.

Cooper's tripartite scheme, wherein two ultimately useless extremes are played off against a socially and personally workable mean, is one common way—perhaps the most common way in his time—of representing the range of feminine personality. The particular substance of each of the three figures varies from author to author, but the idea of a triad is frequently controlling.[5] Regrettably, the predominance of this design has been obscured by later critics who are especially fascinated with another mode of feminine portrayal—the representation of women as polar opposites, the so-called dark-fair contrast. This design is indeed to be found in works of the period, but less often. The neglect of the triad has led to the neglect of the all-important central, viable female figure.

Although Ralph Waldo Emerson is considered a major author, we read him less for literary excellence than for his expression of significant and influential American ideas. As a moral philosopher and inspirational lecturer, he was less concerned with specific circumstances than general issues. He was disturbed by what he believed to be the growing subservience of individuals to conventions and institutions, and he called for a retesting by each person of the routines that enveloped his or her life. His message was not intended for men only, and it seems clear that it was received by both sexes. His day-to-day attitudes toward women seem to have been conservative. He appeared to feel that in the ideal order of things men would be brave and energetic, women beautiful and virtuous. He never questioned the institution of marriage, accepting it in its mid-nineteenth-century version as a given of human existence. Like many New Englanders, he opposed the sexual double standard, and advocated chastity before and fidelity during marriage.

Emerson himself would have been the first to admit that his specific opinions were socially conditioned. He took his stand on his general message of self-trust and self-preeminence. Many whom he influenced went much further in the direction of specific political radicalisms than he did. Among his colleagues who were well known in their own day, perhaps none was more prestigious than Margaret Fuller, whose *Woman in the Nineteenth Century* (1845) was a transcendental manifesto for women's rights. *Woman in the Nineteenth Century* is transcendental in its conviction that specific reforms are secondary to the basic need for a change of attitude toward women on the part of both men and women. Once it is truly felt that women like men have immortal souls, the ending of all discrimination must naturally follow.

Fuller is especially Emersonian in that her chief "message" to women, like his to everybody, advises self-trust, self-reliance, and self-respect. Contemporary women, she believes, are psychologically debilitated by men's low regard for the sex and their own consequent low self-esteem. A bad opinion of self, along with legal and economic dependency on men, leads to servility and degradation both within and without the marriage relation. To counter this, women should hold themselves aloof from men, refusing to marry unless assured of conditions of honesty, respect, and equality. Women on their own should develop their intellects and become more self-enabling and self-controlled. In other words, woman in the nineteenth century is a child who cannot depend on her male guardians and tutors to help her become a responsible adult. On the contrary, they will hinder her. Therefore she must rely on herself, and look for help only from other women.

Far more famous and widely read today than Margaret Fuller is another associate of Emerson's, Henry David Thoreau, who was practically unknown in his own time. Thoreau's *Walden* (1854), however, is an undisputed American masterpiece. As the spiritual autobiography of a year spent in reflection, self-discovery, and self-transcendence, *Walden* could hardly be expected to concern itself with portrayals of women. As a book symbolizing the cycle of withdrawal and rejuvenation it has, like Emerson's essays, a parasexual intention. At the same time *Walden* does have characteristics which involve a sexual reference, characteristics typical of the literary works felt by many critics to form the core of our tradition.

For one thing, although *Walden* lacks a true story line, it alludes continuously to basic narrative patterns which place the work in a context and give significance to particular events. These references are to the great epic and heroic myths. Implicit in *Walden* is a heroic quest in which the hero prepares himself, sets out on a long journey, has many adventures, and finally brings back to his homeland the tangible evidence of his travels. This basic heroic pattern has always been masculine; it has served very rarely as a fundamental plot for women's stories.

Moreover, *Walden's* chief symbol is nature. Although nature symbolism might not seem to imply a sexual limitation, its development in American literature has been almost exclusively masculine in point of view. Partly this is because nature has been developed as a feminine symbol, and the relationship of the hero to "her" is strongly erotic in its overtones. The hero who would live with nature must give up other women. Moreover, nature is often quite hostile toward these other women. In Cooper's works, for example, a woman cannot walk five minutes away from a settlement before she is attacked by savages, wild animals, or natural catastrophes like forest fires and rock slides. On a more realistic level of interpretation, nature stories often center on a type who lives alone beyond the frontier, in the wilderness. Where women come, almost by definition (since they bring home and babies with them) the wilderness ceases to exist. A wilderness story with a female central character would be at odds with real experience.

Perhaps this is why women authors do not appear to have competed with men for possession of the literary territory of nature. The mysteries and challenges of the wilderness do not seem to have exerted psychological or symbolic appeal. Women authors have preferred a more domesticated nature symbolism, like that found in Emily Dickinson's poetry. Whatever the explanations for this fact, the result is that a key motif and a major symbol system in American literature have been developed by men only.

Walt Whitman was also influenced by Emerson, especially in his views of himself as a poet and of the appropriate thematic concerns of poetry. More programmatically than Emerson, he wrote for both men and women. "Has any one supposed it lucky to be born?" he asks in "Song of Myself" (1855). "I hasten to inform him or her it is just as lucky to die." And some lines later, he affirms, "You are not guilty to me, nor stale nor discarded,/I see through the broadcloth and gingham whether or no." The allusions to both sexes show his intent to engage women readers. There are women in his catalogues, evidence that he meant his poetry to encompass their experience.

However, Whitman's poetry is controlled by attitudes that undercut its parasexual surface. Women appear much less often than men; the poetry in fact portrays a largely masculine set of characters and activities. And despite his claim of absolute frankness in physical description, Whitman's account of the female body is euphemistic in comparison to his account of the male, and (in a poem like "I Sing the Body Electric") much briefer. Thus we read, for the male, lines like "Ribs, belly, backbone, joints of the backbone,/Hips, hip-sockets, hip-strength, inward and outward round, manballs, man-root,/Strong set of thighs" and so on. For the woman Whitman gives us "The beauty of the waist, and thence of the hips, and thence downward toward the knees." The disparity of representation implies a disparity of attitude. Say what he will, for Whitman the sexes are fundamentally unequal. This is because women are mothers.

This makes them superior to men in some respects, but by virtue of the sacred charge that has been laid on them rather than by virtue of inherent personal qualities. "Be not ashamed woman, your privilege encloses the rest, and is the exit of the rest,/You are the gates of the body, and you are the gates of the soul." Because he cannot separate his ideas and treatment of the female from the idea of motherhood, Whitman's egalitarian attempts are inconsistent and unconvincing. Men are to be proud of themselves because they are men, women because they are men's mothers. Thus, although it is far more erotic, physical, and biologically explicit than almost anything else written in its time, Whitman's poetry does not really transcend the domestic stereotype of women that controls the literature of his age. On the contrary, his writings dig beneath the stereotype to expose and affirm its psychological foundation—its basis in men's idea of women as their mothers.

Although Whitman criticism has been much interested in sexuality in his poetry, it has been little concerned with his portrayal of woman, and the obvious submersion of the idea of individual woman in the image of mother has not been observed. It has been noted, however, that motherhood and death merge in Whitman's recurrent symbol of the sea (e.g., "Out of the Cradle Endlessly Rocking"). This archaic, or archetypal, image says nothing about women as persons and is indeed another way in which Whitman actually depersonalizes the feminine in his poetry.

In the work of Edgar Allen Poe (mostly written between 1837 and 1849) there is also an equation of the feminine with death, and a depersonalization or transmutation of woman into symbol. Critics often explain the coincidence of death and the maiden in Poe's works by his biography. The tall, beautiful, dark-eyed corpse who haunts so many Poe protagonists is interpreted as the obsessive memory of his mother, who died when he was two. However, images of the beautiful dead girl and the *femme fatale* are both commonplace in the romantic writings which influenced Poe. Moreover, he puts these images to highly theoretic uses, creating works with figures that are only ostensibly women but in fact represent ideas.

Poe employs women in the elaboration of his chief thematic narrative patterns, among which are the following: pursuit of the ideal culminates in madness ("Morella"); denied aspects of the world or the self return to destroy it ("The Fall of the House of Usher"); the ideal is irrecoverably lost in this world, and the soul, refusing to resign itself, dwells in fantasy ("The Raven," "Ul-alume," "Annabel Lee"); reality when compared to the ideal is disappointing and repellent ("Ligeia"); the aspiring soul denies the limits of reality and demonstrates this denial by committing, on the body of the real, what appear to be horrible crimes ("The Black Cat," "Berenice"). By no means does Poe invariably use women to carry out these patterns, and overall only a minority of his stories and poems have women characters. He uses the relationship between husband and wife, or lover and mistress, to represent the relationship between the Soul and the Ideal, or the Soul and the Real. In other words, he uses women when he wants to structure a set of relationships.

Now the attitudes toward women expressed in Whitman's poetry can be imagined as affecting the lives of real women. But it is difficult to imagine an effect that Poe's works might have, hermetic and abstract as they are. Women are not the content of Poe's work, so that the superficial resemblance to popular "grave-yard poetry" is misleading. In that genre, when the dead person is a woman, she really is the subject. But women are signs and not subjects in Poe's discourse, useful because the relations of wife and mistress can stand for the relations between the soul and other parts of the cosmos. There are neither portrayals of women, nor attitudes toward them, in Poe's fiction and poetry.

Melville too, when he writes of women at all, is interested not so much in portraying women as in utilizing them for symbolic purposes, although his purposes are different from Poe's. Melville is mainly noted for works without women, like *Moby-Dick*, *The Confidence Man*, "Bartleby the Scrivener," "Benito Cereno," and *Billy Budd*. Unquestionably these are Melville's best works. He appears to have associated women with society and convention, and consequently found no place for them in the free-ranging and explorative fictions for which he is best known. Connection with women would turn the untrammeled adventurer—as indeed it did turn Melville—into a debt-burdened provider with a large family. Melville idealized manly friendships between equal and indepen-dent spirits as the opposite of (and therefore as a comment upon) the usual female-male association. His pair of stories, "The Tartarus of Maids" and "The Paradise of Bachelors," suggests that women are the prisoners of a ghastly biological and anatomical destiny, while men, if they abstain from women, are free to enjoy life.

Two full-scale works that deal with the problems of male sexuality, and utilize female figures extensively for the purpose, are *Mardi* and *Pierre,* published in 1849 and 1852 respectively *(Moby-Dick* appeared in 1851). The long poem *Clarel* (1876) also treats this subject. The hero of *Mardi* is pursuing his lost ideal love, a fair and pure maiden named Yillah. In turn he is chased by a dark, dangerous, sensual woman called Hautia. After a while the text suggests that Yillah and Hautia are the same, or that Yillah has become Hautia—in short, that innocent romantic love has inevitably become passionate and hence sinful and threatening. The pursuit is not resolved but is transcended in *Mardi* by the introduction of a third kind of love—spiritual or divine love, the love of "Alma," for whom the hero then goes in quest. To translate the allegory: since human love invariably becomes corrupt, the seeker after pure love must turn to the divine. This allegory employs a conventional division of the heroine into the polarity of dark and fair, opposing concepts which yet unite to represent the whole female personality. *Mardi* also displays a conventional tendency to transmute the woman who arouses passion in the male into a sexual aggressor. And it unites passion and guilt in a way that later generations label as typically "Victorian."

The same motifs are found in *Pierre,* though the story is different. The pure naive relationship of Pierre with his angelic fiancée, Lucy, gives way to a heated entanglement with the mysterious Isabel, a relationship especially sinful because Isabel is probably Pierre's illegitimate half-sister. The innocent and sinful women appear to be opposed, but they coalesce in the book's final image to suggest their unity. Pierre consciously tries to have a passionate relationship which is guilt-free, but he cannot. Social pressures are too strong, and he himself is too social a male. *Pierre* does effectively represent the agony of a heterosexual man for whom the sex act is evil. But the saintly Lucy, the demonic Isabel, and Pierre's imperious mother function only to represent that agony. They provide a fine example of how women characters are often realizations of attitudes, fears, and desires, rather than portrayals in a mimetic sense. To be sure, Melville's women are less remote from reality then Poe's, because sexual problems control his presentation of them, while metaphysical problems control Poe's. Nonetheless, Melville's female figures follow the contours of a male fantasy.

When we turn to the works of Nathaniel Hawthorne we enter a different realm, for Hawthorne made women in themselves a central focus in his writing. Among the major nineteenth-century American authors he had the firmest social orientation, and was deeply aware of how much human drama occurs between and among people as well as within them. In his earlier phase, beginning about 1830, Hawthorne wrote short stories and sketches of which we now regularly read only a small number. After 1850 he concentrated on longer works. The formal shift accompanied a thematic shift. The Hawthorne stories that retain interest today concern, quite often, a male protagonist who is isolated by some temperamental coldness, obsessional idea, or secret guilt. For each of these men there is a woman who offers human love and sympathy and consequently salvation from the secular hell of egotistical loneliness. But this offered contact is interpreted by the male as a threat, and he rejects it, frequently abusing or even destroying the female as he does so. One can recognize varieties of this pattern in "Young Goodman Brown," "Rappaccini's Daughter," "The Birthmark," "The Man of Adamant," "Ethan Brand," "Egotism, or the Bosom Serpent," "Roger Malvin's Burial," "Drowne's Wooden Image," and "The Shaker Bridal," to mention only some. In stories where the whole pattern does not appear, the woman is usually a warm, loving, supportive being, unjustly treated by the male.

In Hawthorne's long romances the pattern of a jeopardized man and a saving but rejected woman remains, although with striking changes in the nature of jeopardy and salvation. The males in the long works are oversocialized rather than isolated—timid, conventional, and repressed. The women represent the values of passion, creativity, self-assertion, and sincerity. Where in the stories women offered men a healthy connection to society, now they offer a healthy independence from society. Though the values change, positive values continue to be associated with women throughout Hawthorne's career.

What his fiction does, among other things, is examine the relations between men and women, dramatize male attitudes toward women, and show how these attitudes affect women's lives. Moreover, in his later works he attempts to represent a variety of feminine types and variations within type—to portray women as whole individuals. Although Hester, Miriam, and Zenobia can be roughly assigned to one type and Priscilla, Hilda, and Phoebe to another, within the types there are sharp differences. Phoebe is cheerful, healthy, social, and independent; Priscilla is timid, fragile, dependent, and secretive; Hilda is solitary, stern, insecure, and intensely high-minded. These three characters mainly share an external quality: their emotional range and personal capabilities fall within socially accepted boundaries for women. Therefore they are admired, loved, and protected by men.

Similarly the three "tragic heroines," as they have been called, are chiefly alike in being exceptional women in their needs, talents, and passions. They transgress social boundaries not only in their behavior but in their very being, and they suffer accordingly. Of the three, Miriam is the most high-spirited, spontaneous, generous, and good-natured; Zenobia the most willful, passionate, and inconsistent; Hester the strongest, the most gifted, intense, and serious. Hester is certainly the greatest literary heroine of the period and one of the enduring American female characters. Perhaps she even belongs in an international pantheon. It is not her "sin" that makes her interesting—Hawthorne wisely begins his tale after this event has taken place. She is interesting because of her development after the community discovers and punishes her transgression. Through her Hawthorne touches on many issues of importance to women: loneliness, abandonment, the difficulties of supporting oneself, the conflicts of motherhood, the problems of the powerless. Other aspects of her situation—the fate of passion in a repressive society, the individual against the group, inner morality versus external law—transcend sex.

Though he was not a feminist in any formal sense of the word, Hawthorne was fascinated with the problem of strongly individualized women who try to live with integrity and self-respect in restrictive societies that define their sex as subservient and inferior. He carries this theme from *The Scarlet Letter* (1850) into *The Blithedale Romance* (1852) and *The Marble Faun* (1859). Although neither Zenobia nor Miriam, the heroines of these two later works, has the force and power of Hester, they are interesting women.

Moreover, in these two romances, unlike *The Scarlet Letter,* Hawthorne plays these women off against socially acceptable types, in order to demonstrate the different reactions the types arouse in men, and to increase the complications of the women's situations. In *The Blithedale Romance* the independent and strong-willed Zenobia is rejected in favor of the pale dependent Priscilla. Zenobia is also divided within herself, since despite her great capabilities she is ultimately unable to imagine a destiny for herself other than supporting and aiding—perhaps dominating—a superior male. In *The Marble Faun* Hawthorne contrasts the morally venturesome Miriam and the straitlaced Hilda, who is loved and protected even as the inadequacy of her moral views is acknowledged. Hawthorne's unusual women are too much for themselves, for society, and for the men they love. Women who are more conventional and less demanding, although they are distorted and partial beings in many respects, have a better time of it in life; this is the gloomy overview of woman's condition that emerges from Hawthorne's work.

A different kind of gloom emerges in the poetry of Emily Dickinson, the one certainly great woman writer of the time. Her poems, mostly unpublished until the 1890s, were largely written in the 1860s, and they concern the experience of being female. Although her quality has long been recognized, and she has received extensive, skilled critical attention, her focus on femininity has been seen as a weakness in the poetry rather than a great strength. Her admirers frequently try to show that she rose above her womanhood by writing about universal themes, especially on transcendental or theological topics. Others have stressed the "feminine" aspect of her poetry but have tended to document this more with aspects of her life than with her poetic representation of the experience of being female. Her femininity has often been regarded as a limitation beyond the inevitable limitations of any particular individual view, as though being a woman were some sort of additional handicap. Consequently, many of her admirers have been rather apologetic. In some more sophisticated future era we shall see that being a woman, like being a man, is simply one defining factor among the many that shape a particular artist's point of view.

Clearly, then, it is more important eventually to understand Dickinson as a woman poet than as a portrayer of woman. A lyric poet, she is not interested in characterization. Yet she does present a significant woman character, that of the persona who may or may not be Dickinson herself but is clearly a woman speaking. Her experiences, her range of imagery, and her rhetoric are all inseparable from the facts of her womanhood: the domestic routines, the confinement to home, the particular relationship to physical pain and death, the passivity of outlook, the weight and texture of such appurtenances as feminine clothing, thimbles, butter churns—these are the stuff of Dickinson's poetry. The whole builds to an experience of restricted space and augmented emotional intensity which is unmistakably feminine.

A second important facet of feminine portrayal through the persona centers on the various strategies she adopts to deal with male authority and authority figures, fathers, "masters," and deities. Especially important is her assumption of the mask of a child, a maneuver designed both to express and minimize the seriousness of her rage and rebellion. Sometimes naive, sometimes helpless, sometimes coy or wily or sly, often provocative or mocking, the woman finds refuge and outlet in presenting herself as a child, and this definition is taken seriously by all around her. Safe behind this mask, the woman must still struggle with her social impotence and her anger, and search for the occasional moments of joy or peace that make existence bearable. In sum, Dickinson's poetry gives us astonishing insight into one gifted woman's sense of her own experience.

These major American authors are too diverse to be susceptible to easy generalizations.[6] When it comes to the portrayal of women, perhaps one fact more than any other is determining: most of them had little interest in it. In some works there are no women at all, and in others what appear to be women are really intellectual or sexual symbols. There are several possible explanations for this absence of women in the major literature—Hawthorne and Dickinson, of course, excepted. As was suggested earlier, today's critics tend to prefer the kinds of works that have no women in them to those that do, because they are particularly interested in the wilderness genre of American writing. This bias has probably operated in the selection of the canon which is read and studied today. More important, however, are factors which might have operated in the writers' own time.

One may note to begin with that most of the major authors were not writing novels, and that the novel is the genre in which feminine portraiture is unavoidable.[7] The important question then is why these writers did not compose novels. Some were influenced by the residual Puritan scorn and distrust of fiction, especially those of New England origin. Some were under the influence of literary nationalism, which turned their thoughts to histories or epics in which women would not be likely to figure. And then, too, a writer might easily imagine that by rejecting the popular literary forms of his time and disregarding or even defying popular taste he would demonstrate his high literary aims. Since the popular form was fiction, and popular taste formed by a female audience, such a writer would very likely turn away from women characters, women's stories, and women readers.

The reader who wants to know how women were portrayed during this period, in literature that made such portrayal its aim, must turn perforce to popular fiction, where a typology of feminine characterization can be discerned. From such popular books as *The Wide, Wide World* (Susan Warner, 1850), *Uncle Tom's Cabin* (Harriet Beecher Stowe, 1852), *The Lamplighter* (Maria Cummins, 1854), *Tempest and Sunshine* (Mary Jane Holmes, 1854), *Linda* and *Rena* (Caroline Lee Hentz, 1850 and 1852), *Alone* (Mary Virginia Terhune [Marion Harland], 1854), *St. Elmo* (Augusta Jane Evans, 1867), *The Gates Ajar* (Elizabeth Stuart Phelps, 1868), *Little Women* (Louisa May Alcott, 1869), and many of the dozens of novels produced by Mrs. E.D.E.N. Southworth after 1849, we can abstract a trio of female types: diabolic, angelic, and human women. The diabolic female, when she appears, is the antagonist and never a heroine; the angelic female is occasionally a heroine but more often a model or guide for the human female, the heroine, full of wayward passion and impulse who is disciplined by reality into the mold of gracious womanhood. The basic scheme relates clearly to Christian tradition, as the flawed human soul is attacked by Satan on the one hand and supported and inspired by Christ on the other. As these are stories for women, men figure alternately as the authoritarian figures who establish the rules of the universe within which women must try to define and assert themselves, and as prizes to be won or lost at the game's end. In no case, however, does the male provide validation for feminine existence; settling down to domesticity follows upon the winning of an identity and is never equated with it. Realism rather than submission dictates the heroine's adjustments to the world.

The angel- and devil-women, since they are incapable of change, are not presented with the same degree of realism as is the heroine. The aura of the supernatural or the uncanny clings to them. The angel is almost always physically debilitated; her early death provides an emotional outlet for readers, but even more importantly dramatizes the fact that she does not belong to the world. This is especially evident when the angel is a child, like Stowe's Eva.[8] On the other hand, the striking physical beauty of the diabolic woman, along with her capacity to ensnare men, connects physicality with evil. Together the two character types strongly imply an attempt to deny physical experience and to dissociate woman's sense of identity from her body.

The angel-woman incarnates self-abnegation, humility, piety, openness, generosity, mildness, love, and forgiveness. She totally lacks the forward-driving, self-assertive urge which is the life force itself, and thus the human heroine, though she may emulate her, cannot become such a woman. Or, to put it differently, were she to become such a woman she too would die. The diabolic witch-woman has the drive, but it is linked with vengefulness, duplicity, coldness, and malevolence. Consequently, though the human woman shares some qualities with her, she is quite a different sort of being—warm, generous, and good-natured. The basic plot of all these books is her achievement of happiness and success through self-discipline, with the aid of teachers and examples, and sometimes in the teeth of determined opposition. For one familiar example, *Little Women* tells this story four times over (when Marmee's struggle is included). Beth is of course an angel; *Little Women* is a genial book, and its closest approach to a diabolic character is Aunt March. (The diabolic figure is often a "wicked stepmother" derivative.)

The heroine almost always operates in circumstances of great difficulty. Most often, she is an orphan. She is always poor. She has to live with strangers and indifferent kinspeople. She works for her benefactors but gets neither love nor money for her services. Frequently she must also work—or she decides to work—for wages, as a companion, governess, teacher, shopgirl. She is frequently humiliated, underestimated, and unappreciated. She suffers a good deal and is lonely. Clearly there is much narcissistic self-pity in this portrait, but there is also something more important: although most of the stories bring her peace and security at the end, in the form of a comfortable marriage, they do not always do so, and when they do the heroine has already achieved a degree of self-control and self-dependence that makes this event, strictly speaking, unnecessary. The marriage-and-motherhood syndrome is presented as the most desirable life for a woman, *but it is not required to complete her as a human being.*[9]

If this heroine is confused with the angel-woman whom she emulates (as has regrettably been the case with the critics who see the design of feminine portraiture as polar, rather than triangular), she is certain to be misunderstood as a thoroughly passive being hideously abused by the cruel world. But even when she is recognized as a separate type, she presents something of an enigma to interpreters of her significance. From one vantage point she appears a reactionary capitulation to the forces that wanted women to keep in their places, since all her ability and energy are shaped according to traditional values. From another, she seems a realistic depiction for the time, when women of talent and drive had to learn to accept subservient roles. Yet again, she can be considered an interesting psychological strategy for helping women retain their self-esteem in conditions of life that tended to undermine the female ego. This heroine has psychological strength, moral stamina, and intellectual ability—she is not at all like the weak, clinging, nonrational, and inferior creature of the era's ideology. If the popular books do urge strong women to conform, they also celebrate female strength, ambition, and autonomy. A reader today can much more easily feel the social conservatism of these books than the psychological support they provided in their own time. But since women in the past century were as much human beings as women are today, we can presume that they enjoyed seeing themselves depicted as self-actualizing, self-governing people.

The political views expressed in these books vary, but the

successful women's novels do not seem informed by a feminist consciousness, and women's rights seldom appears as an issue. In *St. Elmo,* indeed, the prodigiously learned and talented heroine, Edna, employs her literary gifts in writing eloquent essays against woman suffrage and in favor of woman's domestic sphere of influence. Like many women at the time, Augusta Evans feared that women would lose what little power they had if they gave up their privileges. Questions of marriage, divorce, and property laws do not intrude in these fictions: although they show almost no intact families, they accept the family ideal as sacrosanct. The reform movements that find expression in these novels are mainly woman's education, abolition, and temperance—the last an important issue for women since they were legally bound to alcoholic husbands or fathers. In general, the orientation of this fiction is private and personal rather than general and political.

We should not leave these books without observing that although they are stylized and sentimental, rife with compensatory fantasy, and often written carelessly, they do tend to pick up characteristics of social and regional life in setting and detail. Offering neither realism nor local color themselves, they are clearly the forerunners of both of these genres which, after the Civil War, absorbed the best energies of our major authors for some forty years. We must look to Susan Warner and Maria Cummins rather than Melville, Poe, or Thoreau for the imaginative sources of the work of Howells, James, Wharton, and Glasgow.

How can such a melange of literary materials, major and minor, popular and elite, be summarized? Of the major authors in this eighty-year stretch, two were specifically concerned with women's rights. Brockden Brown wrote *Alcuin* from a rationalist point of view, while Fuller's *Woman in the Nineteenth Century* is transcendental, but both authors concur in their analysis of a highly discriminatory society which restricted women's field of action and stultified their moral and intellectual being. Washington Irving's genial stereotypes follow the cliché of loving, dependent, domestic female nature. Cooper's women function in a patriarchal framework but exhibit individual variations, and, not infrequently, independence, humor, and high spirits. Emerson's approach was essentially sexless, as was Thoreau's. The latter's work, however, suggests the American symbolic incompatibility between interest in nature and interest in women. Whitman's attempt to speak to both sexes is undermined by his confusion of "woman" with "mother." Poe's women are purely theoretic figures and have no relation to female characterization; Melville's occasional women dramatize male sexual problems.

In contrast, Emily Dickinson, through her persona, defined the world and the personal anguish of a speaker whose gender is the determining factor in her existence, and Hawthorne strove to characterize believable women in social situations. He succeeded in creating the greatest heroine of the period. Hawthorne's uniqueness can be explained in part by the fact that, in his case, the serious desire for popular success led him to turn his attention to popular topics and forms, as the other major authors did not. The popular novels of the day, written largely by and for women, are a repository for examples of female characterization. It is unfortunate that from this sizable group of authors there did not emerge—as there did in England—writers of lasting literary status. Perhaps fresh and unbiased readers will discover some works of quality in this mass of material. In the interim, we can only regret that the split between popular and major literature has prevented us from understanding how women thought about themselves in these important years of American development.

Notes

1 The best summary article on this ideology is Barbara Welter, "The Cult of True Womanhood, 1820-1860," *American Quarterly* 18 (1966), 151-74.

2 At the moment, Page Smith's *Daughters of the Promised Land* (Boston: Little, Brown, 1970) is the only one-volume history of women in America. It is a useful beginning volume, though rather too general. Much information about women is to be found in books about the feminist movement; especially good for this period of American history are Eleanor Flexner, *Century of Struggle* (Cambridge, Mass.: Harvard University Press, 1959), and William L. O'Neill, *Everyone Was Brave* (Chicago: Quadrangle, 1969). Some recent theoretical articles with excellent bibliographies are Gerda Lerner, "The Lady and the Mill Girl: Changes in the Status of Women in the Age of Jackson," *American Studies* 10 (1969), 5-15; Ann Gorden et al., "Women in American Society," *Radical America* 5, no. 4 (1971), 3-66; and Ronald

W. Hogeland, "The Female Appendage: Feminine Lifestyles in America 1820-1860," *Civil War History* 17 (1971), 101-14. Two fine regional books are Dee Brown's anecdotal *The Gentle Tamers: Women of the Old Wild West* (New York: Putnam, 1958) and Anne Firor Scott, *The Southern Lady: From Pedestal to Politics 1830-1920* (Chicago: University of Chicago Press, 1970).

3 The most complete book on popular fiction in this period is still Herbert Ross Brown's *The Sentimental Novel in America 1789-1860* (Durham: University of North Carolina Press, 1940). F. L. Pattee's *The Feminine Fifties* (New York: D. Appleton-Century, 1940) is laughably chauvinistic by today's standards. Helen Waite Papasivily's *All the Happy Endings* (New York: Harper, 1966) is unscholarly but informative on the topic. See also the introduction by Donald A. Koch to the Odyssey Press edition of *Tempest and Sunshine* and *The Lamplighter* (New York, 1968). My approach to these popular works is quite different from all of these studies. More general studies of American popular fiction are Frank Luther Mott, *Golden Multitudes* (New York: Macmillan, 1947), and James D. Hart, *The Popular Book* (Berkeley and Los Angeles: University of California Press, 1950).

4 In his *The Early American Novel* (Columbus: Ohio State University Press, 1971), Henri Petter summarizes many plots of fictions written between 1789 and 1825. The plots are generally either gothic or sentimental, and the sentimental tales are usually novels of seduction and betrayal. Petter calls this genre the "novel of victimization" (p. 28). These early fictions have little in the way of characterization. The heroine is a passive figure, a cipher whose function is to suffer. One often finds a female adversary, a malevolent woman of the world, but she is subordinate. The chief source of distress in these works is the coincidence of feminine weakness with male heartlessness. This vision of male and female nature provides the context for protests like Brown's assertion of female strength and rationality. As this eighteenth-century stereotype gives way to the nineteenth-century view, so too does the content of protest change.

5 In *The Poetry of American Women from 1632 to 1945* (Austin and London: University of Texas Press, 1977), Emily Watts identifies a similar pattern in nineteenth-century poetry.

6 The most influential overall view of American female character portrayal has been, unfortunately, Leslie Fiedler's *Love and Death in the American Novel* (New York: Criterion Books, 1960). Fiedler is not really interested in woman characters. His argument substitutes the portrayal of guilt-free heterosexual males for the portrayal of women, assuming that if the males are normal and healthy, then the women characters must be so also. Two general articles which do actually focus on women characters are Wendy Martin's "Seduced and Abandoned in the New World: The Image of Women in American Fiction," in *Woman in Sexist Society,* ed. Vivian Gornick and Barbara K.

Moran (New York: Basic Books, 1971), pp. 226-39, and Linda Ray Pratt's "The Abuse of Eve by the New World Adam," in *Images of Women in Fiction,* ed. Susan Koppelman Cornillon (Bowling Green, Ohio: Bowling Green University Popular Press, 1972), pp. 155-74. The theses of these articles declare themselves in the titles; though they are offered as general discussions, they draw on a limited selection of works.

7 Richard Chase's popular theory in *The American Novel and Its Tradition* (Garden City, N.Y.: Doubleday, 1957) begs this question by discerning peculiarly "American" version of the novel that disregards many standard examples of the genre written in America.

8 The idea that children who die young are really angels briefly lent their temporary parents is also probably a strategy to help women cope with the loss of their children.

9 This assertion does not hold for the most common narrative pattern in popular women's fiction written before 1820—the plot of seduction. The purport of the seduction story is that a woman has no choices in life except between marriage and death, which is to say that for a woman being alive and being married are synonymous. The disappearance of the seduction genre from American fiction by about 1830 marks a major and significant change in the literary image of woman.

10.

They Shall Have Faces, Minds, and (One Day) Flesh: Women in Late Nineteenth-century and Early Twentieth-century American Literature

Martha Banta

In 1879 when Henry James looked back upon the effects of the Civil War, he was not thinking specifically about women, nor was he intentionally sounding the note of tragedy. The tone given this observation—"one may say that the Civil War marks an era in the history of the American mind"—does not reveal either great anxiety or a bracing against a radical revelation; no more than do the phrases describing the America created by the aftermath of that war: "a more complicated place than it had hitherto seemed, the future more treacherous, success more difficult." [1] Time and World War I would finally reveal to James the import of the process of which he had caught only a glimpse in 1879.[2] What interests us here is that James's own novels and tales began to demonstrate, among other things, what it meant to American women to live on the far side of that Civil War which marked off the Age of Innocence from the Age of Experience.

It was not long before Henry Adams joined James in the absorbing task of assessing the connections between the kind of nation America was becoming and the ways in which women were being affected by the changes of the postwar period. Most of all, both men increasingly sought to know what had gone wrong in America. Somehow, they sensed, the answers might be detected in the lives of its women. Women were the best index of the causes and the consequences of the American tumult; they presented the clearest representations of the illusive tendencies that were bedeviling the nation, the sexes, and the society. As Adams had reconfirmed to his satisfaction every time he turned to his "liveliest neighbor" at innumerable dinners and asked of her why American women were failures, the one true answer came: "Because the American man is a failure!" [3]

Adams spent a lifetime analyzing failure and the cause and effect relationships which brought it about. Why, if the Union had won the war, was there no unity? Why, if the stronger military force had triumphed, was force being wasted in the Age of Energy to such an extent that men were fearful of the day there would be none left to sustain society or life? Why, if the southern slaves had been freed from their status as property, were more subtle forms of property ownership enslaving all sorts of Americans still manifest? Why was there gold everywhere, but little of value? Unity; force; property; value—whatever the nature of his questions, they somehow gathered around the way the American woman was being treated.

For Adams, as well as for James, that treatment found its best expression in images: images being foisted out of uncritical adulation, resentment, lust, sentimentality, and general misunderstanding by the American male; images creating the center of much of American writing, whatever literary forms it took. These were images that indirectly implied the larger social issues that lay behind them, and also images which quite directly declared the nature of the functional types women were being given to enact. Through our examination of these images and the kinds of literary genres that contained them, we can watch the solutions which were evolving on the spot in response to the artistic problems of how best to portray the American woman's passivity or energy, her ignorance of her plight or full awareness of her fate.

The images of women emerging from the period immediately after the Civil War, and the literary forms used to convey them, are as complex or as simplistic as the minds that shaped them. But certain general observations and classifications can be made concerning the questions that led to their creation and the answers they were supposed, however tentatively, to suggest. First, then, let us sketch in the central issues—property, value, force, and unity; later we shall elaborate on the types.

To survive a civil war is one thing; to last out the period of reconstruction is another. There were all those women who said nothing and wrote nothing: the women of New England left behind in decaying villages and collapsing farms while the young men moved on to try to make it out west, the women who went all queer, whose hidden lives Sarah Orne Jewett and, later, Robert Frost tried to fathom; the women of the South depicted by Ellen Glasgow in her novels of Virginia, by Henry James in the reportage of *The American Scene,* and eventually by the fiction of William Faulkner—those women sustained by hatred and their devotion to a failed cause; the women of the Midwest for whom Edgar Lee Masters had to speak, aided only by the mute documents of tombstones and old photographs. Such women represent a lost history that has had to be set down after the fact, by other hands, in a literature dedicated to the memory of silent women, narrow lives, and the economics of deprivation.

The poverty of village or farm and the pinched existence of its women was a major fact of the postwar years, but much of America's attention was focused instead on the gaud of the Gilded Age. The women caught up in its whirl performed important symbolic functions for the Republic's self-congratulatory view of its postwar achievements; they were also visible proof of the self-delusions of the nation and the occasional cause of its nervousness. The Gilded Age took its name from a novel of 1873 on which Mark Twain and Charles Dudley Warner collaborated. Between its publication and Henry James's *The American Scene* (1907) some Americans at least were receiving warning signals about the ambiguous nature of their nation's turbulent economic success.

In *The American Scene,* which emerged from material gathered by Henry James during a visit home from England in 1904, a series of female images and related motifs provide thematic structure and moral significance. Keep this basic fact in mind, and much of James's intricate interpretive activities in the book will come clear: for James the woman is civilization. Whenever civilization is misused or diverted or ignored in America, the same fate is being inflicted upon the women; and vice versa. Both nation and women are being betrayed, and something of great value is lost. Ironically, that value is shunted aside for the sake of gold and property. Even more ironically, that material gain is imaged in terms of the nation whose riches the male passion tries to seize; in turn, the nation is endowed with feminine attributes. Thus the men who lust after monetary possessions have, by their equation of gold with America and America with the woman, lost everything of worth.

Here is Wall Street as imaged in *The American Scene.* It is "the vast money-making structure" where "the assault of the turbid air seemed all one with the look, the tramp, the whole quality and *allure,* the consummate monotonous commonness, of the pushing male crowd. . . ." [4] As a consequence of the city's being put up for sale to benefit her pimps, New York is a "Poor dear bad bold beauty" for whom James feels great compassion *(AS,* p. 109). New York is a whore, tremendously vital, but, alas, "The very sign of its energy is that it doesn't believe in itself . . ." *(AS,* p. 110). The men take as mistress the woman who has lost faith in the purpose of her great charm and energy, corrupted as she is by the male money-passion that only grabs and cannot create.

If the traditional relationship of man and his mistress forms one of the plots offered by *The American Scene* (making it useful to read this nonfiction book as if it were a late novel by James), James characteristically complicates that plot. What has actually happened, James points out, is that the American male has wed his business—that money-force symbolized by the New York whore. The American businessman's true home is Downtown on Wall Street, while, almost surreptitiously, he maintains a second establishment Uptown on Fifth Avenue where his mistress is kept, busying herself with matters of culture and society during the long periods of his absence from her side. The world may believe the

Uptown woman is his legal wife, but James knows that marriage is where passion concentrates itself. For the American male his true union is with the Wall Street woman; his natural element is amidst "the huge American rattle of gold"—that "pecuniary power" which "so beats its wings in the void" (AS, pp. 115, 159).

James, of course, was atypical in his concerns over the grab and waste he found in the relations between the sexes and between America's citizens and its nation. Howard Chandler Christy is truer to the contemporary type in his unquestioning approval of the ways women were being imaged as solid assets. In his book of 1906 on the American Girl, Christy remarked that she is the nation's true royalty; she is the queen whose virtue is always revered since "every American man worthy of the name has been her sworn knight." Christy gravely adds a note that is more bourgeois than feudal when he observes that whether it is their lawns or their women, Americans do no "harm to their property." [5]

With an ironic awareness missing entirely from Christy's glorification of the sound-money policy of investment in the American Girl, William Dean Howells exposes the standard American attitude toward marriage in his A Traveler from Altruria (published during the depression year of 1894). Marriage is a possession which gives a man "the citadel of morality, the fountain of all that is pure and good in [his] private life, the source of home and the image of heaven." Of course, there are "some marriages that do not quite fill the bill, but that is certainly our ideal of marriage." [6]

Sound economics strive to fill the bill every time. The mismanagement of bad economics results only in waste. Henry James saw this when he looked at the women owned by the moneymen of Wall Street: "the ladies, beautiful, gracious and glittering with gems, were in tiaras and a semblance of court-trains, a sort of prescribed official magnificence" (AS, p. 163). These women, like the ones James noted in Saratoga in 1870,[7] suffered a peculiar plight, a variation on the ways in which the worth of women can be wasted. They were all dressed up as if with some place to go and something of importance to do. However, their very look pressed home the irony that their situation contained a total absence of "so many of the implications of completeness, that is, of a sustaining social order . . ." *(AS,* p. 163). James found that "the social empiricism" had put "the cart before the horse. In worlds otherwise arranged . . . the occasion itself, with its character full turned on, produces the tiara. In New York this symbol has, by an arduous extension of its virtue, to produce the occasion" *(AS,* p. 165). What is important to note here is that James was able to discern what was wrong because he could read with such accuracy the evidence that the look of the women before him provided. To other eyes all seemed well: beautifully gowned women meant, did they not, social esteem and tender loving care for them, and a flourishing economy and a healthy culture for America. But James *saw* better, and therefore *knew* better.

If James was unhappy that the Uptown woman had only costly trappings but little social reality, he was concerned with far more than surfaces. If American women are all the society America has (itself a strange, strained situation), this is the result of the man having abdicated his place at the woman's side. This state of affairs, peculiar to America, has come about by "the *successful* rupture of a universal law" that holds that men and women participate together to create cultures of value evolving naturally out of their mutual recognition of one another's value *(AS,* p. 346). What matters to James in all this is not "mere society." Society as the field for human action is too central, too real, to be viewed only as the proper occasion to wear one's tiara. To think this is to reduce the woman's role to the frivolous and to restrict it to Fifth Avenue mansions. The men who woo the Whore of Manhattan might think this, but for James the facts of a nation's society and culture are the genuine reflections of the intelligence and moral fitness of those who create it. The American woman is viewed by James as that sex meant to act as the consummate artist who paints upon the social canvas the full portrait of her character, thereby endowing it with the only value it has. It is a terrible fate, then, that she is too often forced to release her creative energy upon a national void. Lacking the cooperation of men, generally dismissed, the result is that her generation is "addressed really, in the long run, to making a fool" of her *(AS,* p. 348).

In *The Wings of the Dove* (1902) James shows the split in vision held between those of the Lancaster Gate crowd who define Milly Theale only in terms of money in the bank, and those who, like

Susan Stringham, think more closely about what it means that "the truth of truths" about Milly is "that the girl couldn't get away from her wealth." [8] According to the others, what Milly has (thus *is*) are priceless laces and pearls; what James knows, and Susan intuits, is that Milly couldn't have lost her wealth "if she had tried—that was what it was to be really rich. It had to be *the* thing you were" *(WD,* p. 105). James realized that his audience was reading his novel in the midst of a period devoted heart and soul to money; still, he asked them to deal with the strange fact of an heiress whose true value is the quality of her heart, mind, and spirit. His novel turns on the acts of those who scheme to possess by guile what Milly has, without knowing that her finest possession is the ability graciously to give of her love. The tragedy and the comedy of the story swells out of the final terrible realization that those who finally get what Milly *really* offers either do not know what they have been given or, if they do know, find its possession unbearable.

Women rightly viewed as *value,* and wrongly used as *property.* Women also acknowledged as *force*—to be feared for this fact, or honored.

Like James, Henry Adams made out an historical record of America's folly in the abandonment or misunderstanding of its women. Perhaps, he surmised, it was the result of thinking they knew only too well what women are and thus dared not to let loose her particular force. Adams envisioned the man who sat inside the cab of the great machine of the Age of Energy. This man realized that "his living depended on keeping up an average speed of forty miles an hour, tending always to become sixty, eighty, or a hundred, and he could not admit emotions or anxieties or subconscious distractions, more than he could admit whiskey or drugs, without breaking his neck." "He could not run his machine and a woman too, he must leave her, even though his wife, to find her own way . . ." *(EHA,* p. 445).

What Adams observed by the end of the nineteenth century had been sensed before. Hawthorne is only one writer who testified to the deep apprehension over the anarchical power the woman might represent. The symbolism of Hester Prynne's dark hair is frightening in its implications; no wonder society made her confine it under a neat Puritan cap.

What the woman has as her birthright is force, and ways must be found to ignore or to suppress that force; or to let it dissipate itself in harmless gestures. The Lancaster Gate crowd in *The Wings of the Dove* liked to think that Milly Theale was harmless. They preferred to shift their gaze from her to the "embodied poetry" of her pearls. But when Milly comes down the staircase at the Venetian palazzo, she is described as "Milly let loose among them in a wonderful white dress . . ." *(WD,* p. 379). The force of love that Milly is imposes its own kind of emotional and moral havoc once it is set astir; it looks innocent, its intention is to bless, but it is a devastating force that irretrievably alters the lives it touches because it is a force that resists dissipation; because it focuses itself and finds its mark.

Henry Adams was concerned over what happens when the "Woman had been set free—volatilized like Clerk Maxwell's perfect gas; almost brought to the point of explosion like steam" *(EHA,* p. 444). But his concern was more often over forces *not* focused and the threat arising when such energy is scattered like "ephemera." Adams saw "volatilized" women abroad in Europe as skittish tourists, and in Washington, D.C. as

> grave gatherings of Dames or Daughters, taking themselves seriously, or brides fluttering fresh pinions; but all these shifting visions, unknown before 1840, touched the true problem slightly and superficially. Behind them, in every city, town, and farmhouse, were myriads of new types. . . . All these women had been created since 1840; all were to show their meaning before 1940.
>
> Whatever they were, they were not content. . . . The problem remained—to find out whether movement of inertia, inherent in function, could take direction except in lines of inertia. This problem needed to be solved in one generation of American women, and was the most vital of all problems of force. *(EHA,* p. 445)

Women *waiting* to be used well and to make the best of their own value: many of the novels of this period place just such women at their dead center. If a few of these women like to believe theirs is a patience formed of hope, most realize their waiting is no more than dreary resignation and despair. William Dean Howells did very well in depicting the latter type. Howells's heroines—well represented by his Annie Kilburne—often want to do good in their communities; they fret to have their energy put to proper civic use. Another group of Howells's women are like the fatuous Mrs. Makely of *A Traveler from Altruria* who goes in exhaustion each year to summer resorts, moaning, "It is not work alone that kills. . . . There is nothing so killing as household care. Besides, the sex seems to be born tired" *(TA,* p. 24). Howells is excellent in his depiction of women whose nerves are about to snap, neurotics seeking to rouse themselves from lethargy by that "nicest kind of fad"— charity—or even "religion" which may be horrid but is "perfectly safe" *(TA,* pp. 68-69). Together with Mark Twain and Henry Adams, Howells had his own high-strung women at home to care for. As a result these men were able, at least in part, to understand what it might be like to be a woman with nerves unraveling, not because she is silly or shallow like Mrs. Makely, but because her personal force is not sufficiently grounded, converted—made good—as energy.

In the novels of Howells and James, and in the lives of the women they knew personally, there is much potential force, but something often blocks its full, fine release into the world. Often that blockage is caused by the women being underrated. Sometimes it comes in response to the imposition of excessively high, falsely defined ideals upon the reality of their urges and interests. Whether these women suffer by being pressed upon by attitudes that image them as being *less than* or *more than* they actually are, they are caught between social rigidities and inner tensions. We ought not be surprised to realize how many novels of the period emphasize women's frustrations and how many books are set on edge by hypersensitivity and feelings of great lack. What matters is how the women in these books react to their bad lot. Faulty economics, misdefined value, wasted force: these are the factors which make women see themselves as victims. But will they as a result respond by living and dying as "Patient Griseldas" or as "Defiant Heroines"?

Patient Griselda and Defiant Heroine were the types referred to by Henry Adams in a Lowell Institute Lecture of 1876 on the subject "Primitive Rights of Women." [9] Once long, long ago,

Adams the historian discloses, women were strong, will-proud, and resistant to whatever attempted to thwart their personal desires. They were true heroines, possessors of their own destinies; they refused to be merely the purchased or plundered property of men. But by the time of the Roman Empire, and, later, the Holy Roman Empire, state and church allowed women distinction only if they meekly fit the pattern of Patient Griselda. Thereafter, the women who had once—as Adams argues—held power in Egypt and Iceland, Homeric Greece and among the North American Indian tribes, were no longer able openly to enjoy their "direct talent for life."

It is that special talent which is possessed to overflowing by Henry James's defiant heroine, Kate Croy (who shares this role, though with quite different ways of expressing it, with Milly Theale in *The Wings of the Dove*). Kate Croy learns cunning in order to assert her talent; she studies how to act in modes acceptable to the Lancaster Gate gang, the same society which she defies even while she uses it to gain what it, too, names as life's highest goals: money and marriage. No Griselda, Kate is impatient. She does not want to wait very long for anything, but she is willing and able to control her sexual desires for the sake of her counterpassion for the things of "the great life." This is in 1902. Shortly after, American novels came to be peopled by young women with the talents of Kate Croy who, unlike Kate, cannot wait for a moment. Women like Daisy Fay, Faye Greener, and Lady Brett Ashley want, and want now. They want all that the body can give them and all that desire can seize from society. But most of the women in the novels before World War I wait on. The results of that waiting game, how they play it, and the nature of the victories and defeats they experience, make up in large part the plots of the period's novels— the novels we now see with such clarity as moving narratives of potential and of waste.

Property, value, force—and unity: these images mount and intermingle.

In *The Education of Henry Adams* the author notes what the force of the woman had once been for the unification of the human race. "All the steam in the world could not, like the Virgin, build Chartres" (*EHA*, p. 386). In contrast, the modern male—particularly one born in America—was no longer capable of giving instinctual recognition to that fundamental, fertile power possessed by both Venus and the Virgin. At Amiens Adams realized that he responded to the Virgin as "the animated dynamo," as "reproduction," as the fecund sex for which "neither art nor beauty was needed"; his friend, the artist, St. Gaudens, could only see her as "a channel of taste." Adams and St. Gaudens "had but half a nature, and when they came together before the Virgin of Amiens they ought both to have felt in her the force that made them one, but it was not so" (EHA, pp. 384, 387). The male had been "starved" and "blighted" from the start of America's history by a concerted effort to ignore what the Woman and women represent. Even if Adams and his friend were the best of a bad lot, they could not unify sex with culture; they could not become whole in themselves until fully able to recognize the woman's multifold force.

As a novelist Henry James tried to show the way to the needed unity by his careful portrayal of heroines of the mind. Through the acute consciousness with which he endowed his women characters, James attempted first to join sexual passion, cultural force, and intelligence, and second to give them the moral direction which, for him, was the necessary element that transformed what women did into significant and saving value. Even where James succeeded (and many gladly argue that he did not), Adams still had cause to shake his head. Sex and culture had already failed in the western world, Adams believed; all that was left was thought, once the greatest form of human energy, now the mark of its tragic lack of moral purpose.

In "The Rule of Phase Applied to History," Adams's essay of 1908, he suggested contemporary thought might be proceeding into the Ethereal Phase (a period of severe decline) as it neared the time it would become "pure thought." Pure thought cannot act, Adams declared; it is only potential and thus has no force. "Thought in terms of Ether means only Thought in terms of itself, or, in other words, pure Mathematics and Metaphysics, a stage often reached by individuals." [10] "At the utmost," Adams continued, thought "could mean only the subsidence of the current into an ocean of potential thought, or mere consciousness, which is also possible, like static electricity. The only consequence might be an indefinitely long stationary period. . . . In that case, the current would merely cease to flow" (DDD, pp. 308-9). To borrow the idea we have just been working out, the failure of the universe (and America) is analogous to that woman of force who waits and waits, unable to *do* anything with her unused value.

Henry Adams, together with James and Howells, firmly believed that contemporary women had good minds. According to Adams's theory, however, women—in having reached that mental excellence at the greatest personal cost—had only gained a pyrrhic victory. That women had minds as refined as, if not more refined, than those of men was grindingly ironic since it was now the bad time of the Ethereal Phase of human history. Such ability to think might simply assure the death of the human race. To be sure, Adams held out the hope that by means of the mind new sources of energy might yet be released; life might yet be continued and bettered. However, he could make no metaphoric leap from the medieval Virgin as reproductive force to the modern woman of mental energy as the merciful intercessor for humankind.[11]

Just as pessimistic about the advantages to be gained in America through having a large population of women of good minds was Hjalmar Hjorth Boyesen. This Norwegian-born writer, professor of German at Cornell and Columbia, and friend of Howells, was quick to acknowledge the presence of the American bluestocking— the girl possessed of impressive will, independence of spirit, and obvious intelligence. The American girl Boyesen described in his essays actively aspires to the life of the mind and is far more interesting than the American male; but she is apt, while turning about the dance floor, to ask her partner to expound Spinoza's *Ethics*.[12] It would seem, then, that intelligent American women had few choices. They could participate in the tragic apocalypse envisioned by Adams; appear in the slightly ridiculous light shed by Boyesen's praise; or elect to capitulate to the anti-intellectual bent of Howard Chandler Christy when he quite literally set up the American girl in idolatry as a pretty young *thing*.

Christy first introduces his American pride and joy in the chapter, "The Sweet Girl Graduate." Hers is the "pure little heart" which beats freely only on the day she leaves books and thought behind forever *(AG,* p. 86). In their place is lots of healthful summertime play at tennis and golf while she "loafs and invites her soul," readying herself for the really important work of the next season: being "introduced" to society and "getting married."

Whereas Adams's Woman stands on the edge of a great mental Dead Sea and Boyesen's Girl concentrates her humorless gaze inward upon Spinoza's profundities, Christy's Girl focuses banally upon the sleek male prize. A few American males might still share Henry David Thoreau's Transcendentalist distaste for girls who have "regular features" and no intellect. But there were all those who worshipped Christy's débutante or who, like Mark Twain, felt exuberant pleasure over the "dear girls" Twain describes in a piece of 1909: "dear, sweet, loud, familiar, good-hearted, vulgar mechanic's-boarding-house girls, of the eternal pattern, the regulation pattern, the pattern that never changes and never fails. Pretty, too. They always are." [13]

In *The Rise of Silas Lapham* (1885) Howells went beyond conventional views of the female heart and mind; but even he significantly apportions a woman's potential wholeness into schematic halves. There is Irene (the extraordinarily pretty sister who is silent and likes to tend the house) and there is Penelope (the clever, plain sister who reads and talks a lot). The ways in which anti-intellectualism could manifest itself in the fiction of this period are legion and sometimes quite subtle. The praise granted to handsome minds is muted and less frequent. What stands out is that the good head (where it *is* admired) has usually been severed from the physically enticing body. Occasionally there is a pretty face completed by an excellent mind, as with James's Isabel Archer in *The Portrait of a Lady*. But the celebration of what a woman possesses from her neck down is rigorously divorced from the value granted her from the neck up—face or brains.

There are exceptions, of course; and they are usually found in the late novels of Henry James. There are Kate Croy and Charlotte Stant, for example, in *The Wings of the Dove* and *The Golden Bowl*. Even in these works James carefully stresses the *cleverness* of these women. Though to be clever is not to be any less brainy, in the world of James's fiction it is certainly to be far less than morally intelligent. Thus, even in the generous range offered to the female type by James's writing, we are still limited to the lady with the fine mind but without the voluptuous body; or the woman with a sharp mind and a body that arouses disturbing, erotic responses. A distinction is maintained, however subtle, between women who have souls and intelligence and those with physical ripeness and questionable cleverness. Today many women wish to keep the world's attention trained entirely upon their minds. But before this particular turnabout could come to pass it has been necessary to give women bodies so that they might, if they wish, reject them.

The evidence from the period bracketed by the Civil War and World War I overwhelmingly demonstrates that not only was the bulk of the American middle-class reading public excessively shy in matters of the flesh, but that the majority of those who were writing was just as timid about going into the question of a woman's sexuality. Up to and into the twentieth century women in literature were still divided into that classic triad: mothers/sisters/wives; servants/spinsters/relatives; whores. In the midst of real and continuing obstacles which artists (male and female) had to face on the public front, they had to deal with inner struggles concerning their private attitudes toward female sexuality. Howells and Adams wittily, but quite seriously, proclaimed their distaste for love scenes that took place on creaking sofas with women who went in for clawing and biting. Mark Twain's lifelong watchfulness over any overt expression of his sexual impulses has been almost embarrassingly documented. But out of that same sense of recoil experienced by Twain which made him apt to portray his females (peripheral to his "boy-plots" as they are) as pretty and insipid, comes one extraordinary, and highly significant, exception: his portrait of Roxy in *Pudd'nhead Wilson* (1894). Mark Twain once recorded a dream he had had about "a negro wench" gourmandizing "a mushy apple pie—hot" who "made a disgusting proposition." The clarity of his revulsion and fascination for this vivid dream-image prepares us in part for his remarkably strong and ambivalent attitude toward the slave woman Roxy. It is Roxy who takes over the action of this novel until the author finds it necessary to undercut her special power and to destroy the threat of her presence.

In the void between Hawthorne's Hester Prynne and James's Charlotte Stant, Mark Twain's Roxy explodes her energy upon the literary scene out of a bland American sky. Roxy's earthy body is impressively matched by a sharp-edged mind, an implacable will, and stormy emotions. Little wonder that Mark Twain officially assigns Roxy a supporting role. The fact that she refuses to remain on the sidelines of the narrative is good evidence of the centering force such a complete woman could command. Almost as if to punish Roxy's mastery of the novelistic situation, Mark Twain takes from her her role as Defiant Heroine of a tragedy; he "kills" her off by turning her into a weeping, passive, beaten-down Griselda of melodrama and fate. Mark Twain allowed Huck Finn, the social outsider, to take over *his* own story; he could not permit Roxy, another outsider, to retain control of hers. To be an outcast while white and a boy is safer than to be an outcast, black, and a woman passionate both in body and mind.

Under such circumstances it is hardly an overwhelming surprise that *the woman with a body* was either to be ignored altogether or treated in a cautious, limiting, frequently insulting way. Since it was often just as great a trial to represent *the woman with a mind,* all that was left that seemed safe was *the girl with a face.* It was, however, impossible to think that *she* could bear the symbolic weight of the crucial issues exacted of the American female by the best intelligences of the time. It was ludicrous to believe this inane creature could do other than collapse under formidable questions about property and value, force and unity.

Still the questions remained: can a writer portray a true heroine of the mind, while fending off the obvious anti-intellectualism of Christy, the barely disguised biases held by Boyesen, and even (at times) the patronizing tone of Howells? Can this portrait also reveal the woman to be the self-confident possessor of a body that is as interesting, as real, and as much a part of her life as her mind? Or will compromises have to be made by splitting up the whole personality into separate parts, and assigning each part to a different character in the single story—or even delegating those parts to separate books drawn from different literary genres? When we look at even the most interesting of the novels written at the time we find just such fragmentation, as when the heroine of the mind is placed at the center of a tragedy of the intellect and the girl victimized by others' desire for her body becomes the focus of a melodrama of the flesh.

We shall see the consequences of these decisions to parcel out pieces of the whole among distinctive literary forms once we move into the second part of this essay. What we find often comes as the result of responses to the following questions: (1) Is the American girl worshipped because she fulfills the need of the American male for a banal idol? [14] (2) Is the American female looked at hard as a reality only in terms of the disruptive force she represents which must be countered by drastic means? Does she threaten through her forthright sexuality which gives men nightmares of lost self-control or does she rather frighten because of her perfections which are capable of destroying everything in the path of her unbending idealism? [15] (3) Can the American woman be appreciated as someone who is both a human reality (neither demon nor angel) and has much of value to give to herself and to others?

With these questions to work from we are prepared to examine the half-dozen literary types available to women in late nineteenth-century American writing: (1) the Bitch-Virgin; (2) the Mother; (3) the Spinster; (4) the Victim; (5) the Heroine—(a) the Heroine as Idol; (b) the Heroine of Ideas. Notice in particular the ways in which possibilities opened up for the tragic embodiment that moved the woman free from the type of the girl of the melodrama, that literary form which still held out the most appeal for the public mind. Static as this period seems to twentieth-century readers stupefied by its uninventive repetitions and shallow characterizations, something very important is in the process of taking place. If we can be excited by the obvious upheavals brought about by the novels of the 1920s and 1960s, we ought also to find excitement in the real changes, however subtle, taking place by the 1880s and after.

William James, in ways not unlike those of his brother Henry, made an analysis of what drives the American male onward. He personified what he found as the Bitch Goddess Success. This idol of Wall Street represented the degraded lust for money of the Gilded Age; it replaced Henry Adams's symbol for the exalted sexual force of the Middle Ages—the Virgin. Yet in certain instances the Bitch assumes qualities that are paradoxically virginal and maternal, as well as destructive.

In a note written about 1837, Charles Darwin made the following observation on the psychological responses of the Bitch which absorbed William James a generation later when he came at it from the direction of social psychology rather than biology:

I suspect conscience an hereditary compound passion, like avarice. Is there not something analogous to imperiousness of Conscience: in Maternal instinct *domineering* over love of Master & sport etc etc—The Bitch does not so act, because maternal instinct gives most pleasure but because most imperious.[16]

In Darwin's musing the Bitch—examined by him as the literal mother-animal type—seeks to exert a special kind of coercive power. This drive to domineer would seem in human terms, through the associational references made by Darwin, to join both conscience (moral tyranny) and avarice (greed to possess). This linking often appears in American novels of the late nineteenth century, but apportioned between separate women characters: for example, Isabel Archer and Serena Merle in *The Portrait of a Lady,* and Milly Theale and Kate Croy in *The Wings of the Dove.* Furthermore, if the reader happens to think ill of that conscience possessed by the Lady or the Dove which imposes *its* domineering force, then it can be said that both these novels by Henry James contain bitches of conscience (Isabel and Milly) set in contention against, but in kinship with, bitches of avarice (Serena and Kate).

In *McTeague* of 1899 Frank Norris incorporates both the qualities of conscience and greed into his portrait of Trina Sieppe and the terrible effects this "bitch" has upon the "mastiff," McTeague. Poor McTeague, how afraid he is of women! "He did not like them, obstinately cherishing that intuitive suspicion of all things feminine—the perverse dislike of an overgrown boy." [17] It is important to notice how Trina herself is described: "the woman in her was not yet awakened; she was yet, as one might say, without sex. She was almost like a boy, frank, candid, unreserved."

Why is McTeague, the overgrown boy, frightened of Trina? Would Huck be "sceerd" of Jim or Tom, or Ishmael of Queequeg? Perhaps Norris discloses part of the answer when, soon after the description given above, he presents this explanation:

McTeague began dimly to feel that life was too much for him. How had it all come about? A month ago he was perfectly content; he was calm and peaceful, taking his little pleasures as he found them. His life had shaped itself; was, no doubt, to continue always along these same lines. A woman had entered his small world and instantly there was discord. The disturbing element had appeared. Wherever the woman had put her foot a score of distressing complications had sprung up, like the sudden growth of strange and puzzling flowers. *(McT,* p. 39)

Adam before Eve. Natty Bumpo before Judith Hutter proposes. The old-time western hero before the schoolmarm tries to replace his horse. Before: in Paradise; life on the raft that is free, easy, and comfortable: before Aunt Sally or Miz Watson or the Adams's and James's women come along with their terrible urge to "civilize." Certainly this fear of being spruced up past self-recognition is part of McTeague's reaction; on the plane of social behavior at least. But there must be more, deeper down. What we are shown through McTeague's responses to Trina—once the "woman" is awakened in her, as well as what Norris calls the "beast" in McTeague—is the caveman's atavistic desire to possess met in violence by the woman's desire to be seized.

When Trina whispers, "I'm afraid of *you,*" the dentist "did not heed her" for "an immense joy seized upon him—the joy of possession."

> Those instincts that in him were so close to the surface suddenly leaped to life, shouting and clamoring, not to be resisted. He loved her. Ah, did he not love her? The smell of her hair, of her neck, rose to him.
>
> Suddenly he caught her in both his huge arms, crushing down her struggle with his immense strength, kissing her full upon the mouth. Then her great love for McTeague suddenly flashed up in Trina's breast . . . yielding all at once to that strange desire of being conquered and subdued. *(McT,* p. 133)

So far, so good. The two urges (wanting to possess, wanting to be possessed) match. Then Trina whispers to McTeague again, but this time with the warning, "Oh, you must be good to me—very, very good to me, dear. . . ." Alas, Trina is adding the ultimate discord to McTeague's simple mastiff-world; the discord of that force which is shared by both the bitch of greedy desire and the bitch of domineering conscience. "You must be good to me—very, very good." Norris has shown that the male is content as long as his situation is confined to matters of desire and gratification, and so, to a point, is the female. But she also exacts that promise which will destroy satisfaction gained easily, sustained easily.

From the beginning of the novel Norris depicts McTeague as a potential battleground between the beast and the better self. Like Mark Twain's Huck, Norris's McTeague demonstrates that whether the "boy" follows the promptings of the dark or the light angel—follows greedy instinct or restrictive conscience—the male is doomed. To Mark Twain and Frank Norris only animals are happy, since only they are free from the terrible yoke of the "Moral Sense." And the Moral Sense is what civilization is. Civilization, in turn, is everything that the word "woman" represents, even as she simultaneously rouses within the male the dormant beast of violence and anarchy.

After his marriage to Trina and a sharp decline in personal income, McTeague is uneasy. "He had become used to her by now. She was part of the order of the things with which he found himself surrounded. He saw nothing extraordinary about her . . . she was merely his wife. . . . But he sadly missed and regretted all those little animal comforts" which Trina has taught him to desire: cabbage soup, bottled beer, steaming chocolate, "Yale" tobacco, and afternoon walks in a silk hat and Prince Albert coat (*McT*, p. 208). Trina has been the one who has "educated" McTeague's physical needs—who, by "civilizing" them, has caused them to cost the money he no longer can earn. Now, without money but still possessed of the new desires instilled by the Woman, the Beast finds himself denied his "animal comforts." He is told he must be satisfied with what he had been content with *before* Trina came into his quiet boy's life with her avaricious greed for hoarding gold, her civilizing education in the wanting of "things," and her demands that the Beast be "very, very good." Once, the five-cent tobacco brand called "Mastiff" had been sufficient; but for a man to have experienced "Yale" (and Prince Albert coats), and then to have them taken away: *that* is what gnaws and ultimately kills. To remain placidly at the bottom of the Darwinian ladder of human evolution is contentment. To have moved up several rungs—urged on by the Woman's twofold bitch-desires, then to slide backward: this is to slide *all the way down* into Death Valley where the novel's action comes to its terrible conclusion.

In 1906 Howard Chandler Christy wrote that the American débutante is "the culmination of mankind's long struggle upward from his barbarism into civilization. To make her all that she is countless millions have lived and died" *(AG,* pp. 69-70). Such a phrase not only calls up the figure of Trina Sieppe McTeague; it looks toward F. Scott Fitzgerald's portraits of Daisy Fay Buchanan and Nicole Warren Diver. In Norris's novel of 1899 the sexually potent bitch who simultaneously excites the flesh and is excited erotically by thoughts of gold—and who also demands obedience to respectability—brings to a head all the destructive forces suggested by Darwin's jottings of 1837. The end of their story is inevitable: Trina murdered by the Beast within the man she had educated up from the Mastiff; McTeague, handcuffed to a corpse, trapped in the primordial terrain of his ancestors. *McTeague* is the novel of an American Samuel Richardson run amuck among the forces of respectability and marriage, sexual lust and gold, the struggle upward and the plunge downward.

It serves as an informative study in contrasts and similarities to look at Christy's American Girl. She is the sister who becomes the American male's dream-wife. Somehow (since it is unthinkable that it happens by biological means), she also becomes the mother of the nation's future. In all her pretty young thingness, she continues to embody those bitch-values of conscience, love of possessing and being possessed, and disguised sexuality reverenced by her self-deceiving male adorers. In *Sister Carrie* (1900) Theodore Dreiser brought off a companion portrait of the American Girl, even though he included intimate details of social squalor which the Christy Girl would find it hard to imagine as existing "out there." [18]

Carrie Meeber is just another pretty girl from the cornfields near Chicago, one of that legion of native American products whom Mark Twain applauded. Why did this particular girl become a star of the theater? How did she reach public success by one of the few ways open to a woman of her time, however socially questionable such theatrical connections were? Carrie is attractive and sufficiently quick of mind. On stage she has the ability to merge herself into the parts she plays, yet she also stands out in a group and is not just another "pony" in the chorus line. Somewhat passive, she does have hidden funds of will power. If she experiences precious little physical desire, she excites it in others. Carrie is fastidious in her dress and moves with style. That is the real answer: she *moves*.

Carrie moves because she is dissatisfied. She is looking for something even if she does not know what it is. Furthermore, Carrie's unfulfilled desires register on her pretty face, thereby adding something to her mouth and her eyes. The men in the theater boxes lean nearer, focusing intently on that face that seems as if it were about to cry. This is Carrie's great attractive quality: she is "the cosmic waif" men wish to be tender toward. And more: for what Carrie is—lonely, yearning, restless—is what they also are.

Neither Carrie nor the men in the audience can give a name to this ineffable sadness, but its force goes beyond whatever physical excitement Carrie conveys. What is most telling perhaps is that Carrie's beauty—centered in her expression, not her features or her form alone—is worth money on the American entertainment market. Her presence in the theater represents instincts, ideals, emotions—all quite undefinable in words, but directly translatable into cash and public acclaim.

Compared with Trina McTeague Carrie Meeber is the sweet bitch. (She would not have *wanted* Hurstwood to die his shabby, forlorn death if she had ever bothered to think about him.) But she is one just the same: a special version of the Bitch Goddess Success—a goddess worshipped for the blind hopes and desires she manifests in the flesh, and a success because men will pay good money just to circle near her shrine, the theater stage. She is the bitch-designate of that greed to possess, not in the superficial sense of wanting money for its own sake, but because she *is* desire.

It is also necessary to recognize that Carrie is the bitch of conscience as well. Early in the novel the men who use Carrie sexually come, at least in part, to view her as their victim. During brief moments of self-consciousness, they experience that hesitation of purpose which temporarily blocks easy gratification. By the novel's end Carrie's role as carrier of conscience is turned into another, but related, direction. Carrie is admonished by Ames to

aim for "higher and finer" things in life. He wants her to employ
her physical and emotional force on the stage in creating important portraits of deeper ideas. Either way—her present success in
popular romantic comedy or her future in more tragic (i.e.,
"refined") roles—Carrie is meant to stand before men as a
tormenting double lure; the call to desire, and the admonition to
be "very, very good." There is also the ironic implication that if
Carrie decides to try out her powers as a figure of culture she will
make even more money as an actress and attain more social
prestige. Yes, Carrie is the true ancestress of that other famous
manifestation of the American Dream of Fair Women kept forever
a hand's span beyond the reach of men—Daisy Buchanan, whose
voice sounds like coins and who, bitchily, is avarice, restrictions,
enticement, fragility, hardness, and death in one illusive form.

The American woman as mother is the next arresting image
which takes on literary prominence during this period. Mark
Twain often turned weepy over the thought of sainted maternity,
but he enjoyed writing a rip-snorter about Mary Baker Eddy and
the founding of the Mother Church. His portrait of Mrs. Eddy is
simply another imaginative version of the bitch who domineers by
means of the maternal conscience, while greedily taking over both
men's lives and their cash. In contrast, there is the more "pure"
concentration on the maternal image provided by Mary Johnson,
the drunken, brutish Irish Earth Mother of Stephen Crane's
novella, *Maggie: A Girl of the Streets,* published, with difficulty, in
1893. Mrs. Johnson, who survives while the rest of her family goes
to ruin, is one version of the nightmare mother. There is also the
special menace which Henry James provided for his story "Daisy
Miller" in the figure of the passive, absentee mother of the girl who
would also—like Maggie Johnson—die, in part, of a mother's
neglect.[19]

The opposing view of motherhood—one more appropriate to the
age which saw the institutionalization of Mother's Day in 1907—
was held by Walt Whitman. In his belief that American women
fulfill their highest destiny as bearers of the new democratic race,
he expressed his celebration of the bond between a fine nation and
a superb maternity:[20]

I am the poet of the woman the same as the man.
And I say it is as great to be a woman as to be a man,
And I say there is nothing greater than the mother of men.

> ("Song of Myself," stanza 21)

Be not ashamed women, your privilege encloses the rest, and is
   the exit of the rest,
You are the gates of the body, and you are the gates of the
   soul.

> ("I Sing the Body Electric," stanza 5)

... a strong and sweet Female Race, a race of perfect
mothers—is what is needed. *(Democratic Vistas)*

Henry Adams joined Whitman in his notion of the woman-as-mother as the all-important basis for social stability. To Adams—that knight-errant continually on the quest for a home, both in the cosmos and in society—the family was the one dependable unit left to humankind, and the woman was the last living creature fully at home in the world. In *The Education of Henry Adams* he strikes the note he had sounded as early as his 1876 lecture on "Primitive Rights of Women." "She did not think of her universe as a raft to which the limpets stuck for life in the surge of a supersensual chaos; she conceived herself and her family as the centre and flower of an ordered universe which she knew to be unity because she had made it after the image of her own fecundity . . ." *(EHA,* p. 459).[21]

The very fact which Adams revered of the woman's ability to make a home in the midst of the "supersensual chaos" was what F. Scott Fitzgerald shuddered over as the fatal legacy inherited by succeeding generations of American sons. In *Tender is the Night* (1934) Fitzgerald portrays Dick Diver, his married American idealist, as the result of the good and ill done the men of the late nineteenth century by their mothers. It was these women who gave their children "the illusions of eternal strength and health, and of the essential goodness of people; illusions of a nation, the lies of generations of frontier mothers who had to croon falsely, that there were no wolves outside the cabin door." [22] The ability to persuade the men at work settling the American wilderness that there is no harm out there in the night is a masterful one. But when, in turn, the men convince themselves that the women who do the gentle persuading are also "wolfless," illusion is piled upon illusion and there will be trouble.

However important as a symbol, the ways in which the American Mother could be portrayed during the final decades of the nineteenth century were limited, and the readers' responses to her presence in a literary piece were usually stock. She was often used as the excuse for vague sentimentality; was occasionally depicted as a hazard either because of her oppressive "mothering" force or, conversely, because she shirked her duties of "being always there"; or was endlessly elevated as the specific hope of the race through her talent for tidying up the edges of chaos. Whether the mother-image was a son's best sweetheart or his jailer or the rock of his salvation, the mother as a type was well fixed. If the manner in which young unmarried women were portrayed was somewhat narrow, at least there were strong, if isolated, signs that an expansion of that literary type had begun. Not so with the woman who was married with children or with the woman who would never marry and never have children. Mother and Spinster alike were true victims of the popular conventions of the period. Only the Girl on her own and the Woman who dared had the energy to start to break free.

Writ small as a potential force during this period is the Spinster. Indeed, her lack of anything resembling life is what most characterizes the literary type. She often appears in a number of stories and novels, but this frequency is also a guarantee that her portrait will introduce no sexual or cultural discord into the social scene. Sometimes unmarried women are treated as comic subordinates to the main characters; sometimes they are dealt with sensibly, if sketchily; more often than not all writers had to give to their spinsters is sentimental pity for the "life" they never had. The norm is provided by the regional literature of the last decades of the century, which often centers on the manless New England areas or the South stripped by the slaughter of the war. Here the point is reiterated that these women *would* have had a full life "if only" it had not been for the Civil War and its aftermath.

But there was Emily Dickinson. She was the archetypal spinster in the fact of her frustrations, yet she was also the uncommon woman of the literature of her lifetime because she diverted into powerful torrents of poetry whatever blocked currents she suffered privately. Emily Dickinson won the war of antagonistic forces within the heart at the same time the historical events of the Civil War were taking place in a divided nation. This is apparent from the fact that the more bitter the inner disruptions, the more she was able to create. The year 1862 alone saw the completion of 356 poems. That was her *annus mirabilus*—her time of emotional *terribilità* and triumph. The consequence of her struggle was her choice of "just a throne" and her decision to become "The Queen of Calvary." Such choices did not transform her into the queen portrayed in the frontispiece of *The American Girl*. Emily Dickinson's throne and her sovereignty were much nearer to those held by the Virgin of Amiens and of Chartres extolled by Henry Adams. It was a position generally unsought by the American woman (married or not) who had, by ignorance or by fear, tried to avoid the obligations of a force so exacting of the self.

But the Emily Dickinson choice of Queen of Calvary, however unconventional, trembles on the edge of a convention offered, to excess, by many American writers of the period. The Victim was perhaps the single most popular type demanded by the reading public and supplied (with much profit) by its authors. This literary type could obviously be handled with ease at a low level of imaginative merit. What is surprising are the means by which the Victim began to receive excellent literary development. It is this latter phenomenon which will be stressed in the following remarks. The American Girl as victim could, under the inspired pressure of certain writers, come close to, and cross over the line between, the *mereness* of the victim and the *more* of the heroine. She could move from imprisonment in melodramas of pathetic acquiescence to the domination of tragedies of defiance.[23]

Mark Twain allegorized "The Twentieth Century" accordingly:

> ... a fair young creature, drunk and disorderly, borne in the arms of *Satan*. Banner with motto, *"Get what you can, keep what you get."*

> *Guard of Honor*—Monarchs, Presidents, Tammany Bosses, Burglars, Land-Thieves, Convicts, etc., appropriately clothed and bearing the Symbols of their several Trades. *(FM, p. 405)*

In 1901 Mark Twain was thereby indicting the general lust for uncurbed possession and its capacity to victimize an entire century in ways prophetic of Nick Carraway's dream of the drunken woman carried along dark streets, unloved, unknown in *The Great Gatsby* a quarter of a century later.

As a writer Mark Twain always did best by his male characters. From the start he was hampered by deeply emotional responses to innocent young women crushed under betrayal and suffering. His tough old women (like Mrs. Loftus in *Huckleberry Finn* or Mrs. Utterback who brings zest into the *Autobiography)* are strong literary figures; his ingenues are often wincingly embarrassing. He can whip up some linguistic enthusiasm over red-haired Mary Jane Wilks in *Huckleberry Finn* by assigning "sand" to her character, but then she collapses, as do most of his pretty girls, into futility. Men rage in Mark Twain's melodramas over the injustices of the cruel world; the girls weep. A writer cannot get much mileage from so limited a formula (one which at last trapped Mark Twain's men just as much as it had his women characters). Needed in this period of all too idle tears were writers who were capable of seeing women, at the very least, as *interesting* victims; at the best, as victims who finally assert themselves as something more.

Stephen Crane's *Maggie: A Girl of the Streets* is about those streets far more than about Maggie. Crane was fascinated most of all by the New York slums. The characters in his story are treated like fragments of dilapidated tenements struggling to stave off collapse. The people who *do* survive are all, significantly, women. There is Mrs. Johnson whose sheer animal energy cannot be squelched; Nell, the hard, clever whore who knows how to use every man and each occasion to further her ends, undeterred as she is by Maggie's vague hopes and soft idealism; and the old beggar woman downstairs who makes out in a ruthless society because she is outside society, beneath it—thus not vulnerable, as Maggie is, to contending demands that she bring in money from "de toif" and yet remain respectable in order to sustain the good name of the family.

Still, the titular heroine is Maggie, the one who totally fails to survive. Maggie, whose figure is deemed "outa sight" by Pete, has the general physical attributes of Dreiser's Carrie Meeber. But Maggie is a Darwinian sport—an organic whim that cannot possibly make it in an environment into which, by some hereditary fluke, she has been dropped without the will or capacity to adapt. If Henry Adams (who did not have Maggie's economic problems) considered himself a biological and cultural superfluity—a mere "begonia"—what chance has Maggie, a rose that "blossomed in a mud-puddle"?

Maggie is the period's representative victim: too pretty not to be lusted after; too pliant to withstand such demands; too sensitive to be able to bear what is happening to her as she heads downhill toward the dark river of death; too unimaginative to *think* her way out of her deterministic box. Contrast Maggie Johnson with Maggie Verver of James's 1904 novel, *The Golden Bowl.* Maggie Verver is certainly not as pretty as the Irish rose, but she has a fortune that makes her desired by the Prince (James's version of Pete) and she is burdened by just as many ideals as Maggie Johnson (and as many that are suspect and false). Both Maggies are set off in marked contrast to the way of their worlds. But James's Maggie has the imagination both to suffer and to adapt and, finally, to transcend the fatality of her environment and her betrayal. Further, if she adapts, she does it in gracious ways that Charlotte Stant (James's variation on Crane's Nell) cannot.

Contrast Maggie Johnson, too, with Isabel Archer (and even with Pansy Osmond, the parallel victim James's generosity supplies *The Portrait of a Lady*—that novel strongly ruled by traditional elements of melodrama). At the depth of her despair, Isabel sees herself as being as much a prisoner in the Palazzo Roccanera in Rome as ever Maggie Johnson is in the slums of New York.

> She had taken all the first steps in purest confidence, and then she had suddenly found the infinite vista of a multiplied life to be a dark, narrow alley, with a dead wall at the end, instead of leading to the high places of happiness, from which the world would seem to be below one, so that one could look down with a sense of exaltation and advantage, and judge and choose

and pity, it led rather downward and earthward, into realms of restriction and depression, where the sound of other lives, easier and freer, was heard as from above, and served to deepen the feeling of failure.[24]

The major difference between Maggie Johnson and James's victims is that the former is the dupe of fate, the girl who never really knows what is being done to her. Isabel Archer and Maggie Verver, in journeying through their consciousnesses, arrive at last at some real knowledge. Maggie Johnson only stumbles through degrees of misery to end in the dark unknowing of the river. Once James's heroines arrive at awareness—that clearing in the darkness (however surrounded still by its oppressiveness)—they experience far more pain than they did in their earlier innocence. But at least they now know what is happening to them, even though not exactly why they have been made life's victims.

In James's novels the girl as victim, a figure in a melodrama of betrayal and fatality, constitutes one of the literary elements of his basic vision. But what converts his tales of her woe from the pathetic to the tragic is the force of two facts: first, the girl finally says, as it were, to her betrayers, "I may be your victim but I am not your dupe!"; second, even in the midst of her direst pain she makes a difference in the lives of those who betray her; she is a power they must reckon with.[25]

In his preface to *The Wings of the Dove*, James wrote of the problems the artist faces in recording a life wracked by pain, betrayal, and dying; he states how he sought through the figure of Milly Theale to counter the pull of her plight toward mere melodrama.[26]

> ... the last thing in the world it proposed to itself was to be the record predominantly of a collapse. I don't mean to say that my offered victim was not present to my imagination, constantly, as dragged by a greater force than any she herself could exert; she had been given me from far back as contesting every inch of the road.... Such an attitude and such movements, the passion they expressed and the success they in fact represented, what were they in truth but the soul of drama?—which is the portrayal, as we know, of a catastro-

phe determined in spite of oppositions. My young woman
would *herself* be the opposition. . . .

James added at this juncture that he was, indeed, writing about "a
young person so devoted and exposed, a creature with her security
hanging so by a hair," but one whose existence, still, "would create
rather, all round her, very much that whirlpool movement of the
waters produced by the sinking of a big vessel or the failure of a
great business. . . ." Milly thus creates for her oppressors "the
strong narrowing eddies, the immense force of suction, the general
engulfment that, for any neighboring object, makes immersion
inevitable." She was never *not* the victim, but, simultaneously, the
pull of her presence on the others is never to be discounted.

Not so Maggie Johnson, who disappears into the still river
without a sound. The triumphant wail of pleased moral indignation let loose by her mother at the end of Crane's novella has no
connection whatsoever with the reality of Maggie's fate. The
violence of the words that give such satisfaction to Mary Johnson
and the neighbors is self-generated out of a subjective void like the
other illusions Crane has been carefully documenting throughout a
story in which Maggie's reality is quite *de trop*.

James's women are hurt by other people, but those people are in
turn altered, sometimes past self-recognition, by the fact of their
meeting head-on the reality of the heroine's counterforce. However
battered by the private morality they cling to, or threatened by the
impersonal factors of "society" or "fate," Jamesian heroines are
participants in a tragic destiny which has the most personal and
human of causes and consequences. James's plots are not those
suggested by Henry Adams who at times believed that women had
only the choice of what force would crush them. "The Marguerite
of the future could alone decide whether she were better off than
the Marguerite of the past; whether she would rather be victim to
a man, a church, or a machine" *(EHA,* p. 447). For James it was
far more of a contest than that.

We see in the fiction of the period a movement of the American
Girl from victim to victim as heroine to heroine in her own right.
In the shifting from the rigid patternings of melodrama to the
more flexible complexities of tragedy, literature was partially liber-

ated from the traditional expectations it carried over from before the Civil War; it was readied to take on a new kind of woman: the woman who knows; who makes a difference; who is more than the dupe, more than the passive acceptor of her plight. The American literary scene now had a force and a face to be reckoned with.

The American public continued, of course, to prefer its ready-packaged idols. The frontispiece to Howard Chandler Christy's 1906 nonbook is a painting entitled "A Veritable Queen." Viewed from an angle slightly below, the eye is forced to look up at the Girl holding a scepter as she sits upon a throne. She is dressed with shoulders bared and décolletage, but her glance is so coldly haughty no presumptions are thinkable. The book then launches its secular litany by repeating the toast offered daily by the officers of the U.S. Army and Navy to "the 'Sweethearts and Wives' who are the inspiration and the reward of valor." Raising this toast (in ways similar to a priest elevating the Host), Christy dedicates his book "to that 'incomparable she,' the American Girl—*bonne cama-rade*, true friend, and lady born and bred . . ." *(AG*, p. 9).

Today we tend to reject such nursery-sop, but we are still faced with the subtle choices between "Florida" and "California" portrayed by Henry James in *The American Scene.* To James Florida is like the Nile without either Sphinx or Cleopatra *(AS,* p. 462). Florida is "a void furnished at the most with velvet air; you may in fact live there with an idea, if you are content that your idea shall consist of grapefruit and oranges" *(AS,* p. 411). James then contrasts Florida—"the great empty peninsula of weakness"—with California, the kind of "female" he much preferred. The far side of America is "strong," "handsome," and "aristocratic." It is also aware of the terrible things that are yet to be done to it, and defiant of all insults to its integrity. California represents "an instinct on the part of Nature, a sort of shuddering, bristling need, to brace herself in advance against the assault of a society so much less marked with distinction than herself" *(AS,* p. 412).[27]

Yet we, as observers of the literature of a period so frequently marred by complacencies and evasions concerning the reality of a woman's character, dare not rest with our complacent admiration of that new woman—thrusting her way into the American novel—who chose to be both "California" and "Queen of Calvary." Obviously great gains were made once exceptions were given to the rule of the Christy Girl. There is also cause for congratulation that the victim of melodrama, who would linger well into the twentieth century in the silent-film gestures of Lillian Gish and Marguerite Clark, was at least in the process of being supplemented by the heroine of tragedy. But the particular kind of heroine offered to literature at this time was, after all, imaged primarily as the woman of ideas and ideals. She was almost self-destructively the woman of mind. Her position as pure and purifying intelligence was by no means secure or her type all to the good of society or herself. That is, not if she, too, was only a Darwinian sport, unable and unwilling to adapt to the demands of a nation that still continues to worship the Bitch Goddess of a still continuing Gilded Age.

We cannot forget, however much Henry James was pleased to celebrate the feminine consciousness, that Henry Adams remained anxious about the historical and human consequences of "pure thought" in total ascendancy. And we must recall that if James constantly affirmed the value of tragedy and transcendent worth, Howells usually refused to allow his women of fine mind and feelings their full tragic stature. By means of the language of irony, Howells continually undercut whatever in his plots might serve to elevate his women characters to the position of saints or goddesses. For Howells the stand he took was not just a matter of choosing between false or true deities; between illusion and reality. He denied his women all the sublime qualities which James, agnostic and humanist, sought to give to the "princesses" of his final novels because Howells could not credit any version of the sublime as a force in human relations, however "realistic" it might be.

Howells and James were both brave men when it came to writing about women (brave in ways other than the more evident spunk displayed by Crane, Norris, and Dreiser in their determination to introduce some of life's squalor and many of its instinctual drives into literature). It is for each of us now to decide which was the braver—Howells, who refused to write in the elevated language of tragedy, however tragic his narrative situations might be; or James, who was more than willing to grant his women the status of the tragic lover of life and defender of the rights of the self to live totally, responsibly, and perhaps destructively.

American writers of the period had still another problem to face in their dealings with women characters. Flesh was allowed attention in two ways: positively, as the maternal fecundity of the Whitmanian mother or as the pretty face of the Twainian ingenue—that is, as it could be safely treated in domestic dramas and romantic comedies; negatively, through concentration on the melodrama whose prurience was disguised by its focus on the moral plight of the virtuous girl victimized by men's vile lusts or by its cautions against the clever adventuress who uses her brazen physical allure to destroy hapless male innocents. In contrast to these evasions and confusions of the real issues concerning the worth of a woman's body, the woman's mind—comprehensively defined as imagination, intellect, intuition, and moral sensitivity—seemed to be the one force she could be accorded by the writers capable of giving her serious consideration at all.

But wherever the literary combination of heroine and mind was granted precedence, that of heroine and flesh was subtly denied. It would require other decades, other writers, before a Charlotte Stant and a Maggie Verver are merged into one fascinating and forceful figure. For better or worse, by 1915 the mind had won a major victory; but the body had to wait—for Edith Wharton, for one.

C. S. Lewis has written a strange and little-known novel called *Till We Have Faces, A Myth Retold.* This book is his retelling of the Cupid and Psyche legend, and it concerns itself profoundly with the shifting attitudes taken throughout history toward the gods we worship. Once idols were only crude, faceless lumps of stone representing the most elemental of natural forces. But the day came, Lewis tells, when those impersonal, heartless, and mindless gnarls of matter began to have faces, hearts, and minds. This was especially true of those images which traditionally depicted the female forces of life. Psyche herself had to discover what she actually was—a soul, not merely the vague force of superstition her family and the community conceived her to be, or a pretty face and maleable will used for gain by the proprietors of her shrine. This, in brief, is the purport of Lewis's novel. It is also the paradigm of the continuing narrative set down by American writers from the 1860s on into the twentieth century. It is a narrative that moves past Emily Dickinson and Isabel Archer, past Carrie Meeber and Maggie Verver, toward Edith Wharton's Lily

Bart and Ellen Olenska. They shall have faces—expressive of minds, feelings, and a soul—and bodies too.

One day, still further on, there might even be American men (not failures) at the women's sides, ending the terrible loneliness noted by Henry Adams and Henry James. For goddesses are only that because they stand alone.

In *The American Scene* James describes the statute of Aphrodite suddenly encountered in the Museum of Fine Arts in Boston.

> She has lost her background, the divine creature—has lost her company, and is keeping, in a manner, the strangest; but so far from having lost an iota of her power, she has gained unspeakably more, since what she essentially stands for she here stands for alone, rising ineffably to the occasion. She has in short, by her single presence, as yet, annexed an empire. . . . Objects doomed to distinction make round them a desert. (*AS*, p. 253)

One feels that James liked to consider a future time in America when heroines would no longer be "doomed to distinction." James saw to it that Milly Theale, heiress of all the ages, decides to sacrifice voluntarily her nearly superhuman power of aloneness; she chooses to "come down" into the world of love, pain, and life in ways that Emily Dickinson, who mounted into the upper floors of her mind, did not wholly do. By the end of her novel, Maggie Verver has come out of the "desert" where, as the Princess, she has paced alone. But Maggie's movement is complete only if, on his part, the Prince moves toward her.

Immediately after the Aphrodite passage cited above, James speaks of the gifts offered by goddesses to their male worshippers: "For confidence in *them* they make a garden. . . ." James's women figures are ready to act "for love," even at the loss of what they have arduously won in their struggle to become princesses and goddesses of force. But to assure that what these women have sacrificed will result in positive and human benefits, the men must also act out of "confidence in *them.*" Then the Great American Desert will become the dreamed-of American Garden, and even better novels can yet be written.

Notes

1 Henry James, *Hawthorne* (Ithaca, N.Y.: Great Seal Books, 1956), p. 114.

2 In a letter of August 10, 1914 James expressed his shock over the betrayal of his old "belief that through the long years we had seen civilization grow and the worst become impossible." *The Letters of Henry James,* ed. Percy Lubbock, 2 vols. (New York: Scribner's, 1920), II: 389.

3 Henry Adams, *The Education of Henry Adams* (New York: Random House, 1931), pp. 85, 442. This book (first published posthumously in 1918) will hereafter be cited as *EHA*.

4 Henry James, *The American Scene* (Bloomington: Indiana University Press, 1969), p. 83. Hereafter cited as *AS*.

5 *The American Girl as Seen and Portrayed by Howard Chandler Christy* (New York: Moffat, Yard, 1906), pp. 61-62. Hereafter cited as *AG*.

6 William Dean Howells, *A Traveler from Altruria* (New York: Hill and Wang, American Century Series, 1957), p. 20. Hereafter cited as *TA*.

7 In the essay "Saratoga" from *Portraits of Places* published in 1883 by James R. Osgood of Boston, James comments that in contrast to the husbands (who "have lived in every fibre of the will"—p. 328), the women "are the most helpless victims of this cruel situation"—the general "social isolation" which makes it a woman's "inexorable fate" that "she shall be nothing more than dressed . . ." (pp. 330-31).

8 Henry James, *The Wings of the Dove* (New York: Dell, 1958), p. 104. Hereafter cited as *WD*.

9 "Primitive Rights of Woman," *Historical Essays* (New York: Scribner's, 1891), p. 38; hereafter cited as *HE*.

10 "The Rule of Phase Applied to History," *The Degradation of the Democratic Dogma* (New York: Harper Torchbooks, 1969), p. 308; hereafter cited as *DDD*.

11 The dominant note of Adams's apocalyptic admonitions, and their implications for the fate of women, is the one snatched up by D. H. Lawrence in his posthumously published book of 1931, *Apocalypse* (New York: Viking, 1966). For Lawrence the coming of intellectualization pulled down the Magna Mater from her throne on the Crescent Moon, down past the level of the Whore of Babylon riding the great Beast (the Earth Mother in her "malefic aspect"), down to the Policewoman of Lawrence's own day. See pp. 139, 150-51.

12 Hjalmar Hjorth Boyesen, *Literary and Social Silhouettes* (New York: Harper, 1894), p. 14.

13 "The International Lightning Trust, A Kind of Love Story," from *Mark Twain's Fables of Man,* ed. John S. Tuckey (Berkeley and Los Angeles: University of California Press, 1972), p. 91. This volume will hereafter be cited as *FM*.

14 See Henry Adams's review article of two historical accounts of Pocahontas in *The North American Review* 104 (January 1867), 1-30, in which this Indian girl (seen by one early settler as a wanton tomboy somersaulting naked through the camp) is shown to have been quickly converted by the art of mythologizing into the savior of Captain John Smith and the revered lady of royal blood at King James's court.

15 Women as dangerous idealists preoccupied Howells and James. Howells's story about Editha and his Penelope Lapham of *The Rise of Silas Lapham,* Rhoda Aldgate of *An Imperative Duty,* and Hermia Faulkner of *The Shadow of a Dream*—together with James's Euphemia de Mauve and Mrs. Abel Newsome—are but a handful of the total portrayed, with apprehension, by these writers.

16 From *Darwin on Man, A Psychological Study of Scientific Creativity by Howard E. Gruber, together with Darwin's Early and Unpublished Notebooks, transcribed and annotated by Paul H. Barrett* (New York: Dutton, 1974), p. 384.

17 Frank Norris, *McTeague, a Story of San Francisco* (New York: Holt, Rinehart and Winston, 1962), p. 17: the next quotation is from the same page. Hereafter cited as *McT.*

18 The story of Carrie's rise, fall, and recoveries evolved out of the experiences of Dreiser's own sister Emma. The novel was initiated, however, by the simple fact of his writing down the words "Sister Carrie" on a sheet of paper. Dreiser also explicitly linked the love he had felt for his mother with the type of women he constantly drew into his own life or gave over to his fictional males to desire. Whatever his own increasing age, his American girls are usually fixed at age eighteen—"the wonderyear," he called it. They were the sister imaged as both mistress and mother. To Dreiser the male is ever "a waif, an unloved orphan in space," in search of the woman who will give him the complete security of her love. But this woman must come in the guise of sister and mistress—the American Girl sexualized, innocent, ready for possession by men who crave the cessation of their orphaned state; the Girl ready to possess the total devotion given by men to the "unsolved mystery" of her force. (The quotations from Dreiser are from John J. McAleer's *Theodore Dreiser, An Introduction and Interpretation* [New York: Holt, Rinehart and Winston, 1968], pp. 8, 43).

19 The novelistic heroines of Henry James do much better in life when they are orphans. Isabel Archer and Milly Theale are free, at least, from having mothers as inept as Mrs. Miller.

20 The following stanzas are from *Leaves of Grass* and *Democratic Vistas,* pp. 41, 83, and 498 of *Leaves of Grass and Selected Prose* (New York: Rinehart, 1958).

21 In the 1876 address Adams noted that to the male mind the appeal of the family is the same as his basic "love of property"; "for this reason the family is the strongest and healthiest of all human fabrics . . ."

(HE, p. 40). Certainly during the later part of the nineteenth century the question is left unanswered whether the woman as mother is a powerful force because *hers* is the family, or whether the male is in control because he insists upon the property value brought him by his material support. Whichever is in possession, Adams's linkages between certain values continue to play back and forth over the same lines: value in unity, unity as force.

22 F. Scott Fitzgerald, *Tender Is the Night* (New York: Scribner's, 1934), p. 117.

23 In *Sister Carrie* the sequence of theatrical roles taken by Carrie parallels the shifts taking place in the novel which govern how Carrie herself is to be viewed by the reader. Her first performance, given for an Elks Lodge benefit, is of an orphan-victim caught in a melodrama. When Carrie enters the professional theater, she begins in musical comedy where she becomes a "star"—the American Girl as idol. By the novel's end, at Ames's urgings, she is contemplating moving up from comedy to drama. So, too, does Carrie herself move from victim to star, with the possibility that she may yet arrive at the elevated rank of heroine.

24 *The Portrait of a Lady* (New York: Signet Classics, 1964), pp. 391-92. This edition is reprinted from the first London edition of 1881.

25 In an undated note of about 1837 Darwin defined "force" as that which makes a difference in the direction taken by the affected object. See *Darwin on Man,* p. 397.

26 *The Art of the Novel, Critical Prefaces* (New York: Scribner's, 1934), p. 290; the following two quotations are from p. 293.

27 Over the years James's novels increasingly had at their center women of the California type. Isabel Archer has "ideas" quite other than those aesthetic pleasures represented by velvet air, grapefruit, and oranges. Gilbert Osmond (the perfect type of "a society less marked with distinction than herself") decides that Isabel's "California" ideas are "very bad ones" and must "be sacrificed" to those of "Florida."

11.

"Combat in the Erogenous Zone": Women in the American Novel between the Two World Wars

James W. Tuttleton

The major claim made on behalf of American women between the two world wars was, not surprisingly, that of freedom. In fiction this claim took the form of an assertion of woman's need for liberation from domestic and sexual bondage in order to achieve full emotional and intellectual development. During the period the critics of our culture debated whether woman's place was in the home as wife and mother, whether she should move out into the "man's" business world, or whether a combination of homemaking and career was possible or desirable. The issue had been given more or less continuous public attention since Margaret Fuller's *Woman in the Nineteenth Century* (1845) and the feminist convention at Seneca Falls in 1848. Though the bloomer-clad suffragists were scorned and ridiculed throughout the nineteenth century (the neurotic fringes notably satirized in Henry James's *The Bostonians* [1886]), the problems of American women came to be increasingly and sympathetically explored in our public discourse, and in 1920 the Nineteenth Amendment, giving women the right to vote, was finally passed. Elizabeth Cady Stanton, the staunch Genteel Era feminist, had cautioned in *Revolution* that suffrage was a "superficial and fragmentary" aspect of the total woman question and that "the ballot touches only those interests either of men or women, which take their roots in political questions." And she warned that "woman's chief discontent is not with her political, but with her social, and particularly her marital, bondage." [1] Despite her warning, the finally achieved right of suffrage seemed to liberate women from the legal suppression they had hitherto suffered, and a new optimism attended the woman question at the outset of the Jazz Age.

Even before World War I, as William H. Chafe has shown in *The American Woman: Her Changing Social, Economic, and Political Role, 1920-1970,*[2] many women had entered the permanent labor force, and the availability of new job opportunities and a more tolerant attitude toward working careers made women in the twenties *somewhat* more economically independent than they had ever been. Increasing social approval of college education for women, moreover, offered to liberate them intellectually from a conception of themselves as fitted only to be wives and mothers. Though the forces of Victorian conservatism were still strong—Mother's Day was first celebrated in 1907—the tide of Progressive politics, symbolized by the passage of the Nineteenth Amendment, promised to sweep aside all obstacles to woman's fulfillment.

Sinclair Lewis's *The Job* (1917) was one of the more interesting early novels during the period to deal with a liberated woman's struggle to fulfill herself through a career. After much personal unhappiness, Lewis's Una Golden fights her way to the top of the business world, her achievement illustrating the claim—most vigorously argued in Charlotte Perkins Gilman's *Women and Economics* (1898)—that women could find emotional fulfillment and liberation from economic dependency in the labor force. "Even the girls who knew that they were going to be married pretended to be considering important business positions," Lewis observed in *Main Street* (1920). But his heroine Carol Kennicott "was a woman with a working brain and no work." When Carol expresses the wish to do something with her life, her boyfriend gives "the immemorial male reply to the restless woman": "What's better than making a comfy home and bringing up some cute kids and knowing nice homey people?" For Lewis the woman's plight was only part of his general complaint against capitalist society, and he affirmed the cooptation of the suffragist/feminist cause into a vaguely revolutionary socialism. Thus Carol argues:

> "We're all in it, ten million women. . . . What is it we want—and need? . . . I believe all of us want the same things—we're all together, the industrial workers and the women and the farmers and the Negro race and the Asiatic colonies, and even a few of the Respectables. It's all the same revolt, in all the classes that have waited and taken advice. I think perhaps we want a more conscious life. We're tired of drudging and sleeping and dying. We're tired of seeing just a few people able to be individualists. We're tired of always deferring hope till the next generation. We're tired of hearing the politicians and priests and cautious reformers (and husbands!) coax us, 'Be calm! Be patient! Wait! We have the plans for a Utopia already made; just give us a bit more time and we'll produce it; trust us; we're wiser than you.' For ten thousand years they've said that. We want our Utopia now. . . ."

But social change came slowly in small-town America (as elsewhere); and at the end of the novel Carol has deferred her hope to her daughter's generation. She does not change the institutions of a conservative capitalistic society, but she does apparently save her soul by refusing to concede that "dish-washing is enough to satisfy all women!" [3]

That the wife and mother's role *could* be a sufficient source of fulfillment was argued by Elizabeth Cook in "The Kitchen Sink Complex" [4] and by Rose Wilder Lane in "Woman's Place Is in the Home." [5] Both of these essays, published in the thirties in the *Ladies' Home Journal,* are representative of the continuing defense in women's magazines, of the view that women would find greater happiness in the home than at the office. Much of the popular fiction of the time sustained this view by implying that the career-girl betrayed the charm of her sex and her true purpose in life. For "the peace of the home," as S. M. Hutchinson's novel *This Freedom* (1922) put it, "rests ultimately on the kitchen." [6] In "Sex and Achievement," Margaret Mead defined the poignancy of the choice confronting women by observing that a woman could either acknowledge herself "as a woman and therefore less of an achieving individual, or an achieving individual and therefore less of a woman." If she chose to be a womanly woman, she had a greater chance to be a "loved object, the kind of girl whom men will woo and boast of, toast and marry." But if she chose the life of self-assertion and achievement, she stood to forfeit, "as a woman, her chance for the kind of love she wants." [7] In Booth Tarkington's *Alice Adams* (1921), the heroine's enrollment in a business college, at the end of the novel, is the seal of her failure as a womanly woman. (Very few of the novelists of the twenties who pointed to careers as a way out of the domestic trap were prepared to see what became increasingly evident, especially during the Depression—namely, that the work of a stenographer, salesgirl, or even business executive could be as alienating, in the Marxist sense, as domesticity. Lewis eventually conceded the possibility in *Ann Vickers* [1933].) [8]

Looking back, one must concur with Chafe's view, in *The American Woman*, that few of the political and social reforms in behalf of women in the twenties and thirties had much real effect on their situation. The availability of the vote took the steam out of feminism, and when male politicians recognized that women as a sex constituted no real political constituency (and thus no real threat), legislation in their behalf quickly declined. (The Equal Rights Amendment, first proposed in 1923, was quietly entombed in committee, where it languished for more than forty years, and at this writing it still has not been ratified by a sufficient number of state legislatures.) At work women found themselves ill paid, relegated to jobs deemed inferior to those of men, and underpaid even when doing identical work. But toward the end of the twenties, "feminism," as Dorothy Dunbar Bromley noted, had become "a term of opprobrium" for young women, signifying "either the old school . . . who wore flat heels and had very little feminine charm, or the current species who antagonize men with their constant clamor about maiden names." [9]

Nevertheless, feminism was one of the forces which served to create a great deal of *felt* freedom among women in the twenties. And that felt freedom manifested itself most clearly in the relationship of the sexes. Edith Wharton's *The Age of Innocence*

(1920) is a convenient point of departure in discussing "the sexual revolution" of the postwar period because this novel dramatized, among other things, the infantilization of the American girl of the earlier Genteel Era in order to put into historical perspective the failure of the emotional development of the American woman. May Welland, the heroine, is victimized by a conception of female education, of the female role, so narrow that she has little room for action beyond that of domestic manager. With little or no education in books, ideas, art, politics, business, sex, or society (except as circumscribed and constituted by her family's small circle), May has few attractive graces capable of sustaining the attention of her husband.

The "innocence" of that era, according to Wharton, was the innocence of men and women ignorant of the nature of passion and human sexuality. Wharton's New York is intended to be representative of genteel urban middle-class American society, insofar as May, a typical girl, is expected to know nothing about sex before marriage, her husband Newland (theoretically) everything. "What could he and she really know of each other, since it was his duty, as a 'decent' fellow, to conceal his past from her, and hers, as a marriageable girl, to have no past to conceal." And yet overnight, on her honeymoon, May Welland, "the center of this elaborate system of mystifications," would be plunged "into what people evasively called 'the facts of life.' " Mrs. Wharton calls May's innocence "an artificial product," a "factitious purity," which had been "cunningly manufactured by a conspiracy of mothers and aunts and grandmothers and long-dead ancestresses, because it was supposed to be what [Newland] wanted, what he had a right to, in order that he might exercise his lordly pleasure in smashing it like an image made of snow." An American girl who suffers the "innocence that seals the mind against imagination and the heart against experience" [10] can hardly sustain a marriage, and May's husband inevitably drifts toward an extramarital grand passion, requiring her to use all of her sweet guile and cunning to keep the marriage intact. Both she and her husband, according to Wharton, were victims of the double standard and of sexual inhibitions that crippled the emotional well-being of the whole Genteel Era.

Though the conclusion of Wharton's novel forecasts the sexual liberation of both men and women in the twentieth century, Grundyism, the conspiracy of silence against sexual candor, and the domestic enslavement of the American woman continued to vex the imagination of our major writers throughout the twenties. And in varying degrees all of them denounced the crippling effects of the double standard and "respectability." In Dreiser's *Jennie Gerhardt* (1911), Wharton's *Summer* (1917), and Sherwood Anderson's *Winesburg, Ohio* (1919) and *Many Marriages* (1923), the psychosexual pressures of respectability, especially in the small town, victimize and warp men and women into grotesques. In *Winesburg, Ohio,* Kate Swift, Elizabeth Willard, and Alice Hindman, who craves love so desperately that she runs naked through the midnight streets, are all poignant victims of a sexually repressive society which thwarts the emotional development of women. Zona Gale's *Miss Lulu Bett* (1920) explores the pathos of a woman—not really the spinster she is thought to be—who can find no place for herself in a family and society which view female singleness as in itself an anomaly. Willa Cather's heroine in *My Antonia* (1918) suffers social ostracism over her premarital adventures, and in *A Lost Lady* (1923) the plight of Cather's heroine, dislocated from the center of her existence after a sexual scandal, is also poignantly explored. If Cather's tough, practical heroines survive, they do so by linking themselves to some large guiding suprapersonal, suprasocial conception—to nature, particularly to the grandeur of the prairies. Something of this kind of salvation is also achieved by Ellen Chesser in Elizabeth Madox Roberts's *The Time of Man* (1926). Ellen's happiness is achieved and her identity is finally shaped by her development of a metaphysic of time—by her recognition of the place she occupies in the temporal cosmic drama, in the generations of humanity successively unfolding through the time of man. Ellen Glasgow's heroines are strengthened by their deep attachment to the soil of Virginia, which gives them a durable vein of iron. In these novels by women, men and marriage are not the solution but are part of the anguish of living. As Dorinda Oakley says at the end of Glasgow's *Barren Ground* (1925), at the suggestion that she might remarry, "Oh, I've finished with all that. . . . I am thankful to have finished with all that."[11] How time and particularized space temper these women to the hardness of their lot on remote farms or prairies indicates that theirs is as much the ordeal of life itself as the ordeal of being female. As embodiments of the pioneer spirit, they reflect an earlier time rather than the turbulent postwar period. In the period with which we are concerned a new type of woman was emerging of much more moment to the male novelists.

This new social type, the Flapper, was something of a scandal to the Respectables. Bruce Bliven's "Flapper Jane," in a 1925 issue of *The New Republic,* expressed shock at her dress, her cosmetics, and her devil-may-care attitude toward life. Clad in short skirts, rolled hose, and bust-confiner; bedecked with rouge, lipstick, and with bobbed hair; with a cigarette in one hand and a cocktail in the other (despite the Volstead Act); freed by Freud, the Hollywood talkies, and the sex and confession magazines newly popular—the modern woman, the "whoopee mama," danced into the lime-light.[12] One of them, calling herself "Last Year's Débutante," said "Good-Bye, Dear Mr. Grundy" in the *Atlantic Monthly* in 1920. Proclaiming the liberation of the new generation of Flappers and Sheiks, she announced: "We are at war and we may as well acknowledge it. We are just as different in language and customs as if we belonged to different nations instead of different ages. We are foreordained enemies, and we youngsters are not ready to appeal to a court of arbitration, even when justice is administered by so neutral a judge as you [oldsters] try to be." [13] Conservatives were aghast at the New Woman's radical attitudes toward courtship and marriage, the education of children, beauty contests, and companionate marriages. As George E. Mowry has shown, she signaled for them "the downfall of society." [14] The New Woman's declaration of war against traditional values had a profound effect on the writers of the period between the wars. In the following pages I propose to look at the response to her (and to other kinds of women) by three of our major writers—Fitzgerald, Hemingway, and Faulkner. Their treatment of women in fiction is part of the social history of the era. But I should be remiss in my duty if I did not say that, though they admired aspects of her bid for freedom, they were fundamentally ambivalent about her. And at times they were clearly hostile to what they felt as a threat she posed to an older ideal of women to which they clung. Their response to the New Woman is highly personal, sometimes indirect, and ul-timately limited in the sense that their fiction does not tell the full story of women between the wars. But even though imaginative literature is not an adequate mirror of social actuality, by examining what is deeply felt by great writers of imaginative power we may be able to perceive how the sexual tensions in our culture then—created by what the feminist Carrie Chapman Catt called "the world-wide revolt against all artificial barriers which laws and customs interpose between women and human freedom" [15]—came to be used for the purposes of art.

I

Fitzgerald's *This Side of Paradise* (1920) described the rebellion of Flaming Youth against orthodox religion, capitalist politics, and the social organization of the classes. But these issues pale before the real revolution, which for Fitzgerald was a revolution against the sexual restraints enjoined on the middle-class American girl. Fitzgerald understood the rebellious young woman intuitively, described her, and popularized her—with the result that he was charged, wrongly, with engineering the rebellion almost single-handedly. The "terrible speed" who told Amory Blaine that she had kissed dozens of men and supposed she would kiss dozens more was no different from thousands of her contemporaries who engaged in what Fitzgerald called "that great current American phenomenon, the 'petting party.' " Among other things, the novel dramatized how *class* attitudes toward sexual freedom had given way to *generational* attitudes toward it. "None of the Victorian mothers—and most of the mothers were Victorian—had any idea how casually their daughters were accustomed to be kissed." For Victorian mothers promiscuity was the mark of the lower class. "*Servant*-girls are that way," observes one mother: "They are kissed first and proposed to afterward." But as the novel makes clear, American sexual mores were undergoing a change marked by the steady decline of the Popular Daughter from the role of "belle" to "flirt" to "flapper" and "baby vamp." Fitzgerald's protagonist Amory Blaine "saw girls doing things that even in his memory would have been impossible: eating three-o'clock, after-dance suppers in impossible cafés, talking of every side of life with an air half of earnestness, half of mockery, yet with a furtive excitement that Amory considered stood for a real moral let-down. But he never realized how wide-spread it was until he saw the cities between New York and Chicago as one vast juvenile intrigue." [16]

Fitzgerald's revelation of the "desperate adventure" of petting in "the mobile privacy of the automobile," where "confidences were exchanged and the old commandment broke down," [17] created a sensation among mothers, ministers, editors, and other defenders of public morality. Lionel Trilling has remarked "how innocent of mere 'sex,' how charged with sentiment is Fitzgerald's description of love in the Jazz Age," [18] and J. W. Aldridge has observed that "It was an intrigue of manners, merely, conducted by glittering children who could hardly bear to be touched. . . ." [19] But if, as Leslie Fiedler observes, there is "little consummated genital love in his novels," [20] Fitzgerald's treatment of sexuality still had the effect of introducing to many young readers a liberated heroine, a girl emancipated from the sexual Grundyism to which she was still expected to conform. In *F. Scott Fitzgerald: A Critical Portrait,* Henry Dan Piper has noted that "unlike her Western counterpart, who was a product of the more free-and-easy frontier, the Eastern girl was still subject to such old-fashioned European customs as the chaperon, an elaborately formal system of etiquette, and an educational philosophy which advocated the separation of the sexes and the incarceration of girls into prison-like boarding schools." Fitzgerald's Midwestern heroines, modeled on the girls he had known in St. Paul, were egotistical, spontaneous, flip, sensual, calculating, and candid—apparently attractive models of freedom to young Eastern girls chafing under conventional restraints. It is no wonder that Fitzgerald was "so puzzled by the Boston and Philadelphia ministers and editors who accused him of trying to corrupt their daughters," as Piper has observed, or that he was "puzzled by the daughters themselves who saw his novel as a clarion call to revolt." [21]

Although Fitzgerald's heroines reflect this liberated Midwestern social type, they also express a deep fantasy about beautiful, emotionally inaccessible, wealthy, and socially desirable women. His view of women is finally inseparable from his view of wealth. *This Side of Paradise, The Great Gatsby* (1925), and *Tender Is the Night* (1934) all reflect his disastrous loss of Ginevra King to Billy Mitchell and the near-loss of Zelda Sayre because, as he put it in his notebook, "a poor boy shouldn't think of marrying a rich man's daughter." [22] Nevertheless, even though he was strongly attracted to her, Fitzgerald suffered deep anxiety over the rich girl who did not promise to fulfill the conventional role of middle-class wife and mother. If writers of the Genteel Era tended to romanticize the American girl (Howells's Kitty and Lydia, James's Milly Theale, for example), Fitzgerald and other young postwar writers began to create versions of what might be called "the young American bitch" and to explore a new intense hostility between men and women never before seen in the American novel. Gloria Gilbert in *The Beautiful and Damned* (1922) rejects domesticity not out of any libertarian principle or career aspiration but out of sheer theatrical hedonism. "What grubworms women are to crawl on their bellies through colorless marriages!" Gloria records in her diary. "Marriage was created not to be a background but to need one. Mine is going to be outstanding. It can't shan't, be the setting—it's going to be the performance, the live, lovely, glamorous performance, and the world shall be the scenery. I refuse to dedicate my life to posterity. Surely one owes as much to the current generation as to one's unwanted children. What a fate—to grow rotund and unseemly, to lose my self-love, to think in terms of milk, oatmeal, nurse, diapers. . . ." [23]

There is no question that Fitzgerald's inspiration, his muse, was an ideal of feminine beauty. But Ideal Beauty incarnated itself in the style of his time, as *The Beautiful and Damned* makes clear—as "a ragtime kid, a flapper, a jazz-baby, and a baby vamp." [24] Small wonder the attraction-repulsion in his portraits of Rosalind, Isabelle, Gloria, Daisy Buchanan, and Nicole Diver. Attractive as she was, the New Woman could hardly fulfill Fitzgerald's high expectations or realize his dream. In the perception of this fact he found his theme, for he could not help recognizing in the New Woman what she so often recognized in herself—boredom, insincerity, triviality, and hedonistic irresponsibility. "I've got a streak of what you'd call cheapness," [25] Gloria concedes; and this cheapness, desecrating Fitzgerald's ideal of love and beauty, manifests itself in the flapper's addiction to the speakeasy, the squiggling saxophone, and the seductive foxtrot. "I can't make my feet behave when I hear that tune. Oh, baby!" cries one of Fitzgerald's flappers. "God, I'm sophisticated," sighs another.

No wonder that for Fitzgerald, as for Amory Blaine in *This Side of Paradise,* "the problem of evil" solidified into "the problem of sex," and that beauty came to be "inseparably linked with evil"—"most of all with the beauty of women"—because, "after all, it had too many associations with license and indulgence." [26] The association of womanly beauty with license and indulgence is most vividly presented in *The Great Gatsby.* Daisy Fay Buchanan symbolizes for the parvenu hero all the glamour of beauty and wealth in a desirable woman. She, like his own identity, is a creation of his imagination, with little relation to actuality. She is the fairy-tale princess in the king's tower whose voice is full of money—the epitome, in short, of the "golden girl" he has always desired. He cannot perceive "the basic insincerity," the "incurable dishonesty," of her character. And in the end, of course, he is murdered for the crime she commits. Fitzgerald's memorable heroes all suffer at the hands of rich, bored, sophisticated, insincere women who "smashed up things and creatures and then retreated back into their money or their vast carelessness, or whatever it was that kept them together, and let other people clean up the mess they had made...." [27] (Though Fitzgerald's criticism here is principally directed at both Buchanans as representatives of an affluent economic class without ethical values, the moral character of the women of this class, especially Daisy, is the major object of his attention.) Gatsby is a representative of all the sad young men in Fitzgerald's fiction because his ideal of woman, his need for love, cannot find its proper incarnation in an age of vamps and flappers. And in the histories of these young men, entrapped by their own fantasies, we may observe Fitzgerald's anxiety over the emasculating power of the New Woman of the Jazz Age, to whom nevertheless he was powerfully attracted.

All of Fitzgerald's stories have a touch of disaster in them because he was detached enough from his own aspirations to recognize that "living wasn't the reckless, careless business these people thought—this generation just younger than me," "the wildest of all generations, the generation which had been adolescent during the war." He accurately foresaw the moral letdown in store for them as "things were getting thinner and thinner as the eternal necessary human values tried to spread over all that expansion," and finally "the most expensive orgy in history" came to an "abrupt end" when "the utter confidence which was its essential prop" received an "enormous jolt" on Black Friday in 1929, and the whole "flimsy structure" came crashing down. "It was borrowed time anyhow," Fitzgerald later observed, "the whole upper tenth of a nation living with the insouciance of grand ducs and the casualness of chorus girls." [28]

By 1929 and the onset of the Depression, as Elizabeth Stevenson has shown in *Babbitts and Bohemians: The American 1920's,* the Flapper as a type had disappeared—into harlotry, some said, or, as others said, into middle-class respectability.[29] Fitzgerald inclined toward the former view, for he was incapable of imagining that the liberated woman of the twenties, severed from her traditional role, could achieve a happiness and fulfillment he could admire. His essays on the Jazz Age, written in the 1930s, underline the moral implicit in his earlier stories. To his daughter Scottie he wrote in 1937: "For premature adventure one pays an atrocious price. As I told you once every boy I know who drank at eighteen or nineteen is now safe in his grave. The girls who were what we called 'speeds' (in our stone-age slang) at sixteen were reduced to anything they could get at the marrying time. It's in the logic of life that no young person ever 'gets away with anything.' They fool their parents but not their contemporaries. It was in the cards that Ginevra King should get fired from Westover—also that your mother should wear out young. I think that despite a tendency to self-indulgence you and I have some essential seriousness that will manage to preserve us." [30] Fitzgerald's remark to his daughter is paternal, personal, and moralistic; but it also suggests the thirties' view of the twenties' experience. Fitzgerald's saving grace, what preserves him for us, was his sensitivity to the social transformations liberating young American women (and men), the accuracy with which he recorded their moral experience, and the aesthetic power with which he organized and expressed his ambivalent feelings—with the effect that we are as attracted to his heroines as he was, but in the end are equally disillusioned with the self-indulgent uses to which the American girl of the twenties, as he saw her, had put her freedom. "If I had anything to do with creating the manners of the contemporary American girl," Fitzgerald once lamented, "I certainly made a botch of the job." [31]

II

In his early career, Hemingway portrayed the new young woman very much as Fitzgerald did—with fascination and distaste. Hemingway's heroines are not dizzy flappers foxtrotting in New York speakeasies, but many of them are comparably self-indulgent, hedonistic, and deracinated from older stable moral and social values. There is a measure of truth in the commonplace observation that Hemingway's *The Sun Also Rises* (1926) reflects the "lost generation." Brett Ashley is a desexed symbol of the effect of the "dirty war" on Hemingway's generation. Her bobbed hair and man's felt hat, her alcoholism and sexual promiscuity, her drunken consort with male homosexuals in Parisian bars are physical and sexual symbols—like Jake's genital wound—of the spiritual damage the generation had suffered.[32] For several decades of Hemingway criticism the representative character of this novel, as a reflection of our social history, has been accordingly emphasized.

But the characterization of Hemingway's women also suggests that he was profoundly disturbed about male and female sexuality. In particular one may observe that his deep (if masked) suspicion of women reflects a neurotic anxiety, like Fitzgerald's, over their emasculating power. Brett is portrayed with considerable sympathy, but we cannot ignore her incapacity for serious feeling, which wreaks Circean havoc on the men in her life—Mike, Robert Cohn, Romero, and Jake Barnes. Margot, in "The Short Happy Life of Francis Macomber," is presented as "simply enamelled in that American female cruelty"; and Wilson, the British safari guide, remarks of American women that they are "the hardest, the cruelest, the most predatory and the most attractive and their men have softened or gone to pieces nervously as they have hardened." [33]

This fictional view of emasculating American female cruelty and male insecurity and nervousness is doubtless a response to Hemingway's own experience with women. But it may have a more specific origin in his friendship with Zelda and Scott Fitzgerald. For in *A Moveable Feast* (1964) Zelda is portrayed as having virtually emasculated Scott by telling him that, genitally, he was insufficiently endowed. "But why would she say it?" Fitzgerald asked, after he and Hemingway had compared measurements in the men's room of a bar. "To put you out of business," Hemingway replied. "That's the oldest way in the world of putting people out of business, Scott." [34] In "Mr. and Mrs. Elliott," Hemingway presents a husband effectively put out of business by an aggressive (possibly lesbian) American wife. And in "The Snows of Kilimanjaro" Hemingway explores the question of whether the "rich bitch" sapped her husband's writing talent by making life too comfortable for him, by "womanizing" him, with the effect that he failed to realize his literary gift. The rich wife is finally absolved of responsibility for her husband's failures. And we may take note that the hunter Wilson's view of American women is not necessarily that of his author. Yet the recurrence of bitchy women in Hemingway's fiction suggests a continuing deep aversion to the aggressive New Woman of his time. The character of the erogenous combat between Hemingway's couples suggests an incompatibility between the conflicting needs of men and women so deep that his men often find it easier to go it alone. Hemingway continually played variations on the theme of *Men Without Women* (1927) because the new female of the species was in fact, for him, deadlier than the male.

Nevertheless, Hemingway is the tender poet of heterosexual love during the period between the two world wars. And in *A Farewell to Arms* (1929) and *For Whom the Bell Tolls* (1940) he celebrated that love tragically, poignantly, and perhaps even sentimentally. We are asked to admire his heroines, Catherine Barkley and Maria, because they are not New Women, Circes, vampires, or bitches. They appealed to Hemingway's imagination because of their utter sexual willingness, submission, and passivity. Both are idealizations of the womanly woman stereotype. They are old fashioned, self-sacrificing, and totally involved in and devoted to fulfilling the needs (sexual, physical, and emotional—but not intellectual) of the men in their lives, Frederic Henry and Robert Jordan. Catherine says, "There isn't any me. I'm you. Don't make up a separate me. . . . You're my religion. You're all I've got." And Robert Jordan assures Maria, "You are me now. . . . Surely thou must feel it, rabbit." [35] And for her, for both of them, the earth moves.

It is intentional, therefore, that Catherine has long blond hair and that Maria suffers deep shame at her head's having been shaved by the Fascists. Long hair for Hemingway is the physical symbol of genuine femininity, and in these heroines he celebrates an ideal of womanhood which seemed to him to have largely vanished after World War I, except perhaps in Europe. The mindless heroine with no will, ego, or identity of her own is rightly objectionable to many contemporary women. But Hemingway's sensibility required him to idealize that kind of woman, for he was not equal to the emotional skirmishing often present in normal heterosexual relationships. His distrust of aggressive women in marriage grew out of the traumas of his own parents' relationship, devastatingly portrayed in "The Doctor and the Doctor's Wife." "Once a man's married he's absolutely bitched," Bill tells Nick in "The Three-Day Blow." "Fall for them but don't let them ruin you." [36] Yes, Nick agrees, their emotional claims can be devastating. In "Cross-Country Snow," Nick has to give up skiing in Switzerland and settle down in the United States because his wife Helen is going to have a baby. The "domestic enslavement" of the wife, treated in works like Lewis's *Main Street*, here becomes the plight of the husband. But such "enslavement" is only one of the ways women ruin Hemingway's men, "bitch" their lives.[37]

In Hemingway's order of values masculine independence had an extraordinary importance. Its source was his need for emotional self-protection, his fear of damage to the self. His feelings about women were inextricably involved with his perception of the meaninglessness of life—which is nasty, brutish, and short—and his fear of death. Given the valueless world, the problem (as Jake defines it in *The Sun Also Rises*) is "how to live in it," [38] what kind of code to devise in order to protect the self from anxiety arising out of the fear of death. One solution is the "giant killer" of drink, ritually consumed in a clean, well-lighted place (a limited area of self-imposed order): drink blots out the consciousness of nihilism, the *nada* pervading all existence.[39] Another "giant killer" is of course sex, for the ecstasy of orgasm and the attendant emotions of uncomplicated, undemanding, and adoring heterosexual love may alleviate the solitude of existential dread. This is the wisdom of Pilar in steering Maria and Robert Jordan into the double sleeping bag: together, within it, they make an "erotic alliance" against "the things of the night."

But this union offers Hemingway's lovers only a momentary deliverance from the consciousness of *nada*, for even the supreme value of romantic love is shown to be ineffectual before the fact of death, seen by Pilar in the lines of Jordan's hand and symbolized by the rain that terrifies Catherine Barkley. Thus the question becomes, "how to live in it" if love is not enough. "A man must not marry," advises the Italian major in "In Another Country." "If he is to lose everything, he should not place himself in a position to lose that. He should not place himself in a position to lose. He should find things he cannot lose." [40] (This bitter feeling is the consequence of his young wife's having just died.) One is interested here in how Hemingway's men cope with the emotional complication caused by relationships with women. In "Indian Camp," the brave slits his own throat because he cannot bear his wife's agony in childbirth. At Adrianople in *In Our Time* childbirth, the fruit of love, is attended by the chaos of war and death in the steady rain. The speaker in "On the Quai at Smyrna" must resort to irony to cope with the horror of "the women with dead babies. You couldn't get the women to give up their dead babies." [41] And in *A Farewell to Arms* Frederic Henry is left alone at the end with his grief—Catherine's death being the price of his sleeping with her, of his giving himself so fully to a woman that he is absolutely vulnerable to the cruelty of fate. He might have known better. "There is no lonelier man in death, except the suicide," Hemingway once poignantly observed, "than that man who has lived many years with a good wife and then outlived her. If two people love each other there can be no happy end to it." [42]

The need for love, then, the complete gift of the self, dangerously exposes the Hemingway hero to his own emotional vulnerability. Woman is a party to an eventual assault on him by *nada* and death; and the knowledge of this fact often makes him emotionally aloof from her. But even his own body betrays him—through emotions like fear or the need for love, by mental fatigue, physical frailty, and old age. How to live in it: Hemingway's stories suggest that only the disciplined will, resistant to the seductions of happiness and the illusion of its permanence, only the stoic power of endurance, hardened by the cruelties of fortune, can give his protagonists a means of triumphing over the meaninglessness of existence. Though momentarily "unmanned" by his grief, the major in "In Another Country" straightens himself, and walks out of the hospital, his dignity recovered, intact. Nick, Jake, and Frederic Henry all seem "bitched" by the women with whom they become involved. Their histories evidence the author's deep fear—if not of women, at least of man's "weakness" in "succumbing" to his own emotional need for woman. Looking at Hemingway's strong men, the ones who survive, we take note of Santiago in *The Old Man and the Sea,* the major in "In Another Country," and the old man in "A Clean, Well-Lighted Place" as instances of the "undefeated," men redeemed by an inwardness of stoic strength in which, finally, women have no part—except as poignant memories of love the hero once momentarily had but lost.

III

The power of endurance is also a major value in Faulkner's fiction. But he celebrates not the careful old men but the enduring spiritual strength of women. What Faulkner felt about women and how he characterized them have been so frequently misrepresented that the judicious reader of his novels may well be astonished. His New Women are without question unflatteringly portrayed in *Mosquitoes* (1927) and *Sanctuary* (1931). And Joanna Burden in *Light in August* (1932) and Drusilla Sartoris in *The Unvanquished* (1938) are neurotic, even perverted women. It is true that one of Faulkner's characters (Jason Compson) remarks, "Once a bitch always a bitch," and that another regards women as "articulated female genital organs with an aptitude for spending whatever money you may happen to possess." [43]

But it is by no means true, as Maxwell Geismar has claimed in *Writers in Crisis,* that Faulkner has "a suspicion of women when it is not contempt and contempt when it is not hatred" or that he sees "the Female source of life itself as inherently vicious." Nor is Leslie Fiedler correct in claiming that "In no other writer in the world do pejorative stereotypes of women appear with greater frequency and on more levels, from the most trivial to the most profound," or that if Faulkner "dared treat in such terms any racial minority, his books would have been banned in every enlightened school in the country." [44] These remarks distort the fiction of Faulkner by identifying the author's view with the opinion of some of his characters. In fact, Faulkner's novels contain a large gallery of women, of all ages, several races, and many social and psychological types. Though he holds up a mirror to American (particularly Southern) womanhood, his aim is to dramatize conflicts of the human heart at moments when conduct and feeling are at an extremity of crisis.

Like Fitzgerald, the young Faulkner was captivated by an ideal of woman—young, alluring, virginal, inaccessible—symbolized in his recurrent allusions to Keats's "still unravished bride of quietness." The glorification of this kind of feminine ideal is natural to romantic young men. But the Southern tradition of reverencing what a character in *Sanctuary* calls "the most sacred thing in life, womanhood," [45] gave a special intensity to Faulkner's portraits of women. He did not believe in the Southern cult of womanhood, of course, but his imagination was captivated by its effect on sensitive young men twisted by their own sexual idealism. Horace Benbow in *Sartoris* (1929) is one such young man; Quentin Compson in *The Sound and the Fury* (1929) and *Absalom, Absalom!* (1936) is another. Neither of the sisters of these young men is equal to the purity expected of the Southern lady, for the need for love in women, as in men, is powerful; and sex is a drive in Faulkner's women that sometimes masters them. The idealistic young man's incapacity to deal with female sexuality (particularly that of his sister) is often, therefore, his doom as well as hers.

Actual women, as Faulkner well understood, cannot without violence be put to the service of abstract idealism. Despite the American myth that women are purer or more spiritual than men, Faulkner's novels reveal that sex is a great natural procreant urge that cannot be constrained by Calvinism. In "Hair" Ratliff observes: "There's not any such thing as a woman born bad, because they are all born bad, born with the badness in them. The thing is, to get them married before the badness comes to a natural head. But we try to make them conform to a system that says a woman can't be married until she reaches a certain age. And nature don't pay any attention to systems, let alone women paying any attention to them, or to anything." [46] The comedy of Faulkner's rhetoric undercuts the suggestion that sex is in itself evil. But it is clearly an irrepressible energy at the very center of woman's being. In the portrait of Eula Varner in *The Hamlet* (1940), this natural female sexuality is elevated into the myth of the Earth Mother at its highest, wildest, funniest pinnacle. Her brother Jody, her teacher Labove, and the other men of Frenchmen's Bend who have been shaped by "the harsh functioning of Protestant primary education" are powerless before Eula's sexuality, which communicates itself as "a moist blast of spring's liquorish corruption," the men's hysterical desire illustrating "a pagan triumphal prostration before the supreme primal uterus." [47]

The life-affirming, procreative character of female sexuality, irrepressible and hardly subject to theological or social constraint, is also comically presented in *Light in August*. The protagonist Joe Christmas is destroyed by a series of tragic adventures, often with women, who try to minister to his needs. (Feeding him is the giveaway sign of their nourishing function.) Joe cannot reconcile himself to the ambiguity of his racial identity, or to the ministration of women, however, and is eventually destroyed. Lena Grove's story, which envelops Joe's, puts his tragedy into perspective by celebrating her as the embodiment of fulfilled female sexuality in harmony with the natural rhythms of existence. Despite Joe's importance to the novel, "that story began with Lena Grove," Faulkner once observed, "the idea of the young girl with nothing, pregnant, determined to find her sweetheart. It was—that was out of my admiration for women, for the courage and endurance of women." [48] Nature and the female seasons: throughout Faulkner's best work, the two are equivalents for the reproductive, nourishing, life-sustaining and affirming basis of existence—symbolized in *Sartoris,* for example, in Aunt Jenny's gardening in springtime.

It is tempting to generalize the opposing reckless, aggressive, and destructive energy in nature as the male principle. In *Absalom, Absalom!* Aunt Rosa Coldfield ("all polymath love's androgynous advocate" [49]) gives it that name. But there are enough women in his novels devoted to Thanatos, and enough men devoted to Eros, to prevent easy generalizations about the male and female principles in Faulkner's work. The problem for both his men and women is to get into creative, loving relationship with the life-giving force of existence, which is incarnate in nature (for example, in the wilderness in *Go Down, Moses* [1942]) as well as in human sexuality. What usually destroys Faulkner's men is their egotism, self-assertion, or their devotion to some concept of woman which has no relation to her actuality. Horace Benbow poeticizes his Ideal Woman and is blind to the reality of Narcissa and Belle

Mitchell; Bayard Sartoris, in his quest for self-destruction, denies the woman who bears him a son; Joe Christmas throws the food offered by those who would mother him and vomits at this "woman's muck"; Thomas Sutpen callously exploits female sexuality to further his own grand design; and Popeye is impotent and sadistic before it—or before Temple's "playing at it."

The most poignant of Faulkner's self-destructive men who are severed from the affirming principle of life is Quentin Compson in *The Sound and the Fury.* Quentin is the son of an alcoholic father and a neurotic mother who has virtually abandoned her children; he and his brothers turn to their sister Caddie as a mother substitute. As Caddy grows into adolescent sexuality, however, Quentin's static inner world of order begins to disintegrate; he is driven to deny her sexuality and to fight with her boyfriends. But "the minute fragile membrane of her maidenhead" is unequal to sustaining the family's pride and honor, and Quentin eventually surrenders himself to the suicide he so desperately craves. The ideal of womanly purity thus wars vainly against the actuality of female need, so that, for the damaged idealist, woman sinks to the "delicate equilibrium of periodical filth between two moons balanced." [50]

The sources of Quentin's neurotic disorder are expressed in the terrible agony of his cry, *"if I'd just had a mother so I could say Mother Mother."* [51] But Mrs. Compson is a hopeless hypochondriac, swollen in self-pity and egotism, and Caddy is growing into a woman with her own needs. Dilsey comes closest to fulfilling Quentin's profound need for maternal love, consolation, sustenance, and support. But neither he nor the others in the family who so desperately need and rely on Dilsey can recognize the precious gift of mothering she offers. Blacks may complain at Dilsey as an Aunt Jemima stereotype, and radical women may deplore her self-effacement and passivity. But Dilsey is the most important character, let alone woman, in all of Faulkner's fiction because she embodies the highest love Faulkner was capable of imagining. She incarnates the life-affirming principle of selfless love and devotion to those entrusted, by fate, to her care. As the true mothering presence in the disintegrating Compson household, she reflects an aspect of Caroline Barr (1840-1940), the black mammy who raised young Faulkner and to whom he dedicated *Go Down, Moses.* Born in slavery, Faulkner wrote, she "gave to my family a fidelity without stint or calculation of recompense and to my childhood an immeasurable devotion and love." [52]

Faulkner's best women are tough-minded pragmatists who have what Sally R. Page in *Faulkner's Women* has called "a greater commitment to the sustenance of life than do the men, a commitment which enables them to disregard traditional morality and rationality when the preservation of the well-being of life is at stake." [53] If we isolate some of Dilsey's characteristics, Faulkner may seem to be glorifying dependency, guileful submissiveness, and passive self-effacement—behavioral characteristics associated with social enslavement (whether racial or sexual) and moral inferiority. These are certainly not qualities likely to appeal to a militant black or to the modern liberated woman. Nevertheless, Faulkner valued the family as the cornerstone of society and as a repository of the wisdom of the race; and he celebrated those qualities which make for the stability and coherence of the family and the transmission, from generation to generation, of the "old verities of the heart"—pride, compassion, pity and honor, courage and endurance. Asked at Nagano about his view of women, Faulkner observed: "the opinion that women cause the trouble is not my own. . . . They have held families together and it's because of families that the race is continued, and I would be sorry to think that my work had given anyone the impression that I held women in morally a lower position than men, which I do not." [54] As Chick Mallison remarks ironically in *Intruder in the Dust* (1948), "women couldn't really stand anything except tragedy and poverty and physical pain." [55] This view of women as the power making for community is reflected again and again in the novels—in Granny Millard, Aunt Jenny, Lena Grove, and especially in Dilsey. Dilsey is the supreme example, in the words of Ms. Page, of how "through motherhood the Romantic ideals of creativity, self-transcendence, and union with the nature of existence can be achieved without evil or destructiveness." [56]

IV

Faulkner's view of the supreme function of woman reflects what Betty Friedan has called the "feminine mystique." This view of woman's nature and function, widely celebrated in the popular woman's magazines in Faulkner's time *(Ladies' Home Journal, McCall's, The Pictorial Review)*, was, and is, endemic in our culture. And Aileen Kraditor's *Up From the Pedestal* (1968) has persuasively documented the extent to which the persistence of this view of woman's role prevented political and social action from having much real impact during the period between the wars. Looking back over the major American novels of the period, one observes that for most of our writers the New Woman was unattractive, owing to her emotional insincerity, "misplaced" ambition, hedonism, and moral irresponsibility. In the end the best writers of the period—in my view Fitzgerald, Hemingway, and Faulkner—seem to have had greatest sympathy with the prevailing stereotype of the "womanly woman," the woman with an old-fashioned sense of her role as life-giving, nourishing, life-sustaining presence ministering to her husband or family. The power of this conception was endemic in the very way men and women had been reared and educated in America. And given the structure of the family and its distribution of male and female roles, that image powerfully affected the way novelists, male and female, created women characters.

Anaïs Nin has urged the contemporary woman writer "to sever herself from the myth man creates, from being created by him; she has to struggle with her own cycles, storms, terrors which man does not understand." [57] There is no doubt in my mind that Nin points here to psychic and emotional realities never grasped by the male novelists I have discussed. But Nin calls for what neither the major men nor women novelists of the *l'entre deux guerres* period could give; and in this perception Nin, a virtual unknown at the time, was much in advance of the current sisterhood of novelists. For what the major women novelists of this period celebrated— novelists like Cather, Wharton, Glasgow, Gale, and Roberts—does not notably differ from what their male counterparts praised and admired. Hence my reading of the fictive portraits of women can hardly constitute a revisionist literary history. In Willa Cather's *My Antonia,* for example, the final image of Antonia Cuzak identifies her with the beneficence of natural sexual and biological processes, "the goodness of planting and tending, and harvesting." Cather's celebration of Antonia as mother of a large and productive family may suggest to us an idealization of the common maternal stereotype. But Antonia is meant to return us to what Cather called "immemorial human attitudes which we recognize by instinct as universal and true." And Cather's narrator concludes: "It was no wonder [Antonia's] sons stood tall and straight. She was a rich mine of life, like the founders of early races." [58] "Archetype" might therefore be a better word for her.

The social dislocation produced by the Depression reinforced the feminine mystique and intensified literary idealizations of the woman as mother. John Steinbeck's *The Grapes of Wrath* (1939), written at the end of the Depression, seems to me the ultimate celebration of the maternal ideal of the period, for Ma Joad holds the family together, nourishes and sustains it against adversity, and brings it through to California. In the final scene of that novel, her daughter Rose of Sharon (the baby stillborn) is encouraged by Ma Joad to give her milk-full breasts to the starving man in the barn so that his life may be saved. This scene has been called offensively coarse, degrading to women, possibly obscene. But the starkly physical character of the action is intended to present to us a graphic symbol of the highest function—according to some of the best American novelists of the period—that women may have. That the *mother* could be an emasculating destroyer is principally a post-World War II literary phenomenon, evident in the satire of writers like Philip Wylie, Bruce Jay Friedman, and Philip Roth.

Notes

1 "The Ballot—Bread, Virtue, Power," *Revolution,* January 8, 1868, quoted in William L. O'Neill's *Everyone Was Brave* (Chicago: Quadrangle Press, 1969), p. 19.
2 (New York: Oxford University Press, 1972), pp. 48-65.
3 Sinclair Lewis, *Main Street* (New York: Harcourt Brace, 1920), pp. 201-2.
4 Elizabeth Cook, "The Kitchen Sink Complex," *Ladies' Home Journal* 48 (September 1931), 12.
5 Rose Wilder Lane, "Woman's Place Is in the Home," *Ladies' Home Journal* 53 (October 1936), 18.
6 Quoted in Chafe, *The American Woman,* p. 99.
7 Margaret Mead, "Sex and Achievement," *Forum* 94 (November 1935), 301-3.

8 Nan Bauer Maglin, "Women in Three Sinclair Lewis Novels," *Massachusetts Review* 14 (1973), 783-801.

9 Dorothy Dunbar Bromley, "Feminist—New Style," *Harper's* 155 (October 1927), 152-60.

10 Edith Wharton, *The Age of Innocence* (New York: D. Appleton, 1920), pp. 41-43, 145. For an exaggerated case for Mrs. Wharton's "feminism," see Josephine Jessup, *The Faith of Our Feminists* (New York: Richard R. Smith, 1950).

11 Ellen Glasgow, *Barren Ground* (Garden City, N.Y.: Doubleday Doran, 1933), p. 526.

12 Bruce Bliven, "Flapper Jane," *The New Republic*, September 9, 1925, pp. 65-67.

13 "Good-Bye, Dear Mr. Grundy," *Atlantic Monthly* 126 (November 1920), 642-46.

14 George E. Mowry, ed., *The Twenties: Fords, Flappers & Fanatics* (Englewood Cliffs, N.J.: Prentice-Hall, 1963), p. 173.

15 Quoted in Chafe, *The American Woman*, p. 20.

16 F. Scott Fitzgerald, *This Side of Paradise* (New York: Scribner's, 1920), pp. 64-65.

17 F. Scott Fitzgerald, *The Crack-Up*, ed. Edmund Wilson (New York: New Directions, 1945), pp. 14-15.

18 Lionel Trilling, "F. Scott Fitzgerald," in *F. Scott Fitzgerald: The Man and His Work*, ed. Alfred Kazin (New York: Collier Books, 1962), p. 198.

19 J. W. Aldridge, "Fitzgerald: The Horror and the Vision of Paradise," in *F. Scott Fitzgerald: A Collection of Critical Essays*, ed. Arthur Mizener (Englewood Cliffs, N.J.: Prentice-Hall, 1963), p. 32.

20 Leslie Fiedler, *Love and Death in the American Novel* (New York: Criterion Books, 1960), p. 304.

21 Henry Dan Piper, *F. Scott Fitzgerald: A Critical Portrait* (New York: Holt, Rinehart, and Winston, 1965), pp. 60-61.

22 Andrew Turnbull, *Scott Fitzgerald* (New York: Scribner's, 1962), p. 72; see also Arthur Mizener, "Scott Fitzgerald and the Top Girl," *Atlantic Monthly* 207 (March 1961), 55-60.

23 F. Scott Fitzgerald, *The Beautiful and Damned* (New York: Scribner's, 1922), p. 147.

24 Ibid., p. 29.

25 Ibid., p. 73.

26 Fitzgerald, *This Side of Paradise*, p. 302.

27 F. Scott Fitzgerald, *The Great Gatsby* (New York: Scribner's, 1925), pp. 180-81.

28 Fitzgerald, *The Crack-Up*, pp. 21-22.

29 Elizabeth Stevenson, *Babbitts and Bohemians: The American 1920s* (New York: Macmillan, 1967), pp. 138-51. Compare Fitzgerald's remark in *The Crack-Up* that "the flapper never really disappeared in the twenties—she merely dropped her name, put on rubber heels and worked in the dark" (p. 210).

30 *Letters of F. Scott Fitzgerald,* ed. Andrew Turnbull (New York: Dell, 1966), pp. 27-28.

31 Ibid., p. 367.

32 Theodore Bardacke, "Hemingway's Women," in *Ernest Hemingway: The Man and His Work,* ed. John K. M. McCaffery (Cleveland and New York: World Publishing Co., 1950), p. 343.

33 "The Short Happy Life of Francis Macomber," in *The Short Stories of Ernest Hemingway* (New York: Scribner's, 1953), p. 8. For fuller treatments of Hemingway's view of women, see William Phillips, "Male-ism and Moralism: Hemingway and Steinbeck," *American Mercury* 75 (1952), 93-98; Phyllis Bartlett, "Other Countries, Other Wenches," *Modern Fiction Studies* 3 (1957-58), 345-49; and Anne Greco, "Margot Macomber: 'Bitch Goddess,' Exonerated," *Fitzgerald-Hemingway Annual* 1972, pp. 273-80.

34 Ernest Hemingway, *A Moveable Feast* (New York: Bantam Books, 1965), p. 188.

35 Ernest Hemingway, *A Farewell to Arms* (New York: Scribner's, 1929), p. 120; and *For Whom the Bell Tolls* (New York: Scribner's, 1940), p. 463.

36 *The Short Stories of Ernest Hemingway,* p. 122.

37 These remarks are not meant to suggest that Hemingway was a latent or overt homosexual, as is sometimes alleged. (Homosexuality and lesbianism were profound evils for Hemingway, true perversions of right human sexuality.) Nor are they meant to suggest that he was a misogynist, like Henry Miller. Kate Millett's *Sexual Politics* and Norman Mailer's *The Prisoner of Sex* take up the issue of Miller's view of women. I have no wish to rehearse their quarrel here. But to observe the degradation of women in, say, *Tropic of Cancer* (1934) is to realize that Hemingway was no misogynist. For Miller, women were mere receptacles of male lust. "O Tania," Miller rhapsodizes, "where now is that warm cunt of yours, those fat, heavy garters, those soft bulging thighs?" In Miller's fictionalized "genito-urinary" relationships, women are offered no real commitment, compassion, or affection. What is obscene in Miller's prose is not the diction, the graphic description of sexual or excremental acts (though these indubitably shocked Americans in the Depression years and led to the banning of his work), but rather his manifest degradation of women as a sex and his embrace of the narcissism and "inhumanism" by which he justified that degradation.

38 Ernest Hemingway, *The Sun Also Rises* (New York: Scribner's, 1926), p. 148.

39 See "A Clean, Well-Lighted Place" in *The Short Stories of Ernest Hemingway,* pp. 379-83.

40 *The Short Stories of Ernest Hemingway,* p. 271.

41 Ibid., p. 87.

42 Compare Cleanth Brooks's speculation that Hemingway "might very well have taken his motto from the German romantic poet Novalis:

'All passions end like a tragedy. Whatever is finite ends in death' "
William Faulkner: The Yoknapatawpha Country [New Haven: Yale University Press, 1966], p. 207).

43 William Faulkner, *The Sound and the Fury and As I Lay Dying* (New York: Modern Library, 1929), p. 198.

44 Maxwell Geismar, *Writers in Crisis* (Boston: Houghton Mifflin, 1942), p. 180; Fiedler, *Love and Death in the American Novel*, p. 309. For other treatments of this subject, see David M. Miller's "Faulkner's Women," *Modern Fiction Studies* 13 (1967), 3-17; Samuel Yorks's "Faulkner's Woman: The Peril of Mankind," *Arizona Quarterly* 17 (1961), 119-29.

45 William Faulkner, *Sanctuary* (New York: Modern Library, 1931), p. 276.

46 "Hair," *Collected Stories of William Faulkner* (New York: Random House, 1943), p. 133.

47 William Faulkner, *The Hamlet* (New York: Random House, 1940), p. 114.

48 *Faulkner in the University: Class Conferences at the University of Virginia, 1957-1958*, ed. Frederick L. Gwynn and Joseph L. Blotner (New York: Random House, 1965), p. 74.

49 William Faulkner, *Absalom, Absalom!* (New York: Random House, 1936), p. 146. For other views of this subject, see K. E. Zink, "Faulkner's Garden: Woman and the Immemorial Earth," *Modern Fiction Studies* 2 (1956), 139-49; and Thomas M. Lorch, "Thomas Sutpen and the Female Principle," *Mississippi Quarterly* 20 (1966-67), 38-42.

50 Faulkner, *The Sound and the Fury*, p. 147. Compare John L. Longley, Jr., " 'Who Never Had a Sister': A Reading of *The Sound and the Fury*," *Mosaic* 7 (1973), 35-53; and Charles D. Peavy, " 'If I'd Just Had a Mother': Faulkner's Quentin Compson," *Literature and Psychology* 23 (1973), 114-21.

51 Faulkner, *The Sound and the Fury*, p. 190.

52 William Faulkner, *Go Down, Moses* (New York: Modern Library, 1952), n.p.

53 Sally R. Page, *Faulkner's Women: Characterization and Meaning* (Deland, Fla.: Everett/Edwards, 1972), p. 186.

54 *Faulkner at Nagano*, ed. Robert A. Jelliffe (Tokyo: Kenkyusha, 1956), pp. 69-70.

55 William Faulkner, *Intruder in the Dust* (New York: Modern Library, 1948), p. 208.

56 Page, *Faulkner's Women*, p. 46.

57 *The Diary of Anaïs Nin*, ed. Gunther Stuhlman (New York: Swallow Press/ Harcourt, Brace, and World, 1966), II: 234.

58 Willa Cather, *My Antonia* (Boston: Houghton Mifflin, 1949), p. 229.

12.

Second-class Citizenship:
The Status of Women
in Contemporary American Fiction

Martha Masinton and Charles G. Masinton

Contemporary American fiction finds a happy metaphor in John Barth's "funhouse," the house of mirrors in which images of images reflect and distort each other into infinity. While Barth intends his metaphor to apply primarily to fictional technique, the range of experience dealt with in recent American novels similarly offers itself to hyperbolic expression: desperation and hope, murder and madness, innocence and ecstasy—all are represented in the works of contemporary novelists. Given such variety, one might well expect to encounter in these works an extraordinary array of female characters; instead, one discovers, first, that a serious disjuncture exists in the degree of significance accorded the activities of male and female characters, and, second, that the roles assigned to women in contemporary novels derive primarily from myth and stereotype.[1] Further, while one might look to the feminist fiction of the sixties and early seventies for redress of this condition, one finds there also, though imagined from a very different point of view, female characters whose significance lies precisely in their identity as stereotypical products of cultural conditioning. In short, Isabel Archer seems to have died without issue, but the fictional woods are full of the sons of Huck Finn.

The situation of women in fiction in fact reflects rather accurately, if metaphorically, that of women in contemporary society. In every important field of activity control and power rest largely with men: men control the political life of the country, dominate the directorates and management of large corporations, provide the leadership of the more powerful labor unions, and occupy the majority of high-level administrative positions at every level of education. In 1976 there were no women in the U.S. Senate and only sixteen in the U.S. House of Representatives, while of the fifty states, only two had women as governors. On television and in the movies serious roles for women have diminished almost to the point of invisibility. Women, in effect, are second-class citizens of their own country, and their position owes as much to the prevalence of certain beliefs and attitudes concerning them as it does to legal (or illegal) restrictions on their activities. Thus, while it is not surprising that roles for women in contemporary fiction should be so limited in both variety and significance, it neverthe-less appears that the situation as it exists represents a lamentable failure of the literary imagination.

For the American novelist the problem of envisioning significant roles for women is compounded by the existence of a native literary tradition that—with notable exceptions like Nathaniel Hawthorne and Henry James—has always emphasized the masculine and neglected the feminine. From James Fenimore Cooper to Thomas McGuane and James Dickey, in an unbroken if jagged line of descent, the American Adam has moved through or away from his corrupted Eden in search of a satisfactory way of being. The peculiar vitality of the fable derives in part from its validity as an expression of the fundamental American experience (the break with the old, the dream of the new) and in part from its appropriateness to the formulation of existential rather than social levels of reality. The tradition has unhappy consequences for women, however, because its conventions require that they be left on the shore while the hero cruises the river. The world of discovery is masculine, and the experience of becoming is mas-culine; the conventional social world is feminine, and women are static figures within it. The male breaks new ground, and the female follows along behind to consolidate and socialize the territory: at worst, she is anathema to the more fluid hero; at best, someone he must love and leave.

The social myth that gave rise to these literary conventions saw women as the guarantors of stability in the family and consequently in society as a whole. The highest and most important role a woman could assume was that of responsible wife and mother—and, therefore, almost by definition, conservator of social values. The traditional novel as it developed in Europe, and as it was adapted by such American novelists as Howells, James, and Wharton, drew heavily on the informing conventions of the bourgeois social world in its treatment of women. The specificity with which society defined female roles and the almost absolute identification of women with received social values provided the matrix for the creation of female characters. A woman could be used to redeem and socialize the restless hero, or she could be used to show the superficiality of social convention; she could move outside the social world to serve as a temptress or to represent an alternative and perhaps more valuable reality; she could reject the role assigned her by society and herself become the heroine; or she could, like Isabel Archer, be endowed with financial independence and turned loose to see what she could make of the world. Woman's role in the traditional novel derived primarily from the nature of her relationship to an authoritative, normative society, for which sexual irresponsibility in women (but not in men) represented the unforgivable sin and conformity to social expectation the greatest good.

Irving Howe, in an essay entitled "Mass Society and Post-Modern Fiction," describes the effect on the novelist of the breakdown in the traditional relationship between fiction and the social world, and in the course of his discussion refers briefly to two American novels. "If one compares two American novelists so different in formal opinion, social background, and literary method as Theodore Dreiser and Edith Wharton, it becomes clear that in such works as *Sister Carrie* and *The House of Mirth* both are relying upon the same crucial assumption: that values, whether traditional or modernist, desirable or false, can be tested in a novel by dramatizing the relationships between mobile characters and fixed social groups." [2] Both novels deal chiefly with women whose lives represent a challenge to the established social norms, and while the two novelists envision quite different fates for their aberrant heroines, neither work could have been written had not the full weight of social authority been brought to bear against such women. The situation of the woman who rejected her assigned social role furnished the novelist with precisely the dramatic materials Howe describes and in fact constituted the given condition for many of the great nineteenth- and early twentieth-century fictional heroines. In contemporary society the sanctions against "deviant" women no longer apply; the woman "seduced" has many alternatives, and the woman who chooses not to marry, or to end her marriage, no longer must endure ostracism and financial distress. Thus one of the most significant roles open to women in fiction has been foreclosed by a more flexible society.[3] Women may still be used by novelists to represent the social world, but insofar as that world is shown as malevolent, they must in some degree become malevolent themselves.[4] And in those novels in which the center of action is extrasocial, they must remain on the periphery.

It could be argued, however, that if, as Howe maintains, the traditional assumptions about society no longer serve as the stable background of the novel, a new set of assumptions has come to function as a philosophical common ground for contemporary fiction. The central thesis of these assumptions is that society can no longer pretend in any way to define or indemnify value. Norman Mailer's *An American Dream* sets out precisely to show that the dream is poisoned and poisonous, while John Updike's *Couples* shows the flaccidity of lives lived without guarantee of value. In a fiction intensely concerned with the effects on the individual of the breakdown of normative value systems, there is clearly no reason for differentiating between male and female according to the patterns implicit in those systems; yet that differentiation continues to dictate the way women are written about. Three writers who are dissimilar in almost every respect—Mailer, Updike, and Saul Bellow—provide interesting examples of the limitations to which female characters are currently subject.

Because Norman Mailer has always sought the Mother Lode of the definitive American novel, his characters, male as well as female, are meant to be larger than life, and his rhetorical style tends to obscure the fact that his use of women is by no means idiosyncratic. By making explicit what for other writers is only implicit, Mailer has become the favorite target of feminist critics. In the novel that has attracted the most attention from feminists, *An American Dream* (1965), Mailer intends his protagonist, Stephen Rojack, to be seen as the new American hero (specifically a hero of his own time and place, mid-twentieth-century America) and the two women in his life, Cherry and Deborah, as mythic metaphors for the possibilities open to him: redemption and damnation. Rojack is losing his manhood and his life and must reclaim both by killing his wife, Deborah, impregnating his mistress, Cherry (who then dies), and confronting Deborah's diabolical father, Barney Kelly, in his lair on Park Avenue. These tasks completed, Rojack chooses the old-fashioned course of setting out for the frontier, a jungle in Central America.

Deborah and Cherry function almost entirely as metaphors in the novel: Deborah stands for the evil of the American social machine and for a viciously corrupt femininity; Cherry represents goodness, the redemptive quality of American innocence, and the positive values of femininity. Mailer's characterization of the two women is informed by his own perception of women as inherently and absolutely different in nature from men. What might be called the power of the womb exerts a considerable influence over the affairs of his characters. Women, because they are the creators of life, also hold within themselves the authority of death, and Mailer approaches them in fear and trembling, but also with a good deal of bravado. They must be confronted, and mastered, by the man who would achieve his manhood. Rojack masters Deborah by strangling her, and Cherry by willing her to accept his seed into her womb. Cherry must die, however, because she too has been implicated in the corruption personified by Barney Kelly and shown by Mailer as pervasive in American life. But at the end of the novel Cherry is allowed a sort of afterlife: in an imaginary telephone call between heaven and a phone booth in the Nevada desert she assures Rojack that all is well and passes on greetings from "Marilyn," Mailer's favorite blonde.

Cherry is herself blonde, in fact, a sort of essence of blondness: "She had studied blondes, this Cherry, she was all of them...." [5] Deborah, however, is dark (and is associated with the powers of darkness). Cherry is, in sleep, "a golden child" (p. 130); Deborah is a "Great Bitch" (p. 9). Mailer's emphasis on these aspects of the two women suggests a contemporary version of the romantic convention of the fair heroine and the dark lady, but he enlarges the stereotypes by granting each that mysterious power of womanhood which derives, as he says in *The Prisoner of Sex*, from woman's position "one step closer to eternity" than man's.[6] Thus Deborah's evil nature is symbolized by a defective womb: "There had been something malformed about her uterus—she was never explicit— and her ducts had suffered from a chronic inflammation since Dierdre had been born ... she lost the baby, it came brokenly to birth, in terror, I always thought, of the womb which was shaping it" (p. 26). Cherry's womb, by contrast, is fecund, and Rojack counts it a sign of his own rebirth when Cherry says that they have made a baby.

A mythic tone permeates the entire novel, and within that context Mailer's use of his female characters is consistent with his purpose, which is to develop, as D. H. Lawrence before him did, a viable symbolic system for dealing with contemporary experience. Rojack is to be seen as a fallen American Adam seeking to rediscover the springs of his being in a world not merely corrupt but literally deadly. While the women serve to delineate the nature and terms of his predicament, neither can share his experience of it, and thus both must serve as subsidiary characters in the novel.

Certain parallels exist between Mailer's *An American Dream* and Saul Bellow's *Herzog* (1964). Madeline Pontritter Herzog is, in her own way, as mysteriously evil as Deborah Kelly Rojack, and her father, like Deborah's, is a famous American. Herzog would like to kill her, but as Robert Langbaum points out: "[He] does not because he cannot reconcile with ordinary reality his momentary insights into her supernatural evil. Mailer's hero can do what Bellow's cannot because his insight into Deborah's evil transforms reality for him." [7] Herzog, like Rojack, is ostensibly in retreat at the end of the novel, but he is awaiting a visit from Ramona, the woman whose significance for him is analogous to that of Cherry for Rojack. Of Ramona, Bellow says that with Herzog she has experienced "a real Easter. She knew what Resurrection was." [8] The ironic tone that Bellow means to inject here confirms Langbaum's implied point about the different levels of reality in the two novels: Mailer and Rojack believe in the possibility of resurrection; Bellow and Herzog do not. Bellow's Herzog, moreover, is not to be seen as an all-American hero, and Bellow makes that clear by referring several times to his "foreignness" and having him lapse periodically into French. Herzog may, like Rojack, be trapped in his time, but his burden consists of his identity as an end product of the western intellectual tradition. He wants to make it all work as it has not worked before: *"And the peculiar idea entered my (Jewish) mind that we'd see about this! My life would prove a different point altogether"* (p. 106).

Bellow is neither a sexual chauvinist nor a theoretician of the sexual battlefield, but he has Herzog speculate on the differences between men and women. "What was he hanging around for? To follow this career of *personal relationships* until his strength at last gave out? . . . But this is a female pursuit. This hugging and heartbreak is for women. The occupation of a man is in duty, in use, in civility, in politics in the Aristotelian sense" (p. 94). And later: "But at least one thing became clear. To look for fulfillment in another, in interpersonal relationships, was a feminine game. And the man who shops from woman to woman, though his heart aches with idealism, with the desire for pure love, has entered the female realm. After Napoleon fell, the ambitious young man carried his power drive into the boudoir. And there the women took command" (p. 188). The man belongs in the world, can find himself only by experiencing it, defines himself by his activity in it, while the woman is content with the smaller, though equally problematic, realm of personal relations. Although the tone of Herzog's observations is, again, ironic, Bellow's use of female characters in the novel reflects precisely this differentiation between spheres of activity; and part of the conflict of the novel results from the confusion created by Herzog's temporary absorption into the feminine world and Madeline's radically misguided attempt to storm the gates of the masculine.

Madeline serves in the novel as an abrasive surface against which a number of Herzog's illusions are rubbed away: she represents chaos, knowledge divorced from value, personality run amuck—in short, some of the more hysterical reactions to the existential situation. Herzog, having been rejected by her, must learn to reject her also. Ramona, herself successfully engaged in a small business, is intelligent, well educated, and competent; she knows how to organize her life and is willing to help Herzog with his. Madeline is in a sense one of Herzog's foremost "Reality Instructors," but Ramona has her own reality to offer—one that Herzog finally decides to accept, if only conditionally. It is not resurrection that he will achieve with Ramona, but ease, relief from the hazards of being himself. Herzog sees more than either woman, sees the limitations of their respective versions of experience, and has the larger role to play, not simply because he is Bellow's protagonist, but also because Bellow can imagine women only in supporting roles.

John Updike, in *Couples* (1968), creates a male hero who moves almost entirely in what Herzog describes as the feminine realm. The world of the novel is the social world of affluent America in the 1960s. Like Mailer, Updike very carefully identifies time and place and has one of the novel's several parties take place on the evening of the assassination of John Kennedy. Piet Hanema lives in his time, but is not of it; he is identified at the beginning and near the end of the novel, both times by women, as an "old-fashioned" man in a very particular sense. His anomalous position derives in part from the nature of his occupation and in part from the fact that he is a practicing and believing Christian, a worshipper of a "perfectly arbitrary" Calvinist God. In earlier times Piet would have been a master craftsman, but his talents now make him a specialist in the very limited field of restoring old homes, and in the course of the novel he is squeezed out of his business by his partner, Gallagher, who, unlike Piet, is willing and eager to build development housing.

Virtually excluded from the world of Tarbox men, most of whom pursue technological or scientific careers, Piet joins the feminine world of daytime Tarbox. The women of Tarbox are all married, and most of them are mothers. They are not employed, and their lives fit the classic suburban pattern: their husbands go elsewhere to work, and they have time on their hands. Piet is willing to fill that time, but he also brings them something special—"word of a world where vegetation was heraldic and every woman was some man's queen." [9] Piet "loved any woman he lay with, that was his strength, his appeal; but with each woman his heart was more intimidated by the counterthrust of time" (p. 336).

For Piet, as for Rojack, women are the mysterious and sometimes frightening Other, essentially different from men and vested with strange powers.

The two most important women in the novel are Piet's wife, Angela, and his mistress, Foxy Whitman, whom he marries after he is divorced from Angela and Foxy is divorced from her husband. Angela is identified with Diana, the chaste huntress; Foxy, with Venus, the seaborn. Angela lives in the house Piet chose and renovated for her, inland from the sea, true and square, competently enclosing the family within its protective walls. Foxy lives in the house Angela had wanted, facing the sea, built on a sand marsh, in need of every type of repair, and with an inadequate foundation. Angela represents solidity, the integrity of the family, and (as her name suggests) an almost supernaturally forgiving and generous nature. Foxy is an adumbration of disintegration; she begins her affair with Piet while she is carrying her husband's child, and later, when she becomes pregnant by Piet, undergoes an abortion. Her husband's shock over the timing of the affair causes him to demand a divorce, and so, almost without volition, Piet finds himself bound to her. Ultimately Piet and Foxy marry and move to another town, where they live "among people like themselves ... as another couple" (p. 458), and their fate would seem to be a perfect expression of the arbitrariness of Piet's God.

Updike imagines his women more sensitively and less programmatically than Mailer or Bellow, but he too sees them as different from men in their concern for the personal and the everyday as opposed to the objective and the transcendent. He suggests at one point that men are frightened of death and defy it, while women accept it. Piet needs something that Angela and Foxy don't need and can provide only in a limited way—a hedge against death; and even though they both suffer as a result of his anguish, they are affected only vicariously by the world that taxes him so acutely. Piet's situation at the end of the novel is reminiscent of that of Lawrence's gamekeeper, Mellors, who always has understood that he needs the world of men as well as the world of Constance Chatterley's bed, but cannot find a way into that world. Piet, by abandoning the existential framework that held his life together and helped to ward off his fear of death, has, in effect, capitulated to the secular forces of the modern world, and, as a consequence, must now confront a life stripped of metaphysical significance and devoid of stabilizing values. His new job, as an inspector of government building projects, symbolizes the particular horror of his new situation.

The pattern that emerges here recurs again and again in contemporary American fiction: the male hero is shown as experiencing his time in whatever manner the novelist defines that time, while the female characters whom he encounters are exempted from the burden of contemporaneity and allowed refuge either in myth or in stereotypical female roles.[10] The male hero must establish an identity or a life for himself in an amorphous society itself stricken with anomie; the typical female character exists only referentially: she may offer redemption or damnation, or she may serve merely to define the terms of his dilemma, but she may not herself experience that dilemma. Whether the writer sees the protagonist's problem as a matter of dealing with the void at the heart of the universe, or, more simply, as a matter of achieving manhood, the essential question can be formulated only in masculine terms.[11]

The circumscribed and conditional existence allotted to women in contemporary fiction reflects not only the major themes of the American literary tradition and the condition of women in American society but also a self-serving cultural myth of extraordinary power, one that has served both to explain what women are and to dictate what they ought to be. The myth holds that women are so inherently different from men that the world they perceive and thus experience is in effect not even the same as that of men. Erik H. Erikson, in his well-known essay, "Inner and Outer Space: Reflections on Womanhood," finds that while males seek to thrust themselves outward into space, females attempt to enclose and organize space, and his conclusions are frequently cited as the definitive exposition of the difference between men and women.[12] David G. McClelland, in "Wanted: A New Self-Image for Women," argues that since the evidence makes clear what women are, women should use the information to construct a positive self-image.[13] The scientific "proof" concerning the nature of women that contemporary psychologists and sociologists furnish accords very nicely with what a male-dominated society wishes to believe about women; it establishes that by nature women belong in the home with the family, and, by inference, confirms the more mystical aspects of that belief. Thus women are also imagined to be much less affected than men by the notion of time as a limiting dimension because, presumably, they exist on a more elemental and eternal plane: they are an integral part of the cycle of birth, love, and death. Paradoxically, this condition allows them to concentrate on the everyday world, frees them from the existential dilemma that men experience. Because of their inherent nature, they exist virtually as creatures in the cave, their world defined by shadows and governed by the needs of men. In social terms the myth authorizes women to be as they are, even though the behavior considered desirable and natural in women—submissive, self-effacing, and compliant—would be considered abnormal and undesirable in men, while the qualities valued by and rewarded by society as a whole—initiative and independence—mark the woman who possesses them as unnatural. Thus women, caught in a classic double-bind situation, have the peculiar task of learning to be what society values least.[14]

The feminist movement of the 1960s and 1970s has recognized not only the oppression implicit in the myth but also its increasing irrelevance. Elizabeth Janeway suggests that an inverse ratio exists between the relevance of a cultural or social myth and the society's need to insist on its validity, and that as myth moves further from a descriptive function, it tends to become more prescriptive.[15] In a more concrete sense Ann D. Gordon, Mari Jo Buhle, and Nancy E. Schrom argue that the motive for society's insistence on the myth is economic. "The reason for perpetuating this traditional ideal in spite of its increasing incongruity with historical reality has been a simple one: As consumers, middle-class women have filled a vital and indispensable role in an economy based on mass consumption. In order to carry out this prescribed role, women had to be educated to accept their economic function."[16] Clearly, when one of three marriages in the United States may be expected to end in divorce, and when nearly half of the married women in the United States work outside the home, it is less than accurate to maintain that marriage is a stable institution and folly to insist that woman's place is in the home. Moreover, things are happening in the home that do not fit well with the goddess-of-the-hearth notion; woman have begun to question the most fundamental of society's expectations concerning them, and their discontent has found expression in such works as Betty Friedan's *The Feminine Mystique* (1963). The feminist movement requires of society a recognition of these new realities and positive measures to help women to deal with them. The feminist demands are by no means unreasonable, but the hysterical reactions they have provoked attest to the fact that the changes they ask for would entail a radical revision in the way men and women think about each other and themselves. Earlier feminists in the United States concentrated on acquiring the rights of full citizenship for women; the new feminist movement asks for nothing less than full humanity.

Contemporary feminist fiction has served the movement primarily by showing in personal terms what is wrong with the myth. In novel after novel women writers have detailed the effects on the individual woman of cultural stereotyping and of the double-bind in which society encases them. Feminist novelists—among them Sue Kaufman and Alix Kates Shulman—confront a technical difficulty, however, when they attempt to write about characters whose lives are intended to show the effects of cultural conditioning: how to make interesting a character whose life has been largely devoid of free choice and action. The technical problem here is related to an apparent contradiction in the feminist position. If women are no more than what the culture has made them, then how can they be expected to break with or alter the culture? (In practical terms this ontological conflict—which, philosophically, may find resolution in phenomenology, with its stress on intentionality [17]—has had little effect, for in fact women do break away and are working hard for change, but it does create difficulties for the writer attempting to deal with "the woman question.") For a number of feminist novelists the use of first-person narration has proved to be the solution to the problem, for this strategy allows the writer to endow the heroine with a consciousness capable of commenting on and to a certain degree transcending the limited (and limiting) circumstances of her life.[18] Still, this approach has its pitfalls, because it is often difficult to believe that a narrator obviously possessed of intelligence and considerable self-awareness could consent to the conditions of the life she describes.

The heroine of Sue Kaufman's *Diary of a Mad Housewife* (1967) is just such a character. Tina Balser is a woman successful by most of society's standards. Married to a rising young lawyer, the mother of two daughters, she has no financial worries and lives in a large, comfortable New York apartment. She discovers, however, that she seems to be slipping away from reality, and in order to hold on to some sense of herself, she decides to keep a diary. We learn that her husband is pathologically demanding and that her life consists of a series of exertions on his behalf which almost always somehow fall short of his expectations. In the course of the novel she has an affair with a cynical writer and is vilely abused by her husband, her children, and her lover. The tone of her diary, as she records her experiences, is moving, but also witty and ironic, and we are prepared to accept her as a woman of our time. Having achieved the goals that society encourages women to value, she nevertheless recognizes the essential emptiness of her life. Ultimately, however, her husband admits to a need for psychiatric help and confesses his own problems to Tina, who has never been allowed to know that he had any. Thus her despair turns out to have been a function of his mental disorder, and the implication is that things will return to normal as soon as he can find help. There is ambiguity at the core of the novel, and the ending sharply disappoints our expectation that she will have learned something that will cause her to change her life. Presumably, once his demands have become reasonable and his attitude toward her more positive, she will no longer suffer.

Ellen Morgan, in an essay entitled "The Neo-Feminist Novel," describes Alix Kates Shulman's *Memoirs of an Ex-Prom Queen* (1972) as "truly neo-feminist in every sense . . . the first such work to have emerged to date from the American movement." Specifically, Morgan notes, "the patriarchal institutional mechanisms which neo-feminists have identified are shown as they function to oppress." [19] Shulman's heroine, Sasha Davis, goes much further than Kaufman's character; she divorces her first husband, and at the end of the novel, now the mother of two small children, she is preparing to leave her second husband. She has declared her independence from men, but we do not know precisely what she will do or how she will support herself and her children. Morgan identifies the novel as a *Bildungsroman,* the story of the coming of age of a woman, and while this characterization seems accurate, there are sections of the novel that seem wrenched into shape primarily by the novelist's need to show all of the ways in which a woman is oppressed by society. When Sasha marries her second husband, for example, she has already learned much about herself and about the nature of marriage, yet she very quickly has two babies, even though she has quite firmly rejected motherhood in the past. The experience of a particularly awful abortion apparently influences her decision to have children, but Shulman does not make clear the reason for her choice. The woman in the novel who has already made the break, Sasha's friend Roxanne, is never fully developed as a character and seems instead to function as a symbol for Sasha of an alternative possibility. Shulman does not deal with Roxanne's problems or with the processes by which she has achieved her independence; instead, she concentrates on Sasha's developing consciousness.

The opposition between conditioning and will asserts itself very strongly in *Memoirs;* Sasha is extremely intelligent, interested in philosophy, and at one point prepared to pursue a career in that field, yet her only sense of her own worth derives from men's responses to and recognition of her great beauty. The transition from bright, worldly graduate student to oppressed mother of two, worried about why Willy keeps coming home late from the office, seems arbitrary, and, in its implication that most women would have followed the same course because of their conditioning, even rather offensive. The men in the novel define Sasha's life even after she has learned that their purposes are inimical to hers, and until she decides to leave her second husband (on the very last page of the work) her will is virtually immobilized. Still, the consciousness revealed through the first-person narrative technique constitutes a valuable contribution to the male-female dialectic and an interesting contrast to the image of women presented in essentially masculine novels.

Three other novelists—Joyce Carol Oates, Joan Didion, and Marge Piercy (the latter the only one of the three specifically identified with the feminist movement)—have written about women in a different and larger context, combining their perceptions concerning the nature of contemporary experience with a vision of women as sharing equally with men in that experience. Piercy, in her feminist novel *Small Changes* (1973), imagines an alternative world in which the power politics of sexual relationships are replaced by something better—a concern for each person as an individual and a respect for mutual needs. Piercy takes her two central characters, Beth and Miriam, through a variety of experiences with men, but she shows very carefully that male-female relationships as they now exist are intimately bound up with a capitalist social structure that defines roles for men and women according to its economic needs. Piercy is a radical feminist, and she sees radical social change as the only resolution for the problems of women. The woman who succeeds in breaking through to a new type of relationship (with another woman rather than with a man) has gone underground at the end of the novel, and with her lover and her lover's children will have to remain in disguise indefinitely. *Small Changes* is indeed doctrinaire and occasionally polemical, but Piercy's formulation of the feminist problem acquires validity through her recognition of the need for revolutionary change in society at large and through her careful attention to the details of the intricate relationship between sexuality and cultural role playing.

Maria Wyeth, the heroine of Joan Didion's *Play It As It Lays* (1970), superficially resembles the heroines of Kaufman and Shulman. Like Sasha Davis, she is near the end of an unhappy marriage, and, like Tina Balser, has been driven nearly mad by the conditions of her life, but Didion shows both the marriage and those conditions to be part of a world so completely without value or meaning as to make the suicide of one of Maria's friends seem a valid act. In *Slouching Towards Bethlehem* (1968) Didion described the bleak psychic landscape of Southern California from the point of view of a journalist, and in *Play It As It Lays* she uses it as a paradigm for contemporary culture. Maria is afflicted not only by the absolute lack of value in this world but also by its peculiar unreality, for in it nothing seems real or lasting. She will play the hand that she is dealt with as much courage as possible, but she realizes that the cards are stacked against her; and by the end of the novel, now dangerously close to madness, she realizes that winning has been reduced to a question of sheer survival. Didion's treatment of Maria's role as a wife and as a woman living in a region where youth and beauty are apotheosized reflects a feminist perspective, but the wider context of the novel is the corrupt social world in which Maria and her husband exist. The sense of pervasive despair recalls Camus's *L'Etranger;* as a statement of a particular existential condition, *Play It As It Lays* is neither masculine nor feminine but simply human.

Joyce Carol Oates, like D. H. Lawrence and Norman Mailer, is concerned with somatic states of being,[20] and in *Do With Me What You Will* (1973) she writes about a woman moving from near-catatonia to the expression of a powerful will. Elena, like Sasha Davis, is extraordinarily beautiful, and her beauty has been the controlling fact of her life; she is perceived by all who come in contact with her as a lovely, but useless, object. Her husband makes her a part of his collection of beautiful things, and her mother trains her carefully to be whatever men find desirable and thus to make her way in the world. Elena finally overcomes her extreme passivity (which has masked her refusal to become involved with other people) and in response to an irresistible need for love, leaves her husband and takes her lover from his wife and family. Both husband and lover are lawyers, and while the deracinated world of contemporary mass society constitutes the milieu of the novel, Oates concerns herself particularly with the nature and function of law and its relation to the individual. By dramatizing the inherent opposition between the demands imposed on the individual by the law as the vehicle of social authority and the imperatives dictated by the anarchic forces of passion, she brings on a collision between the world of men in the novel and Elena's private world. The novel could be described as feminist in a peripheral sense, but Oates rejects any absolute differentiation between men and women because she sees that at the deepest levels of being, culture, society, and myth are all equally irrelevant.

Piercy, Didion, and Oates treat women as serious human beings actively seeking to understand and shape their own lives. In this they differ from the majority of contemporary novelists who continue to see women primarily in terms of certain deeply ingrained cultural attitudes. American fiction of the last generation has dealt extensively with the effects on men of existing in a world uncertain of its values and seemingly beyond the comprehending powers of reason in its excesses. While the best of that fiction illuminates the case for women as well as for men, it has no heroines of the stature of Doris Lessing's Anna Wulf, the protagonist of *The Golden Notebook* (1962), a woman whom the writer endows with full responsibility for her own choices—sexual, political, moral, and ethical. In the face of radical social change only a few writers have begun to see beyond those rigid concepts of sexual identity that have always implied inequality and denied women the freedom of action accorded men, and fewer still have gone so far as to examine the grounds for a commonality of experience. It is time for American novelists to move beyond the intellectual and artistic limitations that accompany the stereotyping of women and to recognize the rich fictional possibilities inherent in the struggle of women to achieve full equality with men.

Notes

1 Joanna Russ, "What Can a Heroine Do? Or Why Women Can't Write," in *Images of Women in Fiction: Feminist Perspectives,* ed. Susan Koppelman Cornillon (Bowling Green, Ohio: Bowling Green University Popular Press, 1972), p. 5, in a different context, describes women in western fiction as "not women but images of women.... They do not really exist at all—at their best they are depictions of the social roles women are supposed to play ... at their worst they are gorgeous, Cloudcuckooland fantasies about what men want, or hate, or fear."

2 *Partisan Review* 26 (Summer 1959), rpt. in Marcus Klein, ed., *The American Novel Since World War II* (New York: Fawcett, 1969), p. 128.

3 Elizabeth Hardwick, *Seduction and Betrayal: Women and Literature* (New York: Random House, 1974), p. 208, describing this pattern as "the plot of the illicit, the plot of love," makes this observation: "Now the old plot is dead, fallen into obsolescence. You cannot seduce anyone when innocence is not a value. Technology annihilates consequence. Heroism hurts and no one easily consents to be under its rule."

4 Diana Trilling, "The Image of Women in Contemporary Literature," in *The Woman in America,* ed. Robert Jay Lifton (Boston: Houghton Mifflin, 1965), p. 63, describes "the new impulse of the writer to identify the destructive female force with the destructive social force: woman *is* society in all its dark, unspecifiable lust and horror."

5 Norman Mailer, *An American Dream* (New York: Dial Press, 1965), p. 97. All quotations are from this edition. Subsequent references will be found in the text in parentheses.

6 Norman Mailer, *The Prisoner of Sex* (New York: New American Library, 1971), p. 86.

7 Robert Langbaum, "Mailer's New Style," in *The Modern Spirit: Essays on the Continuity of Nineteenth and Twentieth Century Literature* (New York: Oxford University Press, 1970), p. 150.

8 Saul Bellow, *Herzog* (New York: Viking, 1964), p. 185. All quotations are from this edition. Subsequent references will be found in the text in parentheses.

9 John Updike, *Couples* (New York: Knopf, 1968), p. 384. All quotations are from this edition. Subsequent references will be found in the text in parentheses.

10 Mary Allen's *The Necessary Blankness: Women in Major American Fiction of the Sixties* (Urbana: University of Illinois Press, 1976) develops the thesis that female figures in the major fiction of the period have a kind of vacant, bland, "blank" quality—an emptiness that does not afflict the more active and aggressive males. Although she treats the work of Barth, Pynchon, Purdy, Kesey, Roth, and Updike, she does not comment on Mailer or Bellow (who has recently won the Nobel Prize). And among women writers of the sixties she deals only with Plath and Oates. Yet the line of argument she takes strongly tends to support the conclusions made in the present essay because she acknowledges the severely limited and demeaning roles usually assigned to women in the fiction of that decade.

11 Mary Ellmann, in her chapter on "Feminine Stereotypes" in *Thinking About Women* (New York: Harcourt, Brace & World, 1968), pp. 67-68, observes that while women obtain their "ideal condition" by "rising above themselves," men achieve theirs "by their *becoming,* and (with luck) remaining, simply men."

12 *The Woman in America,* ed. Lifton, pp. 1-26.

13 Ibid., pp. 173-92.

14 Elizabeth Janeway, *Man's World, Woman's Place: A Study in Social Mythology* (New York: Morrow, 1971), pp. 103-4.

15 Ibid., p. 140.

16 "Women in American Society: An Historical Contribution," *Radical America* 5 (July-Aug. 1971), 3-67. In this extremely useful, voluminously documented, and closely argued essay, Gordon, Buhle, and Schrom propose a new theoretical basis for the study of women's history in America.

17 Christopher Morris, "A Post-Structuralist Psychology," *The Ohio Review* 15 (Spring 1974), 8-9.

18 The problem of selecting the appropriate literary form, as well as the most appropriate conventions within that form, often proves especially troublesome to women writers of these times. The first-person narrative strategy allows the writers discussed here to inject more of their deeply felt personal experience into the fiction they write than would be possible with the third-person point of view. The need to communicate the strong feelings and emotions generated not only by their own individual situations but also by the social situation which

denies women full equality with men is obviously of paramount importance to a majority of contemporary American women writers. Some extremely well-known figures among them—such as Sylvia Plath, Anne Sexton, Adrienne Rich, and Erica Jong—have turned to poetry, and to the lyric in particular, because it more easily allows them to give voice to the intimate, subjective experiences than the form of the novel, which demands more in the way of objectification and dramatic action, readily permits. (The realm of the novel has traditionally been that of shared public experiences and widely accepted social values. Since those values have until recently strongly tended to perpetuate the rigid and confining roles open to women, and since these roles have been generally reflected in the novel as stereotypes, this literary form in America has not evolved many useful formulas for women today to use in translating material from their own personal and private lives into fictional terms.) Moreover, when Jong does write a novel *(Fear of Flying,* 1973), she makes it carry the load of many rearranged and transmuted autobiographical facts. Likewise, Sylvia Plath's novel, *The Bell Jar* (1963), is autobiographical.

19 *Images of Women in Fiction,* ed. Cornillon, pp. 189, 197.
20 Langbaum, in "Mailer's New Style," p. 150, mentions the "somatic characterization" of Lawrence and Mailer and says that in *An American Dream* "the submerged or potential becomes manifest." It is equally true to observe that in much of Oates's writing—but perhaps most noticeably in *Wonderland* and *Do With Me What You Will*—we find "somatic characterization."

13.

"Free in Fact and at Last":
The Image of the Black Woman
In Black American Fiction

Elizabeth Schultz

The invisibility of the black American woman is frequently commented upon. On national wage scales she has always been the lowest paid; in national political life she has only recently been seen; in national statistics she is categorized as the unwed mother, the welfare recipient, the maid; in national myth she is designated by multiple names, all of which conceal her identity—Aunt Jemima, Mammy, Matriarch, Sometimes Sister, Black Bitch, Girl. If, however, the factor of invisibility provides the possibilities of freedom, as Ralph Ellison in his *Invisible Man* suggests, perhaps the black American woman, ironically, has achieved a freedom beyond that of other Americans. W. E. B. DuBois maintains in a classic statement written in 1920 that "so few women are born free, and some amid insult and scarlet letters achieved freedom; but our women in black had freedom thrust contemptuously upon them. With that freedom they are buying an untrammeled independence, and dear as the price they pay for it, it will in the end be worth every taunt and groan." [1]

In the novels written by black Americans, the black woman has not been invisible, however. Although the writings of black men occasionally have idealized her in reaction to her degradation by both black and white communities, whereas the novels by black women represent her as complex and struggling, novels by black Americans have generally shown her as resisting the racist and sexist controls that have sought to make her invisible. These novels fully reveal the marvel of her capacity to survive and to be free.

The black American woman's struggle for survival and liberation has been won against the dual traditions of racism and sexism in America. Shirley Chisholm, the first black American congresswoman, while recognizing the power of both traditions, asserts that "Of my two 'handicaps,' being female put many more obstacles in my path than being black." [2] Yet in spite of Chisholm's testimony and the recent creation of the National Black Feminist Organization, most black spokeswomen have argued and continue to argue that racism has been a more oppressive force than antifeminism, that sexual liberation for black men and women is contingent upon racial liberation for both.[3] Indeed the history and literature of black America make it apparent that racial myths have spawned the sexual myths which have kept the black woman in her place. The indifference, or even hostility, with which most contemporary black women regard the women's liberation movement should be considered in the light of this fact as well as in terms of women's traditional position within the black community. Here they have often known a freedom from sexist categories which their white sisters have not known; yet they have remained oppressed racially.

The freedom so contemptuously thrust upon black women results in the first place from the demands of the dominant society that they work. During the days of slavery the black woman was forced to labor in the fields and kitchens of the white master. After slavery she continued to be pressed into farm and domestic work, with factory work only opening to her in the forties with any regularity, and clerical and professional positions only in the past decade. Slavery and poverty have kept the majority of black American women working whereas the majority of white American women, either through lack of economic necessity or lack of motivation, have not worked outside their homes. Consequently, the white woman has submitted to the cultural stereotypes of passivity and femininity, while her black counterpart has become burdened with the stereotype of masculine aggressiveness. A black woman's assessment of this situation is, "There are two kinds of females in this country—colored women and white ladies. Colored women are maids, cooks, taxi drivers, crossing guards, school-teachers, welfare recipients, bar maids and the only time they become ladies is when they are cleaning ladies." [4]

Observing her in the role of breadwinner, sociologists E. Franklin Frazier and Daniel P. Moynihan have classified the black American woman as controlling the affairs of her family and community, as emasculating black men, and as being responsible for the breakup of black marriages.[5] Robert Staples and Joyce Ladner negate this matriarchal classification by considering the black woman's role historically as economic provider. They also point out the viability of the extended kinship family and the limitations of judging the black family in terms of the nuclear family or of judging the black woman in terms of femininity, both of which prevail as ideals in white America.[6] A predicament nevertheless still faces the black woman. She must and does continue to work in order to help support her family; however, because she can qualify for the lowest-paying jobs, she is often able to find work when the black man cannot, thereby leaving herself open to the accusation of being an emasculator.

In black American fiction, the image of the working woman is the most prevalent.[7] In those novels which portray the long life of one woman, she is shown moving from place to place, mastering a variety of skills. In Margaret Walker's *Jubilee* (1966), Vyvry Ware Brown becomes cook, housekeeper, gardener, weaver, midwife; in Ernest Gaines's *The Autobiography of Miss Jane Pittman* (1971), Jane chops cotton, cuts cane, manages a kitchen, organizes a plantation household. The stories of both women in some sense follow the form of a picaresque novel. But neither woman resembles the lonely and isolated picaro. Not only is their labor endless and exhausting, but its tedium and brutality are endured for the sake of their families and communities. These women are never alone.

Other novels, focusing on the black family, reveal the effects of a system which will provide low-status work for the woman but none at all for the man. Lutie Johnson in Ann Petry's *The Street* (1946) clearly sees the effect of this system in her community: "... [a] place where the women had to work to support the families because the men couldn't get jobs and the men got bored and pulled out and the kids were left without proper homes because there was nobody around to put a heart into it." [8] Poverty, precipitated by racism, sets up a relentless chain of events in the life of the black woman; it puts the man out of work, forcing his wife to become a domestic as is the case with Lutie, Mrs. Coffin of Louise Meriwether's *Daddy Was a Number Runner* (1970), Silla Boyce of Paule Marshall's *Brown Girl, Brownstones* (1959), Sissie of John Williams's *Sissie* (1963), and Mrs. Breedlove of Toni Morrison's *The Bluest Eye* (1970). Without work, the black man, like Lutie's husband, Jim, "... went to pieces.... He got used to facing the fact that he couldn't support his wife and child. It ate into him. Slowly, bit by bit, it undermined his belief in himself until he could no longer bear it. And he got himself a woman so that in those moments when he clutched her close to him in bed he could prove he was still needed, wanted" (p. 7).

The black working woman is left physically exhausted by her labor, with little energy to tend to her own children and her own home; she is also left emotionally exhausted, for throughout the day she has had to contend with the degrading comments of her white employers. She is met with condescension or indifference as is Min from *The Street:*

> ... her madams—short ones, fat ones, harried ones, calm ones, drunken ones—none of them had ever listened when she talked. They issued orders to some point over her head until sometimes she was tempted to look up to see if there was another head on top of her own—a head she had grown without knowing it. And the minute she started answering, they turned away. (p. 136)

Gwendolyn Brooks in *Maud Martha* (1953) and Alice Childress in *Like One of the Family* (1956), however, have created women whose self-respect prevents their being degraded by their employers. Maud Martha refuses to return to her job for the overbearing Mrs. Burns-Cooper, and Mildred, Childress's loquacious domestic, not only deflates her employer's patronizing platitudes with her sarcasm, but also asserts her rights:

> "You think it is a compliment when you say, 'We don't think of her as a servant . . .' but after I worked myself into a sweat cleaning the bathroom and the kitchen . . . making beds . . . cooking lunch . . . washing the dishes and ironing Carol's pinafores . . . I do not feel like no weekend guest. I feel like a servant, and in the face of that I have been meaning to ask you for a slight raise which will make me feel much better toward everyone here and make me know my work is appreciated." [9]

The working mothers of *The Street, Number Runner, Brown Girl,* Kirstin Hunter's *Sister Lou and the Soul Brothers* (1968), and *Sissie* try to keep their homes together alone. They do so, always hoping that the absent husband and father will return, always yearning for his loving and his moral support. The emphasis in these novels is not upon the woman as an emasculating matriarch; it is upon her attempt as a mother to foster life and love in her family. She may fail. She may betray her husband by going to the welfare office as does Mrs. Coffin in *Number Runner*. She may scorn her husband's dreams, spurn his gaiety, and finally send him to suicide from shame and despair as does Silla Boyce in *Brown Girl*. She may, also like Silla, transform her frustrations into rage against her children, or generate, as does Sissie, only "pain, guilt, hate, rage, and much too little love." [10] Yet when Sissie writes to her daughter, " 'Lord, I wanted this family to be a great strong tree, like some of those oaks on your grampa's place. But something is eating that tree from the leaves and branches right down to the roots' " (p. 63), her cry of anguish does not evoke the guilt that a similar cry from the stereotypical Jewish mother might. Hers is a cry directed toward an amorphous "something": racism and its ensuing poverty and demoralization. Yet these women continue against such odds to provide the material necessities for their children and to be examples of spiritual strength. They are not idealized in these novels, largely by women, for all their strength and self-sacrifice. They may be represented as agents of emasculation and demoralization, but they are never principals; the principal is the racist society.

The mothers of John O. Killens's *Youngblood* (1954), Frank Brown's *Trumbull Park* (1959), and James Baldwin's *If Beale Street Could Talk* (1974) are also strong-minded women, concerned with the well-being of their families. However, in these novels, all by men, the man supports his family; respect between wife and husband, parents and children is mutual, and racial pride is high; the black nuclear family is alive and well and loving. In these novels Killens, Brown, and Baldwin implicitly refute the Frazier-Moynihan thesis of the emasculating matriarch, the negligent father, and the broken family. However, Petrie, Meriwether, Marshall, and Williams—three women and one man—seem to understand the dilemma of the black woman who is a wife and a mother and must also be a breadwinner; their novels thus refute the Frazier-Moynihan thesis by revealing the woman's inner turmoil. Even when a family is able to stay together, the effects upon the woman who must work are severe as another woman writer, Sarah Wright, demonstrates in *This Child's Gonna Live* (1969). Here Mariah Upshur, to save her family from disease and starvation, joins her husband in doing seasonal harvesting, canning, and fishing, but she cannot save herself from the terrors of guilt and of death.

For Janie of Zora Neale Hurston's novel, *Their Eyes Were Watching God* (1937), work is not always a matter of necessity, and motherhood seems never a consideration; therefore Hurston can speculate on the black woman at work without the pressures of poverty and children though she can never be free of the pressures of sexism and racism. Married first to Logan Killicks, Janie is expected to slave in his kitchen as well as in his fields, but when she marries Joe Starks, he tells her, " 'You behind a plow! You ain't got no business cuttin' up no seed p'taters neither. A pretty doll-baby lak you is made to sit on de front porch and rock and .an y'self and eat p'taters dat other folks plant just special for you.' " [11] Starks aims to lock his new wife into the image of white Southern ladyhood. Both these men try to possess her, the one forcing her to work for him, the other keeping her from work; yet the desire for possession in both is derived from their own sense of racial insecurity. In her third marriage, however, to Tea Cake, a man who loves her and their race, Janie is able to create what Freud would call a state of sound mental health: a balance between love and work. Janie picks beans on the Everglades muck simply because she wants to keep Tea Cake company; the job is a joy. When black women are able to work in harmony with and for their loved ones, as can Vyvry of *Jubilee,* Miss Jane of *The Autobiography,* and Janie, the work, no matter how laborious, may be liberating.

Some survive their work and their mean existences by escaping into religion as do Min in *The Street* and Mrs. Thomas in Richard Wright's *Native Son* (1940); a few others survive by substituting religion for revolution, Christianity for communism, or a flatiron for a pistol. But in general, despite the physical and emotional erosion upon herself and her family, the woman and mother makes her own and her children's survival possible through work. She survives with "grit, shit, and mother wit." And with such survival a form of freedom, albeit contemptuously thrust upon her, she proves a model of resistance to racism. Arguing that "survival . . . was the prerequisite of all higher levels of struggle," Angela Davis points out that the black woman's survival-oriented activities were—and are—a form of resistance.[12] With the powerful demands of poverty always pressing upon her and with the desire to have her husband proud in his own eyes and the eyes of others, she does not fulfill the criteria for being a matriarch; a figure of strength, she is not a figure of power.[13]

White America has sought to perpetuate the slave system by imprisoning the black woman in menial labor and prompting matriarchal behavior, but more effective bondage has perhaps been created by the psychological images which the dominant society has created to keep her subjugated. W. E. B. DuBois describes a veil hanging between the black American and the white society around him, a veil that allows him to see only "a world which yields him no true self-consciousness, but only lets him see himself through the revelation of the other world. It is a peculiar sensation, this double-consciousness, this sense of always looking at one's self through the eyes of others, of measuring one's soul by the tape of a world that looks on in amused contempt and pity";[14] this veil has given the black woman a peculiarly distorted view of herself. The Afro-American novel suggests that the prison of an image of ugliness has been more difficult for the black woman to free herself from than the prison of work. Black psychiatrists William H. Grier and Price M. Cobbs, through numerous case studies, have been able to illuminate the psychological effects a perpetual confrontation with a debased self-image and an elevated image of the white woman have had upon the black woman:

> Her blackness is the antithesis of a creamy white skin, her lips are thick, her hair is kinky and short. She is, in fact, the antithesis of American beauty. However beautiful she might be in a different setting with different standards, in this country she is ugly. . . . There can be no doubt that she will develop a damaged self-concept and an impairment of her feminine narcissism which will have profound consequences for her character development.[15]

The judgment by white America of the black woman's beauty and worth has also affected the black community's judgment of her. As Grier and Cobbs observe, she is not only rejected by the dominant society, but she may also be shunned by her own community. In Wallace Thurman's *The Blacker the Berry* (1929) Emma Lou Morgan's family tried every remedy—"bleachings, scourgings, and powderings"—to make her conform to Caucasian standards of beauty. Had she been a boy, she is told, her dark skin wouldn't have mattered so much, "for a black boy could get along, but a black girl would never know anything but sorrow and disappointment." [16] Emma Lou's family's color-consciousness perverts her ability to judge herself and others. Black herself, she is inferior in her own eyes to anyone of lighter skin; consequently, she gladly gives herself to a "yaller nigger," who is both a drunk and a homosexual, and acquiesces to becoming "a black mammy" for his deformed child. "What she needed to do was to accept her black skin as being real and unchangeable, to realize that certain things were, had been, and would be, and with this in mind begin life anew, always fighting, not so much for acceptance by other people, but for acceptance of herself by herself" (pp. 226-27). This realization at the end of the novel, however, seems hardly as credible as the account of Emma Lou's psychological bondage to the standards of white beauty which had caused so much laceration of self-hatred and self-pity.

More poignant than her story is the story of Pecola Breedlove in *The Bluest Eye;* rejected and tormented because of her blackness by her neighbors, by her classmates, by her own mother, Pecola prays each night for blue eyes. "Thrown, in this way, into the binding conviction that only a miracle could relieve her, she would never know her beauty. She would see only what there was to see: the eyes of other people." [17] She is raped by her father and betrayed into believing that her wish for blue eyes comes true; assaulted physically and psychically, racially and sexually, she goes insane, and Morrison convinces us fully of the waste of a fragile and potentially beautiful life.

In the Afro-American novel the most emasculating of black women is the light-skinned woman who trades on a false sense of superiority based solely on her fair complexion and who embraces a standard of sexual purity associated with white standards of beauty. The black woman who pursues these standards might be called the Black Matriarch as White American Bitch. But again the black novelist implies that the tragedy of the black woman who becomes a sexual emasculator derives from America's racist traditions.

The most devastating portrait of such a woman occurs in Chester Himes's *The Third Generation* (1954). Mrs. Lillian Taylor feels herself superior to her husband, her sons, her neighbors, for none have her pale skin, silky hair, and refined features. She married Dr. Taylor not because of his professional position but because he had done homage at the shrine of her beauty; however, his sexual assault on the shrine the night of their wedding makes it impossible for her "to separate the blackness of his skin from the brutality of his act," and forever afterward she seeks only to humiliate him. The heritage she wants to leave her three sons is "to grow up to love and respect fine white people as she did." [18] Her efforts, however, lead her husband to poverty, her sons to self-destruction and crime, and herself to a red wig, and, ironically, identification as a "white whore."

In his first novel, *Go Tell It on the Mountain* (1953), and his most recent, *If Beale Street Could Talk,* Baldwin also describes the effects which a black woman, given over to hair-straighteners, facial bleaching creams, and her own deification, can have on her husband and herself. Scorning their husbands' jokes, songs, laughter, friends, and sexual urges, they drive their husbands away and themselves to endless self-vindication. Toni Morrison in *The Bluest Eye* gives a detailed account of the growth of the Black Matriarch as White American Bitch:

> They wash themselves with orange-colored Lifebuoy soap, dust themselves with Cashmere Bouquet talc, clean their teeth with salt on a piece of rag, soften their skin with Jergens Lotion. They smell like wood, newspapers, and vanilla. They straighten their hair with Dixie Peach, and part it on the side. At night they curl it in paper from brown bags, tie a print scarf around their heads, and sleep with hands folded across their stomachs. They do not drink, smoke, or swear, and they still call sex "nookey". . . . They go to land-grant colleges, normal schools, and learn how to do the white man's work with refinement. Here they learn the rest of the lesson begun in those soft houses. . . . The careful development of thrift, patience, high morals, and good manners. In short, how to get rid of the funkiness. The dreadful funkiness of passion, the funkiness of the wide range of human emotions. . . . [The man who marries her does not] know that she will give him her body sparingly and partially. He must enter her surreptitiously, lifting the hem of her nightgown only to her navel. He must rest his weight on his elbows when they make love, ostensibly to avoid hurting her breasts but actually to keep her from having to touch or feel too much of him. (pp. 64-65)

Other light-skinned women, rather than tormenting, are tormented in their relationship with their community. The most memorable stories in Jean Toomer's *Cane* (1923) concern such women. The heroines of such novels as William Wells Brown's *Clotel* (1853), Charles Chesnutt's *The House Behind the Cedars* (1900), Nella Larsen's *Passing* (1929), and Gaines's *Catherine Carmier* (1964), all of whom are light skinned enough to be able to "pass," substantiate the convention of the Tragic Mulatto. Although the affections of these women are divided between the white and black communities, they are forced to choose one or the other, to make a decision which, when not actually death-dealing, destroys their personal integrity and psychological well-being. The light-skinned woman who does not trade on her complexion is in a particularly precarious position, for the black community, assuming that she will assert a sense of superiority, may force her to identify with the white world and then debase her when she refuses to do so. The attempt of Brownfield in Alice Walker's *The Third Life of Grange Copeland* (1970) to humiliate his quiet, intelligent wife reveals as much about his insecurity as it does her strength in the face of such cruelty:

> "Just remember you ain't white," he said, even while hating with all his heart the women he wanted and did not want his wife to imitate. He liked to sling the perfection of white women at her because color was something she could not change and as his own colored skin annoyed him he meant for hers to humble her. He did not make her ashamed of being black, though, no matter what he said. She had a simple view of that part of life. Color was something the ground did to flowers, and that was an end to it.[19]

Light-skinned Laurentine of Jessie Fauset's *The Chinaberry Tree* (1933), Vyvry of *Jubilee,* Janie of *Their Eyes,* and Louretta Hawkins of Hunter's *Sister Lou,* however, can joyfully choose to be black. For Laurentine, Vyvry, and Lou, doing so means they must suffer in the name of their mothers whom they hear accused of having had affairs with white men; the assumption, made because of their light skin, is that they, as well as their mothers, prefer white men to black, that they, therefore, seek to debase black men. They may be isolated or confused by these charges, but these women, all in novels by women, are not tempted by them, and with the love of their families behind them, they are resolute. Called prudish and proud for her fair skin, Vyvry proclaims to her former lover, " 'You done called me a white folks' nigger and threw up my color in my face because my daddy was a white man. He wasn't no father to me; he was my Marster. I got my color cause this here is the way God made me. I ain't had nothing to do with my lookin' white no more'n you had nothing to do with you looking black.' "[20] She enumerates the wrongs done to her on her Marster's plantation and bares the scars she received, identifying herself fully with the black experience. Janie recognizes that because she had endorsed her Grandma's and her second husband's notion that ladies should spend their time sitting on their porches, she had been prevented from knowing herself or the joy of living. Discovering the perversions of such a philosophy, she is able to leave Starks and join Tea Cake and the work and play of the black community.

The black American male writer has sought occasionally in his works to counter the elevated image of white beauty by specifically endorsing dark-skinned beauty. The character of Viola Martin of Sutton Griggs's *Imperium in Imperio* (1899) undermines the myths associated with the light-skinned black woman with high melodrama. Described as "charming" in manner, talent, and feature, and as sexually elusive, light-skinned Viola seems to resemble the white virgins of the nineteenth-century genteel tradition on whom the black American bitch is modeled. Griggs, undoubtedly conscious of this tradition, is also conscious of the tradition of the Tragic Mulatto, for Viola's suicide, following a marriage proposal from the black hero of the novel, fulfills both. She is not, however, "tragic" because of her inability to choose between the two races but rather because of her fear that her white ancestry will taint future generations of her beloved black people. She destroys herself, implicitly remaining sexually pure, but explicitly seeking racial purity, and in her note to her rejected lover, she demands that he carry forward her banner of racial purity.

In Chesnutt's early story, "The Wife of His Youth" (1899), Mr. Ryder, a gentleman of refined tastes and manners and an active leader in the Blue Veins Society, a club for black people whose skin was white enough to show blue veins, learns on the day of the ball held to announce his engagement to a fair-skinned woman that the very dark woman he had married during slavery had found him after years of searching and suffering. He recognizes the value of her devotion and sufferings and introduces her with pride to the Blue Veins as "the wife of his youth." Similarly, Eldridge Cleaver's *Soul on Ice* (1968) might be considered a work in which a black man discovers his own worth and freedom by discovering the worth and beauty of the black woman. From the analysis in the first essays in the autobiography of his infatuation with the white woman, he moves to an analysis of the interlocked social and sexual roles of the "ultrafeminine" white woman and the "Amazonian" black woman, to conclude with a hymn of praise for the black woman. He thus displaces the white woman from her traditional pedestal and enshrines a black queen, creating a new image. His overreaction is perhaps extravagant, but uplifting in light of the black woman's long degradation by black men as well as white.

That degradation is, in large part, sexual. Robert Staples argues that the conditions of poverty in the black community expose black women to the many dimensions of sex at an early age, with the consequence that they have been able to accept sexual relations as normal without struggling with the shackles of sexual repression. He suggests that the black woman may provide a "model of sexual liberation" for the inhibited white woman.[21] However, the relative sexual freedom of the black woman has also been "contemptuously thrust upon her." It can only be understood in relation to the conditions of poverty in which, as Petry says in *The Street,* "... people were so damn poor they didn't have time to do anything but work, and their bodies were the only source of relief from the pressure under which they lived; and where the crowding together made the young girls wise beyond their years" (p. 206). It can only be understood in relation to her bondage as a result of the continual abuse of her body and the generation of the myth of the "bad" black woman.

The historical account of this abuse is best given by slave narratives. They document how the black woman was used as a "breeder" and an outlet for the white man's sexual needs; they document how she was subjected to public fondling and exposed naked on the auction block. The narratives reveal that she lived in fear of these abuses and only occasionally could succeed in resisting them.

The brutal story of the white man's direct use of the black woman to satisfy his sexual needs is not frequently told by the black fiction writer, although the effects of this long exploitation reverberate throughout American life and the black American novel. But certainly early black novels and those novels with a historical bent reinforce the authenticity of the historical records. Brown's *Clotel* is concerned with the fate of a light-skinned black woman and her daughters, supposedly her children by Thomas Jefferson. They are separated on the auction block and bought by white men. The purchaser of Clotel, one of the daughters, after making use of her in the guise of love, abandons her because of the demands of his white wife. Chesnutt in *The House Behind the Cedars* and Fauset in *The Chinaberry Tree* indicate that the lives of women whose white masters have provided them with a house and yard and their casual attentions are happy, but in both novels the lives of the fair-skinned girls from these unions are miserable. Toomer's "Blood-Burning Moon" describes explicitly the horrors resulting from the sexual exploitation of black women by white men. Louisa, loved by white Bob Stone and black Tom Burwell, is confused by the passions in her life, by the struggle between the two men, one of whom sees her as a "nigger gal" to come at his call and one of whom dreams of marrying her. The only resolution can be the lynching of the black man. In *Jubilee* and *Miss Jane Pittman,* recent novels dealing with the historical past, black women are free game for the owners and overseers of the plantation during slavery and for the "Patrollers" during Reconstruction; they are pictured as trying to defend themselves though they die in the attempt.

By defining her as sexually promiscuous, as well as menial and ugly, white America has attempted to sustain the sexual exploitation of the black woman. Calvin Hernton in *Sex and Racism in America* writes:

> Being *torn* from the sexual restraints of her native culture (Africa) and universally *forced* to behave like a "naked savage," the relatively restrained African woman was transformed sexually into a beast. Ultimately, after experiencing the ceaseless sexual immorality of the white South, the Negro woman became "promiscuous and loose," and could be "had for the taking." Indeed, she came to look upon herself as the South viewed and treated her, for she had no other morality by which to shape her womanhood, she had no womanhood so far as the white South was concerned.[22]

Gerda Lerner further explains:

> Every black woman was, by definition, a slut according to [the] racist mythology; therefore, to assault her and exploit her sexually was not reprehensible and carried with it none of

the normal communal sanctions against such behavior. A wide range of practices reinforced this myth: the laws against intermarriage; the denial of the title "Miss" or "Mrs." to any black woman; the taboos against respectable social mixing of the races; the refusal to let black women customers try on clothing in stores before making a purchase; the assigning of single toilet facilities to both sexes of blacks; the different legal sanctions against rape, abuse of minors and other sex crimes when committed against white or black women.[23]

The internalization of this image as well as poverty and discrimination in employment have led many black women into prostitution. Studies indicate that the majority of prostitutes in American cities are black.[24] Yet it is also well known that "because open prostitution is only allowed in Black neighborhoods, white men are frequently found in these areas seeking to buy some passion . . . [and] often they accost Black women who are not prostitutes . . . making the streets at night unsafe for 'respectable' Black women." [25] Black fiction suggests that for both the "respectable" woman and the prostitute, forced to view themselves as sexual objects, there seems little possibility of growth and freedom. The image of the "bad" black woman in black American fiction is the image of a woman anxious and afraid, seldom able to shake off her persecutors, black and white.

The fear begins for these women when they are girls. Thus the small-town girls of Toni Morrison's *Sula* (1974) have to devise byzantine routes home from school in order to avoid the physical and verbal harrassments of white boys. Harlem girls, Francie and Sukie, in Meriwether's *Number Runner* may occasionally be able to earn a nickel by dropping their bloomers for the bums, but constant pressure from the white butcher, the white baker, and the bald-headed white man who begins by exposing himself on their tenement roof and then takes to following them to the movies— from the white men who are everywhere asking for a feel—leaves Francie feeling that scorn may be the best resistance, but that fear lurks around every corner. In a scant five pages, Toomer in *Cane* tells the life story of Karintha, who "even as a child . . . carrying beauty, perfect as dusk," [26] is doomed to sell her beauty as a woman; who is doomed, too, to kill the child she bears illegitimately. We do not know whether she acts to save herself or to save the child from a life similar to hers; we know only the validity of Toomer's moral: "Karintha is a woman. Men do not know that the soul of her was a growing thing ripened too soon" (p. 4).

Despair, anger, and hatred, rather than the carefree nonchalance of the stereotyped whore, are characteristic of the prostitutes in black American fiction. The easy women of Harlem novels such as Claude McKay's *Home to Harlem* (1928) and Charles Wright's *The Messenger* (1963) have a variety of characters, but gaily resilient or suicidal, they are all dependent on the whims of men or on drugs and alcohol. In Alice Walker's *Grange Copeland,* Josie has become the most prosperous black in the small Southern town of the novel's setting because of her thriving juke-joint and brothel. She raises her daughter in the atmosphere of the brothel to a similar profession. Yet when Grange Copeland comes along with a marriage offer, she sells her business, and turns her fortune over to him, only to be abandoned by him to a state of poverty and bitterness. Suggie, a good-natured Caribbean woman in Marshall's *Brown Girl,* can only endure her degrading work as a domestic or as a factory-worker if she can take a man and a bottle to bed on Saturday night; but neither offers her protection from the self-righteous accusations of her neighbors or from her poverty. The three prostitutes of *The Bluest Eye* in their arrogance and hatred have been created with irony in contrast to every stereotype of the whore:

> Three merry gargoyles. Three merry harridans. Amused by a long-ago time of ignorance. They did not belong to those generations of prostitutes, created in novels, with great and generous hearts, dedicated because of the horror of circumstance, to ameliorating the luckless barren life of men, taking money incidentally and humbly for their "understanding." Nor were they from that sensitive breed of young girl, gone wrong at the hands of fate, forced to cultivate an outward brittleness in order to protect her spring-time from further shock, but knowing full well she was cut out for better things, and could make the right man happy. Neither were they the sloppy, inadequate whores who, unable to make a living at it alone, turn to drug consumption and traffic or pimps to help

complete their scheme of self-destruction, avoiding suicide only to punish the memory of some absent father or to sustain the misery of some silent mother. (p. 42)

Black writers of both sexes recognize that the black woman is a victim of the sexual myths created about her. The black male writer, however, seems to view her more often than not as the pathetic victim of sexual violence or the helpless catalyst of violence between men. He rarely fails to sympathize with her sexual degradation, however.[27] Conscious of the white man's attempt to undermine the black man's sense of his masculine responsibility by prohibiting him from protecting the black woman, the black male novelist frequently represents her as needing his protection as well as his respect. This is the theme of Frank Yerby's "Health Card" (1944), in which a black soldier attempts to escort his girl safely through a jeering crowd of white G.I.s; the cause of the only harsh words between Tish and Fonny in Baldwin's *Beale Street* is Tish's attempt to dispense with a white molester without Fonny's assistance. Rob Youngblood of Killens's *Youngblood,* having just made love to a good woman who fears a scandal should she become pregnant, remembers the uproar in the black community when "the nicest quietest little girl in the whole school" was discovered pregnant; he determines he will "never take advantage" of a woman, though should he, he would be responsible for his acts.[28]

Black women novelists seem to have less faith, for they present the black woman as having to protect herself. Her form of resistance is liberating, but it is resistance by reaction, through hatred, anger, and violence. The three prostitutes of *The Bluest Eye* protect themselves magnificently by their hatred of all men, all women, and all innocence. In *Number Runner,* China Doll murders her pimp Alfred for putting the evil eye on her younger sister, for beginning to turn her too into a whore. Lutie Johnson's story in *The Street* is that of a young woman's struggle to provide for herself and her son according to the standards of material comfort she sees everywhere available for white America. She imagines herself the young Ben Franklin on arrival in Philadelphia, except that she is arriving in New York and is black and female. She works successively as a domestic, a secretary, an entertainer to keep herself and her son free, but she finds herself being trapped by her fear of the moist-eyed glances of white men on the subways and the hostile glances of white women, of the lecherous man at the school for singers and the brutality of the superintendent of her apartment house, of the presence of the "little lost girls" in the Madame's apartment downstairs and the invitation of the Madame to join them herself, of her husband's desertion for another woman when she begins domestic work and of her lover's demand that she work for him and his boss as their whore. With this final assault to her sense of pride, she kills her lover, striking him repeatedly with blows representing the pent-up rage against all sexual and racial factors that seemed determined to bring her to prostitution, to return her to her historical status as a slave.

Certainly the desire of the Black Matriarch as White American Bitch to withold sex and to humilate her husband is a reaction not only to the image of the "ugly" black woman, but also to the image of the "bad" black woman. The unflattering portrait of the matriarch and bitch by Himes, Toomer, and Baldwin as well as the occasionally derogatory picture of the black woman as sex freak by such novelists as Charles Williams, Claude McKay, and Barry Beckham suggest that the black male writer may see the black woman as completely circumscribed by sex. It is a black woman writer, however, who can describe the total immersion in sexuality as oppressive. Helga Crane in Nella Larsen's *Quicksand* (1928) is a light-skinned woman who seeks to transcend racial and sexual categories through education, travel, and finally religion, but who is bound first by race and then by sex. She is classified as a "snob" by blacks and an "exotic" by whites, and rejects the black man for his limited goals and the white man for his disguised lust. Miserably alone, in reaction she turns to religion, marriage, and motherhood, where she finds herself more irrevocably trapped than before. Religion she comes to recognize as an opiate, her husband as a small-minded lecherous man, and her successive children as obligations. From the concluding sentence in the novel—"And hardly had she left her bed and become able to walk again without pain, hardly had the children returned from the homes of the neighbors, when she began to have her fifth child" [29]—it seems that

Larsen implies that sexual shackles may be more binding even than racial shackles, as Helga seems doomed to endless submission to her husband and endless exhaustion in childbirth.[30]

The black woman as she is represented in black fiction has also, however, inverted the image of ugliness and found beauty and strength in blackness; she has redefined the image of "loose and promiscuous" and found sex to be natural and joyous. Liberation from these racist and sexist images, however, could conceivably lead to the generation of new varieties of limiting stereotypes, e.g., the Black Queen, the Arrogant Whore, the Overprotected Bride. Yet the fiction of black women writers in particular demonstrates especially convincingly that free from these racist and sexist images to embrace her black heritage and her woman's heritage, the black woman also flourishes very much as herself.

The liberated black woman is frequently a girl on the brink of womanhood. Several black women have written the story of the rites-of-passage for the black girl in America. Morrison's *The Bluest Eye* and *Sula,* Meriwether's *Number Runner,* Marshall's *Brown Girl,* Hunter's *Sister Lou,* and Walker's *Grange Copeland* suggest that the young black girl is traditionally subjected to a series of special trials in America in addition to the natural trials of puberty. At the same time she must acknowledge the strange changes in her body, she must also acknowledge changes in the community's relationship to her. She is able to accept the natural changes easily (because of the care and explanations of girlfriends, sisters, or mothers), but the attitude of the male toward her as female and of whites toward her as black, which leads her to anxiety and futility, seems unnatural.

In *Number Runner,* Francie Coffin's earliest dreams were of a handsome white man on a great horse who would come riding down into New York City to free her. However, as her mother becomes the family breadwinner, her brother a pimp, and her father a figure of despair; as she learns that her best friend is being seduced and that her father doesn't mind if she walks down the street where the whores linger in doorways, her dream fades to a faceless, colorless figure. She comes, however, to understand her mother's shame, sorrow, and strength at defying her father; to enjoy the sexual jibes she receives from boys; and to accept her "own rusty self." She can respond to her situation with a single word—"Shit"—and make it descriptive of all the factors causing her feeling of hopelessness as well as a defiant imperative. Selina Boyce's final action in *Brown Girl* is similar to Francie's. Having betrayed the Caribbean community's and her mother's expectations, she confesses to her betrayal, realizing finally that she belongs to them. Confronting her own image in the hostile eyes of a white woman, for the first time she appreciates her mother who has had to confront this image daily and for the first time understands her mother's degradation of her father. Yet she is independent; she leaves her lover who will not himself leave, and sets forth from the community, embracing as she goes her sense of its vitality and despair and flinging back the silver bangles of her childhood which attach her to it. The *sine qua non* for the young black girl to understand herself is to understand her mother; to do so is to understand both the racist and sexist traditions of America and the harsh means of survival the black woman must adopt. Lou Hawkins's story in *Sister Lou* is one of disillusionment, first with the white Protestant work ethic and then with black revolutionary ideals. Her growing appreciation for her own principles is simple in comparison to Francie's and Selina's; yet even Lou must spend a day at her mother's tasks before she can begin to know herself.

The Third Life of Grange Copeland is the remarkable story of Grange Copeland's coming-of-age in the process of bringing up his granddaughter, Ruth. Alice Walker insists that before black girls can grow, black men must resist the ostensible psychological necessity to brutalize black women as the only outlet for the hatred, anger, shame, and envy resulting from their own brutalization by whites. Grange causes his wife's demoralization and suicide; a pattern which is repeated when his son, proving "more cruel than any white man or twenty," constantly beating her physically and psychologically for being "a black ugly nigger bitch," causes in turn his wife's demoralization and death. Grange, however, on becoming Ruth's guardian, is redeemed and determined to teach her everything he knows about the practicalities of keeping books and running a farm, about the uses of nature, about world geography and world literature, about the treacheries of American racism. He would have her self-sufficient:

> And still, in all her living there must be joy, laughter, contentment in being a woman; someday there must be

> happiness in enjoying a man, and children. Each day must be spent, in a sense, apart from any other; on each day there would be sun and cheerfulness or rain and sorrow or quiet contemplation of life. . . . Survival was not everything. *He* had survived. But to survive *whole* was what he wanted for Ruth. (p. 213)

At the novel's conclusion, Ruth has absorbed his teachings, enough even to defy him, and when he is murdered, we are made to believe that her training has made her fully self-sufficient.

Sula and Nel of Morrison's second novel pass their coming-of-age trials to become unique individuals, denigrating traditional stereotypes of black women. Nel seems to become a conventional, "good," self-righteous, middle-class black housewife, and Sula seems to become a "bad" black woman. The strength of Morrison's novel lies in the fact that Nel really does become good in a conventional sense, but cannot forgive Sula for having taken her husband; and that Sula, who has become a pariah in the community for sleeping nonchalantly with any and all men, for sending her grandmother to the old-folks' home, and for watching her mother burn to death, dies free of pain and guilt, of fear and judgment, her mind proudly her own. She will not be bound by the image of the Granny as is her grandmother, nor the image of the whore as is her mother, nor the image of the "good" self-righteous woman as is Nel—eccentric as these women may also be. Nel tells her on her deathbed, " 'You can't act like a man. You can't be walking around all independent-like, doing whatever you like, taking what you want, leaving what you don't.' " And Sula replies,

> "You say I'm a woman and colored. Ain't that the same as being a man? . . . You think I don't know what your life is like just because I ain't living it? I know what every colored woman in this country is doing. . . . Dying. Just like me. But the difference is they dying like a stump. Me, I'm going down like one of those redwoods. I sure do live in this world. . . . my lonely is mine." [31]

Had it been possible for black women to be artists in the America of the thirties, Sula with her spirit of creativity and her independent vision might have thrived.

The black woman in the black American novel also achieves freedom within or through a sexual relationship. If sexual freedom is thrust upon her, she has to make it the basis of hers and the black man's personal freedom. But wondrously in black fiction, relationships do work, with both the man and the woman growing as a consequence. Janie in *Their Eyes* and Ideal in Carlene Hatcher Polite's *The Flagellants* (1967), both characters created by black women, are alone at the conclusion of their stories. Their solitary condition, however, does not define their independence so much as the fact that they have learned self-love through loving and being loved. Ideal's grandmother, in encouraging her "to walk tall" when she was a child, gives her much better advice than Janie's grandmother. Ideal, therefore, is not troubled with the constricting standards of white Southern ladyhood which plague Janie. Proud and yet seemingly terrified of life's multiple unknown powers and demands, Ideal struggles not only with racist and sexist categories, but existential ones as well. Her sounding boards are her own consciousness and her lover, Jimson; she beats them both regularly with questions and accusations. Her freedom comes through the process of openly probing these categories as well as her fears and her hopes, though doing so necessitates her leaving Jimson in the novel's conclusion. Fully realizing that she and Jimson have been "living a myth which the white man has given us," Ideal expresses the faith that nevertheless they "are transformed by being loved in [their] ugliness and imperfection." [32] Janie does not come to a sense of self, as does Ideal, by forcing the unconscious to become conscious, but by the trials and errors of experience, with her marriage to Tea Cake fulfilling her vision as a sixteen-year-old of the glories of natural creation. Because he accepts himself and her, she too comes to self-acceptance: as a woman (not an older woman exploited by a younger man); as a black woman (not a black woman who should have been white); as a vital human being— revelling in hard work, laughter, and long loving. She kills Tea Cake when, crazed by a rabid dog, he begins to assert himself as a stereotypically possessive husband. Her act, which is literally in self-defense, is figuratively in defense of the memory of their joyous, creative life together.

In the novels of James Baldwin, black women are, with varying degrees of complexity, always represented in relation to men. In his first novel alone, he shows her variously. In the role of victim is Deborah, raped by white men; in the role of victimizer is Florence, castrating with her sense of white propriety; in the role of mother, the mature Elizabeth, trying to give her family love when hate and shame are the prevailing emotions; in the role of the beloved, the young Elizabeth, happy in her love for Richard and learning suffering from his futile death. Baldwin's more fully developed portrayals of black women, Ida Scott in *Another Country* (1962) and Tish Rivers in *Beale Street* reveal women gaining their strength and their sense of identity in relation to men. Tish, for whom young Elizabeth in the earlier novel might have been a model, is the center of consciousness for *Beale Street;* and her centers are her family; her man, Fonny, in jail on a trumped-up rape charge; and increasingly the child in her womb. Nothing happens in this novel except that the centers hold. It is because of the love the Riverses have as a family and that Fonny and Tish have for each other that injustice does not prevail. But in loving each other, each individual knows his or her responsibilities. Tish learns early in her relationship with Fonny that "a woman is tremendously controlled by what the man's imagination makes of her," that he makes her a woman (p. 44). She therefore learns that she must allow Fonny to protect her when she is molested by white men, even if his doing so will lead to his being sent unjustly to jail. Baldwin seems to imply in *Beale Street* that in a society where racial injustice and irrationality are institutionalized, love, creating an order of clearly defined roles, is the only defense.

In *Another Country,* love is still the only defense, but love is not a given as it is in *Beale Street;* it is reached after excruciating search. Baldwin in this novel broadly implies that America's redemption is possible only through the obliteration of every kind of racial and sexual stereotypes; the grip of these images upon the American imagination, however, has first to be fully acknowledged: unrecognized and hence unresolved, they lead to madness and suicide. In the novel's conclusion, however, Ida, the black heroine, having confronted the grip sexual and racial myths have had on her own psyche, educates her white lover, and together they pass beyond the barriers of race and sex to that other country of love and wisdom.

The strength of Zora, the heroine of W. E. B. DuBois's *The Quest of the Silver Fleece* (1911), is similar to that of Ida, for she, too, after learning from her own trials, is finally able to educate her lover. Like Griggs and Chesnutt, also writing in the early twentieth century, DuBois treats sex obliquely and conventionally, but Zora is not a conventional character. Raised by her mother who is both whore and sorceress, Zora has been used by white men; when she tells her lover of her past and of her purity since knowing him, he proves more prudish than she and abandons her. To this point in the novel, DuBois describes Zora as a feminine version of the natural savage, running wildly through her swamp, imaginative and amoral, passionate and unruly. As a result of her lover's rejection she evolves into an intellectual and moral paragon. It might be said that her attributes, which are first those of the conventional nineteenth-century Dark Lady, are transformed into those of the conventional nineteenth-century Fair Lady, and yet Zora remains dark. Not only is she conscious of her repressed passion for her lover, but as a black woman she is tormented by white trash who would abuse her sexually and spurned by white financiers and lawyers who cannot take her intelligence seriously. She confronts her adversaries with courage and courtesy as well as with a knowledge of law and economics, but she is saved from Victorian self-righteousness by her continued flights of fantasy and passion. Zora does not achieve the personal independence of Sula and Ideal—nor does she long for it; but, like Janie and Ida, as she asks Bles to marry her in the last lines of the novel, it is clear that she has dissolved racial and sexual barriers to achieve a sure sense of her character and life's possibilities.

Self-fulfillment and freedom for Janie, Ida, and Zora reside finally in a relationship with a man, though each knows herself fully. For Gwendolyn Brooks's Maud Martha, Alice Childress's Mildred, and Sarah Wright's Mariah Upshur, a relationship with a man is only one aspect of their rich lives. Created by black women writers, their full and complex characters seem to be givens. Mildred, who reveals herself through a series of soliloquies comparable to Langston Hughes's Jesse B. Semple, is interested equally in politics and black history, her friends and the neighbor children; Mariah, who lives just at the edge of survival, is consumed by her love for her children, by her guilt for deeds past, and by her dreams of death. Of Maud Martha, Paule Marshall writes:

> Nothing happens in *Maud Martha*. A girl grows up, marries, makes a modest home for herself and her husband, has a child. . . . As a little girl she loves the few dandelions that grow in her yard. When she grows she is disappointed with herself for not being more the "acceptable" type of Negro beauty. She feels occasional contempt and disappointment with her husband although she loves him. At the onset of the birth of her child, she feels, in Miss Brooks' lovely words, "something softly separate in her." And always, she lives with a muted desire for something to happen in her life, even though she reminds herself that with most people, "nothing at all ever happens. . . ." Miss Brooks quietly but firmly insists on the human aspect of her character.[33]

But perhaps in the fiction of black America it is neither the young girl nor the young woman but the older woman who is most likely to achieve freedom. In a marvelously concise summary of the lives of Southern black women, Toni Morrison writes that when young, they

> [Edged] into life from the back door. Becoming. Everybody in the world was in a position to give them orders. White women said, "Do this." White children said, "Give me that." White men said, "Come here." Black men said, "Lay down." The only people they need not take orders from were black children and each other. But they took all that—and re-created it in their own image. . . . Then they were old. . . . They were through with lust and lactations, beyond tears and terror. They alone could walk the roads of Mississippi, the lanes of Georgia, the fields of Alabama unmolested. They were old enough to be irritable when and where they chose, tired enough to look forward to death, disinterested enough to accept the idea of pain while ignoring the presence of pain.

They were, in fact and at last, free. And the lives of these old black women were synthesized in their eyes—a purée of tragedy and humor, wickedness and serenity, truth and fantasy. (p. 108)

Morrison's portrait is of the black grandmother, who, like Faulkner's Dilsey, is free in being beyond sexual and racial turmoil, beyond self-consciousness and time. In black American life and in black American fiction, the Grandmother, as E. Franklin Frazier points out, is the source of continuity in the often fragmented black family and the repository of the folklore and history of black people.[34] We note too that "in contrast to mainstream America's elderly, who usually spend their waning years in subsidiary or parasitic roles, the grandmother in the black family traditionally has held a commanding position." [35] Such figures as Aunt Hager Williams in Langston Hughes's *Not Without Laughter* (1930), Mary in Ralph Ellison's *Invisible Man* (1952), the grandmother in *The Messenger,* or Miss Thompson in *Brown Girl* fulfill Frazier's descriptions and indeed are Dilsey-like; they suffer and endure. Unlike Dilsey, however, in black American fiction, the Grandmother is not always passive and neutral in her wisdom. She can be represented as an individual as well as a symbol. Eva, Sula's grandmother, for example, is full of eccentricities and common sense, "fun and meanness." She thrives on hatred and pride, and until her granddaughter throws her out, she controls the household from her room on the third floor.

Especially memorable as maternalistic figures whose long lives and memories encompass the fullness of black American experience are Vyvry and Miss Jane Pittman. They too suffer and endure, never engaging in active resistance against the constant racist brutalities they encounter during slavery and Reconstruction and always keeping faith in God. Yet they are never passive. Vyvry pleads for her freedom and attempts escape during slavery; during Reconstruction she determines to build a home although she is defeated first by the sharecropping system and then by the Ku Klux Klan; Jane brings her boy's murderer to insanity by shame, and, one hundred years after her own emancipation, marches with the Freedom Riders. And they are always practical; Vyvry's faith reinforces her determination to create a good and prosperous life for her family on this earth, and Jane switches to Voodoo or talks to trees if the need arises. Secure in their racial identity as well as in their marriages, both characters suffer more because of their race than because of their sex, though Jane has been made barren by the brutalities of slavery, and Vyvry must defend herself against the sexist and racist slurs of her former lover. Vyvry, caught between her passion for Randall Ware and her respect for Innis Brown, and Jane with her love for Joe Pittman are hardly sexually neutral as Dilsey and other grandmother figures seem to be. Nor can either be construed as a moral equivalent in an allegory or a melodrama. Vyvry becomes the center of her family and Jane of her community not only because of their sense of moral conviction and of freedom from envy and hatred, but also because of their capacity for love, their enjoyment of themselves, others, chickens, ice cream, baseball.

The personal freedom found by Sula and Ideal takes them beyond the black American community; for these young women, however, love—other than self-love and the vague yearning for communal love—remains another country. The personal freedom found by Ida and Janie with a man, Maud Martha and Mildred with family and friends is largely self-satisfying. The personal freedom of Vyvry and Jane, however, comes to represent an ideal for the entire black community, past and future. Too individualistic to be symbolic, these older black women nevertheless demonstrate by their lives that freedom and love of community need not be incompatible.

It might be said that all black American literature celebrates two aspects of black American life: the fact of survival and the search for freedom. Yet it seems that the black American woman in life and fiction, oppressed into invisibility by race and sex, by the necessity of being menial and matriarchal, by the opprobrious images of "ugly" and "loose," against all odds, has survived and has found freedom. She has survived with "grit, shit, and mother wit"; she has found the freedom to love her race, her family, and herself. Hers is a life to celebrate in story.

Notes

1 W. E. B. Du Bois, *Darkwater,* reprinted in *To Be a Black Woman,* ed. Mel Watkins and Jay David (New York: Morrow, 1970), pp. 234-35.

2 Shirley Chisholm, *Unbought and Unbossed* (Boston: Houghton Mifflin, 1970), p. xii.

3 See Toni Cade, *The Black Woman: An Anthology* (New York: Signet Books, 1970), and Robert Staples's chapter "Black Women and Women's Liberation," in *The Black Woman in America: Sex, Marriage, and the Family* (Chicago: Nelson Hall Publishers, 1973), pp. 161-82, for discussions of the black woman's attitude toward the women's liberation movement.

4 Quoted in Gerda Lerner's *Black Women in America: A Documentary History* (New York: Random House, 1972), p. 217.

5 This is the general thesis of E. Franklin Frazier's *The Negro Family in America* (Chicago: University of Chicago Press, 1939), a thesis which became the basis for governmental policy upon the publication of Daniel P. Moynihan's *The Negro Family: The Case for National Action* (Washington, D.C.: Government Printing Office, 1967).

6 Frazier's thesis went largely unchallenged until Moynihan's work prompted the publication of such thoroughly documented counterstudies as Joyce Ladner's *Tomorrow's Tomorrow: The Black Woman* (Garden City, N.Y.: Doubleday, 1971) and Staples's *The Black Woman in America.*

7 A general survey indicating the discrimination pattern against the black woman in employment and her low status as a wage earner is available in Gerda Lerner's work and updated by Aileen Hernandez's article "Small Change for Black Women," *Ms.,* August 1974, pp. 16-18.

8 Ann Petry, *The Street* (Boston: Houghton Mifflin, 1946), p. 206.

9 Alice Childress, *Like One of the Family* (Brooklyn: Independence Publishers, 1956), p. 8.

10 John A. Williams, *Sissie* (Garden City, N.Y.: Doubleday, 1969), p. 267.

11 Zora Neale Hurston, *Their Eyes Were Watching God* (Greenwich, Conn.: Fawcett, 1969), p. 27.

12 Angela Davis, "Reflections on the Black Woman's Role in the Community of Slaves," *The Black Scholar* 3 (Dec. 1971), 7.

13 See Ladner, *Tomorrow's Tomorrow,* pp. 34-35.

14 W. E. B. DuBois, *The Souls of Black Folk* (Chicago: A.C. McClurg, 1903), pp. 2-3.

15 William H. Grier and Price M. Cobbs, *Black Rage* (New York: Bantam Books, 1968), p. 33.

16 Wallace Thurman, *The Blacker the Berry* (New York: Macmillan, 1970), p. 4.

17 Toni Morrison, *The Bluest Eye* (New York: Holt, Rinehart and Winston, 1970), pp. 64-65.

18 Chester Himes, *The Third Generation* (New York: Signet Books, 1956), p. 9.

19 Alice Walker, *The Third Life of Grange Copeland* (New York: Harcourt Brace Jovanovich, 1970), p. 58.

20 Margaret Walker, *Jubilee* (New York: Bantam Books, 1967), p. 400.

21 Staples, *Black Woman in America*, p. 94.

22 Calvin Hernton, *Sex and Racism in America* (New York: Grove Press, 1965), p. 124.

23 Lerner, *Black Woman in America*, pp. 163-64.

24 See Staples's chapter "Bodies for Sales: Black Prostitutes in White America," in *Black Woman in America*, pp. 73-94.

25 Ibid., p. 90.

26 Jean Toomer, *Cane* (New York: Harper & Row, 1969), p. 1.

27 There are, however, some notable exceptions. Jake in Claude McKay's *Home to Harlem* berates "the commercial flesh of women" [(New York: Pocket Books, 1965), p. 173], and Pearl Mibbs of Barry Beckham's *My Main Mother* (1969) betrays her family trust for material success and sexual kicks in the big city, simultaneously fulfilling the stereotypes of the emasculating matriarch and the slut.

28 John O. Killens, *Youngblood* (New York: Dial Press, 1954), p. 464.

29 Nella Larsen, *Quicksand* (New York: Collier Books, 1971), p. 222.

30 See Hortense E. Thornton's study of Helga's dilemma in "Sexism as Quagmire: Nella Larsen's *Quicksand,*" *College Language Association Journal* 16 (1973), 285-301.

31 Toni Morrison, *Sula* (New York: Knopf, 1974), pp. 142-43.

32 Charlene Hatcher Polite, *The Flagellants* (New York: Farrar Straus Giroux, 1967), p. 189.

33 Paule Marshall, from a panel discussion on "The Negro Woman in American Literature," in *Keeping the Faith: Writings by Contemporary Black American Women,* ed. Pat Crutchfield Exum (Greenwich, Conn.: Fawcett, 1974), p. 38.

34 See Frazier, *Negro Family,* pp. 146-59.

35 Watkins and David, *To Be a Black Woman,* p. 202.

Index